A CULTURAL HISTORY OF THEATRE

VOLUME 6

A Cultural History of Theatre
General Editors: Christopher B. Balme and Tracy C. Davis

Volume 1
A Cultural History of Theatre in Antiquity
Edited by Martin Revermann

Volume 2
A Cultural History of Theatre in the Middle Ages
Edited by Jody Enders

Volume 3
A Cultural History of Theatre in the Early Modern Age
Edited by Robert Henke

Volume 4
A Cultural History of Theatre in the Age of Enlightenment
Edited by Mechele Leon

Volume 5
A Cultural History of Theatre in the Age of Empire
Edited by Peter W. Marx

Volume 6
A Cultural History of Theatre in the Modern Age
Edited by Kim Solga

A CULTURAL HISTORY OF THEATRE

IN THE MODERN AGE

VOLUME 6

Edited by Kim Solga

BLOOMSBURY ACADEMIC

LONDON • NEW YORK • OXFORD • NEW DELHI • SYDNEY

BLOOMSBURY ACADEMIC
Bloomsbury Publishing Plc
50 Bedford Square, London, WC1B 3DP, UK
1385 Broadway, New York, NY 10018, USA
29 Earlsfort Terrace, Dublin 2, Ireland

BLOOMSBURY, BLOOMSBURY ACADEMIC and the Diana logo are trademarks of Bloomsbury Publishing Plc

First published in hardback in 2017
Reprinted 2019, 2020
This paperback edition published 2022

Copyright © Kim Solga and contributors, 2017, 2022

Kim Solga has asserted her right under the Copyright, Designs and Patents Act, 1988, to be identified as Editor of this work.

Cover image: *An Inspector Calls* by J.B. Priestly. UK Tour, September 2015, directed by Stephen Daldry. © Mark Douet / ArenaPAL

All rights reserved. No part of this publication may be reproduced or transmitted in any form or by any means, electronic or mechanical, including photocopying, recording, or any information storage or retrieval system, without prior permission in writing from the publishers.

Bloomsbury Publishing Plc does not have any control over, or responsibility for, any third-party websites referred to or in this book. All internet addresses given in this book were correct at the time of going to press. The author and publisher regret any inconvenience caused if addresses have changed or sites have ceased to exist, but can accept no responsibility for any such changes.

A catalogue record for this book is available from the British Library.

Library of Congress Cataloging-in-Publication Data
Names: Solga, Kim edited.
Title: A cultural history of theatre in the modern age / edited by Kim Solga.
Description: London ; New York : Bloomsbury Academic, 2017. | Series: Cultural History of Theater | Includes bibliographical references and index.
Identifiers: LCCN 2016048848 | ISBN 9781472585837 (hardback)
Subjects: LCSH: Theater–History–20th century. | Theater and society.
Classification: LCC PN2189 .C785 2017 | DDC 792.0904—dc23 LC record available at https://lccn.loc.gov/2016048848

ISBN:	HB:	978-1-4725-8583-7
	HB Set:	978-1-4725-8584-4
	PB:	978-1-3502-7777-9
	PB Set:	978-1-3502-7782-3
	ePDF:	978-1-3501-3549-9
	eBook:	978-1-3501-3548-2

Series: Cultural Histories

Typeset by RefineCatch Limited, Bungay, Suffolk

To find out more about our authors and books visit www.bloomsbury.com and sign up for our newsletters.

CONTENTS

LIST OF ILLUSTRATIONS — vii
NOTES ON CONTRIBUTORS — xi
SERIES PREFACE — xv
EDITOR'S ACKNOWLEDGEMENTS — xvi

Introduction: The Impossible Modern Age — 1
Kim Solga

1 Institutional Frameworks: Theatre, State, and Market in Modern Urban Performance — 17
   Michael McKinnie

2 Social Functions: Consumers and Producers — 35
   Nicholas Ridout

3 Sexuality and Gender: New Stories and New Spaces on the Modern Stage — 55
   Kirsten Pullen

4 The Environment of Theatre: 'Home' in the Modern Age — 75
   Kim Solga and Joanne Tompkins

5 Circulations: Visual Sovereignty, Transmotion, and Tribalography — 95
   Jill Carter, Heather Davis-Fisch, and Ric Knowles

6 Interpretations: The Stakes of Audience Interpretation in
   Twentieth-Century Political Theatre   117
   Dassia N. Posner

7 Communities of Production: A Materialist Reading with an
   Offstage View   139
   Christin Essin and Marlis Schweitzer

8 Genres and Repertoires: Redressing the Nation in Ireland
   and Japan   159
   Michelle Liu Carriger and Aoife Monks

9 Technologies of Performance: Machinic Staging and
   Corporeal Choreographies   181
   Ashley Ferro-Murray and Timothy Murray

10 Knowledge Transmission: Media and Memory   201
   Sarah Bay-Cheng

NOTES   221
BIBLIOGRAPHY   241
INDEX   259

LIST OF ILLUSTRATIONS

INTRODUCTION

0.1	Horse in full gallop, study by Eadweard Muybridge.	7
0.2	The Woolworth Building, New York.	10
0.3	Fallingwater, by Frank Lloyd Wright.	11

CHAPTER ONE

1.1	Hoarding outside The Theatre Centre, Toronto, during refurbishment, 2013.	18
1.2	Hoarding outside The Theatre Centre, Toronto, 2013.	18
1.3	The Theatre Centre, Toronto, 2014.	19

CHAPTER TWO

2.1	Attendees at the Metropolitan Opera crowd around the bar for drinks and cigarettes during an intermission.	40
2.2	India, Kolkata, rubber factory.	41

CHAPTER THREE

3.1	Mae West in *Sex*.	61
3.2	Cast celebrating the twelfth anniversary of *Oh! Calcutta!*	64
3.3	Charles Ludlam in *Vogue*, 1971.	68
3.4	Ben Gazzara and Barbara Bel Geddes in *Cat on a Hot Tin Roof*, 1955.	72

CHAPTER FOUR

4.1	The interior lobby and bar area of the Young Vic theatre on the South Bank, London.	86
4.2	Exterior of the Young Vic theatre, London.	87
4.3	Sam Troughton as Tuzenbach and Vanessa Kirby as Masha in Chekhov's *Three Sisters* at the Young Vic, London.	90

CHAPTER FIVE

5.1	Production still from *Nanook of the North*.	101
5.2	Alethea Arnaquq-Baril interviewed in Iqaluit, Nunavut.	102
5.3	Costumes used at Potlatch Ceremony, 1919.	103
5.4	Filmmaker Kevin Nikkel watches footage from *The Romance of the Far Fur Country* with Trevor Issac, at the U'mista Cultural Centre, Alert Bay, British Columbia.	104
5.5	This is ceremony – woman's ceremony.	109
5.6	Indigenous transmotion for a world in peril.	110

CHAPTER SIX

6.1	Anton Lavinsky, scene design for *Mystery-Bouffe*.	124
6.2	Audience questionnaire completed after a performance of *Mystery-Bouffe*.	126

6.3	Production still of Saul, performed simultaneously by puppet and puppeteer (Basil Jones), in *Tooth and Nail*.	129
6.4	Pa Ubu (Dawid Minnaar) in *Ubu and the Truth Commission*, by Jane Taylor.	133
6.5	TRC witness puppet and puppeteers (Adrian Kohler and Louis Seboko) in *Ubu and the Truth Commission*.	135

CHAPTER SEVEN

7.1	Storming of the Winter Palace, 1920.	140
7.2	Striking chorus girls turn Manhattan sidewalks into sites of spectacular protest, 1919.	144
7.3	Provincetown Players setting stage for *Bound East for Cardiff* at 139 Macdougal St, New York, 1916.	145
7.4	Midge Lucas working in the Hudson Scenic paint shop, New York.	148
7.5	Scene from the Australian production of *War Horse*, 2013.	151

CHAPTER EIGHT

8.1	Example of Stage-Irishman costume, in an image by Samuel De Wilde of Mr Rock as the Irishman.	165
8.2	Takarazuka theatre's *The Rose of Versailles* final rehearsal in Tokyo, 17 February 2006.	172
8.3	Jean Butler and Colin Dunne in *Riverdance*, 1996.	175
8.4	Michio Ito in costume as the Hawk Spirit in *At The Hawk's Well*, 1916.	177

CHAPTER NINE

9.1	Loïe Fuller in *La Danse Blanche*.	187
9.2	Alex Hay, *Grass Field*.	195
9.3	Micha Cárdenas and Elle Mehrmand, *technésexual*.	199

CHAPTER TEN

10.1 Film still from *Workers Leaving the Lumière Factory in Lyon* (*La Sortie de l'Usine Lumière à Lyon*), 1895.   205

10.2 Patrick Magee in Samuel Beckett's *Krapp's Last Tape*, 1959.   211

NOTES ON CONTRIBUTORS

Sarah Bay-Cheng is Professor of Theater and Dance at Bowdoin College, where she teaches digital media and contemporary performance, modern drama, American theatre, and researches the intersections among technology, literature, theatre, and history. Her book publications include *Performance and Media: Taxonomies for a Changing Field* (2015), *Mapping Intermediality in Performance* (2010), *Poets at Play: An Anthology of Poetic Drama* (2010), and *Mama Dada: Gertrude Stein's Avant-Garde Theater* (2004). She currently co-edits the book series, Avant-Gardes in Performance, for Palgrave Macmillan, and serves on the editorial boards for several journals in theatre, digital media, and contemporary art. Her essays have appeared in *Theatre Journal*, *Contemporary Performance*, and the *Journal of Dramatic Theory and Criticism*. In 2015 Bay-Cheng was a Fulbright Scholar in American Studies at Utrecht University, Netherlands. Her current monograph project focuses on digital historiography and performance.

Michelle Liu Carriger is an assistant professor in the Theater Department at the University of California Los Angeles. Her current research project examines the historiography of clothing and the performance of self in Britain and Japan through nineteenth-century fashion controversies and contemporary subcultural fashions. Her article '"The Unnatural History and Petticoat Mystery of Boulton and Park": A Victorian Sex Scandal and the Theatre Defense' won the 2012 *TDR* student essay contest and the 2013 Gerald Kahan Prize from the American Society for Theatre Research.

Jill Carter (Anishinaabe/Ashkenazi) is a Toronto-based theatre practitioner and Assistant Professor with the Centre for Drama, Theatre and Performance Studies; the Aboriginal Studies Program; and the Transitional Year Programme at the University of Toronto. Her research and praxis base themselves in the mechanics of story creation (devising and dramaturgy), the processes of delivery (performance on the stage and on the page), and the mechanics of affect. She has worked with Turtle Gals Performance Ensemble (Assistant Dramaturg and Performer), the *Chocolate Woman* Collective (Researcher, Assistant Director, Remount Director, Workshop Director), and the *Omuskego Cree Water Stories* Project (Workshop Director). In 2014, she directed the Canadian Premiere of Gloria Miguel's *Something Old, Something New, Something Borrowed, Something Blue* at Native Earth Performing Arts' Aki Studio. Recent publications include 'Discarding Sympathy, Disrupting Catharis: The Mortification of Indigenous Flesh as Survivance-Intervention' for *Theatre Journal* (2015), 'The Physics of the Mola: W/riting Indigenous Resurgence on the Contemporary Stage' for *Modern Drama* (2016), and a review of Yvette Nolan's *Medicine Shows* for *alt.theatre: cultural diversity and the stage*.

Heather Davis-Fisch is an Associate Professor of Theatre and English at the University of the Fraser Valley (Canada). She is the author of *Loss and Cultural Remains in Performance: The Ghosts of the Franklin Expedition* (2012). Her work has also been published in *Theatre Research in Canada, Canadian Theatre Review, Cultural Studies ↔ Critical Methodologies*, and *Performing Arts Journal*.

Christin Essin is an assistant professor at Vanderbilt University in Nashville, Tennessee and the author of *Stage Designers in Early Twentieth-Century America: Artists, Activists, Cultural Critics* (2012), winner of the United States Institute of Theatre Technology's 2015 Golden Pen Award. Her essays on the cultural history of theatrical stage design and backstage labour have appeared in *Theatre Journal, Theatre Topics*, and *Theatre History Studies*.

Ashley Ferro-Murray is Associate Curator, Theater/Dance at the Experimental Media and Performing Arts Center (EMPAC) at Rensselaer Polytechnic Institute. Ferro-Murray's article 'Dancing the Hardware: Rachid Ouramdane's embodied performance' is published in *Media-N*, she has published book reviews in *Dance Research Journal* and *The Drama Review*, and she has numerous online publications with venues such as -empyre- new media listserve and Dancers Using Technology blog. As an intermedial choreographer and dramaturge, Ferro-Murray has produced projects with organizations including the Zero1 Art and Technology Biennial, the Contemporary Jewish Museum, The Milkbar, and AS220.

Ric Knowles is Professor Emeritus of Theatre Studies at the University of Guelph, past editor of *Canadian Theatre Review, Modern Drama*, and *Theatre Journal*, and author or editor of eighteen books on theatre and performance. His eight authored books include *The Theatre of Form and the Production of Meaning, Reading the Material Theatre, Theatre & Interculturalism*, and *How Theatre Means*.

Michael McKinnie is Senior Lecturer in Drama at Queen Mary University of London. His research focuses primarily on theatre and urban development and the cultural economics of contemporary performance. He is the author of *City Stages: Theatre and Urban Space in a Global City*, which was awarded the Ann Saddlemyer Prize for outstanding book by the Canadian Association for Theatre Research. He is also the editor of *Space and the Geographies of Theatre* and has contributed articles to edited collections and journals such as *Theatre Journal*, *Modern Drama*, *Contemporary Theatre Review*, and *Theatre Research in Canada*.

Aoife Monks is Reader in Theatre Studies in the Department of Drama, Queen Mary University of London. She is the author of *The Actor in Costume* (2010) and with Ali Maclaurin, *Readings in Costume* (2015). She is Consulting Editor for *Contemporary Theatre Review* and is working on a monograph on stage Irishness and virtuosity.

Timothy Murray is Professor of Comparative Literature and English, Director of the Society for the Humanities and Curator of the Rose Goldsen Archive of New Media Art at Cornell University. He is the author of *Digital Baroque: New Media Art and Cinematic Folds* (2008), *Zonas de Contacto: el arte en CD-ROM* (1999), *Drama Trauma: Specters of Race and Sexuality in Performance, Video, Art* (1997), *Like a Film: Ideological Fantasy on Screen, Camera, and Canvas* (1993), and *Theatrical Legitimation: Allegories of Genius in XVIIth-Century England and France* (1987). He is editor of *Mimesis, Masochism & Mime: The Politics of Theatricality in Contemporary French Thought* (1997), and, with Alan Smith, *Repossessions: Psychoanalysis and the Phantasms of Early-Modern Culture* (1997). He was Editor of *Theatre Journal* from 1984 to 1988.

Dassia N. Posner is Assistant Professor of Theatre at Northwestern University. Her books include *The Director's Prism: E. T. A. Hoffmann and the Russian Theatrical Avant-Garde* (2016), a contextualized analysis of the vivid theatre work of Meyerhold, Tairov, and Eisenstein, and *The Routledge Companion to Puppetry and Material Performance* (2014), a collection of contemporary puppetry scholarship co-edited with Claudia Orenstein and John Bell. Her articles appear in *Theatre Survey*, *Theatre Topics*, *Slavic and East European Performance*, and *Puppetry International*. She is also a professional dramaturg; recent projects include *Grand Concourse* (2015), *Russian Transport* (2014), and *Three Sisters* (2012) at Steppenwolf Theatre Company.

Kirsten Pullen is Associate Professor and Director of Graduate Studies in the Department of Performance Studies at Texas A&M University. Her books include *Actresses and Whores: On Stage and in Society* (2005) and *Like a Natural Woman: Spectacular Female Performance in Classical Hollywood* (2014). She has also published articles and delivered conference papers on Internet fandom, theatre audiences, dance on film and television, and actresses.

Nicholas Ridout is Professor of Theatre at Queen Mary University of London. His books include *Passionate Amateurs: Theatre, Communism and Love* (2013), *Theatre & Ethics* (2009), and *Stage Fright, Animals and Other Theatrical Problems* (2006).

Marlis Schweitzer is Associate Professor in the Department of Theatre at York University in Toronto, Canada. She is the author of *When Broadway Was the Runway: Theater, Fashion, and American Culture* (2009), *Transatlantic Broadway: The Infrastructural Politics of Global Politics* (2015), and co-editor (with Joanne Zerdy) of *Performing Objects and Theatrical Things* (2014). Her articles on topics ranging from phrenology and ocean liners to fashion shows and the Disney store have appeared in *Theatre Journal, Theatre Survey, TDR, Theatre Research International, Theatre Research in Canada,* and *Canadian Theatre Review*. Her current book project traces the movement of child actors along Anglo-American theatrical circuits in the early to mid-nineteenth century.

Kim Solga is Professor, Theatre Studies, in the Department of English and Writing Studies at Western University, Canada. She is the author of *Violence Against Women in Early Modern Performance: Invisible Acts* (2009), *Theatre & Feminism* (2015), and the co-editor of four award-winning volumes: *Performance and the City* (2009), *Performance and the Global City* (2013), and *New Canadian Realisms* (2 vols, 2012). Her writing has also appeared in *Theatre Journal, Contemporary Theatre Review, Shakespeare Bulletin, Theatre Research in Canada,* and *Canadian Theatre Review*. She is the current editor of *Theatre Research in Canada*.

Joanne Tompkins is Associate Dean Research in the Faculty of Humanities and Social Sciences at the University of Queensland, Australia. She is the co-author of *Post Colonial Drama* (with Helen Gilbert, 1996), *Women's Intercultural Performance* (with Julie Holledge, 2000), and *A Global Doll's House: Distant Readings of Ibsen* (with Julie Holledge, Jonathan Bollen, and Frode Helland, 2016). She is author of *Unsettling Space: Contestations in Contemporary Australian Theatre* (2006) and *Theatre's Heterotopias: Performance and the Cultural Politics of Space* (2014). She is Editor of *Theatre Journal*.

SERIES PREFACE

A Cultural History of Theatre is a six-volume series examining a cultural practice that emerged in antiquity and today encompasses practically the whole globe. Theatre is generally acknowledged to be the most social of artistic practices, requiring collectives to both produce and consume it. Theatrical performance's ability to organize and cohere markers of cultural belonging, difference, and dissonance are the hallmarks of social life. Its production and reception have, however, altered significantly over the past two-and-a-half thousand years. Despite these changes, the same chapter headings structure all six volumes: institutional frameworks, social functions, sexuality and gender, environment, circulation, interpretations, communities of production, repertoire and genres, technologies of performance, and knowledge transmission. These headings represent significant cultural approaches as opposed to purely regional, national, aesthetic, or generic categories. This allows for comparative readings of key *cultural* questions affecting theatre both diachronically and synchronically. The six volumes divide the history of theatre as follows:

Volume 1: A Cultural History of Theatre in Antiquity (500 BC–1000 AD)
Volume 2: A Cultural History of Theatre in the Middle Ages (1000–1400)
Volume 3: A Cultural History of Theatre in the Early Modern Age
　　(1400–1650)
Volume 4: A Cultural History of Theatre in the Age of Enlightenment
　　(1650–1800)
Volume 5: A Cultural History of Theatre in the Age of Empire (1800–1920)
Volume 6: A Cultural History of Theatre in the Modern Age (1920–2000+)

Christopher B. Balme and Tracy C. Davis, General Editors

EDITOR'S ACKNOWLEDGEMENTS

I would like to thank Tracy Davis and Chris Balme for entrusting this project to me and for supporting my vision for it, especially when that vision clashed with some of the larger aims of the series.

I would also like to thank the contributors to this volume for all of their hard work, their dedication, their willingness to take risks as collaborators, and their unwavering patience as we moved through multiple iterations of each chapter. I want to acknowledge how much effort they have put into this volume, and to note that its strengths are their strengths. Its weaknesses are my own.

Finally, my greatest love and thanks to those dear friends who stood me up when I fell down during the darkest days of building this book: Steven Bruhm, Peter Schwenger, Alison Lee, Joel Faflak, and Jeremy Greenway.

Kim Solga, December 2016

Introduction

The Impossible Modern Age

KIM SOLGA

MODERN, MODERNITY, MODERNISM... AND THE THEATRE

There may be no modern age. Clearly, this is a counterintuitive way to begin an introduction to a book that takes this term as central to its title, and yet 'the modern' is perhaps less a generational or historical marker than it is an idea, an ideal, even a means of cultural organization that makes a deliberate break from a clearly marked past. To call something modern – a nation or group of nations (modern France; modern Europe), a person (the modern woman), or even a theatre – is to assert something fundamental about the social, cultural, economic, and technical sophistication of that thing, over and against the things that have come before – ideas, people, worldviews, forms of representation. It is also, as Michael McKinnie and Nicholas Ridout argue forcefully in the opening chapters of this volume, to make a claim about the relationship of that thing to free market capitalism, perhaps the pre-eminent organizing force of those things we label modern – whether they obtain in the twentieth and twenty-first centuries, or in centuries past.

This book begins, then, from the premise that the modern is not an historical marker so much as a cultural fantasy, one in which human beings across the earth invest and share unequally. Along with its cognate, 'modernity', it is also a fantasy that came, during the twentieth century, tenaciously to take hold as 'nature' or 'reality', business-as-usual, broadly invisible as the often-coercive social framework it actually is. This is not to say that the period of historical time this book investigates – theoretically 1920 through 2000, but pragmatically the late nineteenth century through to the moment of this writing – is not structured by externally verifiable events, from world wars to environmental crises to politically motivated genocides. It is to argue, however, that the organization of these and related events into a discourse about the modern is a performative act rather than an historical inevitability. As speech-act theorist J.L. Austin and his most famous inheritor, queer cultural theorist and philosopher Judith Butler, define it, a 'performative' is a discursive act (a speech act, or an embodied action) that makes real the thing it talks about. It does this largely by citing previous acts that do the same thing, thus generating from within language itself a sense of shared cultural certainty about a world presumed to exist beyond language.[1] Further, because the modern is performative[2] – because the idea of modernity is something we, as humans, *speak and act* into being, rather than simply exist within – that also means it may be, and has been, subject to extraordinary investigation, interrogation, and also celebration at the theatre.

Modernity describes a state of human affairs obtaining within the periods scholars traditionally label as modern.[3] It refers to the shifting social, economic, and intellectual conditions that accompany changes in science, technology, and expanded human movement around the globe beginning in the later fifteenth century, and which reach fever pitch in the years following the machine-driven innovations of the industrial revolution (mid–late 1800s). As film historian Ben Singer explains, modernity as an ethos is characterized by a linear progress narrative which implies we can always build more, better, and faster things, and that such building (despite plenty of evidence to the contrary) will always mean increased benefits for all human beings. This narrative, however, is enabled by relationships of alterity both to the past and to other cultures and geographical places, as scholars including Michel De Certeau and Denise Albanese have understood. In Albanese's summary of De Certeau's argument, modernity 'produces itself through othering, through discursive and material mechanisms that effectively bifurcate regions of culture, the better to legitimate some and delegitimate others'.[4] This (culturally violent) practice of absorbing and then eliminating that which it is not, coupled with the impact of its addiction to rapid change, means that modernity tends to produce fragmented experiences of living that reverberate traumatically across individual human bodies no longer embedded in stable community networks; it is a sociocultural framework that generates human progress at significant human cost. No wonder, then, that for Sigmund Freud (1856–1939) the modern subject is buffeted by both conscious and unconscious forces, where the latter act upon the former in order to help the subject cope with the trauma produced by modernity 'at full throttle'[5] – even while that subject moves gamely along in the speeding stream.

The term 'modern', similarly, implies a relation to past times and practices, but it functions as a historiography, a methodological move that draws a line between past and present, and often renders these ideas in critical relation one to another. This dialectic – between what we understand as modern and what we do not, or between what our culture wishes to believe is modern *about us* in relation to what came before us/is other than us – has been one of the subjects of greatest concern for artists at the theatre in the period we here call 'the modern age'. In Chapter 10, Sarah Bay-Cheng tracks some of the ways in which artists investigate modern culture's preoccupation with memory and its rupture, with modernity's prized forward momentum as a function of memory's refusal or failure – even as artists, technicians, historians, and theorists remain preoccupied with the best ways to capture performance events more and more precisely on film or in digital files.[6] Questions about how cultures remember, and when and how they forget, reverberate across the century scarred by the Holocaust against the Jews, and form part of a larger artistic compulsion in the late modern period towards matters of social justice and the ethics of exploring them at the theatre. Artists interested in these issues, as Dassia Posner explains in Chapter 6, often deploy dialectical strategies as a tool of inquiry. Posner argues that theatre makers across the long twentieth century invested heavily in audience engagement and political activation, creating frameworks that would allow spectators to question their most revered social truths and traditions by making the binary divisions undergirding them visible on stage. The use of dialectics as a directorial strategy at the theatre was pioneered, Posner notes, in early Soviet Russia, and brought into the mainstream in Europe and the Anglosphere by Bertolt Brecht and those influenced by him. It is now standard fare for performers working in a range of traditions, from devised theatre to clown to puppetry.

The chapters in this volume all start from an understanding of modernity as culturally performed, fundamentally socially unequal, imbricated in relations of capital (and the often violent political machinations capitalism encourages), and therefore unstable, flexible, volatile, and for all this subject to powerful re-imaginings. Each chapter then looks differently at the several ways that theatre practitioners have negotiated – and helped the societies in which they take part to negotiate – the tenets of modernity. Because our authors do not begin from any other shared definition of 'the modern', the stories told in this volume are eclectic; some authors make provocative interventions into existing historical narratives about modern theatre and performance (for example, Chapters 1, 4, and 7), while others challenge existing historiographical practices (for example, Chapters 5 and 8). The larger picture that emerges may sometimes appear counterintuitive; this is intentional. The goal of this book is not to capture *the* story of the modern theatre, but rather to demonstrate emphatically the impossibility of such a task at this time. It aims instead to tell a wide range of stories about the way theatre (as an imagination-driven, intensely political, highly social human art form) works alongside the paradoxes of human relations under cultural modernity, in order to illuminate and challenge but also to support and reinforce.

In light of our sometimes contrarian approach to this volume, the purpose of this introduction is to offer readers a set of coordinates, an aid to navigating our stories about the theatre of multiple ages-modern. I organize these coordinates around the following questions.

First, when and where is 'the modern age'? Modernity may be social rather than empirical, actively imagined into being rather than passively observed as an already-formed thing, but that does not mean that the modern age as we understand it does not come with a set of spatial and temporal markers. The modern, as it has been understood from Anglo-European perspectives, might begin during the continental Renaissance, or during the Enlightenment, or perhaps with the invention of the steam engine, but above all it connotes that which moves forward: it carries momentum, it is tomorrow and not yesterday. It is also spatially enactive: Anglo-European modernity, for example, organizes and grows cities but abandons rural townships; it is positioned as West and not East, North and not South. How does modern theatre and performance engage with these spatial and temporal markers, reinforce them, reframe them, or challenge them?[7]

Second, whose lives 'count' as 'modern'? Although modernity's progress narrative promises net benefit for all, in fact modernity's founding ideology is organized around a division between the human beings (philosophers, economists, robber-barons, scientists, technological innovators) understood as its practitioners, and human beings labelled pre-modern (typically because they live outside the spaces demarcated as modern, whether geographically or culturally). In Albanese's terms they are 'othered'; in the language of modern capitalism, they are not developers, but 'developing'). As the previous volume in this series demonstrates, the Age of Empire was driven by the modernizing impulse otherwise known as colonialism: the arrival of European settlers in vast numbers in North America, Australasia, and (along with brutal conquering armies) Central and South America, Vice-regal aristocrats in India, and soldiers and bounty-hunters in Africa was in each case precipitated by an understanding of the colonizer as modern and the colonized as anything but.[8] If the division of the world's humans into modern (often white, often male) and pre-modern (often black or brown, often female or not normatively gendered or queer) is modernity's pre-eminent condition of possibility, how does the theatre and performance of the late-nineteenth through early twenty-first centuries take up, interrogate, or even entrench this division – contribute to its modernizing project, or seek to undo it entirely?

Utopic dreaming 'at full throttle' may be modernity's greatest hallmark, but it is also its most dangerous fantasy; this tangle lies at the heart of much art we label 'modernism'. Modernist movements in painting, literature, architecture, and of course theatre variously reflect modernity's progress narrative, demonstrating its beneficence, and refract that narrative darkly, challenging in particular its founding claim to be inherently culturally progressive. Rarely, however, does any work of modernist art do only one of these things at a time. Modernism at the theatre, as in many related art practices, embodies the cognitive and aesthetic fracture into multiplicity that Freud and others[9] view as central to modern subjectivity; modern drama is often discussed in terms of paradox and contradiction, as it reflects upon the paradoxical qualities of modernity itself.[10] This kind of work trains upon modernity what performance theorist Elin Diamond provocatively calls a 'double optic'.[11]

In her ground-breaking article, 'Modern Drama/Modernity's Drama', Diamond argues for a distinction between the drama 'of' the modern period and what she labels 'modernity's drama': theatrical works that actively ostend the ideologies and assumptions (including those about time and space, about technological improvement, about capital and its use-value, and about racial, gender, and cultural difference) underpinning the modern project. We might imagine the quintessential drama 'of' the modern to be work that actively models the linear progress narrative's sense of inevitability or of universal positive outcome, whether or not it fully endorses that outcome; for example, although they are often ultimately critical of modernity's social Darwinism, stage realism and naturalism frequently come under attack for their parallel investments in a unified dramaturgical journey towards what appears, on reflection, to be an inevitable end, and in the material practices (audience cut off from the stage by lighting and set design; casting choices) they have used to reinforce this textual tendency.[12] 'Modernity's drama', by contrast, fractures this unity and exposes instead the doubled consciousness it embeds; crucially, it may do this consciously, or not. This is work that demonstrates 'modern time' to be syncopated (then *and* now, running swiftly ahead yet leaving many behind the times), and the spaces of modernity to be various and frequently in collision with one another (East *and* West, the slum adjacent to the glittering urban centre, defining its boundary lines). It is work that foregrounds modernity's central paradoxes, its reliance on bodies and experiences deliberately marginalized by its progress narrative and 'full throttle' aspirations; and it is work invested, in turn, not only in audience comfort and pleasure but also in audience challenge, debate, and even disgust.

WHEN IS MODERN?

There is no single year in which the idea of modernity took hold, nor one location that birthed it. Instead, we might more productively call the time and place of the modern age processual, in constant motion. Rebecca Solnit opens her influential book on the first modern photographer and cinematographer, Eadweard Muybridge, by identifying the peculiar contradictions that shape modern conceptions of space and time, beginning during the industrial revolution and extending well beyond it.[13] Modern space and time, Solnit argues, are defined by how they seem to expand and contract in ways previously unimaginable to human beings: technological, scientific, and aesthetic innovations from the middle and later nineteenth century literally appear to slow time down – photography and geology, for example, isolate and foreground events previously imperceptible to the human eye (the detail available in a still photo; the layers of time embedded in rock formations) – while the building of railways and other inventions linked to manufacture, trade, and the expansion of free market capitalism have the opposite effect, speeding time up and shrinking huge distances.[14] Innovations like railway-building enabled movement and migration on a vast scale for the first time in the middle of the nineteenth century, and changed human perceptions of time in the process; by the middle of the twentieth century, not only had time shrunk once more – from horseback-time (15 kph) through railway-time (100 kph) to jet-plane time (1,000 kph) – but ongoing innovations in cinematic technology meant that humans could do routinely, with increasing precision, and increasingly in the comforts of their own homes, what Muybridge's primary innovation, the zoopraxiscope, had allowed him to do to widespread astonishment and acclaim a century earlier: freeze time in order to observe the human and animal worlds on film in detail never previously imagined (see Figure 0.1). The result of these parallel developments in how we see and perceive the shape and pace of our world has been – and continues to be, in an historical epoch driven by lightning-fast digital innovation – extraordinary cultural as well as cognitive change. As it changes human time, modernity also *literally* leaves its imprint on human bodies: we become creatures of relativity. Solnit notes, 'Early in the twentieth century, when Albert Einstein reached for metaphors to explain his theory of relativity, he repeatedly seized upon the image of a train running across the landscape, a train whose passengers were experiencing time differently than those on the ground'.[15]

The elasticity of modern spatio-temporal experience is one of the grounding logics underpinning modern art in all media. At the theatre, we see modernity's aggressive technoculture revelled in and refracted by the purposefully loud, chaotic works of the Italian Futurists early in the period, its emotional fallout in Antonin Artaud's Theatre of Cruelty, and its conflicted embrace in late twentieth-century trends towards performances enabled by WiFi technology or staged in cyberspace, such as in the work of the Builders' Association (USA), the UK's Forced Entertainment, or Germany's Rimini Protokoll. The principles of geographical, temporal, and social disorientation also lie behind the labours of some of the twentieth century's most influential experimental directors, from Edward Gordon Craig (and his mechanistic theatre of actor-marionettes), to

INTRODUCTION 7

FIGURE 0.1: Study of a horse at full gallop in collotype print. Photo by Eadweard Muybridge/The LIFE Picture Collection/Getty Images.

Konstantin Stanislavsky (as he reconceived the actor to be an independent, creative, artist-agent whose work relied on the precise observation of his or her own subjective experiences), to Bertolt Brecht (whose 'epic theatre' grounded itself in the on-stage collision of multiple, conflicting social perspectives, held up for debate and critique). Later in the century, examples as diverse as Brazilian director Augusto Boal's spect-actors (through whose improvisational labour the structure and outcome of a play is rearranged in performance), British playwright Caryl Churchill's reorganization of her characters' temporal realities (perhaps most famously in *Top Girls* [1982], her critical response to Thatcher-era neoliberal feminism), and Canadian auteur Robert Lepage's seemingly effortless transformations of props from one object to another as his characters appear at once human, then again as the embodiment of machines (his company is called 'Ex Machina') attest to the lasting impact on the performing arts of this extraordinary cognitive shift from human-scale to machine-scale, as well as its ongoing imbrication with late capitalism and its social fallout.

Solnit calls the nineteenth-century renovation of human perception 'the annihilation of time and space': the destruction of the pre-modern notion that either of these concepts is fixed rather than framed by the perspective of individuals and groups on the move. Hans Ulrich Gumbrecht makes a similar argument for modernity as an experience of spatio-temporal re-ordering in his 1998 book, *In 1926: Living on the Edge of Time*. Ironically, that volume pivots the modern tear in space/time around a specific year, though not around any specific location, and the book is organized by key cultural innovations, 'codes', and concepts in order to encourage readers to sample, travel, move around, and experience the moment coalescing around 1926 from any number of perspectives. Taken together, Solnit's and Gumbrecht's works present an emerging modern world in a swirl of motion, a phenomenon that touches down in key places at crystallizing moments (Sarajevo in 1914; Berlin in 1936; Memphis in 1968; Beijing in 1989)[16] but otherwise takes *movement itself* as its defining characteristic, the railway station or airport as its most cherished locale.

Just as Gumbrecht uses 1926 as exemplary of the modern 'moment' rather than as a point of origin, for the authors of this volume 1920 – the year our modern age is to begin – is a fulcrum. Each chapter broadly construes the here-and-now of the modern age as a function of intersecting cultural trends and artistic practices that begin long before 1920 and extend well into the new century in which we now live. In its tether to the events of the First World War (1914–1918), however, 1920 points us all at an essential aspect of modern habitation and art-making: the experience of living constantly in the shadow of international warfare and the human and cultural crises it brings. Human beings have always experienced war as normative, but in the twentieth century modern innovations – from aeroplanes to nuclear armaments to international alliances such as NATO and the Warsaw Pact – meant that violence could never again be isolated as 'abroad', simply 'over there'. Through this lens, 1920 lets us look not only back at 1914 (and at 1917, the year of Russia's October Revolution), but also ahead to 1939 (the beginning of the European conflict that became the Second World War), to 1950 (the beginning of the Cold War), to 1955 (the beginning of the conflict known in Anglo-America as the Vietnam War), to 1990 and 2003 (the first and second American-led wars against Iraq), to 1994 (the genocide against the Tutsi people in Rwanda), to 2011 (Syria, ISIS ... and beyond). If previous moments in human history might be characterized by frequent, isolated conflicts taking place simultaneously *around* the globe, the modern age features *global* conflict: the *same* conflict, waged on multiple fronts over prolonged periods of time, and impacting large numbers of nations or supra-national groups.[17] These kinds of conflicts not only shape modern human perceptions of location, dividing the globe into safe and unsafe spaces, 'haven' versus 'war zone', but throughout the twentieth century they have spawned waves of human displacement that in turn have impacted dramatically on senses of self and community.

As the definition, scope, and spheres of human-made violence shifted under modernity – from local to global, but also from Cold Wars to drone warfare to a fresh, popular interest in post-traumatic stress disorders and other social aftermaths of war – the impact of such events embedded themselves deeply in the fabric of modern cultural production. At the theatre, the idea of 'total war' appears again and again not only as a byproduct of modernity, but as central to its self-fashioning via the myth of unrelenting human progress. War works as a trope for theatre makers to explore the circumstances under which human beings are permitted to inhabit the time and space designated as modern, and to think about how modernity's boundaries are policed by institutions that often find themselves in thrall to the political and economic power conflict brings. British feminist Churchill packs the decades-long conflict between Israel and Palestine into less than 10 minutes in her controversial *Seven Jewish Children* (2009), ironically compacting the seeming endlessness of that fight in a dark mirror of modernity's bulldozing, accelerating impulses; in *Far Away* (2000), she imagines a world at war with plants, animals, trees – everything – at the centre of which lies a gruesome, enabling co-dependence of commodity fetishism and cultural genocide. Churchill's influences include Brecht, whose interrogation of war's imbrication with market capitalism is the main topic of debate in his *Mother Courage and Her Children* (1941), written in exile from Hitler's Germany, but Churchill's later work, as Elaine Aston has recently argued,[18] owes much to Samuel Beckett, whose own writing for the stage imagines the very idea of 'being human' to be under siege from a modernity shaped by the division of life into those who wait (Vladimir and Estragon), those who bring a blend of debilitating violence and diverting entertainment to the waiting (Lucky and Pozzo), and those who can afford never to arrive (Godot).

SO *WHERE*, THEN?

If modern time is untethered by the railroad, then sped up by the jumbo jet, fighter jet, and the internet, the essential fluidity of modern space ironically locates its origin in the hoped-for stability embodied by late nineteenth- and early twentieth-century European conceptions of home. As I argue with Joanne Tomkins in Chapter 4, 'homeliness' and its unmooring (what Freud, in 1918, described as the 'uncanny') has been central to both modern drama and scholarly investigations of it. The rapid urbanization and technological innovation characteristic of the later nineteenth century provoked a need to distinguish firmly between one's private and public lives, with the former vested in the home kept by one's wife and servants as a refuge from the chaos of modernity at full throttle. Home-as-refuge is no less an imagined ideal than modernity itself, of course, and in practice the modern home reflected the very divisions – between capital and labour, work time and leisure time, spaces of violence and spaces of safety, humans who count and those who count for less – on which modernity at large was constructed.[19] For this reason, the fantasies shaping the modern home, and the fantasy of *escaping from* the modern home and into the wider world, now more accessible than ever, have been of intense interest to modern artists.

Architecture's twin obsessions through the twentieth century were the large-scale public building, with the sky-scraper as its apotheosis, and the modern house for which the most celebrated architects of the modern period (van der Rohe, Le Corbusier, Frank Lloyd Wright) earned their fame (see Figures 0.2 and 0.3).[20] As Michel De Certeau demonstrates in his landmark essay, 'Walking in the City', the division between the view from on high – the god's eye view typically occupied by those privileged enough to make it to the top of modern capitalism's food chain – and the street-level view of modern urban denizens, as they trace the city's contours with their hurrying bodies, symbolizes the two poles of modern spatial practice.[21] At the theatre, European and American realists and naturalists interested in dissecting the minutiae of bourgeois private life set their plays in well-dressed rooms in modern houses; impresarios such as André Antoine built small-scale, intimate playhouses to mirror the stage work of the theatrical naturalists and create a feeling of privacy in public. But as tenacious as they have been across the long modern age, because realism and naturalism literally embody modernity's compulsion towards the private home and its

FIGURE 0.2: The Woolworth Building, once the tallest building in the world and completed in 1913, as seen on 28 May 2016 in New York City. Photo by Gary Hershorn/Getty Images.

FIGURE 0.3: Exterior view of Fallingwater, in Bear Run, Pennsylvania, designed by architect Frank Lloyd Wright for Edgar Kaufmann. Bettman/Getty Images.

assumptions about coherence, stability, and singularity of world-view, they have also come repeatedly under fire from theatre-makers determined to explore modern space's expansive, and coercive, dimensions.

Early stage realism and naturalism were quickly and often vociferously challenged by alternative avant-garde practices (Dadaism, Expressionism, Surrealism, among others) wishing to blow up the comforts of home and provoke critical thinking about war, trauma, human displacement, and other experiences thought to be quintessentially modern; by mid-century theatre makers were increasingly leaving theatre buildings themselves behind, working in found spaces and creating performance on the street, in site-specific locations, or, later, on the web. This was an aesthetic decision – a break with the theatre building as representative of the mainstream (home as stifling) – but also a pragmatic one (theatrical homes, as Michael McKinnie notes in Chapter 1, are very expensive to build and maintain in the modern period). Yet abandoning the physical space of 'home' at the theatre did not mean disposing of its politics entirely: the hierarchies and divisions that organize quotidian space under modernity into public and private, local and global, financially valuable and taken-for-granted, extend beyond it and are – as in all things modern – far more complicated than any binary can adequately represent.

State investment in theatre as a public and social good anchored many theatre artists across Europe, the Americas, and Australasia through the mid-twentieth century, but has now been for some time in decline, most acutely in North America; this leaves artists subject to the vicissitudes of finance capital and its vested interests, and in turn influences where and how theatrical homes may be found, made, or negotiated (and what kinds of work may be created there). Meanwhile, targeted investment by both public and private stakeholders in theatrical products and practitioners deemed culturally valuable permitted the development of global festival networks beginning in the later twentieth century; today, the most celebrated artists' works travel worldwide on a much-expanded touring circuit geared towards affluent tourist audiences, and earn immense cultural capital for a privileged substrate of (mostly) white, male auteurs like Peter Sellars, Robert Lepage, Simon McBurney, and Julie Taymor (one of the few women amongst this company). In an era of cuts to state art budgets, large state-funded companies with permanent physical homes (such as England's National Theatre) increasingly shore up their revenues with 'live' viewings of their productions beamed to massive global audiences via transnational cinema networks (such as Cineplex Odeon); by contrast, most smaller theatre companies work without an anchor auditorium (or even rehearsal space), not out of a vestigial counter-cultural desire to resist the modern logic of home, but because fiscal and other material constraints mean they simply cannot afford one.

Modernity's spatial parameters rest on the myth of home and hearth in other ways, too. Imagining the globe to be infinitely accessible and yet safely anchored and shaped by Western worldviews, the Anglo-European modern takes itself as the norm and understands its base as the global North and West, pulling inspiration from and exporting influence to the global South and East. Modern theatre is in no way immune from this resolutely colonial spatial practice – as examples ranging from Artaud's interest in Balinese dance to Peter Brook's controversial South Asian productions demonstrate – but as the twentieth century progressed theatre practitioners increasingly recognized, and became attuned to the critical possibilities extended by, the fact that modern performance happens in places beyond the so-called 'global North'.

With this recognition comes a fresh understanding of modern space as not just unfixed, expansive, as wide as the globe or as small as the bourgeois sitting room, but also as *layered* – as a series of spaces built one on top of the other, a palimpsest derived from the mass physical and cultural violence modernity's othering actions produce. In Chapter 5, Jill Carter, Heather Davis-Fisch, and Ric Knowles remind us that the nations known today as modern Canada, the modern United

States, and modern Mexico are also – in fact always already were – Turtle Island, the most common English term for the homelands of thousands of Indigenous nations on whose cultural genocide modern North America and its own cultural heritage has been crafted. Chapter 5 story of theatrical circulation begins from *that* space, and ends with the revelation that one of modern America's founding theatrical mythologies is, in fact, located inside 'Indian' space and 'Indian' time.[22] As Tracy C. Davis argues in a related context, 'this is mythos expressed as history', a deliberate upending of the modern telos that is both forward-driving as well as anxious about its receding pasts.[23]

WHO COUNTS AS MODERN?

As they crack open the space and time of the modern to reveal the Indigenous folkways and worldviews it buries, Carter, Davis-Fisch, and Knowles also return Indigenous peoples to the modern-age stage as subjects rather than objects of modernity (as developers, not simply developing). They turn our attention to the ways in which modernity's founding mythos has relied for its self-fashioning upon both the labour and the invisibility of a host of bodies deemed 'other', and they ask questions about theatre's power to return agency to those dust-binned creators. Here, they are in good company throughout our volume. In Chapter 2, Nicholas Ridout explores the difference between a 'theatre of consumers' and a 'theatre of producers', working through the social and economic structures that shape modern theatre made *by* some people *for* others, in contrast to an alternate modern theatre made by and for the same individuals who seek in that theatre a way to render their everyday lives more economically stable, politically efficacious, and socially just. In Chapter 7, Christin Essin and Marlis Schweitzer consider constituencies of service workers – including backstage labourers, retail personnel, and paratheatrical labourers in some of the biggest theatre markets in the modern, urban world – as central to modern theatre's 'communities of production'; these are the labourers conventionally sidelined by popular (and, indeed, academic) interest in actors, directors, and designers as the only producers whose work is worth marking. In Chapters 3 and 9, Kirsten Pullen, Ashley Ferro-Murray, and Timothy Murray each bring women's bodies differently into focus as central to modern theatrical making, dwelling on the ways in which those bodies have both shaped and been shaped by popular narratives of theatrical modernism as simultaneously central and marginal, desirable to and abject for the modern project. In Chapter 8, Michelle Liu Carriger and Aoife Monks explicitly address – as do Carter, Davis-Fisch, and Knowles – the Eurocentrism of much modern theatre scholarship, cathecting Japanese and Irish performance repertoires as they complicate our understanding of orientalism in practice – as well as our understanding of what counts as modern repertoire.

The question of whose bodies and experiences count, how, and to what ends has become increasingly urgent in later twentieth-century theatre and performance practices, as the uneven representation of women, queer, and visible minority artists on English, American, European, and Australasian stages has become a matter of significant industry, academic, and even popular debate. At the same time, the shift from a glut of work made *about* those without power and agency *by* those with both, toward a critical mass of work made *by and about* those seeking cultural and economic power, agency, and recognition for themselves, has framed one of the most remarkable trajectories of the later modern period. To be sure, early twenty-first-century theatre remains unevenly weighted towards the experiences of white, straight, privileged men, but increasingly access to the means of theatrical production for non-male, non-white, and queer subjects has allowed the theatre to become a site for the active exploration of this ongoing misrepresentation in modernity's cultures beyond.

Artists use a variety of techniques to interrogate who counts on (and behind) the stage, but (as the chapters ahead also demonstrate) two stand out as key trends in the re-orienting of human representation in late modern-age theatre and performance. First among these is metatheatre, a practice that reflects actively upon the relationship between theatre and the everyday, and that often includes an awareness of the history, context, and processes of its own making.[24] Metatheatrical practices are inherently political, and, as Dassia Posner notes in Chapter 6, although the concept is often linked to Shakespeare and early modern drama ('all the world's a stage'), metatheatre demonstrates its greatest critical power in the late modern period. For example, in *The Shipment* (2008), Korean-American director Young Jean Lee and her collaborators style the performance's first half as an exaggerated minstrel show, shaping contemporary black performance stereotypes (from the aggressive, vulgar stand-up comic to the drug-addled rap star) knowingly into a confrontational display that culminates in members of the cast singing directly, and uncomfortably, to their audience. In its second half the performers put on a conventional living-room drama in the American realist tradition, only to reveal in the final moment – again, nodding to context, convention, and process – that they have been playing white characters all along. Running a broad gauntlet of late twentieth-century performance repertoires, referencing the *long durée* tradition of blackface, and landing back in the living rooms of the modern realists, Lee's thoroughgoing metatheatricality here reveals the extent to which so much modern art, culture, politics, and even social structure relies on black bodies as tools and foils, never as subjects of genuine human experience and need.

The second technique modern theatre and performance artists often use to address the politics of who counts is to foreground those bodies literally, backgrounding in turn those that are typically perceived to count for more, and thus framing the relations of dependence among them in new and revealing ways. In *Harlem Duet* (1997), black Canadian playwright Djanet Sears tells the story of Othello's first wife, Billy, alive and working on her dissertation in contemporary Harlem; Desdemona appears as a hand, briefly, mid-way through the story, while Billie and Othello debate the ways in which black women's bodies are undervalued, both by white society and by many black men. (*Harlem Duet* of course deploys metatheatre as well; the two practices are often used interdependently.) English playwright Sarah Kane wrote scenes of astonishing violence against disabled, queer, and low-class male, female, and transgendered bodies in works such as *Blasted* (1995) and *Cleansed* (1998), attracting mountains of scorn from the reviewing establishment (largely white and male!) but also critical acclaim for her unflinching representations of modern British society's least-regarded bodies. Earlier in the twentieth century this trend can be seen emerging with playwrights ranging from Elizabeth Robins – who was famous for originating Ibsen's textbook hysteric Hedda Gabler in London but whose *Votes For Women!* (1907) included a mass suffrage rally, and a cast of forty, in its middle act – to Tennessee Williams (see also Chapter 3), who frequently used both men's and women's bodies to demonstrate queer modes of living in some of his most celebrated plays, including *A Streetcar Named Desire* (1947).

In performance throughout the twentieth and early twenty-first centuries, the foregrounding of marginalized bodies is increasingly made possible by technology, returning us full circle, but queerly, to the 'full throttle' of modernity. Chapter 9 takes up fully the imbrication of body and technology in the modern period, but here, and by way of conclusion, recent work in live cinema by the British-born, increasingly Europe-based director Katie Mitchell is instructive. In 2010's *Fraulein Julie* – an adaptation of August Strindberg's exemplary naturalist play *Miss Julie* (1888) – Mitchell and her team of collaborators reorient the narrative away from the manservant Jean and his social aspirations, and towards the female servant Kristen, who in Strindberg's original functions as a retrograde religious conscience, exemplary of the 'old ways' against which Jean rebels. At the centre of Mitchell's stage sits a classic realist 'fourth wall' space, fully contained by a literal box set – on stage is a real room, for all intents and purposes, in Julie's 'real' home. The cinema apparatus exists all around this space and is the primary object of audience view; we see interiors via a large screen above the stage but barely glimpse the room with our own eyes. Instead we watch Kristen hovering at the edges of the box set, darting in and out, her internal monologues captured as visual montages on screen alongside the movements of Jean and Julie inside the box.

Mitchell and her team deploy classic modernist but also brand-new digital film practices and technologies in order to restructure Strindberg's play as the story of its least regarded character – the young woman in service; the woman (in this adaptation) pregnant out of wedlock. All the while they innovate new theatrical technologies[25] and focus audience attention on artistic, technical, as well as service labour – Kirsten's, but also the cast's and the crew's (most are onstage as actors, camera operators, and managers of tech and props throughout). They channel Muybridge, using camera technology to bring a complex mix of previously ignored or assumed human experiences into our view. They also capture the rebellious spirit of the modern world's 'annihilation of time and space' at its best – when it is a means not just of throttling humanity forward, but of stopping to regard and revalue that which is trashed in its wake.

CHAPTER ONE

Institutional Frameworks

Theatre, State, and Market in Modern Urban Performance[1]

MICHAEL MCKINNIE

In 2013, new hoardings were installed outside a construction site on Queen Street West in Toronto, Canada's largest city (Figure 1.1).

Spelled out in large block letters, the message on them read: 'COMING SOON TO THE NEIGHBOURHOOD: NOT ANOTHER CONDO'. This was accompanied by the reassuring, 'Don't worry, we're not tearing this beautiful heritage building down. We're revitalizing it and turning it into a new live arts hub and incubator' (Figure 1.2).

The heritage building under renovation was a modest brick structure first opened in 1909 as the west-end branch of the Toronto Public Library. Designed in the Beaux Arts style commonly employed by architects of the thousands of public libraries, like this one, sponsored by American industrialist Andrew Carnegie in the early twentieth century, the site had more recently been occupied by the City of Toronto's Department of Public Health and was badly in need of attention. Following a CDN$6.2 million renovation, the building was reopened in 2014 as the latest home of The Theatre Centre, a modest-sized theatre company that has produced a mix of experimental performance and community arts in a variety of downtown venues since its founding in 1981 (Figure 1.3).

The opening of any new theatre facility is an important event in a city where demand for performance venues has long outstripped supply. But this one is especially notable in that it involved The Theatre Centre, whose recurring difficulties in establishing a 'permanent home' have, perhaps more than for any

FIGURE 1.1: Hoarding outside The Theatre Centre, Toronto, during refurbishment, 2013. Photo: Lilya Sultanova. Reproduced with kind permission of The Theatre Centre.

FIGURE 1.2: Hoarding outside The Theatre Centre, Toronto, 2013. Photo: Lilya Sultanova. Reproduced with kind permission of The Theatre Centre.

FIGURE 1.3: The Theatre Centre, Toronto, 2014. Photo: Tiana Roebuck. Reproduced with kind permission of The Theatre Centre.

other theatre company in Toronto, symbolized the difficulty of those companies gaining secure tenure in the city's high-cost property market during the past four decades.[2] The location of The Theatre Centre's new home is also significant: this stretch of Queen Street West is a historically working-class part of the city now experiencing large-scale urban transformation, as private developers build thousands of apartments marketed for sale to affluent professionals. The message on the hoarding during construction of the new Theatre Centre – 'NOT ANOTHER CONDO' – acknowledged, in a tongue-in-cheek way, the disquiet of many Torontonians about the scale and speed of development in their city, which has been encouraged by the municipal state and accelerated by global financialization.[3] It also illustrates how the building's heritage and its history as a civic institution (a lineage theatre may also claim) are key to managing the anxieties that such developments provoke.

The redevelopment of The Theatre Centre prompts a number of important questions that go beyond a single theatre company in one city. How might we begin to conceive the relationship between theatre and other institutions, such as the state and the market economy? How does doing this call into question modern (or more precisely, modern Euro-American) theatre's historically agonistic stance toward institutions? What are some of the changing ways that theatre, as an institution, is embedded with capital and the state? And how should we regard theatre's promise that it can simultaneously capitalize upon and resolve the social antagonisms that market relations entail?

My use of the term 'embedded' here echoes political economist Karl Polanyi, who sought to theorize the emergence and spread of the market economy in Europe from the late eighteenth century onwards.[4] For Polanyi, this involved a historical transition from 'societies with markets' to 'market societies'. Marketization entails the market no longer being seen as a social institution among many other social institutions, but rather appearing, as Jean-Christophe Agnew puts it, as 'a timeless, natural arrangement for human needs'.[5] The problem, however, is that the market is an inherently volatile institution; regardless of the doctrines of neo-classical economics, it is unable to subordinate social relations and subjects to the motive of gain entirely, and so it cannot marketize on its own. Marketization, therefore, has historically involved a lot of heavy lifting by an array of other 'embedded' social institutions (primarily, but not only, the state and the law) whose purview is not primarily economic. These help manage – sometimes successfully, sometimes not – the social tensions and contradictions that marketization inevitably produces.

To be sure, Polanyi's argument has its limitations. As the Marxist sociologist Michael Burawoy points out, Polanyi tends to subsume multiple historical phases of marketization within a 'singular wave of marketisation giving way to a singular countermovement—what he calls the "great transformation"'.[6] Polanyi also arguably underestimates the ability of capital to overcome the crises that marketization involves and, although he notes the importance of institutions other than the market, the state, and the law within marketization, his consideration of these is limited (and characterizing them as supplying 'protective covering' for the market during the process risks being reductive about their purpose within a highly complex institutional scene).[7] But for my purposes here, Polyani's key contribution is less empirical than heuristic: he prompts us to consider how any number of social institutions, including cultural ones such as theatre, need not be subsumed within the market in order still to be caught up with marketization. And it is worth asking what distinctive role theatre might play, however ambivalently, as a result of this imbrication.

In order to do this, though, it is necessary to set aside any inherited resistance to thinking of theatre as an institution in the first place. As I will discuss, scholars of modern theatre have given remarkably little thought to theatre as an institution – what sort of institution it might be, how it might come into being, and what it might do in the public sphere. This disinterest partly results from disciplinary training and conventions but also reflects a general unease about institutions within modern theatre practice and scholarship, a (sometimes well founded) suspicion most obviously directed towards the state and towards theatre itself. It has also inflected the ways in which the history of modern theatre has been told and how theatre's relationship to other institutions – and to itself as an institution – has been understood.⁸ If taken at face value, though, it risks distracting from the complex ways in which theatre's efficacy often depends on its interpenetration with key political and economic institutions, and on its own institutionality.

One place where this embeddedness has historically been most evident is in the sites where performance happens, especially during periods of significant urban change. Theatre and urban planning have been closely entwined since the shape of European cities began to be determined less by happenstance and more by conscious design during the eighteenth and nineteenth centuries. Seen as forms of urban and economic development, the earlier modern theatres built in, say, Berlin and Paris find their more contemporary analogues not only in the monumental arts centres built by welfare states following the Second World War but also in the networks of smaller theatres upon which the creative city strategies that cities around the world have adopted in recent years depend. In the latter part of this chapter, then, I will consider modern theatre as an institution implicated in the related processes of urbanization and marketization, through one of its most recent iterations: a form of property development within a financialized urban economy. I argue that venues such as the new Theatre Centre in Toronto are made possible by theatre's institutional intimacy with the municipal state and the urban real estate market, and by the company's agility in working with the political economic scripts they supply. But the same urban development that opens up new opportunities for theatre-building may also produce significant social unease, and The Theatre Centre also recognizes this. Here the institutionality of theatre is important as well, since it helps make tenable theatre's promise that it can ameliorate the social antagonisms that large-scale urban change entails.

Given the scale of these forces, why examine a relatively modest theatre development like The Theatre Centre? And why focus on Toronto as an exemplary 'modern' theatre city? First, the particular way that the 'mixed economy' model of theatre financing – comprising some combination of income derived from box office, public subsidy, and private philanthropy – that has evolved in Canada means that most not-for-profit theatre companies occupy a kind of middle position between the more market-dominated model of the United States and the much more generously state-funded model common in continental Europe.⁹ This often necessitates theatre engaging in a rather intricate and improvisatory choreography with the state and the market simultaneously. On the one hand, it would be untenable for arts organizations like The Theatre Centre to operate without public funding, and so they must be attuned to the constantly shifting terms that obtaining this subsidy involves. On the other hand, the amount of public subsidy available is often insufficient to cover such organizations' production costs, so the market cannot be ignored either. But given that an experimental and community arts company is likely only to generate limited box office and philanthropic income, engagement with the market may occur by somewhat refracted means; in the case of The Theatre Centre and a growing number of arts organizations in Toronto, this has been through the urban planning and governance regimes of the municipal state.

Second, although theatre-building and urban planning share a common history, their conjunction gains new and distinctive force in contemporary Toronto. For approximately the past decade Toronto has been experiencing one of the world's largest urban real estate booms, and the building of arts infrastructure, such as the new Theatre Centre, has become tied to this development boom in novel and unanticipated ways. The new Theatre Centre illustrates some of the significant ideological work that theatre, as an institution, is attempting in relation to financialized capital and the urban state. Agnew highlights the 'discrete and retrograde amnesia [that] appears to repeat itself each time experience rediscovers and relives the antagonism of market relations in a form that ideology has yet to resolve'.[10] The Theatre Centre's reassurance that it will be 'not another condo' both acknowledges the social unease that results from large-scale urban development in Toronto – even if this development is no historical accident – and, more broadly, proposes theatre as an exemplary institution to salve it. Through theatre-building it makes a kind of civic promise, one that depends not on theatre opposing the state and the market, but, instead, on mobilizing its deep association with them in imaginative, if sometimes discomfiting, ways.

THEATRE AND INSTITUTIONS

The modernist ideal of cultural autonomy continues to have significant political and aesthetic purchase, especially at a time when struggles over institutions are significant not only for political and economic theory but have material consequences for millions of people every day – consider, for example, the thousands who gathered in the theatre at Epidaurus during the summer of 2015 for performances of Aristophanes' *The Assembly Women*, in response to the austerity regime imposed on Greece by the Eurozone governments and their financial allies. More broadly, though, the relationship between modern theatre and institutions has been characterized by a kind of institutional agonism, both in terms of theatre's relation to other institutions and relative to its own institutionality. This agonism is so pervasive that it can be difficult to know how to unpick it, and this is complicated by the fact that theatre scholarship has demonstrated little interest in doing so. As Christopher B. Balme points out: 'Most scholars have little difficulty in thinking of theatre as an institution – even if most are not particularly interested in that aspect of the medium – yet there has been little work done in actually defining the concept of institution in relationship to theatre.'[11]

When thinking about theatre as an institution we are usually trying to work out three distinct but overlapping problems: how to define theatre as an institution; how theatre is institutionalized; and the material effects of theatre's institutionalization. The first problem – what it is – is conceptual. The second – how it comes into being – is processual. And the third – what it does – is agential. All three are historically and culturally circumscribed, and each is deeply ideological.

It is worth taking these problems in turn. Conceptually, Balme observes that there is no single definition of institution that crosses all of the disciplines and fields in which the term arises.[12] Institutions have been considered most extensively in sociology and political economy, where, he points out, they are commonly seen to share three main characteristics: duration (they persist over an extended period of time); legal status (they are constituted through and function according to some sort of juridical framework, the nature of which changes over time); and 'supraindividual functionality' (their operation and persistence are not dependent on particular individuals).[13] Institutions are usually understood to be different from organizations, which are singular bodies, such as theatre companies, organized around achieving a particular purpose. (To use Balme's way of framing the distinction, an organization is a team and the institution is the game, with its attendant rules and codes.) As organizations, theatre companies may look very different from each other, with divergent mandates, repertoires, performance styles, artistic personnel, and histories. But this diversity is usually underpinned by shared, culturally circumscribed institutional structures that condition the way these companies work, regardless of their distinctive attributes. The shape these structures take delineate theatre's institutional form during a given historical period and social context.

In many modern theatre cultures, a significant number of these structures are related to theatre's widespread adoption of a now-familiar, but historically relatively recent, legal form: the non-profit, or not-for-profit, company. Taking on this form may involve theatre companies registering as charities (which are particular variants of the non-profit company that often entail specific governance arrangements, such as having a board of directors or trustees, to whom artistic leadership reports), accepting public funding (which may require specific reporting procedures, such as producing an annual report of activities), or seeking private philanthropy (which may involve producing certain types of documentation that donors require in order to offset the value of their gifts against tax owed). The non-profit form also illustrates that significant structures and mechanisms that have shaped theatre as an institution and become part of its daily operations may have arisen for reasons having little to do with it; to use the technical terminology, these structures have developed *exogenously* rather than *endogenously* to theatre. For example, the key legal mechanisms granting charitable status to American theatres, and permitting tax exemptions to their donors, have their roots in the introduction of the federal income tax in 1913 and the national War Revenue Act of 1917, respectively.[14]

Such formal mechanisms are accompanied by an array of institutional rules, norms, value systems, conventions, and cultural scripts that condition the way that modern theatre functions on a daily basis. Each of these terms has a slightly different shade of meaning and degree of reflexivity, but taken together they indicate the importance of underlying customs in the functioning of modern theatre as an institution, whether these are tacit or explicit, inherited or invented. Anyone who spends time in a rehearsal room, in whatever capacity, becomes aware very quickly of the extraordinary density of collective expectations and codes of behaviour that its operation involves, and of the ferocity with which these may be enforced when transgressed (woe betide the actor who is late more than once for rehearsal, or the assistant director who gives notes to performers without the permission of the director). Whether formal or informal, these mechanisms help ensure some degree of predictability in the theatrical production process, so that it may continue even as artistic directors depart, cast members change, new directors join the board, and so on. At the same time, and as in any institution, they also contribute to the relative resistance of theatre to sudden change, for better or worse.[15]

Conceiving theatre in these ways, however, stands at odds with the decidedly anti-institutional terms on which modern theatre scholars and practitioners have commonly understood the theatrical arts (and articulated their cultural value, as well as defended them from perceived attack). Insofar as modern theatre has been seen in relation to institutions it has often been imagined that theatre is subjected to institutions – predominantly the state or private corporations, but sometimes arts institutions – which are at best uncomprehending and at worst malign. This subjection can take explicitly punitive forms, such as when governments remove controversial plays from school curricula or private sponsors influence programming. It may also take insidiously benevolent forms, such as when state bureaucrats and theatre administrators, who direct policy-making and arts funding, are seen to preserve their shared bureaucratic interests at the expense of artistic creation. The American director Peter Sellars has argued that in such cases arts functionaries 'simply say "I am going to keep my job no matter what", so policy is put forward that does not perpetuate the art, it perpetuates the institution. Right now we're saving our institutions and killing the art forms'.[16] In this way of thinking, theatre continues to be made in spite of institutions, rather than through them. Of course, Sellars's rhetoric should be treated with some circumspection, given that so much of modern theatre – including Sellars's own work – has historically involved public subsidy, and this subsidy always involves extensive institutional networks. (This is especially true since the mixed economy model of theatre financing that rose to prominence in many countries during the twentieth century involves a complex mix of legal, fiscal, political, and artistic mechanisms.) If, as Shannon Jackson rightly observes, theatre's potential to articulate a radical politics has often been thought to reside in its adoption of an antagonistic position vis-à-vis institutions, in actuality such a politics is as likely to be secured through some form of institutionalization as not.[17]

The problem remains, however, that institutions are usually abstractions, and, as a result, it can be challenging to discern how theatre's institutionalization happens. While we might insist on distinguishing institutions from, say, organizations, in the interest of conceptual rigour, institutionalization only intermittently presents itself transparently as such for consideration.[18] Instead, we often glimpse this process through other entities, practices, and forms that materialize institutional structures in distinctive and sometimes unpredictable ways 'on the ground', through a process of translation and transposition, often with unpredictable results. It may be by examining, for example, particular theatre companies, or rehearsal conventions, or styles of theatre architecture, that theatre's institutionalization becomes visible. Alongside this, and without wanting to elide a small number of notable exceptions, such as Jackson, the critical inattention to institutions to which Balme alludes not only reflects scholarly indifference, it is also a methodological effect of the ways that theatre scholars have commonly conceived and approached their material. Modern theatre scholarship has tended to prioritize the analysis of singular instances of performance (for example, individual plays, productions, or practitioners) over social processes and networks. It has also often assumed, explicitly or implicitly, that its hypotheses are best tested within the spatio-temporal boundaries of theatre events ('but how can we see it in a performance?'). These critical practices can make it difficult to discern theatre's institutionalization because the contours and mechanisms of the process will not always be visible, or best grasped, in such instances or events.

Moreover, if 'institution' implies continuity and custom, such qualities seem at odds with accounts of modern theatre's ostensible unruliness and its potential to provoke social change. As Balme comments: 'By its very definition the term institution is inimical to our preferred understanding of theatre as a bubbling cauldron of resistance, subversion and perpetual innovation.'[19] This is undoubtedly the case in scholarship about modern Euro-American theatres, especially given the central role granted within it to the idea of the 'avant-garde' (both as a historical body of work and as a set of aesthetic aspirations that persist today). In his analysis of Alfred Jarry's famed production of *Ubu Roi* in Paris in 1896 and its subsequent recuperation by theatre scholars as a founding moment of theatrical modernism, Thomas Postlewait points out the extent to which modern theatre history relies on tropes of aesthetic rupture and social provocation, whether or not these are warranted by the available evidence. The 'reigning idea of modern theatre history', he claims, is that modern theatre unfolds as 'a series of new – preferably shocking – events'.[20] This is true both for individual theatre practitioners and the artistic movements into which their work supposedly coalesces. 'We may disagree on which of the controversial events launched the avant-garde revolution in the most significant manner', Postlewait argues, 'but we concur that the shock tactics of various artistic works and movements, including Futurism, Dadaism, Surrealism, and Expressionism, demonstrate and delivered the adversarial mission of modernist art'. Thus, the 'historical narrative ratifies not only the value of the ideas and works but also our role as the keepers and defenders of the heritage'.[21]

Of course, even when an event as extreme as a theatre 'riot' occurs (and the desire for modern theatre to provoke controversy is validated nowhere better than through a riot), this may actually signal a struggle over the terms of theatre's institutionalization rather than a rejection of its institutionalization *per se*. W.B. Yeats's famous use of the word 'riot' to characterize Irish nationalist protests against the National Theatre Society's production of J.M. Synge's *The Playboy of the Western World* at the Abbey Theatre in Dublin in 1907 casts the controversy as a struggle between an individual playwright's freedom of expression and mob rule. (For more on the role of the riot in the shaping of modernist repertoires, see Chapter 8.) But as Lionel Pilkington persuasively argues, the controversy lay, instead, in conflicting institutional visions of the National Theatre Society (NTS) and a dispute about what its relationship to other national institutions (existing or, if the aim of Irish independence were realized, imagined) should be. While 'the protests that followed the first performance of *The Playboy of the Western World* were an opportunity for nationalists to insist that a national institution like the NTS should be sensitive, if not wholly responsive, to majority opinion', Yeats's response was less a cry for artistic freedom and more a call for law and order.[22] Pilkington observes that for 'Yeats and the defenders of the theatre . . . it was a matter of principle not only that the police be invited to the theatre and asked to make arrests, but that those arrested should be prosecuted in the courts'.[23] Keeping one eye firmly fixed on the future, Yeats, by staging the play and denouncing nationalist protest in the way he did, was undertaking a form of inter-institutional positioning on behalf of the NTS. He recognized that its future institutional status would not depend on its popular standing but, rather, lie 'in its ability as a national institution to lay claim to the cultural and symbolic apparatus of an envisaged Irish state'.[24]

Taken together, the above examples suggest that modern theatre's institutional agonism signals not so much a rejection of institutions altogether, but indicates instead a nexus of other phenomena: a discomfiting recognition of the extent to which institutionalization is a necessary condition of theatrical production and consumption; the challenge of satisfactorily representing how complex processes of theatrical institutionalization unfold; and the difficulty in sustaining romantic notions of theatre's essentially oppositional mission once its institutionalization becomes apparent. Given the impossibility of disavowing its own institutionalization, then, the question becomes how modern theatre might manage it, and even capitalize upon it.

MODERN THEATRE AS AN EMBEDDED INSTITUTION

By its assurance that its new home would not be 'another condo', The Theatre Centre made a kind of civic promise that theatre can mitigate the social unease that rapid urban development involves. In pointing to this promise, my aim is not to determine whether or not it is possible for it to be kept (the most likely outcome of such a determination being, 'in some ways yes, in some ways no'). From a cultural historical perspective, other questions are potentially more fruitful. What prompts such a promise to seem necessary in the first place? Why is it plausible? And on what does it depend?

Public concern about urban development in early twenty-first-century Toronto encompasses several strands of urban unease. In the first place, the city's wave of development at this time occurs primarily through a model of housing – condominium apartments, many of which are subsequently rented out to tenants – that fails to conform to the longstanding North American ideal of the owner-occupied, single-family house. The growth of Toronto's suburban areas after the Second World War (largely in Scarborough, North York, and Etobicoke) followed the low-density model pursued in many North American cities at the time. As elsewhere, this longtime model was followed by widespread policy consensus that Toronto's post-millennium growth must involve greater urban density. The tenure of Toronto's infamous right-wing 'crack mayor', Rob Ford, from 2010 to 2014, and the reluctance of his successor, the conservative mayor John Tory, to address car dependency, however, indicate that what is accepted in policy circles remains very much still up for debate among residents at this time. The fact that Toronto's suburbs are so low in density also permits post-millennial downtown residents to imagine that their neighbourhoods are denser than they actually are. Most early twenty-first-century condominium development in Toronto is located downtown, and, as a result, lays bare the fact that its neighbours were not quite the ideal urbanists they might have imagined themselves to be.

The Theatre Centre's civic promise is also about the speed of urban development. The changes to Toronto's skyline in the first decade of the new millennium, especially along Lake Ontario, have been startling. In 2013 *Canadian Business* magazine claimed that 'no city in the Western Hemisphere is putting up more high-rises than Toronto', and, whether this is strictly accurate or not, there has been unprecedented growth in residential and commercial developments in the city, far exceeding that of many international cities.[25] For several years running, Toronto has had more high-rise buildings under construction than any other city in North America, and it now has the second greatest number of high-rises of any city in the world.[26] Although the city has experienced development booms in the past, most notably in the 1980s, these tended to be concentrated in commercial areas of the city, such as its downtown financial district, rather than in older, predominantly residential, neighbourhoods or along the lakeshore. The sense that these developments are rapidly 'changing the character' of downtown Toronto – whose relative resistance to change is what is thought to make it a healthy urban environment in the first place – is very much in the air.

Against this backdrop, The Theatre Centre's impulse to reassure Torontonians that it was not building 'another condo' makes sense, since at the present time 'condo' is a metonym for increasing density and rapid urban transformation. That this assurance should seem believable – and I think it does – is another matter. This has to do with the way that the new Theatre Centre draws on theatre's history as an almost paradigmatically urban and civic institution. In the *longue durée* of urban modernity, theatre-building has been one of the constitutive features of city-making in Europe and North America, and theatre's involvement with nationalist movements and the geographical expansion of capitalist relations has ensured its familiarity in places and cultures around the globe. As Marvin Carlson has shown, urban planning and theatre building have been deeply entwined since at least the mid-eighteenth century, beginning with Frederick the Great's commissioning of the Berlin Opera House and followed by any number of prominent examples since (including the Opéra in Paris in the mid-nineteenth century, Lincoln Center in New York, and the South Bank complex of arts venues in London in the latter half of the twentieth century).[27] More modest, and decidedly less dirigiste, theatre developments, such as the group of small theatres in Toronto that refashioned former manufacturing buildings as performance venues during the 1970s, are the flipside of the same urban coin. This is not to suggest that theatre-building has been without controversy or that all theatre developments have had the same aims or outcomes. But theatre-building has been so historically associated with urban development – as a constitutive institution of the modern city, as a way to negotiate the process of urbanization (and, by extension, globalization), and as an agent of political and economic governance of the modern city – that it seems entirely appropriate for a mid-sized experimental theatre company to make such a claim.

That this claim might be at all persuasive is also at least partly due to theatre's position as a civic institution generally, and the history of 1115 Queen Street West as a civic building particularly. Media coverage of the new Theatre Centre repeatedly invoked the building's origins as a public library, and The Theatre Centre itself drew attention to this history in its own promotions.[28] Like theatres, public libraries have been historically associated with sentiments of civic well-being and urban affluence; in the face of economic transformation, they testify to the existence and durability of a (sometimes actual, sometimes idealized) local community that persists in spite of broader changes over which its residents appear to have little control. The Theatre Centre's invocation of the building's designation by the City of Toronto as a heritage site only amplified this civic claim, positioning the company as the contemporary descendent of the values the library embodied, both as an institution and in terms of its built form.[29]

That a single theatre company could seek to resolve social antagonisms produced by urban development, and that this aspiration could even seem plausible in the first place, also depends, perhaps ironically, on a deep and extensive institutional embedding of theatre vis-à-vis the market and the municipal state. This embedding increasingly involves institutional mechanisms that fall outside theatre scholarship's familiar critical interests in, for example, public funding of the arts or forms of state regulation such as legal censorship. But many of these instruments – such as loan guarantees, lines of credit, and below-market leases – are increasingly important if we wish to understand the basis on which theatre makes its civic promise today.

In order to access new forms of financing and build badly needed cultural infrastructure, Toronto's theatre industry has come to depend on the municipal state playing an important intermediary role, as both a bridge to capital and a buffer against it. In the case of the former, theatre relies on the municipal state's recognition of some distinctive challenges it faces in order to operate within a major city. Theatre requires substantial capital investment in order to make its spaces viable for performance, since in most cities with healthy economies the stock of potential spaces is limited, and theatre is a highly specialist type of use. But it would be risky for a not-for-profit theatre company to undertake this investment alone, since doing so would involve assuming a substantial debt secured against its property (even if a bank would agree to lend the capital in the first place, which it would likely do only if the company's property were valuable as real estate, not as a performance venue). Theatre depends, therefore, on the state sharing some of this risk, but here through indirect mechanisms that are less visible than direct spending, and so less likely to generate public opprobrium or censure from self-styled guardians of the public purse. Such mechanisms are a way for the municipal state to play the traditional role of the state within market societies of lubricating the flow of capital to theatre, even if this is on a fairly modest scale, but not to be seen to do so.

At the same time, however, theatre depends on the municipal state acting as a buffer against the excesses of capital. In market societies this has historically been an important role for the state, in order to smooth out the effects of marketization, which tend towards bust and boom. In a high-cost, inflationary property market, the drive to commoditize land is strong. Without some sort of state intervention it can be difficult for theatres to remain in the city core, either because they will be physically squeezed out, or priced out, or both. This could mean stepping in when the normal operations of the property market would produce an undesirable result, such as displacing theatres from the city centre. Or it could mean intervening when theatres' exposure to the market threatens their financial health, such as when they struggle to repay loans secured against the equity in their properties. One possible response to both of these scenarios is for the municipal state to act as landlord in the last instance, by assuming ownership of the properties involved and leasing them back to their occupants at a nominal cost. Through such an intervention the municipal state shields theatre from some of the more extreme effects of a volatile property market.

Here is how this institutional logic plays out in practice in Toronto's theatre industry, and for The Theatre Centre specifically. Like many cities, Toronto has an arm's length funding body, the Toronto Arts Council (TAC). And like many theatre companies in Toronto, The Theatre Centre receives a modest annual operating grant from the TAC (in 2014 the company received a grant of CDN$121,000, within an annual operating budget of approximately CDN$900,000, along with grants from the provincial and federal arts councils as well).[30] But the construction of its new facility involved other municipal mechanisms necessary to finance the project that are important but would be easy to overlook.

The City of Toronto owns a large number of properties scattered throughout the city. Among these are what the City calls its 'cultural portfolio': heritage buildings in the downtown core occupied by a number of important local theatre companies and arts organizations, including Canadian Stage Berkeley Street, Theatre Passe Muraille, Buddies in Bad Times, Young People's Theatre, and now The Theatre Centre. These theatres' tenancies are governed by Below Market Rent (BMR) agreements with the City, which allow non-profit organizations, like theatre companies, to lease City properties at a nominal rent in return for assuming responsibility for the operating costs of these spaces.[31] For the City, its BMR policy is part of broader municipal service delivery, and most of the approximately one hundred BMR agreements in operation are with community or social services organizations rather than arts companies. But its cultural portfolio, in particular, helps the City retain high-profile arts activity in the downtown core that would likely be priced out otherwise, given that these properties are in locations that would be very attractive to private developers. The cultural portfolio also helps the City claim that it is achieving the spatial goals of its Culture Plan and its various creative city strategies (as in many early twenty-first-century cities, the concept of the 'creative city' has figured prominently in Toronto's urban planning regime).

The counterpart to the cultural portfolio and the BMR policy is the City's Loan and Loan Guarantee Portfolio. For theatre companies leasing City properties, the Loan Guarantee programme is especially important, since it provides them with access to capital that would otherwise be difficult, if not impossible, for them to gain. The Loan Guarantee programme addresses a problem particular to tenants of the City's cultural properties, in that they often require loans to improve these properties and adapt them to artistic use (heritage buildings may be in poor repair and were designed for other purposes). Banks, however, are usually unwilling to lend the substantial sums of money involved to non-profit organizations with few tangible assets. The way that theatre companies in Toronto have commonly raised such financing has been by securing bank loans against the equity in properties they own, but this option is not open to tenants of City buildings. (In any case, such an approach is not without significant risk. The reason why the cultural portfolio includes Theatre Passe Muraille's property in the first place is because that theatre could no longer sustain repayments on its secured loans, which led to the acquisition of its property by the City in order to safeguard the facility's continued use as a theatre and provide the funds to pay off Theatre Passe Muraille's debts.) In order to make a loan from a bank to one of its tenant organizations possible, therefore, the City may agree to guarantee a portion, or even the entirety, of the loan.

The Theatre Centre's new home has been made possible by these mechanisms. Prior to the departure of Toronto Public Health from 1115 Queen Street West in 2012, The Theatre Centre was awarded the tenancy of the building and signed a BMR agreement with the City.[32] But the building required significant renovation in order to be used as a theatre facility, both in order to improve its physical condition and to expand it to accommodate The Theatre Centre's programme. Although the company secured funding for approximately 70 per cent of the CDN$6.2 million refurbishment budget, it required bridge financing to cover the remaining CDN$1.5 million.[33] The City ultimately agreed to guarantee a bank loan for The Theatre Centre and, after works were completed, the company opened its new home in the spring of 2014.

This is not, however, the whole story. Approximately CDN$1 million of the financing for The Theatre Centre development consisted of what is known in Toronto arts and urban planning circles as 'Section 37 money'. This refers to Section 37 of the Planning Act, the provincial statute that governs municipal planning in the province of Ontario. Section 37 is the part of the Act that allows municipalities to 'authorize increases in the height and density of development' beyond what is allowed by their official plans in exchange for the landowner providing (unspecified) 'facilities, services or matters'.[34] This seemingly innocuous provision has existed for many years, and most municipalities in Ontario use it infrequently. There are similar legal provisions in planning law elsewhere in the world; for example, 'Section 106' agreements in England and Wales also trade exemptions to planning regulations for payments to local authorities (and, as in Toronto, these have become contentious as developers seek to avoid them). In

Toronto, Section 37 agreements have become an increasingly important mechanism through which the City has secured funding or other benefits for public amenities such as affordable housing, parks, libraries, transportation services, community centres, and cultural venues such as theatres. Given the cost of, and competition for, development sites in downtown Toronto, it also is usually cheaper for a developer to absorb the cost of a Section 37 agreement in order to secure the greater occupancy that a planning variance would permit than it would be to scale back a development (thus foregoing revenue) or assemble a larger site (thus adding much greater cost through land acquisition). Moreover, there has historically been strong political pressure for low residential property tax increases in Toronto, which has reduced the fiscal capacity of the municipal state to address the City's enormous infrastructure needs. Early twenty-first-century Toronto has the lowest residential property taxes in the Greater Toronto Area, but, like any big city, has very large infrastructure requirements and these must be paid for primarily out of the local tax base.

While the City of Toronto has been inventive in its use of Section 37 agreements to fund public amenities, they are not without their pitfalls, and any theatre company wishing to make use of the provision must successfully navigate these. To start with, Section 37 agreements are almost entirely ad hoc; developers are not legally required to enter into them (though they may determine that doing so will make approval of their application for exemption from the requirements of the Official Plan more likely) and there are no formal requirements in relation to the size of their contribution or the type of amenity funded (with the result that these can vary greatly from development to development). The projects supported are very much subject to political pressure, and, while this has resulted in some welcome civic activism in Toronto, it makes the provision of basic urban infrastructure increasingly dependent on the organizing capacity and planning expertise of local residents and organizations, who are often in a subordinate power relationship with developers (if developers refuse to negotiate, and the area city councillor does not intervene effectively, there is little they can do). The largest number of Section 37 agreements is also in the downtown core, with few in suburban areas of the city. This makes sense in some ways, because that is where development is concentrated and politically progressive downtown councillors have been more aggressive in brokering agreements than their more conservative suburban counterparts. But it also tends to reproduce the existing geographical distribution of municipal infrastructure (including theatres), which is already best developed in the downtown core, and it can make agreements especially subject to the patronage of individual city councillors (thus using arts projects to resuscitate, to some degree, an older clientelist model of municipal politics that modern planning regimes were intended to supplant, or at least mitigate).[35] And, because Section 37 benefits are not provided until building permits are issued, theatre developments become tied even more tightly to the planning schedule of the municipal state and the construction cycle of private capital than in the past. Thus, the provision of theatrical infrastructure has come to depend to a great extent on the booms (and inevitable busts) of the property market; The Theatre Centre's civic promise is underpinned by some very complex political and economic relations indeed.[36]

CONCLUSION

It is likely that without institutional mechanisms such as Section 37 agreements, a number of theatre and arts developments in Toronto, including the new Theatre Centre, would not have happened. Certainly, there was a long period where few new theatre venues were developed in the city, in spite of the enormous growth of its theatre economy, and Section 37 agreements have made new forms of capital financing for building projects available where it did not exist previously. At the same time, however, the ingenuity of The Theatre Centre in capitalizing upon such institutional mechanisms should not be underestimated, and the successful conscription of developers and city planners in the process suggests not only their recognition of the cultural capital that theatre often brings to the table in modern urban development, but also their acknowledgement of its institutional competence. In creating its new home, The Theatre Centre testified not to theatre's institutional hostility but to its institutional agility.

In a number of broader ways, then, modern theatre can be seen as an exemplary institution. Many of the characteristics of theatre that we now take for granted are the result of its deep and extensive institutionalization, not only in and of itself but in relation to the dominant institutions of the modern age: the market and the state. Theatre's role in contemporary urban development, furthermore, demonstrates its institutional embeddedness and, equally importantly, its skill in capitalizing upon it. That theatre can simultaneously participate in modern marketization and hold out the promise of ameliorating the social antagonisms that marketization entails illustrates that the relationship between modern theatre and institutions is rather more complex – critically and politically – than our inherited ways of thinking about their conjunction suggest. Whether this civic promise can ultimately be realized is open to question. But the fact that it is plausible to make it in the first place is revealing, and more than a little unsettling.

CHAPTER TWO

Social Functions

Consumers and Producers

NICHOLAS RIDOUT

There is no modern age. As the introduction to this volume has already suggested, to write a cultural history in terms of this universalizing category would be to practise a form of intellectual violence. It would be to embrace the idea of a state of affairs, called modernity perhaps, to which everyone aspires, and it would be to ignore the reality that modernity is often simply the word used for capitalism by those who pretend that actually-existing capitalism marks the horizon of human possibility. Since the late twentieth century, as the option of an avowedly non-capitalist modernity (actually-existing socialism) seemed to disappear from view, modernization and modernity have become ever more synonymous with maximum participation, by individuals and collectives, in a globalized capitalism.

For many of these individuals and collectives this participation is on terms established in the West. But as much recent scholarship has shown, the origin of this globalized capitalism is not the West, so much as it is in the encounters between Europeans on the one hand, and a wide range of cultures and societies in the Americas, Africa, Asia, and the Pacific on the other. This has three significant consequences for the way modernity is understood. First, the specific form of modernity (or capitalism) as it is known in the West turns out to be dependent, for its very existence, on the exploitation of the labour and resources of millions of supposedly non-modern people, who were taken into slavery, forced into indentured labour, dispossessed of their land and of their natural and cultural resources by colonizing Europeans. Second, modernity refers not just to the prosperous and predominantly urban industrial societies of the West, but also to those societies shaped at the other side of this violent interaction. The 'supposedly non-modern' people enslaved and exploited in the colonial encounter are just as 'modern' as their colonizers. Furthermore, the process of 'modernization' that I am here calling colonization was in fact the very means through which the distinctions between modern and pre-modern, European and non-European were first established. Third, there have been multiple experiences of modernity, not because it has been exported worldwide to consumers, but because modernity, in this broader understanding, came into being in multiple locations, in each of which specific encounters took distinctive forms and led to the formation of particular institutions and social relations. This, finally, is why there can be no 'modern age'. The term itself presupposes a universal modernity, modelled on one specific experience alone: Western Modernity. It not only limits the range of experiences that might be understood to be modern, it effectively hides from view the historical reality that the story of universal modernity is forged in and subsequently maintained by violence, and that it continues to be an occasion for political and cultural struggle.

The work of subjecting this universal modernity to critical analysis and articulating alternate modernities has been under way in many parts of the world for some time, and some of it, as we shall see, has been done in the theatre. This work has often been led by those who are not normally included as the subjects of a universalizing, 'Western' modernity. As Partha Chatterjee, speaking in Bengali in Kolkata, observed:

> because of the way in which the history of our modernity has been intertwined with the history of colonialism, we have never quite been able to believe that there exists a universal domain of free discourse, unfettered by differences of race or nationality. Somehow, from the very beginning, we have made a shrewd guess that given the close complicity between modern knowledges and modern regimes of power, we would forever remain consumers of universal modernity; never would be taken seriously as its producers. It is for this reason that we have tried, for over a hundred years, to take our eyes away from this chimera of universal modernity and clear up a space where we might become the creators of our own modernity.[1]

THREE SOCIAL FUNCTIONS: SOCIAL CHANGE, THE LOGIC OF WORK, NEGATION

To think responsibly about the social function of theatre in the modern age is therefore to abandon attempts to think in universal terms of either modernity, or social function, or theatre. It is to consider theatres as practices in a range of different modernities, and therefore as capable of performing more than one social function. In doing so I take up Partha Chatterjee's distinction between 'consumers' and 'producers' of modernity and carry it over into a distinction between two different ways of understanding theatre and its possible social functions, to distinguish, that is, between a theatre for consumers on the one hand and a theatre for producers on the other. I start with what I have elsewhere named 'the theatre of modernity'.[2] In this earlier, and it now turns out, rather restricted definition, the theatre of modernity was where most people sat in the dark during their leisure time watching and listening to some other people at work in the light. In other words, this modern theatre is a theatre for consumers. It encompasses everything from the Broadway musical to experimental art theatre often called 'modernist' or 'avant-garde', and associated with canonical names from August Strindberg to Romeo Castellucci. Understood in terms of both the material and ideological features by which a certain European modernity has been characterized, this 'modern theatre' is clearly part of an economics of exchange, it is predominantly an urban practice, it frequently takes as its subject the life of the individual, it tends to assume an audience of rational and autonomous individuals, and it assumes a broadly secular social environment. This is not to say that such theatre may not sometimes either seek to remove itself from exchange, take place in rural settings, present collectives rather than individuals on stage, address its audience as a public from whom a collective response might be solicited, or seek to explore religious or non-rational experiences. But when it does any of these things it does so knowing itself to be both contained within and in dialogue with these dominant features of everyday modernity.

This indicates a range of possible social functions for such a theatre, many of which might be gathered loosely under the heading of critique. In this modernity, at least, theatre-makers frequently understand themselves and other artists to be engaged in a practice because they want to make a difference, in their society, for their audiences. Theatre in this modernity is in the business of change and transformation, whether it be psychological, spiritual, social, or political. Most theatre in this modernity, and nearly all the theatre that is understood to be art, carries with it a commitment of some kind to the production of the new, to the idea that something might be progressed. It is a kind of modernization. Only very rare examples of critique in this theatre of modernity actively seek to send modernization into reverse. Even a critic of the secular, rational, individualistic modern world as fierce as Antonin Artaud conceived his 'theatre of cruelty', for all its celebration of the irrational, its mystical language, and its fantasies of authentic and primitive culture, as a summons to his spectators to leap forward into a better future – a newer modernity – rather than to make a return to a pre-modern past.

This theatre for consumers, as it is found in its most familiar locations (and with perhaps the widest range of variant forms) in cities such as London and

New York, Buenos Aires and Berlin, can offer its consumers opportunities for reflection upon the conditions in which they live and their relations with one another. What might distinguish theatre from other artistic practice is that it offers these opportunities in a social setting. This theatre looks social. It is associated with sociability. It frequently represents the social, in that the medium itself (with notable exceptions) tends, when it represents things (which it does most of the time), to represent people in relationships. It often does this in ways that organize the characters in a play so that they can be understood to stand for larger collectivities (professions, classes, generations). Amid the consumption, this theatre encourages spectators to relate the society of the stage to the social world they themselves inhabit, and to imagine their responses to the performance as contributions to a dialogue or debate about that social world and how it might be improved. This theatre might constitute part of a 'bourgeois public sphere': that actual and virtual social space imagined by Jürgen Habermas to have emerged in the cities of eighteenth-century Europe, in which a free and disinterested conversation between social equals promises rational solutions to social and political problems. This 'public sphere', which had long since, in Habermas's account (written in the early 1960s), been contaminated by the twin evils of marketing in actually-existing capitalism and propaganda in actually-existing socialism, is of course a modern (European) idea par excellence, part of what Habermas himself later came to call 'Modernity: An Unfinished Project'.[3]

The work of this theatre of critique, debate, and social reflection is part of an ongoing project of modernity, then, even, perhaps, of modernization. It seeks, as I have already suggested, to contribute to some kind of transformation, offering experiences, within the realm of the social, that might encourage its consumers to experience the world differently, both during and after the performance. It offers such experiences in the hope that those who attend and respond might feel differently about themselves and their relations with one another, or even with others who are not (yet) imagined to be part of the social realm in which this theatre is consumed; that it might contribute to some enduring change in perspective and understanding. Very often this hope is a hope, too, for the social function of theatre, a desire and a determination to see that the production and consumption of theatre might contribute, directly or indirectly, to something that might loosely be called 'social change'. Its social function is to encourage a broader process of desirable social change. This is the first of the three social functions that might be attributed to theatre.

Of course, theatre may also play a role in inhibiting social change, preserving ideological coherence for existing social organization. For, although most people involved in making theatre and producing critical material about it in the liberal democracies of actually-existing capitalism tend to identify themselves with causes and ideas they consider socially progressive, the immediate pre-history of this European theatre reveals theatre as a practice intimately involved in the production and reproduction of state power. Even leaving aside this pre-history, and with it the suspicion that state-funded companies such as the Comédie Française, the Royal Shakespeare Company, and any number of 'national' theatres might point to the persistent consolidation of state power over potentially progressive social forces and movements, this theatre's participation in the entertainment industry threatens to limit any potentially progressive social function for the theatre. This is not because by its mere participation in the market this theatre has 'sold out' to 'the man'. It is not inevitable that all progressive 'messages' should be fatally contaminated by the contradiction that the messenger is paid, or because everyone involved in the event is participating in capitalism. It is rather that as part of the entertainment industry, the modern theatre – the one with the consumers in the dark and the producers on stage in the light – performs a second social function, one that arises directly from the economics of this encounter.

The modern theatre participates in the organization of human capacities, in the interest of production, into work and non-work. Going to the theatre, in the evening, after work, spending the money one has earned through work, is a way of 'recreating' oneself, of making oneself available once again, reinvigorated, for the expenditure of labour power upon which capitalist productivity depends. The second social function of theatre is therefore to confirm, in the most personally rewarding and socially pleasurable manner, the logic of work upon which the existing social order is founded. No matter that the entertainment offered permits its consumers to think new thoughts about the shortcomings of that social order, or that the act of gathering around critical representations of their own society might generate feelings of community and solidarity and ignite desires for social change, it does so while extending an organization of life by work that limits what kind of change can be imagined. Theodor Adorno and Max Horkheimer describe this situation as follows:

> Amusement under late capitalism is the prolongation of work. It is sought after as an escape from the mechanised work process, and to recruit strength in order to be able to cope with it again. But at the same time mechanisation has such power over a man's leisure and happiness, and so profoundly determines the manufacture of amusement goods, that his experiences are inevitably after-images of the work process itself. The ostensible content is merely a faded foreground; what sinks in is the automatic succession of standardised operations. What happens at work, in the factory, or in the office can only be escaped from by approximation to it in one's leisure time.[4]

Inasmuch as it remains a theatre for consumers, then, theatre can perform only a very limited social function, beyond its confirmation of the logic of work in capitalism. This goes some way to explaining why, in *Aesthetic Theory*, Adorno offers a third social function for theatre (or, in Adorno's case, art in general). This third social function is to have no social function ('Insofar as a social function can be predicated for artworks, it is their functionlessness').[5] It is precisely in its abstention from a direct engagement with the social world of which it paradoxically forms a part that art can serve as a negation of that world as it is, and in so doing present itself as an instance of truth, freedom and the possibility of an entirely different social world. Of all the activities that go by the name of art, it is particularly difficult to think of theatre behaving in this way. It is, as we have seen, a social activity. Chamber music, lyric poetry, and certain kinds of prose fiction are far better equipped to perform such negation, and Adorno frequently turns to such forms for examples of the art he values. In the theatre it is mainly in the plays of Samuel Beckett, which, at the level of their representations, at least, seem to repudiate even the possibility of the social, that Adorno identifies the negation he seeks in art. But even Beckett's plays hardly escape their implication of the prolongation of work by means of leisure. They are, after all, just like West End musicals, usually performed in the evening, as work for their actors, technicians, and other theatre employees, and as leisure

FIGURE 2.1: Attendees at the Metropolitan Opera crowd around the bar for drinks and cigarettes during an intermission. Getty Images.

for their spectators. The choice for theatre-makers might be either to relinquish any aspiration that their work might perform a progressive social function, or to abandon that mode of theatre I have characterized here as characteristic of modernity – where people sit in the dark in their leisure time watching other people working. This means that the progressive social function for theatre might lie with a theatre for producers rather than a theatre for consumers (see Figure 2.1).

THEATRE FOR PRODUCERS

I turn now to the modernity to which Partha Chatterjee refers in the quotation above, in the Indian state of West Bengal, and to a theatre that claims to produce its own modernity rather than consume one imposed upon it by others. West Bengal, like the rest of the contemporary states of the Indian subcontinent (India, Pakistan, Bangladesh, and Sri Lanka), was subject to British colonial rule until independence in 1947. Kolkata, its major city, had been the headquarters of the East India Company from 1690 and then, following the imposition of direct rule from London in 1858, the capital of 'British' India itself (see Figure 2.2). Today, along with the rest of India, it is routinely viewed, in a neo-colonial perspective, as a society in need of 'development', one in which modernity has not yet been reached and in which all sorts of tradition (religion,

FIGURE 2.2: India, Kolkata, rubber factory. Photo by Lillehaug/ullstein bild. Getty Images.

perhaps most obviously) is thought to persist. In such views the people's poverty is seen as backwardness, rather than as the result of colonialism, and it is on this basis that a neo-colonialism can be and frequently is offered as a solution to the damage it has already wrought. It is against that damage, and in the name of a different and more complex conception of what it might be to be modern, that the theatre of Jana Sanskriti has been working since its foundation in the mid-1980s. Its work, and the historical situation in which it emerged, offers another way of thinking about theatre, modernity, and social function.

Jana Sanskriti does cultural work in rural West Bengal, combining theatre-making with social and political activism. It is one of the longest-standing groups of practitioners of Theatre of the Oppressed, a participatory political theatre practice first developed in the 1970s by Augusto Boal, a Brazilian theatre director and writer. I consider the particular example of Jana Sanskriti, not simply because it works in the very same location – West Bengal – in relation to which both Partha Chatterjee and Dipesh Chakrabarthy have articulated their ideas about alternate modernities, but also because of the attention paid to it from outside theatre and performance studies, most particularly in recent work by the sociologist Dia Da Costa, who views it not simply as theatre practice, but, more broadly, as 'cultural work'.

Dia Da Costa is interested in the work of Jana Sanskriti because she wants to challenge normative understandings of 'development' of the very kind I am also concerned to trouble here by unsettling commonsense and ideological conceptions of 'modernization'. Crucially, Da Costa sees the work of Jana Sanskriti as a form of 'productive labour' which seeks its effects against the logics of 'development' and 'modernization' required by capitalism, in the active and collaborative making of a culture of social solidarity and political resistance to state and corporate power. I am indebted to her work and to the work of other Indian scholars and theatre-makers for whatever limited understanding I possess of this ongoing work and its historical and political antecedents in Bengal.

Theatre in West Bengal has a complex relationship with Bengali modernity. The theatre culture that developed in Kolkata in the first half of the nineteenth century largely involved the adoption and adaptation of Western forms of 'proscenium' theatre, understood by its Bengali enthusiasts as a modern practice through which they could affirm a national cultural capacity. As Rustom Bharucha affirms, '[i]t was a means by which the "natives" could assert their cultural heritage. The irony, of course, is that the theatrical heritage of the Bengali theater was intrinsically colonial. Before it could develop an indigenous tradition, the Bengali theater slavishly imitated the proscenium tradition of the nineteenth-century theater in England'.[6] Sudipto Chatterjee characterizes this relationship slightly differently, arguing that from its beginnings in the 1830s the theatre of the so-called 'Bengali Renaissance' – including the influential work of the playwright Michael Madusudhan Datta (1824–1873), the actor, playwright, and director Girish Chandra Ghosh (1824–1912), and the playwright Dinabandhu Mitra (1829–1873), to name three of its most canonical figures – were examples of a 'creative hybridity', that 'registers difference and sameness, mimesis and alterity at the same time'.[7] For Dia Da Costa, Bengali theatre under British colonial rule involved bringing 'native traditions into a political modernity that would make them fit for self representation'.[8] These perspectives allow this theatre to be seen as a modern theatre in at least three senses: it responded to the distinctive experience of the modernity coming into being through the colonial encounter; it critiqued colonial rule and articulated a nationalist consciousness; it was an urban middle class practice that excluded peasant and working class participants and 'popular' experiences. It was also a 'modern' theatre in the sense I have outlined in the preceding section: a theatre for consumers, rather than a theatre of producers.

This is one way of understanding why Rustom Bharucha, while recognizing 'the emotional power and entertainment value of the commercial theater in Bengal', chooses to focus instead on examples of avowedly 'political theatre' for which entertainment and its consumption is not the primary purpose.[9] In *Rehearsals of Revolution* – a book whose title is an adaptation of a term made popular by Augusto Boal, and which was published at more or less the same time as the first experiments in theatre that led to the formation of Jana Sanskriti – Bharucha traces a development away from this largely middle-class theatre for consumers, towards a theatre which addresses itself to the interests of India's producers – its rural and urban workers. His primary focus is on two key theatre-makers of the post-Independence period, Utpal Dutt and Badal Sircar, but he also pays some attention to the earlier work of the Indian People's Theatre Association (IPTA).

Formed in 1942 with the intention of mobilizing a people's theatre movement opposed simultaneously to fascism and to British colonial rule, IPTA quickly expanded beyond its original groups in Mumbai and Kolkata to become a national organization.[10] Its workers made theatre for mass audiences, made use of popular forms (in Bengal, this often meant *jatra*, a participatory and processional performance form featuring figures and stories from Hindu mythology), as well as adapting European and American drama (Ibsen, Odets) for local audiences. Productions were topical and engaged, with early subjects ranging from the anti-fascist struggle in Singapore (*Four Comrades*, 1942) to the Bengal famine of 1943 (*Nabanna*, 1944). IPTA was affiliated with and functioned effectively as a cultural arm of the Communist Party of India (CPI). However, despite its address to the masses, it was still a theatre for consumers, in that it saw theatre itself as a medium through which meanings could be communicated from one group of people to another, in order to awaken them to consciousness of the reality of their social and political conditions. Its socialist, anti-fascist, and anti-colonialist vision was also a modernizing one, representing, as Dia Da Costa observers, a conception of modernization in which the 'unhealthy' aspects of rural culture were to be eradicated in the interests of a secular, socialist nationalism led by the middle class: it sought a 'progressive transformation of their [the rural masses'] culture'.[11] In other words, it invited the rural poor to consume a socialist version of modernity offered by an enlightened and progressive sector of the urban Bengali middle class.

The same observation might also apply to the work of Utpal Dutt. Dutt had directed productions of Shakespeare for Kolkata's Little Theatre Group in the late 1940s, and worked briefly in IPTA in 1950, which introduced him to the potential of working politically with mass audiences. Returning to the Little Theatre Group, he led its transformation into a company making work in Bengali for working class audiences on increasingly political subjects, sometimes engaging directly with specific political campaigns, such as the CPI's 1967 election campaign. In the 1970s he turned, as had artists in the Bengali IPTA a few decades earlier, to the conventions and techniques of *jatra* to develop a popular 'theatre for revolution' that sought, according to Da Costa, to 'politicise rural indigenous forms [such as *jatra*] by modernising them in a socialist narrative'.[12]

The work of Dutt's contemporary, Badal Sircar, was more oriented to a middle-class urban audience. But in his articulation of what he called the Third Theatre, Sircar placed the question of the urban–rural divide at the centre of his practice. Sircar's Third Theatre would be an attempt to synthesise two existing modes of theatre: making a bridge between a rural folk theatre and an urban theatre derived from Western practices. This synthesis at the level of theatrical practice would not resolve the dichotomy, but theatre might play a part in a broader social and economic struggle to do so. In a series of productions from *Spartacus* (1972) to *Bhoma* (1979), a play adapted from the real life struggles of a rural Bengali everyman, Sircar's company Satabdi sought to represent to urban audiences the political struggles of the rural poor, abandoning the proscenium stagings of his earlier work in favour of stagings in an intimate space at the Academy of Fine Arts in Kolkata and regular open air performances in Surendranath Park in central Kolkata. The first performance of *Bhoma* was presented on an open-air platform in a village in the region in which the man on whom its central character was based had lived. The company also led workshops with villagers alongside their work in this production, and, from the mid-1980s, undertook regular rural tours of their productions.

Writing in 1983 about the future potential of Sircar's work, Bharucha suggested an affinity with Boal's Theatre of the Oppressed, observing that the village workshops demonstrated that 'Sircar shares Boal's faith that the people can create a theater for themselves that will enable them to understand and shape the conditions of their life'.[13] Less optimistic assessments of the social and political value of Sircar's theatre have emphasized his romanticization of the rural poor,[14] suggesting that Sircar's conception of an urban–rural dichotomy may have rested on precisely the distinctions between modernity and tradition or development and 'backwardness' that others have sought to complicate. While Sircar's subsequent work did not take up the techniques of Theatre of the Oppressed as Bharucha clearly hoped it might, a group of activists working in villages outside Kolkata were about to do so. In his account of the formation of Jana Sanskriti in 1985, its founder and present-day artistic director Sanjoy Ganguly describes how a group of mainly middle-class activists, members of the CPI(M) (which had formed a Left Front government in West Bengal in 1977), turned to theatre as a way of engaging more fully with the lives of the rural people with whom they were doing political work. Initially this turn to theatre, inspired by folk performance, took the familiar form of plays presented to audiences, representing popular struggles and highlighting pressing social and political issues in episodic structures incorporating music and dance. Looking back on these early experiments, Ganguly recalls a realization that performance itself was not enough, and that the transmission of ideas through theatre to an audience, with the aim of 'empowering' them, failed to account for the creative and intellectual capacity of the rural audiences. It resembled too closely the kind of 'theatre for development' that, even though it had been embraced enthusiastically by socialists and nationalists in multiple locations (including India) who saw it as an instrument of progress, could also reproduce a conception of development, based on industrialization, technological innovation, and economic growth uncritically acquired from capitalist modernization theory.

This is what led to the decision to develop future work along the lines suggested by Boal's Theatre of the Oppressed, which Ganguly had encountered through Boal's writings at around this time.[15] It meant abandoning the idea that theatre could function as a bearer of progressive modernization, requiring instead that theatre be re-functioned into an open-ended process in which the theatre makers would listen as much as speak. Crucially, it also involved thinking of theatre as just one among a range of practices constituting one's social and cultural work. It is significant that this understanding of the potential social function of theatre was achieved by a group of people with no *à priori* investment in theatre as such. Rather than asking themselves how theatre might be given a social or political function, they asked whether theatre might be socially or politically useful.

In turning to Theatre of the Oppressed, Jana Sanskriti were taking up a theatrical practice also formed under conditions of neo-colonial oppression, and which had, from its inception, sought to address precisely the political difficulty that Jana Sanskriti and others before them had been confronting in India. How, asked both Jana Sanskriti and Boal, can educated and politicized middle-class activists avoid adopting and transmitting models of development and modernization that may have no relevance to the lives of the people with whom they want to work, and whose oppression they wish to end? A brief account of the emergence of Theatre of the Oppressed and a description of one of its core techniques, Forum Theatre, should suggest the nature of the solution, its appeal to Jana Sanskriti, and its significance in terms of the social function of theatre in (and against) modernity.

Augusto Boal had been a successful director at the Arena Theatre in São Paulo between 1955 and 1971. As the Brazilian military dictatorship that seized power in a coup in 1964 intensified its repression, including, increasingly, attacks on intellectuals and artists in the late 1960s, Boal was directly threatened. He was imprisoned and tortured over a three in month period in 1971, and although he was cleared of all charges and released, he was forced into exile. He moved to Buenos Aires, which he used as a base through the first half of the 1970s for a range of work in several American countries. It was while working in Peru as part of an educational project (Operación Alfabetización Integral or ALFIN) that he started to develop the techniques that would become Theatre of the Oppressed. ALFIN's work was strongly influenced by the radical pedagogical theorist Paulo Freire (a fellow Brazilian whom Boal had met over a decade earlier, and who was one of the major political and intellectual influences on his work), and the term Theatre of the Oppressed is a very public acknowledgement of the significance to Boal of Freire's book *Pedagogy of the Oppressed* (first published in Portuguese in 1968). Education, for Freire, must be a dialogue of equals that acknowledges its own politics, rather than the transmission of knowledge from those who presume to know to those who are presumed not to.

One of the core techniques of Theatre of the Oppressed is Forum Theatre. A play is performed. It dramatizes a situation of oppression. The play is repeated. A facilitator (the Joker) invites spectators to intervene by interrupting the play at any moment they choose in order to take over the role of an oppressed protagonist and change the scene or situation. Spectators thus become, in Boal's terms, 'spect-actors', or, in the terms I have been using so far, they transform themselves from consumers to producers of theatre. Their intervention will in turn be judged by other spect-actors, in an evolving sequence of actions. Actors playing the roles of oppressors use all their wit and ingenuity to foil the efforts of the oppressed to change the situation. This realizes what Boal sought for participants in his theatre work for ALFIN, that they should 'learn to "speak" theatre for themselves'.[16] Forum Theatre does not in itself propose solutions. It does not offer images of a better (more modern, more developed) future. It is rather a process through which solutions might be found, a politicized struggle (staged as a playful competition) over possibilities. It is also a theatre that rejects the idea of professionalism or expertise (either in politics or in theatre), and with it, too, the division of theatrical labour between producers and consumers. Everyone produces.

Theatre of the Oppressed does not end with the performance, however liberatory or joyous its momentary sense of possibilities might be. For those who work seriously with its techniques – and particularly for practitioners such as Jana Sanskriti who came to it as activists first rather than as theatre-makers wanting to work politically – it has to be accompanied by all sorts of other work, before and after, as part of a social and political struggle. The work of Jana Sanskriti, then, is composed of two related practices: on the one hand there is performance (workshops, rehearsals, plays, Forum Theatre, organizing festivals) and on the other there is fieldwork, which includes meetings, debates, ideological training, and participation in political campaigns (for rights to cultural spaces, for example, or against dowry and domestic violence).

Sanjoy Ganguly describes how these activities combine. A play is prepared on a chosen topic (in his example, the lack of good education in one hundred villages in the South 24 Parganas district of West Bengal). Ten teams take the play out into villages as Forum Theatre. Spect-actor interventions are recorded so that they can later be accessed by people who were not there. Before the teams return to perform the plays again, Jana Sanskriti circulate in their magazine information about education policy. The plays are performed three times, with periods for reflection between them. This process will, Jana Sanskriti hope, lead to the consolidation of a social movement with specific, informed and collective political demands and proposals for change. Ganguly describes this process as a movement from 'joint social action' – doing things together, via reflection – to 'rational collective action'. The rational collective action may contradict the supposed rationality of government agencies and other proponents of modernization and development.[17] In some cases it may involve mobilization against state policy, as in the case of the Jana Sanskriti play *Unnayan* (the title means 'Development'), which, as Dia Da Costa has observed, pitted its rural protagonists against the West Bengal CPI(M)-led government's programme of purchasing agricultural land for industrial use. What is crucial, for Da Costa, about the work done through and around this play, is that it does not simply empower rural tradition against the force of industrial modernization; it puts modernization and its 'rationality' in question. It keeps open an alternative conception of 'development' to the normalization of 'coercive dispossession', insisting that 'another development is possible'.[18]

The purposes of such a theatre, in producing 'rational collective action', are multiple. It is not only about securing social or economic improvements, expanding cultural rights, raising political consciousness, or creating a situation in which the subaltern speaks, although it is all these things. What Dia Da Costa suggests is that it constitutes 'political theatre as daily political action', involving 'the productive labour of meaning-making, refusing epistemic closure, and making particular historically-available meanings and practices count in public, institutionally-valued, and normative ways'.[19] That is to say, it is productive labour that is not about exchange or accumulation, but is instead directed towards what is often called 'reproductive labour', and therefore often left out of both capitalist and socialist versions of development and modernization. This (re)productive labour contributes, Da Costa argues, to the strengthening of popular histories, ways of living and organizing that have been 'dispossessed of significance and legitimacy within capitalist history', and it makes available and tangible (again) the possibility of different ways of living and organizing.[20]

The social function of such a theatre offers a form of collective and productive labour that constitutes, in its very practice rather than in what it represents, an alternative way of living to that offered by capitalism. It creates the conditions in which that practice in the theatre might be coordinated with complementary cultural activities and political struggles. Randy Martin suggests something very similar in his study of socialist theatre groups in Cuba and Nicaragua in the 1980s, when he notes that theatre, in its making and in its presentation, is not merely a representation but also, crucially, an instance of social interaction. 'Theater', he writes, 'is a particularly elastic expression of aesthetic and organizational form that can prefigure broader social developments.'[21] Here, prefigure means more than simply 'present an image of a future' and becomes instead a moment of participation in the future experimented with in the present. It becomes a rehearsal for revolution.

THEATRE FOR CONSUMERS

In the final section of this chapter I consider a fourth possibility for theatre's social function, one that appears to have been available even within a theatre for consumers, and which Theodor Adorno himself glimpsed in an opera by Bertolt Brecht and Kurt Weill entitled *Aufstieg und Fall der Stadt Mahagonny* (hereafter *Mahagonny*). The opera received its first production in Leipzig in 1930, two years after Brecht and Weill had enjoyed commercial success in Berlin with *Die Dreigroschenoper (The Threepenny Opera)*. It presents the story of the foundation and destruction of a city dedicated entirely to the pleasures of consumption. Two men and a woman, on the run from the law in an imaginary America, stop right where they are in the middle of nowhere and start up an entertainment industry. Their enterprise begins with prostitution before expanding to encompass food, drink, tobacco, cabaret, and boxing. The city attracts eager customers, including a quartet of Alaska lumberjacks, seeking recreation after the almost unendurable pain of 'seven years of felling timber / seven years of cold and squalor / seven years of bitter toil'.[22] At the height of its economic boom the city narrowly and miraculously avoids destruction by a hurricane and thereafter enshrines as its governing principle the radical free-market motto that 'everything is permitted'. When Jimmy Mahoney, one of the four Alaskans, fails to pay his bar bill, however, he is arrested, put on trial, convicted and condemned to death, 'for the penniless man / is the worst kind of criminal / beyond both pity and pardon'.[23] Everything is permitted, as long as you can pay for it.

Although *Mahagonny* does not enjoy the same enduring popularity as *The Threepenny Opera*, it remains part of the operatic repertoire today. This is significant because a major aspect of the work is its attempt to undo the form of opera itself, from within. It is from their work together on *Mahagonny* that Weill and Brecht developed the idea, subsequently developed more extensively by Brecht, of the culinary properties of opera (and indeed, all art) under capitalism. By 'culinary' opera or art Brecht and Weill refer to works that consist of nothing more than the sensually appealing aspects of their own form, retaining nothing that might resist the work's unthinking consumption by an audience.[24] As Lydia Goehr argues, building on ideas first articulated by Theodor Adorno, *Mahagonny* is the 'last' culinary opera.[25] Instead of merely being culinary, *Mahagonny* exposes its audience to its own culinary relationship with opera. Its audience is invited to consider its pursuit of pleasure at the opera house as a social and political fact, and as just one dimension of an economic order (capitalism) that depends for its survival upon precisely this uncritical attitude to consumption. *Mahagonny* shows how this consumption depends upon a draconian approach to poverty (punishable by death), which, the opera proposes, is its inevitable consequence (or, indeed, its founding law).

At least one element of *Mahagonny* has largely escaped the role it initially played in the opera and has circulated much more widely. 'The Alabama Song', with which Jenny and the other prostitutes announce their arrival for work in *Mahagonny*, has become, alongside 'Mack the Knife' from *The Threepenny Opera*, the most widely covered and most well-known of all Brecht–Weill songs ('Oh show us the way / to the next whisky bar'). Detached from its place in the critical framework of the opera, the song circulates as a perfect musical commodity, conjuring for most listeners a vision of Weimar decadence. Theodor Adorno almost anticipates the song's successful 'solo career' when he writes in his 1930 essay on *Mahagonny* that 'The Alabama Song' is 'one of the strangest pieces in *Mahagonny*; nowhere does the music display the archaic power of remembering long-gone, lost songs recognized in pitiful melodic phrases more potently than in this song, whose mindless repetitions give it the air of a homecoming from the realm of dementia'.[26] The song seems to perform, in its later circulation, precisely the culinary function for which it was designed in *Mahagonny*, but does so – in its general reception, at least – without activating the critical reflection that its place in the opera also invites. Wrenched, like all commodities, from the conditions of its production and freed to circulate in a marketplace, one suspects that 'The Alabama Song' rarely provokes listeners to ask themselves why they fall so completely for this particular kitschy musical artefact, or how their enjoyment of the song might involve an unacknowledged affective investment in, say, prostitution. But that is what the opera itself, which Brecht and Weill insisted was to be played in an opera house and sung by opera singers, invites its consumers to consider.

An evening at the opera house, like most evenings at the theatre, proceeds in a familiar fashion. The Royal Opera House production of *Mahagonny* in London in 2015 was no exception. In the West End, where the Royal Opera House is situated, there is a large associated leisure industry, including bars, cafés, and restaurants catering specifically to theatre-goers, and which offer, for example, 'pre-theatre' menus to customers on their way from work to a performance. Admission to the auditorium is by ticket only. Priority booking is available to Friends of Covent Garden (a membership scheme with packages ranging from £90 to £1,900 a year, depending on the benefits chosen), and to the 'general public' thereafter. Ticket prices for opera currently range from £10 for the cheapest amphitheatre seats to £190 for the best seats in the Orchestra Stalls, Grand Tier, and Dress Circle. Ticketholders tend to arrive at the theatre from about half an hour before the advertised time of the performance. Some bring tickets that have been mailed to them at home, others collect them from prepaid ticket desks in the foyer. Surrounding the auditorium, but often within the areas subject to ticket control, are bars serving both food and drink. At the Royal Opera House part of the entertainment package, both implicitly and explicitly, is a sense that the ticketholder is admitted to a world of privilege and luxury. The refreshments available reflect this, as promotional material on the theatre's website suggests:

> A unique collaboration with Ruinart Champagne, the Paul Hamlyn Hall Champagne Bar is what many people instantly think of when they hear about the Royal Opera House. Enjoying a glass of chilled, crisp champagne before curtain up or during the interval is, for many people, a part of the ritual and enjoyment of a night at the opera or ballet. So, too, is a plate of our smoked salmon, prepared exclusively to our unique recipe by Severn and Wye.

Summoned to the auditorium by a series of bells and announcements that 'this evening's performance is about to begin', ticketholders take pre-assigned numbered seats, often purchasing and consulting lavishly produced programme booklets, whose production is clearly funded by advertising from luxury brands wishing to associate their commodities with the high culture experience that opera purportedly offers. As the audience assembles in the auditorium, the orchestra gathers in the pit below and in front of the stage, and players variously warm up, practice fragments of music or exercises, and then, as the moment for the performance to begin nears, tune their instruments to one another, taking their note from the principal oboist. Once the orchestra is ready, its leader, a violinist, enters the pit, to applause from the audience. She or he is then followed, to much greater applause, by the conductor for this evening's performance. Once the applause for his or her appearance has subsided, the conductor commands the attention of the orchestra and the music begins.

Many operas open with an overture that precedes the action, although many stage productions typically enliven this musical inauguration with some kind of action or image. Some operas (especially those written before the nineteenth century) are clearly composed in 'numbers' – discrete musical-dramatic units, such as solo arias, duets, quartets and choruses – and this frequently creates a relationship between performance and audience in which individual numbers are applauded. This practice carries over even into nineteenth-century and later operas that do not exhibit this 'numbers' format, being 'through-composed' instead. In such cases only the most notable arias are typically applauded, and the applause is often related, at least in principle, to the degree of virtuosity the public reckons to have been displayed in the performance of the aria. Most productions are interrupted by intervals. During these intervals ticketholders typically take refreshments in the bars, often consuming drinks pre-purchased before the performance began. At the conclusion of the performance the curtain falls (or the lights on the stage go out), coming up again (in either case) to permit a series of often elaborate and usually hierarchical curtain calls in which first the chorus and other supernumeraries, then, in ascending order of importance, the principal singers, and finally, at the ostensible but entirely ceremonial invitation of one or more of the principal singers, the conductor, appear to acknowledge the applause of the audience. On the opening night of a production (which is also, typically, the evening attended by newspaper critics and other reviewers) the director and sometimes other members of the theatrical production team also take a bow. In opera productions it is far more common than it is in other forms of theatre for the nature of the applause to vary markedly from one artist to another: special performances or house favourites are rewarded with denser and more energetic applause than others as well as with cries of 'Bravo!', or, for the gender-sensitive cognoscenti, sometimes, 'Brava!'. On the not-infrequent occasions when members of an opera audience consider that the theatrical production has violated some mysterious but agreed-upon standard of fidelity to the 'work', the stage director and her or his team will sometimes be boo-ed vigorously, with those responsible for the musical aspects of the production often applauded all the more vigorously just so that it is very clear where the blame is to be lodged.

Clearly all these dimensions of the opera-going experience are an integral part of the meaning and social function of the performance event. One might even speculate that this strong codification of the entertainment relationship in the reciprocal actions performed during the course of an evening at the Royal Opera House might be precisely the means through which the 'amusement' provided by this branch of the 'culture industry' achieves its approximation of the standardized procedures of the workplace. In other words, the actions of producers and consumers alike make it very clear that one group of people are working for another, even at a time when the consumers, at least, might imagine that they have escaped from the world of work. It is also, of course, what Brecht and Weill meant when they described opera as 'culinary' and what makes *Mahagonny* a crucial point of reference for Adorno's account of the fate of opera in modernity. In Adorno's account, 'traditional opera' has been 'totally eviscerated without this being in the slightest apparent in official culture'.[27] An art form or cultural practice that has outlived its moment of radical aesthetic potential nevertheless continues to exercise a powerful, and often primarily sensuous, appeal. The problem is that this sensuous appeal, which had once been properly integrated into the construction and content of the work, is now pursued for its own sake, with the effect that beauty in either sound or image has become mere 'kitsch'.

In his review of *Mahagonny*, Adorno explains how Weill's music, specifically, achieves this effect:

> This music, except for a few quasi-polyphonic moments such as the introduction and a few ensemble passages, uses the most primitive of means – or rather, it wraps the worn-out, scratched-up household items of the bourgeois parlour to a children's playground, where the other sides of the old items spread terror as totem figures; this music, cobbled together from triads of wrong notes, the nails hammered down with the strong beats of old music-hall songs that are not known but remembered as parts of the genetic make-up, and glued with the stinking adhesive of softened opera pot-pourris – this music, made from the ruins of past music, is entirely contemporary [. . .] its construction, it montage of dead material, makes its dead and illusory nature evident, and from the attendant terror draws the power for a manifesto.[28]

Brecht and Weill's *Mahagonny* is the primary, if not in fact the only example of an opera which takes as its subject this very predicament. It compels its audience not only to experience its sensuous pleasures but also to confront the extent to which the pursuit of such gratifications is the basis for a violent and inhuman society: the world of *Mahagonny* where everything is permitted apart from being unable to pay for one's pleasures (a failure which will be punished by death). In other words, it contains an immanent critique of the art form of which it is an example. The effect of this critique is to make visible the relationship between the condition into which the art form has fallen and the society in which it has been produced. The music of *Mahagonny* simultaneously appeals to its audience – bypassing consciousness to tap into inherited cultural desires and satisfactions – and appals them, by revealing the very objects that satisfy these desires as so many dead things, now uncannily and terrifyingly returned to life, undead.

The social function of this theatre, then, is to reveal in the moment of consumption something of the relationship between consumption itself (including the consumption of culture) and death, or, in other words, to offer pleasure and death simultaneously. Is it possible that, in this encounter with their own culture, recognized as both dead and deadly, an occasional modern person might wonder whether it might be possible to do culture differently (even while feeling one's own pleasure in the way it is done now)? And if so, to wonder whether one way of doing that would be to make it themselves rather than have someone else serve it up for them? That such questions might have been in Brecht's mind seems likely. At precisely the time that Brecht and Weill were serving up the ambiguous delights of *Mahagonny*, Brecht had also embarked on an experimental development of his own theatre practice. Brecht's *Lehrstücke* (learning plays) were created for their participants – thinking and politicized actors – as much as for audiences. Rather than products, they were intended as processes, through which participants could explore, through the acting out of scenes, the range of possible political decisions available within each hypothetical and fictional scenario. In other words, they were something a little like the Forum Theatre devised by Augusto Boal and adapted for use by Jana Sanskriti as a theatre for producers (of their own modernity) in West Bengal.

CHAPTER THREE

Sexuality and Gender

New Stories and New Spaces on the Modern Stage[1]

KIRSTEN PULLEN

In 1920, Arthur Schnitzler's 1900 play *La Ronde* (*Reigen*) was produced for the first time in Berlin; the following year it opened in Vienna. *La Ronde* begins with a prostitute and her soldier client; the soldier has sex with a maid, who has sex with the young son of her employers, who has sex with a married woman, who has sex with her husband, who has sex with a young stranger, who has sex with a poet, who has sex with an actress, who has sex with a count, who has sex with the whore who began the daisy chain. Cutting across class lines and offering a casual view of sexual relations, *La Ronde* was an immediate scandal. After riots at the Vienna production, the actors, directors, and theatre managers were brought to court and charged with obscenity, though they were eventually cleared.[2]

The so-called '*Reigen* Scandal' is but one of many public outcries against theatrical representations of sex that erupted in Europe, the UK and North America during the modern period; these shared many similarities, and usually ended in a trial at which all or most of the charges were dropped. At the same time, as Theodore Ziolkowski points out, the outcry in this case was certainly connected to growing anti-Semitism in Vienna: Schnitzler was a prominent Jewish writer and thinker, and he became a scapegoat for the presumed moral failures of Vienna's Jewish community.[3] This too follows a familiar pattern; during the late nineteenth and through the twentieth centuries, controversies over theatrical productions about sex often masked other social pressures, sometimes only tangentially related to questions of sex and gender. The *Reigen* scandal thus demonstrates clearly the kinds of cultural work that sex at the modern theatre can do: both mirroring contemporary attitudes but also providing a space for new narratives of identity to emerge and grow (however imperfectly). Importantly, theatrical representations of sex, gender, and sexuality can entice audiences into the theatre with the promise of revealing new, 'secret' stories about bodies and their experiences, and then can help make those stories publicly acceptable.

La Ronde also references another important trend in modern theatrical sex, however. It was frequently adapted throughout the twentieth century – and each adaptation became less controversial than previous iterations.[4] Beginning with Max Ophüls's 1950 film, moving through David Hare's 1998 *The Blue Room* (starring Nicole Kidman in the nude in both London and on Broadway), and reaching its zenith in London in 2009, when it spawned four simultaneous adaptations, subsequent versions of *La Ronde* increasingly replaced shock with boredom. *The Guardian* theatre critic Andrew Haydon explained the multiple 2009 adaptations, as well as the dozens of others before, by noting 'the play's enormously seductive structure', but he also complained that millennial productions lack 'the original gleeful subversion and the feeling that the play is lifting the lid on a dirty secret', and so '[become] something much more banal'.[5]

One particular adaptation reflects well the responses elicited by most others. Michael John LaChiusa's 1994 musical *Hello Again* not only reveals the shift Haydon charts, but also reveals the importance of location – *where* sex is staged, and for whom – to this story. The premiere opened in one of off-Broadway's most prestigious houses, the Mitzi Newhouse Theatre at Lincoln Center in New York City; it set ten linked sexual encounters across every decade of the twentieth century, sung to music inspired by each. The *New York Times* review described it as 'a lovely expression of fluid motion. . . . Even when the characters are . . . rolling indecorously on the ground, there's a grace about the work that keeps it from being smutty'.[6] Its 1998 revival at the Second Stage Theatre, a less prestigious off-Broadway venue, was less successful: *Variety* warned readers that '[e]ach scene dwells on a misguided soul utilizing sexual corruption as a means of finding personal fulfillment, always accompanied by a meandering musical ditty or two'.[7] Still later, about the 2011 revival staged by The Transport Group in a 'shadowy loft in Soho', Ben Brantley warned *New York Times* readers that they would be so close to the action that they should be prepared to stare 'straight into a pair of bared, pumping buttocks', likely more than once.[8] Importantly, as the musical moved from large, prestigious theatres to ad hoc venues, it became less interesting (perhaps even less acceptable) to critics.

The relative merits of *Hello Again* aside, the reviews never suggest the musical is especially controversial. Perhaps Haydon's and Brantley's criticism is the only explanation necessary: removed from a context (the early twentieth century) where casual sex is shocking, the play is facile, clichéd, and prosaic. However, I want to suggest another potential explanation for the power of the 1920s German productions (as well as Ophüls's 1950 film) over and against the relatively unremarkable post-1970s adaptations.

On one hand, theatrical representations of sex necessarily follow other public discourses about sex, gender, and sexuality in the modern period. As sex becomes more openly discussed, as gender identities come to be understood as multiple and fluid, and as gender inequities inside and outside the theatre are ameliorated, so sexual representations on the stage proper grow less shocking. On the other hand, theatrical representations of sex and gender reflect not only shifting social mores about sex (especially casual, commercial, and queer sex), but also changes to the cultural spaces those mores occupy, the spaces in which sex is understood to take place, to 'fit' into the modern public sphere. Brantley's review of the 2011 revival of *Hello Again* points out that bare buttocks and casual sex are no longer shocking, but it also focuses on the production's location (a 'shadowy loft' not usually used for theatrical performances) and the subsequent proximity of the actors to the audience (bare buttocks in spectators' faces). The modern age saw sex in public become not just normal but expected; *Hello Again* on Broadway sated that expectation, but in Soho it played dangerously with the line between public and private spaces in performance – and caught Brantley's attention for just that move. Just as the *Reigen* scandal serves as a metonym for loosening attitudes toward 'public' sex in the modern age, then, Brantley's review reveals another key trend in the way theatrical representations of gender and sexuality are viewed during this period. As representations of sex on stage become less and less noteworthy throughout the twentieth century, critical and popular responses to sexually explicit work come more and more to be marked by assumptions about the *space* of sex, about the appropriateness of certain venues for the performances taking place there. Explicit sex on stage thus comes, in the modern period, to embed important insights about where sex – especially non-heteronormative sex – should and should not be found in a newly open, post-liberation public sphere.

THE SECRET OF SEX: CONTEXTUALIZING MODERN THEATRICAL REPRESENTATIONS OF SEXUALITY

Michel Foucault, in his groundbreaking *The History of Sexuality*, asserts that modern societies have 'dedicated themselves to speaking of [sex] *ad infinitum*, while exploiting it as *the* secret'.[9] Though his definition of 'modern' encompasses several centuries and focuses on mostly European contexts, Foucault's claim aptly describes the situation on North American, European, and UK commercial and avant-garde stages during the twentieth century. Discourses of gender, sex, and sexuality in the twentieth century reflected a steady loosening of both laws and attitudes; the theatre followed but also influenced these changes. The Progressive Era, marked in the United States by the 1920 passage of the 19th Amendment granting women the right to vote (women earned limited voting rights in England and Canada in 1918), and in England by the 1919 Sex Disqualification Act allowing women to work as lawyers and civil servants, saw numerous domestic dramas that seriously considered adultery, prostitution and premarital sex as well as notions of marriage as a partnership between equals. (Alfred Lunt and Lynn Fontanne's success in Noël Coward comedies and Shakespeare, Shaw, and Chekhov revivals typifies these kinds of plays.) In 1957, the British Report of the Departmental Committee on Homosexual Offences and Prostitution (colloquially known as the Wolfenden Report) advised that 'homosexual acts between consenting adults in private should no longer constitute an offence';[10] around that time, work including Roger Gellert's *Quaint Honor* (1958), Robert Anderson's *Tea and Sympathy* (1953), and John Van Druten's *I Am a Camera* (1952) took advantage of more relaxed attitudes about male homosexuality and advocated for its decriminalization through theatrical representation. These preliminary explorations of male homosexuality in turn made space for the more explicitly queer plays of the 1960s and 1970s, such as Edward Albee's *Who's Afraid of Virginia Woolf?* (1962), James Rado and Gerome Ragni's *Hair* (1967), Matt Crowley's *The Boys in the Band* (1968), David Mamet's *Sexual Perversity in Chicago* (1974), and Wendy Wasserstein's *Uncommon Women and Others* (1977). The sexual revolution that took hold in North America, Britain, and Europe in the second half of the twentieth century was shaped by greater accessibility of reliable birth control, the loosening of sodomy laws, the decriminalization of interracial marriage in the United States, the release of William H. Masters and Virginia E. Johnson's studies of human sexuality, and the legalization of abortion, and meant that theatrical representations of sexuality increasingly took these topics as subject matter.

Following Foucault, but also marching in step with these major social and legal changes, sex plays at the modern theatre have come to constitute a key condition of modernity: illicit and thrilling representations of sex – both heterosexual and homosexual, from male perspectives but also, increasingly and importantly, from female perspectives – are central to the 'modern' theatrical canon. As these works were introduced, popularized, and then became increasingly mainstream, specific venues for producing and staging sexually explicit work were created or redefined. Avant-garde and experimental spaces first pushed the boundaries of sexual representation; Richard Schechner's Performing Garage, for example, opened its doors with *Dionysus in '69*, a play instantly notorious for its bacchanal frenzy, performer nudity and breakdown of the barriers between actor and audience. Mainstream spaces – such as New York's Broadway, London's West End and the Toronto Theatre District – increasingly played host to new and sometimes shocking narratives of sex and sexuality, offering audiences alternative articulations of sexual experience in public zones previously imagined to be inappropriate for such things. In general, representations were shocking when they offered something new – more explicit language, nudity, narratives of what some might consider perversion – though of course what was shocking in 1926 was often banal by 2011, as *Hello Again* demonstrates. At the same time, women, queers, and other sexually marginalized performers, playwrights, and producers moved into theatres both commercial and, more typically, avant-garde as labourers and artists; they began to exert more control over the means of production, carefully and sympathetically nuancing sexual representations in the process.

In the case studies that follow, I trace first the scandalous impact of a woman's sexual desire, and the freedom she claims to sell her body, on Broadway in 1926, before looking at the relative paucity of concern over explicit heteronormative (and largely male-authored) pleasure in the 1969 adult musical *Oh! Calcutta!* These two examples suggest how the open representation of sexualized bodies challenged received distinctions between commercial and avant-garde performance; they also demonstrate the spatial limits placed on some kinds of sexual representations (women's; for-profit) over others (male; straight; 'fun'), even as both shows opened in historical moments rife with 'liberation' discourse (the moment of women's suffrage and first-wave feminism; the middle of the sexual revolution). I then turn to two representations of queer sexuality – Charles Ludlam's 1970 off-off-Broadway production, *Bluebeard*, and the original 1955 Broadway production of Tennessee Williams's *Cat on a Hot Tin Roof* – to explore the ways in which their very different venues impacted the cultural work each show was permitted to do. In each case, a close examination of sexual content in relation to the social spaces that content was allowed to occupy demonstrates how theatrical sex helped to move conversations about sex and gender openly into the modern public sphere, even as certain aspects of those discourses deemed too private, too unseemly, remained at the theatrical margins, their appearance in public rigorously policed by the theatrical tastemakers of their day. These four productions are certainly not uniquely transgressive, nor are they the only ones in which questions of appropriate venue and audience clashed with narrative content, language, and explicit *mise-en-scène*. Rather, they stand as exemplars of key trends, offering especially compelling evidence of the ways in which the spaces occupied by sex in theatrical production were as important as sexual content on stage in the modern period.

NUDITY AND NAKED DESIRE: MAE WEST AND KENNETH TYNAN'S COMMERCIAL SEX SHOWS

In April 1926, when Mae West's *Sex* opened at the Daly Theatre on Broadway, it joined several other productions about female sex and/or sexual desire already running on the Great White Way, including the annual *Ziegfeld Follies* revue (1907–1931, revived 1934 and 1936) of scantily clad women, comedians, and musical acts (and its ever more risqué copycats *George White's Scandals* [1919–1939], *Earl Carroll's Vanities* [1925–1932], and *Artists and Models* [1923–1925; 1927, 1930]). From David Belasco's *Lulu Belle*, about 'a flamboyant prostitute who pounds the pavements of San Juan Hill and Harlem',[11] to a revival of *Hedda Gabler* with its sexually free protagonists Hedda Gabler and Thea Elvsted, nine plays during the 1926 season included stories of sexually independent women and the repercussions of their dangerous desires. But West's *Sex*, which *Variety* decried as 'a nasty red-light district show – which would be tolerated in but few of the stock burlesque houses in America',[12] was the lone production closed for indecency, its cast and crew arrested, and West herself jailed and fined. Its crime, to be sure, was explicit sex – female sex – but also its daring to locate that sex directly on Broadway, in full view of American middle-class audiences.

Efforts to regulate West's representation of prostitution ultimately included police intervention. On 9 February 1927, after approximately 350 performances,[13] *Sex* was raided. West, producers John Timony and C.W. Morgenstern, theatre owner John Cort, and the entire cast were arrested for corrupting the morals of youth through *Sex*'s 'wicked, lewd, scandalous, bawdy, obscene, indecent, infamous, immoral, and impure' content.[14] Though Timony and Morgenstern filed an indictment against further police interference and *Sex* continued until May 1927, West served a short sentence in June 1927 at the New York City Women's Penitentiary. She framed the raid and arrest in terms of censorship, suggesting that she understood her arrest as part of official discourse's attempts to suppress the expression of female sexuality. Her sexuality, deemed inappropriate for the Broadway stage, was literally confined to the margins of society, as she spent ten days in jail.

Sex was criticized as 'nasty, infantile, [and] amateurish' by *Variety*, the *New York Times* called it 'crude and inept', and *Billboard* complained that it was 'the cheapest, most vulgar, low show to have dared to open in New York this year',[15] but the sticking point for critics was clearly the power of a sexually strong and independent female lead for whom sex was a financial transaction, and unabashedly so. As Margy LaMont, as in all of her stage and screen star turns, West played a prostitute or 'kept woman' who rose through society by rejecting one lover when a richer one came along (Figure 3.1). She was not punished at the end, nor did she accept a conventional marriage arrangement. Instead,

FIGURE 3.1: Mae West representing prostitution on Broadway in *Sex*, 1926. Bettman/Getty Images.

Margy left the socially stratified suburban United States for further adventure as the sexual and financial partner of a former client.

Though *Sex* was a popular success, West's play was condemned for its sympathetic portrayal of the criminal underworld and the unmediated sexuality of Margy LaMont was singled out.[16] Marybeth Hamilton suggests that *Sex* was deemed too realistic because it 'presented sexuality in a style that legitimate theatre scorned'.[17] West foregrounded the cash exchange fundamental to prostitution, rather than euphemistically presenting Margy and her cohorts as accepting the gifts of admirers. Further, West's particular body language and vocal style – 'raw', 'crude', and 'unvarnished' in the words of several critics – offered a portrait that was too close to audiences' idea of a 'real prostitute' for comfort. West's play brought into public view the kinds of sexual transactions most wished to keep private, and it did so in a space (the Broadway theatre) marked for entertainment, but also for 'art'.

Critics' and audience complaints about the 'realism' of West's show can be linked to concerns about modernity more broadly, and specifically about the compartmentalization of modernity's public and private spaces. Ralph Borsodi's popular 1929 polemic against the ills of life in American cities, *This Ugly Civilization*, argued that modernity offers great comforts to humans (cars that move quickly, goods that are produced cheaply) but imposes 'conditions which destroy [people's] capacity for enjoying' these comforts.[18] Modern civilization, he asserts, is 'a civilization of noise, smoke, smells, and crowds' that assaults citizens on all sides.[19] That West's too noisy, too crowded, too dirty, too sexy play appeared on Broadway (which the critics who vilified *Sex* seemed to believe was a temple to art and beauty) was especially troubling; Borsodi contrasts the rowdy modern city with a pastoral, pre-modern utopia, longing for a private, domestic sphere untainted by the commercialism of the city's public spaces. According to critics such as Borsodi, in the modern city, things (such as sex) that should be kept hidden and even sacred are made public, and their potentially transcendent qualities are cheapened and become dirty.

Anxieties over the distinction between modernity's public and private spaces, and the (sexual) contents proper to each, were reflected in different kinds of theatre venues early in the twentieth century. Critics and audiences knew that sex was common in burlesque houses in both North America and continental Europe: the *Folies Bergère* and *Moulin Rouge* in Paris offered chorus girls dancing the can-can and exposing their underwear (or lack thereof); Berlin was notorious for its racy cabaret scene; and The Windmill Theatre in London featured nude *tableaux vivants*. In the United States, burlesque theatres were popular leisure destinations for male audiences, attracting the same number if not the same kinds of crowds as Broadway productions: they were not typically patronized by women or the middle classes. Featuring songs and comic skits that relied on double entendre and sexual content and were performed by both men and women, by the 1920s burlesque increasingly included striptease or exotic dance performances as well.[20] Early burlesque spaces were located adjacent to but not directly in a city's fashionable theatre district, though this began to change in the 1920s too; in 1922, for example, Earl Carroll built a theatre on Broadway to house his annual *Vanities* review, moving his productions a few blocks uptown from his previous venues, which had catered to a largely male and working-class audience.

By 1926, then, the potential slip between burlesque and Broadway content, burlesque's new interest in attracting Broadway audiences, as well the fresh geographic proximity of both kinds of theatre, made *Sex*'s blurred boundaries especially vexing. Its style was expected and even acceptable in burlesque houses and other working class venues, but its jazz score, slang, and performance techniques were not considered acceptable for the Daly Theatre. The problem was not so much content as it was form, and the fit (or lack of fit) between form and locale. At the same time that West appeared on stage in *Sex*, other canonical plays about sexuality and its discontents were also trafficking in realist conventions and naturalist plots. Henrik Ibsen's *Little Eyolf* (written 1894, premiered 1895) blames the tragic life and death of its title character on his parents' neglect as they are having sexual intercourse; Sean O'Casey's *Juno and the Paycock* (written in 1924 for the Abbey Theatre, Dublin) includes an illegitimate pregnancy; Eugene O'Neill's *The Great God Brown* (1926) weaves sexual obsession into its manifesto of artistic expression at all costs. Clearly, frank treatments of sexuality were hallmarks of modern, 'realist' theatre as early as the later nineteenth century. What *Sex* did not have, however, was the literary pedigree that accompanied productions of plays written by Ibsen or associated with the Abbey Theatre or the Provincetown Players. Of course, it also had a female playwright, starring in her own work and playing the character that became her presumably autobiographical persona. West's performance style, the play's language, and its focus on the seamiest aspects of commercial sex threatened the rules for theatrical representations of female sexuality *in the 'legitimate' theatre*: simply put, *Sex* was deemed inappropriate for its space, and critical demands for it to be removed before it infected Broadway audiences demonstrate how West pushed the boundaries for what women might say, do, and write on the mainstream American stage.[21]

Forty years later, another play seemed to embrace the conventions of legitimate theatre but also depicted sexuality in a disturbingly forthright fashion that contravened that theatre's agreed-upon boundaries. Devised by respected theatre critic Kenneth Tynan and directed by Obie winner Jacques Levy, *Oh! Calcutta!* is a musical revue featuring sketches by literary figures including Samuel Beckett, Sam Shepard, and Edna O'Brien. The adult musical opened in June 1969 in a converted burlesque house renamed the Eden Theatre; its thirty-nine previews all sold out and it played to crowded houses before moving to Broadway's Belasco Theatre in February 1971.[22] It ran there until August 1972, and was revived in September 1977 at Broadway's Edison Theatre. When that production closed in August 1989 it was the longest running musical in Broadway history, largely because it had become a popular tourist attraction.[23]

Like *Sex*, Kenneth Tynan's 1969 production of *Oh! Calcutta!* provides a limit case for examining how sexuality reflects but also defines modern life, expands the modern theatrical canon, and challenges notions of appropriate venue for sexual content in the modern public sphere. In important ways, *Oh! Calcutta!* is both an avant-garde performance of provocation and a prurient and titillating example of popular theatre for the twentieth century. Elizabeth Wollman explains that it is one of the earliest and certainly the best known of the 1970s 'adult musicals', 'commercial musicals that were directly influenced by the sexual revolution'.[24] Though most of these musicals started in off- or off-off-Broadway theatres, like *Oh! Calcutta!*, many eventually shifted to Broadway houses and attracted mainstream audiences. According to Wollman, they therefore reflected 'the slow absorption of the sexual revolution into

64   A CULTURAL HISTORY OF THEATRE IN THE MODERN AGE

FIGURE 3.2: The cast of *Oh! Calcutta!* celebrating twelve years of on-stage nudity. Photo by Ron Galella/WireImage. Getty Images.

mainstream America'.[25] Both *Oh! Calcutta!* and *Sex* are examples of how explicit sex at the theatre challenge audiences in new ways when they are produced in mainstream venues.

Oh! Calcutta! included the kind of nudity and naked dancing that was and remains illegal outside of specially zoned erotic dance clubs in most American cities (Figure 3.2). A series of sketches and songs, it opens with Samuel Beckett's *Breath*, commissioned by Tynan and purportedly sent on a postcard from Beckett for inclusion in the revue.[26] (To Beckett's stage direction, 'littered with miscellaneous rubbish', Tynan added 'including naked people'.[27]) Except for Beckett's prologue, the other fourteen sketches are unattributed. The production closed with a company number, 'Coming Together, Going Together', with all the performers 'naked, dancing wildly to the blues rock'.[28] Though only Beckett is specifically credited (likely an attempt on Tynan's part to add artistic legitimacy to his production), all the listed writers except O'Brien are male; all contributors are heterosexual and white. Despite the nudity and sexual candor, it is not an especially progressive text.

When he produced *Oh! Calcutta!*, Kenneth Tynan was a respected theatre critic, championing Samuel Beckett, the Berliner Ensemble, and Tennessee Williams in his position as literary manager for Britain's National Theatre.[29] He was also a staunch opponent of theatrical censorship in the UK, and though he told the *New York Times* in 1969 (before the revue opened) that the producers were not 'trying to prove anything', it seems clear that he understood *Oh! Calcutta!* as a challenge to at least more mundane theatrical fare.[30] Though the New York production was subject to bad reviews, it was not subject to censorship. Writing for the *New York Times*, Clive Barnes assured readers that there was 'no more innocent show in town – and certainly none more witless – than this silly little diversion'.[31] The 1970 London production was scrutinized, but Attorney General Sir Peter Rawlings opted not to close it.[32] An editorial in *The Economist* agreed with Rawlings that the revue was not 'likely to deprave or corrupt', the legal statute for public obscenity, as it was a 'bundle of weak sketches, sprinkled with four-letter words, chock-full of sex play (and some very good dancing and singing) and performed partly in the nude'.[33]

Even so, as Beckett scholar Graham Saunders notes, the production 'was heralded as a landmark cultural event in espousing the spirit of sexual liberation that came to define the late 1960s'.[34] *Oh! Calcutta!* was part of a larger Broadway trend to use nudity to create 'honest depictions of the human condition' and to challenge barriers between art and life, and audience and performer, by the time of the sexual revolution; forty years after West's troubled turn, what had been impossibly racy for Broadway was deemed a diversion at worst – though critics still felt it necessary to denigrate the show for witlessness, safeguarding Broadway's highbrow bona fides in the process.[35] Both *Sex* and *Oh! Calcutta!* in their own moments brought explicit narratives and spectacularly sexualized bodies into mainstream spaces, providing the kinds of thrills otherwise regulated to burlesque theatres and strip shows. They blurred lines between 'legitimate' and 'low-brow' productions, making sexual representations to some extent 'safe' for art-loving patrons. Mainstream theatres increasingly borrowed the illicit styles and genres of burlesque clubs, introducing audiences to new discourses of sex and sexuality and educating them about the realities of modern sex. At the same time, these new narratives helped define the modern theatre as sexually forward, sexually open, and interested in debates about how and where discourses of sex, sexuality, and gender belong in the public sphere.

QUEER PLAYWRIGHTS AND QUEER SPACES: *CAT ON A HOT TIN ROOF* AND *BLUEBEARD*

Though *Oh! Calcutta!* was heterocentric if not homophobic, other modern American theatres explored queer sexualities extensively during the twentieth century. At roughly the same time that adult musicals were moving into the mainstream, on- and off-Broadway theatres embraced queer subject matter and queer artists, much to the chagrin of some critics. Harold Taubman's 1963 *New York Times* editorial 'Modern Primer: Helpful Hints to Tell Appearances vs.

Truth' is justly reviled for its promise to aid theatregoers in ferreting out 'the intimations and symbols of homosexuality in our theater' and then avoiding them. Taubman notes that several plays from the 1963 season are 'palpable specimens of homosexual content', before warning readers about the clandestine queerness of some male and female characters. Taubman's diatribe begs playwrights to 'define their themes clearly and honestly', presumably so that unwitting audiences could avoid offensive and secret queer themes, characters and playwrights.[36] In 1966, Stanley Kauffman took up Taubman's provocation, again urging gay playwrights to 'write truthfully of what [they know], rather than try to transform it to a life [they do] not know, to the detriment of [their] truth and ours'. Though Kauffman's editorial purports to support more queer representations in the theatre, its language does the opposite. He refers several times to 'normal' (his quotations) people who are justly dismayed by the fact that 'three of the most successful American playwrights [presumably Tennessee Williams, William Inge, and Edward Albee] of the last twenty years are (reputed) homosexuals' whose plays offer 'a badly distorted picture of American women, marriage and society in general'. Further, Kauffman explains that homosexuality is a nearly inevitable scourge of the theatre because 'of the defiant and/or protective histrionism [gay men] must employ in their daily lives'. Their plays are therefore 'streaked with vindictiveness'.[37] Though Taubman and Kauffman may seem like isolated voices, their editorials for the *New York Times* can reasonably be understood to speak to broader concerns of the New York and national theatre communities.

This homophobia was part of a larger postwar preoccupation with depravity and dissidence in the United States, where anxieties about queer sexuality partially supplanted anxieties about female sexuality at mid-century. At the height of the Cold War and during the ongoing investigations of the House Un-American Activities Committee, not only communism but 'sexual perversion' – meaning male homosexuality – threatened American security. As Elaine Tyler May observes, '[a]fter the war, which had fostered the emergence of same-sex communities and the increasing visibility of gay men and lesbians, the post war years brought a wave of official homophobia'[38]; homosexuals were hunted down and vilified, often arrested and liable to lose their homes and jobs if their orientation was discovered.

Stephen Bottoms convincingly argues that some academic theatre critics echoed this homophobia, borrowing the argument that plays by queer artists distort the theatre and its representations of US national identity. He details Richard Schechner's scathing *TDR* critique of *Who's Afraid of Virginia Woolf?*, suggesting 'that Schechner's outrage is built on the assumption . . . that Albee, as a gay man, had "in actual fact" written a play about two homosexual couples, thinly disguised as straight ones',[39] and points out that Donald Kaplan, writing in 1965, parallels Kauffman's assertion that 'homosexuals find homes so easily in the theatre'.[40] Further, in *Playing Underground*, Bottoms explains that both academic and popular critics recognized the 'queer spirit' of much avant-garde theatre and held it 'at manly arm's length' for much of the 1960s.[41] On Broadway or in other commercial theatres, then, queer representations were ostensibly problematic when they were masked as heterosexual or could be interpreted as revealing too much of the performers', directors', and playwrights' 'natural' homosexual histrionics. Presumably, openly queer characters were acceptable, though as I demonstrate below, openly queer characters on Broadway during the Cold War years were typically recuperated into heterosexual unions, creating a theatrical as well as a critical Catch-22.

For both popular and academic critics, queer representations at this time needed to follow particular conventions and remain in particular, appropriate places – that is, queers on Broadway needed to be open but troubled victims, like Brick in Tennessee Williams's *Cat on a Hot Tin Roof*. Off- and off-off-Broadway, however, queers signalled an experimentation with sexuality in plays that also pushed the boundaries of form and style. By the end of the period, the avant-garde's investment in queerness eventually went mainstream, as Charles Ludlam's *Bluebeard* demonstrates. Just as West and Tynan provided audiences with new narratives of explicit (hetero)sexuality, so too did Ludlam educate audiences in new ways to think about gay sexuality. The avant-garde theatre, quintessentially modern in its focus on experimentation and ambiguity, was the primary site where queer representations developed, and from there they were able to move into the commercial, legitimate sphere.

In 1967, actor/director/playwright Charles Ludlam founded the Ridiculous Theatrical Company, after Ludlam's break with John Vaccaro's Play-House of the Ridiculous, based in part on Vaccaro's conservative stance towards overt depictions of homosexuality.[42] Ludlam worked collaboratively with his actors, though he claimed all writing credits in the company's first decade. The company drew on many sources, perhaps most especially from their interest in popular film and television, to create characters that capitalized on the performers' specific talents.[43] Ludlam explained to Ronald Argelander that '[r]oles are interchangeable ... personality is an artifice in life, and ... it can be changed or interchanged'.[44] This interchangeability allowed company members to play cross-gendered characters (see Figure 3.3) and the Ridiculous to embrace 'androgynous sexual sensibility', in turn creating a theatrical space where 'pansexuality is a reality'.[45] Though Ludlam was gay (and died of AIDS in 1987), and the Ridiculous 'has long been considered by gays to be part of their cultural heritage',[46] Ludlam insisted that he did not 'have an ax to grind' and squirmed under the label of 'gay theatre'.[47] Nevertheless, Ridiculous plays ultimately depended on cross-gendered casting and foregrounded multiple character, gender, and sexuality switches within one play, as is especially evident in their biggest critical and commercial success, *The Mystery of Irma Vep* (1984).

FIGURE 3.3: Charles Ludlam, bending genders for *Vogue* magazine, 1971. Photo by Jack Robinson/Hulton Archive. Getty Images.

Before *The Mystery of Irma Vep* but shortly after leaving Vaccaro, Ludlam's company premiered *Bluebeard: A Melodrama in Three Acts*. According to Ludlam biographer David Kaufman, *Bluebeard* was a breakthrough, the first time that 'Ludlam had finally written a real play and the company had become a real company'.[48] In fact, *Bluebeard* has a traditional three-act structure, clear and coherent characters, and a relatively straightforward plot. At the same time, it is a pastiche of Gothic horror texts. Khanazar von Bluebeard (Ludlam, in the original production) experiments to produce a third genital in pursuit of transcendent sexual pleasure. His niece Sybil (played by Black-Eyed Susan), her fiancée Rodney (Bill Vehr), and her chaperone Miss Cubbidge (Lola Pashalinski) arrive on Bluebeard's island; they meet Lamia the Leopard Woman (Mario Montez, cross-dressed), Bluebeard's housekeeper Mrs Maggot (a cross-dressed Gary Tucker), and Sheemish (John Brockmeyer). Bluebeard exchanges vows and has sex with Miss Cubbidge, seduces Sybil, conjures Hecate, and successfully sutures a third genital, described as 'a loofah sponge with a movable bird claw'.[49] In the melodramatic conclusion, Bluebeard shoots Lamia, and Sheemish turns on him. Mrs Maggot is revealed to be Sybil's birth mother and Miss Cubbidge announces she is pregnant with Bluebeard's child. The three women and Rodney leave the island. Despairing over his failed experiments and faithless wives, Bluebeard storms out of the laboratory and Sheemish and Lamia exit 'into a magnificent golden shaft of light'.[50]

Bluebeard opened at La MaMa in March 1970, at a moment when that experimental theatre space was shifting its ticketing, producing, and renting policies in order to become more profitable. As Bottoms explains, when Ludlam realized that La MaMa's contracts stipulated that it was entitled to a percentage of any play that premiered on its stages, he refused to sign. Though he had planned for a long run, founder and proprietor Ellen Stewart cut the run to a week and refused press viewings.[51] The Ridiculous Theatrical Company transferred the play to Christopher's End, which built a stage for the performances. The change in venue is significant. La MaMa was recognized as a legitimate theatre, a leading venue for avant-garde work in the late 1960s and 1970s. Christopher's End was 'a dingy gay bar',[52] physically and psychically removed from other off- and off-off-Broadway theatres. Further, Ludlam was characteristically vocal about his split with La MaMa and Ellen Stewart, inviting critics to take a trip way downtown to see his production; they did, and *Bluebeard* became a critical and nearly commercial success. Ludlam exploited the controversy surrounding its production in order to demonstrate his play's relevance and importance.

Ludlam's campaign to generate controversy in part by occupying new theatrical space was successful, at least in terms of its impact on the reviewing community. *Times* critic Mel Gussow explained to his readers that the show played Thursday through Sunday 'at the Christopher's End Theater, which is at the far west end of Christopher Street', directions rarely included in *New York Times* reviews.[53] He raved that 'the plot is complicated and digressionary, and great fun to follow ... Ludlam's performance is deliciously rococo, and obviously he has infected everyone in his Ridiculous Theatrical Company'.[54] This review thus heralds Ludlam's new company and underlines its status as extremely off-Broadway. Clearly, Ludlam's Christopher's End production signalled his desire to claim a new space for queer work and to mark his company as interpreters of queer narratives. Most importantly, he made mainstream reviewers come to him, forcing them to reckon not only with these narratives but also with the kinds of venues in which they were housed.

Audiences were invited to visit new places and there encounter new performances and performers, educating themselves not only in the conventions of modern, avant-garde theatre but also in sexual identities and practices not previously available for view in the public sphere.

Other reviewers who travelled to Ludlam's makeshift theatre recognized *Bluebeard* as a singular and significant production. John O'Connor's review for *The Wall Street Journal* was enthusiastic in its praise for Ludlam's 'drawing room grotesque'.[55] *The Village Voice* reviewed it twice: Martin Washburn's first review focused on the acting, praising Black-Eyed Susan and Ludlam in particular for 'their reverence for their vehicle ... It makes their acting unique'.[56] Richard Schechner also reviewed the play for *The Village Voice*, giving it an unqualified rave. Comparing Ludlam to Molière, he wrote that the play demonstrates 'the only way that traditional theatre – the theatre of texts, costumes, stages, impersonations, stage lights – can flourish in our society'.[57] The review, then, firmly placed *Bluebeard* inside a theatrical canon, making it legitimate, artistic, and mainstream, even as it played in a gay bar without a real stage, let alone a real claim to theatrical legitimacy.

Schechner's support of this play went further. Determined to move it into a recognizable theatre, he rented his Performing Garage to Ludlam for a four month run of *Bluebeard*, during which time Ludlam won a Special Citation at the May 1970 Obie Awards for his performance.[58] *Bluebeard*'s move from the respectable La MaMa to dingy Christopher's End, then back to respectability in the Performing Garage may have allowed it to remain relatively free of controversy, at least in terms of its representation of sexual identities. The story of *Bluebeard*'s progress, however, also marks how crucial venue and framing were to the representation of queer sexualities at that historical moment. Less than a year after riots protesting police raids on the homosexual clientele at the Stonewall Bar in New York City ushered in the contemporary gay rights movement, Ludlam's decision to move *Bluebeard* to *another* gay bar for its premiere suggests how both the lived experience and theatrical representation of queer sexualities were still often marginalized. But Ludlam's ability to bring major theatre critics to that marginal space also signals the ways in which both queerness and its experimental, explicit representations were beginning to move into the mainstream. What was once private, secret, and illegal was increasingly visible and present. The production's third move, to the Performing Garage, further established *Bluebeard* as legitimate theatre at the same time that it offered Schechner further credibility as an avant-garde producer and director, willing to champion other works, even queer works, not directed by himself nor featuring his company. Schechner, who decried the secret homosexuality of mainstream, commercial theatre, embraced experimental sexuality in avant-garde spaces – and ensured that it remained in those 'proper' venues. Ludlam's success with *Bluebeard*, then, is crucial to understanding how explicitly transgressive queer sexualities came to occupy particular spaces within the US theatrical community – both accepted, and affecting change on some levels, and yet socially contained to the margins at the same time.[59]

Though *Bluebeard* exploited its off-off-Broadway location to advocate for the importance of queer performance to the American avant-garde, other, more canonical plays treated queer sexualities in a strategically guarded fashion, and gained acceptance in the mainstream as a result. Tennessee Williams's *Cat on a Hot Tin Roof* opened at Broadway's Morosco Theatre on 24 March 1955, starring folk singer Burl Ives as Big Daddy and Mildred Dunnock as Big Mama, Ben Gazzara as their troubled son, Brick, and Barbara Bel Geddes as Maggie the Cat (Figure 3.4).[60] Though produced nearly a decade before Howard Taubman's diatribe against secretly gay writers and their not so secretly gay plays, Williams's melodramatic masterpiece of Southern gothic was one of the first Broadway plays to reference homosexuality, and certainly the first of its kind to win a Pulitzer Prize. Brooks Atkinson's two *New York Times* reviews (the first published after the play's 24 March 1955 opening and the second for the next week's Sunday edition) were both rapturous. Undoubtedly taking his cue from Brick's fight against 'mendacity', Atkinson writes that the play 'is not only part of the truth of life; it is the absolute truth of the theatre'.[61] His review does not, however, mention 'mendacity' – code for homosexual experience, and in particular life in the closet, in the play – nor the hidden truths of Brick's character. His second review does not hint at the potentially explosive subject matter either, though he does admit that 'there is plenty of obscenity' in the play. Importantly, both reviews suggest that Williams's famously ambiguous play offers a 'crystal clear' vision of human nature.[62]

Not surprisingly, some viewers felt duped by the stellar reviews as well as the approbation signalled by the New York Critics Circle Award and the Pulitzer Prize. Reader Helen Price found the play 'revolting'; she believed it unfit for even 'the most vulgar burlesque theatre' and refused to believe that fathers and sons ever discussed their sex lives.[63] A few days later, Frederick Pappus agreed, aghast that the Pulitzer Prize was 'awarded to a play that makes a disgusting mockery of women, love, marriage, and children'.[64] Notably, however, Broadway audiences seem primarily to have objected to the bawdy and brutal heterosexual content of the play rather than its intimations of homosexuality; perhaps the success of *Tea and Sympathy*,[65] which had its one hundredth Broadway performance soon after *Cat*'s opening, had prepared audiences for ambiguously queer characters who ultimately affirm their heterosexuality. Like *Oh! Calcutta!* a decade later, *Cat on a Hot Tin Roof* had the imprimatur of art as well; Williams had won multiple New York Critics Circle Prizes and a previous Pulitzer Prize, and Elia Kazan was a noted director, with two Tony Awards, one Academy Award, and two nominations at the time of *Cat*'s production. Though Broadway in the 1950s was known for its musicals, serious

FIGURE 3.4: Passionate Maggie (Barbara Bel Geddes) and cool Brick (Ben Gazzara) in *Cat on a Hot Tin Roof*, capturing the 'truth' of American marriage at mid-century. Photo by Gjon Mili/The LIFE Picture Collection. Getty Images.

drama still flourished and several plays that might legitimately be termed art were produced. *Cat on a Hot Tin Roof* joined Arthur Miller's *A View from the Bridge* (Miller was famous for 1949's *Death of a Salesman*), and William Inge's *Bus Stop* (his play *Picnic* won the Pulitzer Prize in 1953). Certainly, Broadway's relatively highbrow status and its willingness to tackle moral issues in dramatic form may have made Brick's queerness – notably diluted by Kazan's revisions to the play script for the Broadway production – palatable for audiences.

Brooks McNamara points out that Broadway audiences expect to enjoy 'the products of an industry that sees itself as a provider of an alternative to the majority of light movie and television fare'.[66] *Cat on a Hot Tin Roof*'s transfer from stage to screen underscores this point. In July 1955, MGM purchased the rights to the play. The *New York Times* reported that '[s]ome persons familiar with the drama expressed surprise that it could have been handled for the movies in a manner to meet production code approval'.[67] In fact, the production code could not handle Brick's ambiguous sexuality; what Broadway audiences were willing to watch and what the Production Code Administration (the precursor to today's cinema ratings system) could allow were quite different. R. Barton Palmer and William Robert Bray explain that in the film, 'the ambiguities of Williams's original stage play are drastically simplified'.[68] In the film, Brick loves and lusts for Maggie, but cannot forgive either Skipper or his wife for sleeping together. More importantly, his anger with the 'mendacity' that so marks the stage version is changed to a son's anger at an absent father; Big Daddy (again played by Burl Ives) reconciles with Brick in the plantation's cluttered basement, paving the way for his reunion with Maggie. Even if Broadway at mid-century was an appropriate venue for telling stories – however carefully couched – of closeted and ambiguous sexuality, Hollywood film was not.

By the end of the twentieth century the secret of sex was well and truly out: no longer relegated to burlesque houses and off-Broadway stages, nudity and narratives of homosexuality and prostitution were widely available to mainstream audiences in legitimate theatres. Always commercial but no longer necessarily controversial, theatrical representations of sex are deemed acceptable and appropriate subjects for contemporary audiences; the story of sex in the modern theatre parallels the story of sex's emergence into modern society, as shifting social attitudes about sex and gender allowed for new, alternative representations on public stages. In important ways, this story is also about how venue can determine appropriateness, and how a production's theatrical location can frame audience and critical response, allowing some works to have broader social and cultural impact than others. As *La Ronde, Sex, Cat on a Hot Tin Roof, Oh! Calcutta!, Bluebeard,* and *Hello Again* demonstrate, a particular production is titillating, controversial, successful, and significant because of where it is performed as much as because of what that performance includes.

CHAPTER FOUR

The Environment of Theatre

'Home' in the Modern Age

KIM SOLGA AND JOANNE TOMPKINS

In Stephen Daldry's 1992 production of J.B. Priestley's *An Inspector Calls* for London's National Theatre, the (property) house that the Inspector visits literally comes off its foundations at the performance's end. This shocking displacement announces a dismantling of conventional assumptions about the safety and security of 'home' (and, metonymically, of late twentieth-century British society) as the piece's endgame. The production – and its shifting underpinnings – must have touched a chord, because it played to packed houses in London from 1992 to 1995 before embarking on two large-scale international tours.

The climactic cracking open of Daldry's set made physical the emotional upheaval of the family at the centre of Priestley's narrative, but it also echoed starkly the landmark breakup of another theatrical household over one hundred years earlier: Nora and Torvald Helmer's. When Nora first slammed the door on her husband's apartment during the controversial final scene of Henrik Ibsen's *A Doll's House* (1879), she introduced home's fracture as one of the principal obsessions of modern performance. Ibsen's naturalist plays are indelibly linked to the attractively furnished, aspirational bourgeois living spaces in which they are set, which – despite these spaces' inevitable unravelling over the course of each play – may be one of the reasons they have remained so popular, worldwide, throughout the long twentieth century.[1] Indeed, at the height of global recession in June 2012 – with communities across Europe staggering under EU-imposed austerity, Occupy London's last encampment forcibly dismantled, and the property market in that city raging out of control – the Young Vic theatre's production of *A Doll's House* became the smash hit of the summer.

For modern theatre in Europe and North America, no location physical or imagined has been so vexed, and so obsessively revisited, as that of *home*. Scholars have long argued that the history of modern realist (or narrative) drama in particular can be traced through home's failed comforts, dramatic dissolutions and impossible fantasies[2]: in the tense, tightly-scripted domestic plots of Anton Chekhov, Ibsen, and August Strindberg; the representations of family turmoil in the homes of Arthur Miller, Tennessee Williams, Marsha Norman, August Wilson, Sam Shepard, and Yasmina Reza; the grappling with banality and dehumanization in the absurdist homes of Eugene Ionesco; and the broader political and social crises embodied on stage by home's dark negatives (think of Samuel Beckett's barren road in *Waiting for Godot* [1953], or Sarah Kane's now-infamous 'generic' hotel room, blown to pieces in *Blasted* [1995]). As this chapter argues, however, the legacy of modern drama's imbrication with home extends far beyond its starring role in fourth-wall realism. The surrealist, Dadaist, absurdist, and other anti-realist modes that dominated avant-garde performance through the mid-twentieth century, as well as the environmental, site-specific, and immersive performance works that continue to challenge realism's canonical status in the early twenty-first, have struggled with, negotiated, but also re-animated the central contradictions that home poses for modern subjects – including for those displaced in the wake of neoliberal globalization. In that same wake, theatre companies have found 'houses' of their own – homes for their creative work and its audiences – hard to come by, and the precarious balance between social security for themselves, and cultural value for their labours, ever harder to maintain. Eric Hobsbawm notes that home in the late nineteenth-century bourgeois imagination promised privacy, security, and the social sanction of children and family. These are promises to which early twenty-first-century subjects cling, even as the neoliberal 'precariat' grows, migrant 'crises' continue to dominate news cycles internationally, and property booms in mega-cities ensure fewer of us will ever be safely and comfortably housed for the long term.[3] More than ever in the long modern age, the promise of a home of one's own is badly kept in the societies over which it holds the greatest emotional power.[4] This, in turn, is a home truth to which contemporary theatre and performance makers continue relentlessly, and creatively, to respond.

This chapter sketches a map of modern performance by interrogating home as *the* environment that em-places twentieth-century theatre within the larger social, political, and economic frameworks of modernity. We begin with an historical overview of the interlocking relationship between early modernist theatre, the domestic house, and its social and mythical correlatives in order to unpack the cultural history of that theatre's obsession with 'home' as both a literal place and a space central to the modern imagination. We intervene in existing debates that have framed home as above all pathological for European and American realism to argue instead that home at the modern theatre should be regarded through the lens of modernity's 'double optic' – as an environment toxic yet also creative, limiting but expansive, physical yet open to powerful re-imaginings in a post-modern, neoliberal world.[5] We then examine two late expressions of this environmental double optic in contemporary London: the work of the Young Vic theatre (whose motto, 'It's a big world in here', captures the spirit of modern theatre's variant, often contradictory, commitments to home), and Platform's *And While London Burns* (2006–), an audio-walk about climate catastrophe that reimagines the 'house' of modern performance as the post-national global city itself.

The Young Vic's motto – 'It's a big world in here' – tantalizingly catches the mythical spirit of finding a 'home' at the theatre (if nowhere else) on which so much modern drama pivots, and within London's early twenty-first century theatre ecology the Young Vic literally offers, via its innovative 'Two Boroughs' programme, a home-from-home for many residents in the poor communities of Lambeth and Southwark in which the theatre building is located. As we trace the contours of home at the modern theatre – reading at turns materially, theoretically, and institutionally – we contend that both the popular, money-earning modern 'classics' frequently revived at the Young Vic and the now-ubiquitous site-specific and immersive performances exemplified here by *And While London Burns* animate the contradictions *not between but within* 'belonging and exile, home and homelessness' that Una Chaudhuri identifies as key to the geography of modern theatre.[6] In the early twenty-first century, these tensions define the extra-theatrical lives lived under neoliberal globalization by so many middle and working class theatre makers and theatregoers across Europe, North America, Eurasia, and beyond: the more precious home becomes to us at the theatre, the further it recedes from our everyday grasp. 'Home', in this chapter, is not simply modern drama's founding trope, its narratological ground: rather, home – in all its powerful, modern-age paradoxicality, its painful aspiration and our longing for it nevertheless – is at once the literal as well as the imaginative environment that enables the production and consumption of new ways of living in twentieth- and twenty-first-century performance.

'AT HOME' IN MODERN(IST) EUROPEAN THEATRE

Modern theatre begins with the material configuration of home on stage. The turn to the use of naturalistic settings in the 1870s and 1880s coincides with the new prominence granted the domestic sphere in social life as a result of nineteenth-century post-Industrial Revolution European and American economic prosperity. Ibsen's play offers an object lesson: *A Doll's House* takes place over Christmas, and the opening scene shows Nora Helmer returning to her family's apartment laden with treats to give to the children, place on the Christmas tree, and even consume in private. The scene is one of domestic labour, to be sure, but its true subject is not child-rearing or cooking – it is *shopping*.[7] David Morley refers to Mary Douglas on the origins of home in the nineteenth-century imagination: 'while home is located, it is not necessarily fixed in space – rather, home starts by bringing space under control' through 'regular patterns of activity and structures in time' that might include cooking and eating, bathing and sleeping, but also the accruing, ordering, displaying and maintaining of *things*.[8]

The modern history of 'home' thus incorporates a house *plus* all of its attendant belongings, as well as the feelings we attach to those things; this framework emerges first with the massive increase in urban populations in the nineteenth century, and then with the urgent need physically to accommodate such an enormous demographic shift.[9] The population booms of the late nineteenth century, and the housing crises they generated, in turn provoked 'home' to take on metaphorical value in nineteenth-century middle-class life: it became synonymous with the private sphere, an imagined space that was strictly separated from the busy, crowded public streets as 'a place of refuge – a "sanctuary" or a "walled garden" – in which the husband could recover from the pressures of business life while his wife and children remained inviolate from the temptations of the wicked world'.[10] One version of this sanctuary was staged annually, beginning in 1908, for the middle-class masses at London's Ideal Home Show. '[D]isplay[ing] the very latest models of desirable home life', the Ideal Home Show sold a fantasy for purchase, encouraging householders (especially wives) to accumulate the several things – from soft furnishings to flowers to *mises-en-scène* – that could signify the succour home was meant to hold.[11] The nature of this exhibition, and its enduring success, reinforces John Rennie Short's perception that the modern home is 'idealized [. . .] more often than other places'.[12]

From its inception, the modern Anglo-European home was both physical – a place literally sequestered from increasingly congested public spaces – and desired, *consumed* into being as a refuge from a dangerous world. Yet the relationship between physical home and 'dream home' was not straightforwardly binary. Hobsbawm uses the linked German words *Heim* and *Heimat* to nuance the nineteenth-century formula of home/private and work/public. '*Heim*' – or what 'belongs to me and mine and nobody else' – represents the private, physical modern home, whereas '*Heimat*', which denotes bonds of birth and citizenship and links people to a network of ethnic and community relations, 'is essentially public [and] by definition collective. It cannot belong to us as individuals'.[13] Hobsbawm's discussion of *Heim* and *Heimat* demonstrates that within the ideal of home as private and sequestered space lies the reality that such an ideal is culturally invented, and that in its purest imagining it is shared by one and all. The modern home's ideal may be predicated on the possessive – the '*Heim*' that 'belongs to me and mine and nobody else' – but it also contains the inherent acknowledgement that its roots (and responsibilities) lie in a much larger, messier, evolving social space.

This contradiction is not an accident or mistake, but rather an essential component of modernity's notion of home – and it was not lost on theatre artists in the early modernist period. The perfect-looking bourgeois drawing room sets of late nineteenth-century naturalism were designed to appear claustrophobic, spaces less of refuge than of awkward negotiation; moreover, they were deliberately meant to be more challenging for some characters than others to call home. Ibsen's Hedda Gabler discovers this when her new husband, Tesman, spends money he does not yet have on a grand house she has claimed, offhandedly, to be her dream dwelling. For Hedda, living inside London's Ideal Home Show is a painful chore: she quickly realizes that her job as a wife in this fantasy space is to provide the 'sanctuary' for her husband that Burnett notes above, supporting his ambitions instead of pursuing her own. Hedda ends the play by committing suicide; with bitter irony Ibsen stages her death within the inner sanctum at the heart of the play's intricate living room set. Nora Helmer, who similarly finds herself unable to bear the gendered weight of home's expectations at the end of her play, chooses instead exile, shutting the apartment door emphatically behind her.

For characters in modern narrative drama, especially female characters, finding 'home' at the theatre often meant moving into a prison that resembled a shop window. For audiences, visiting such characters at the theatre meant experiencing a profound sense of psychic *emplacement* (succour from the rapidly changing world outside the theatre building) coupled with a strong awareness of psychic fracture emanating from the home-space represented on stage. Sigmund Freud, who drew inspiration for his psychological theories from the theatre of this moment, called this defining contradiction 'uncanniness': literally in the original German '*Unheimlichkeit*' or un-homely-ness, this is the feeling of being at once physically 'in the house' and yet emotionally untethered from that place's comfortable associations. With its domestic settings rendered in minute detail yet matched to narratives of powerful psychosocial dispossession, early realist drama returned the bourgeois individual to Freud's scene of *Unheimlich* rupture again and again. In her groundbreaking study, *Staging Place* (1995), Chaudhuri theorizes this return for theatre criticism, defining 'geopathology' as modern drama's quintessential disease: the experience of longing to belong, linked inherently to a powerful sense of, and even need for, exile from a suffocating home.

'Geopathology' may be the modern realists' locational poison, but the surrealist and expressionist works that challenged realism's dominance in the early twentieth century were no less interested in the psychosocial conundrums of unhomely modernity – though they were aesthetically far removed from the naturalist fourth-wall set. Strindberg's *Ghost Sonata* (1908) offers a compelling example of this trend. The play was first staged in the Intimate Theatre in Stockholm, one of a host of chamber spaces across Europe designed to offer shelter to avant-garde performance amidst the crowded streets of industrial modernity. *Ghost Sonata* takes place in an apartment block haunted by figures who represent the failure of traditional familial bonds on one hand, and the new industrial normal on the other: they are a community of cultural oddities living on top of each other in a rapidly urbanizing city. Alfred Jarry's *Ubu Roi* (1896) similarly grounds its foul-mouthed proto-Dadaist politics in the messed-up domestic battles of the despotic rulers Mère and Père Ubu; they foreshadow the tyrants of the 1920s and 1930s from a base that is half children's puppet show, half waking nightmare. Picking up on this connection brilliantly, Cheek by Jowl's French Company set its 2013 revival of *Ubu Roi* in a sleek contemporary living room, gleaming white and decorated as though for the pages of *Architectural Digest*. While their son, stalker-like, ominously filmed scenes of backstage domesticity on his handheld camera, the Ubus hosted a chic dinner party. But try as they might, they could not keep the veneer of urbane respectability in place: chaos and violence erupted continuously from all sides, overwhelming both the party and its hyper-realist staging as it swept all guests into the grotesque. The immediate political effect was to draw attention to the untenable pretensions of glorified *Heimlichkeit* in the wake of 2008's Great Recession: at each performance's climax Père Ubu entered the audience – to a round of awkward laughter – to ask any bankers in the crowd to identify themselves.

THINKING BEYOND GEOPATHOLOGY: 'HOME' AS MYTHO-POETIC SPACE

Since the publication of Chaudhuri's *Staging Place*, theories of space in modern drama have taken the period's geopathological interest in home somewhat for granted. In the process, modern theatre criticism has caught something of geopathology's disease, leaving undertheorized the several other ways that home signifies across a range of styles, genres, and performance modes in the long twentieth century. As examples such as Cheek by Jowl's *Ubu Roi* demonstrate, modernity's 'home' is not confined to fourth-wall realism, and it is more than the sum of its illnesses: it can also be the site of forceful stylistic collaboration, raucous comedy, and a space from which to imagine new, vibrant ways of engaging communities in the project of building a fairer, shared world. *Ubu Roi* blended a Stanislavsky-influenced, British directorial team (Declan

Donnelan and Nick Ormerod) with a company of French artists trained in a highly physical performance style, a forcefully naturalistic design concept, a tragi-comic aesthetic, and an exemplary anti-realist play – all to expose the bankruptcy of neoliberalism's investment in the nuclear household as the primary unit of economic consumption. The eclecticism of the resulting work demonstrates the extent to which 'home' at the modern theatre remains an urgently political idea, but operates also as a source for exploration and creative undoing. Inspired by Cheek by Jowl's production, we look afresh in this section at modern drama's homecomings through the lens of mythic space. What would it mean if modern drama's obsession with home's frustrations and limitations was understood not as an illness born of cultural anxiety that drives inevitably towards exile, but rather as foundational to its creativity, its longevity, and its cultural expansiveness? What if modern drama's greatest strength is not its ability to stage an escape *from* a socially, ethically, culturally bankrupt home, but its urge to dive *into* home as imagined – and thus re-imaginable – space?

Chaudhuri's geopathology articulates 'place as problem', and home above all as a launch pad for escape.[14] Beginning with Ibsen, she explains that 'the crisis of the concept of home appears as the collision therein of two incommensurable desires: the desire for a stable container for identity and the desire to deterritorialize the self'.[15] She argues that the nature of theatrical geopathology shifts through the twentieth century as modernism moves beyond realism, and as geopathology is thus 'exposed, ironized, deconstructed' in works that 'respond to the pressures of a world increasingly defined by the actual dislocations of immigration and refugeehood'.[16] Nevertheless, even in this later work home remains troubled for Chaudhuri, and is often a site of violence. The 'failed-homecoming plot' remains ubiquitous,[17] and the trauma of failed return is often inescapable.[18]

If, however, we place Chaudhuri's geopathology into dialogue with Elin Diamond's notion of modernity's 'double optic', a somewhat different relation among the physical, psychic, and social spaces of 'home' obtains. Diamond argues that 'modernity's drama' contains a 'tendency to foster a double optic' that is 'necessarily transgressive of modernity's historical project'[19] – by which she means the progress narrative that Ben Singer describes as 'modernity at full throttle', the relentless, forward industrial motion that drives agitated modern subjects home to seek comfort, quiet, and safety – and never quite to find it. In contradistinction to this powerful, often coercive linear force, Diamond's double optic 'places at least two irreconcilable [modern] realities in view', echoing the doubled consciousness of Freud's psychical theories but also the historical materialist texts of Bertolt Brecht, the experimental works of Zora Neale Hurston, and the labours of other writers for whom modernity's drama is defined by the open acknowledgement of, and revelling in, contradiction as an instructive, even pleasurable social condition.[20] The binary that Chaudhuri identifies between belonging and exile is itself an effect of and creative response to modernity's contradictory tendencies, yet Diamond's 'double optic' framework suggests something more nuanced still: the possibility that geopathology may represent only one side of modern drama's environmental consciousness.

Freud is the theorist best placed to identify the modern home as the preeminent site of modernity's double optic: his *Unheimlichkeit* describes not an 'either/or' relation, but a sense of simultaneous comfort and horror, a repressed feeling from one's past made manifest as both fear *and* desire in a particular, familiar place. The non-binary relation between *Heimlich* and *Unheimlich* is crucial here: as Freud notes, '*heimlich* is a word the meaning of which develops towards an ambivalence, until it finally coincides with its opposite, *Unheimlich. Unheimlich* is in some way or other a sub-species of *heimlich*'.[21] Freud's discussion of this concept in 'The Uncanny' (1919) grows directly out of the bourgeois cultural moment that produces both the Ideal Home Show and the terror of 'modernity at full throttle' as inseparable partners in signification. The glorious shoppers' fantasy dressing the streets of London, Chicago, Paris, and New York is heightened by the equally fantastic (and phantasmatic) frisson of fear that comes with imagining being downed by a speeding tram on the way home with one's purchases.

Turning now to modernist spatial theorists Yi-Fu Tuan and Gaston Bachelard, we might further expand modern theatre history's understanding of 'home' to include the fundamentally *creative* experiences of modern subjects living in what are always already the imagined spaces of *Unheimlichkeit*. The resulting, doubled conception of home – as a physically, psychically, and socially limiting place that also contains its own imaginative 'cure' for limitation – may then open up fresh interpretive angles on the post- or even anti-realist scenes conjured in performance by modernist and postmodernist designers, actors, and directors. The scenographic trend towards devising worlds that cannot be physically captured by the literal spaces of a given theatre building shapes many of the environmental innovations of later twentieth-century site-specific and immersive, as well as feminist and critical race, theatre and performance artists – from New York's Living Theatre and Wooster Group, to Quebec's Ex Machina and Britain's Punchdrunk, to Split Britches, Caryl Churchill, Suzan-Lori Parks, Ariane Mnouchkine, and many others. As we argue in the final section of this chapter, the late modern trend away from a detailed physical verisimilitude and towards fully phantasmatic spaces in performance can be liberating, politically activist, and fundamentally democratic; it can also, however, be at times sympathetic to a late-capitalist economy all too willing to substitute images of a utopic, shared world of mobile global citizens for truly safe, affordable housing for those individuals still trapped in specific places by economic, migration, or other social factors.

Tuan's mythic space differs from but does not oppose the literal places we associate with realist mimesis at the theatre; rather, it exists alongside them. For Tuan, mythic space persists because of the very human urge to imagine a location that is 'not here', and in this it coincides perfectly with the compulsion to make (and attend) theatre, in any place or time: '[i]n mythical thought the part can symbolize the whole and have its full potency', just as in theatre, a very limited range of signs (props, lighting, gestures) can generate a room in a castle, a whole kingdom, or even 'history' as such.[22] Tuan's mythic space is 'an intellectual construct' that can intersect with 'real' spaces, but differs from them in that it 'ignores the logic of exclusion and contradiction' central to architecturally or geographically bounded forms.[23] Here, Tuan reveals the democratic impulses of mythic space, as well as its feminist, queer, anti-colonial, and differently-abled potential. When Peggy Shaw and Lois Weaver turn the modest-sized La MaMa theatre into first a tiny, disused storeroom and then into the open road from New York to Michigan to California (in 1987's *Dress Suits to Hire*), they prompt us, in Tuan's words, to 'wonder what lies on the other side of the mountain range or ocean', to '[construct] mythical geographies that may bear little or no relationship to reality'[24] – but which therefore may also allow us to imagine a better, safer, more pleasurable reality than that lived by lesbian and other queer subjects daily in a homophobic nation. Similarly, when an actor playing the head of the Johnson & Johnson company dances on a table to 'tap out' a letter to architect Frank Lloyd Wright (in Ex Machina's *Geometry of Miracles*, 1997), an 'everyday object' is transformed 'through the subtle alteration of perspective, lighting [and] a performer's movements'[25] to produce what Tuan calls 'a world view or cosmology' that allows audiences to 'make sense of [the play's] environment' but also to take real pleasure in and inspiration from virtuosic, imagined, alternative universes.[26]

As these brief examples illustrate, mythic space has for Tuan specific architectural as well as psychical effects. The venue of a performance (a theatre, a park, a disused warehouse), coupled with the imaginary spaces created on stage to conjure the world of a play, work together to articulate aspects of Diamond's double optic, generating simultaneous familiarity and distance ('distance from the self'[27]) for spectators and performers alike. This theatre – La MaMa in New York; La Caserne in Quebec City – is familiar to us, but its stage-world, refreshed since we last sat or walked here, is new (and thus also bears the quality of the uncanny, an unexpected thing in a known location). If we find a 'home' in this place, it is never a stable or entirely safe one, yet that instability and unsafety are often more provocative and enjoyable than they are unnerving. In contrast with Tuan, Bachelard focuses on a much more specific, much more comforting locale – the tiny, secret location within one's house where one feels, even if just for a moment, completely secure.[28] In the 1950s and 1960s, at the height of the Cold War, Bachelard argued for a different order of the space of psychic interiority to that proposed by Freud. His word 'topoanalysis' refers to the 'topography of our intimate being';[29] according to Bachelard we retain the memory of our childhood home, 'our first universe, a real cosmos in every sense of the word', in ways not simply uncanny and terrible but also potentially supportive and encouraging.[30] Our early home-memories, he argues, bear directly on how we understand other structures as adults, and these memory-effects have a material existence in 'real' space and time. Bachelard notes that the intimate spaces of our memories intersect with exterior 'world space' every day, and that each resulting space is metaphysically immense in its own way.[31]

Bachelard and Tuan both argue for a specificity of location through what might at first appear to be the purely ephemeral, but their claims link back to the theatre through a perhaps unlikely conduit: modern acting practice. They reference above all a *perception* of home, whether imperfectly remembered or simply imagined, as the *material* ground on which an idea of home takes the place of the thing itself, and this blending of the concrete with the imagined in the shaping of modern space in turn has much in common with the influential practice of Russian director Konstantin Stanislavsky. Stanislavsky's 'System' of acting was developed throughout the first three decades of the twentieth century and imported to North America and beyond by his students, as well as through the related work of Lee Strasberg and Stella Adler; it stems from the premise that dramatic character must be built on a base of physical actions performed in real space and time, but blended with actors' active imagining of those actions, imagining made possible through their 'experiencing' of the world both within their own bodies and outside the theatre.[32] Although Stanislavsky's focus on physical actions, especially in his later writings, appears to foreground the centrality of physical mimesis in the crafting of a role, in fact human imagination is the cornerstone of all of his acting exercises. For Stanislavsky, modern actors' successes are determined not only by their ability to copy real actions and emotions accurately, but by their ability to project themselves into situations that *could* be real in order to do so. Whether that 'real' is a living room set, a cloud in the sky, or an alternate universe is immaterial: what matters is that actors articulate the space of performance as a genuinely immanent place of human dwelling.

Read back into the auditorium via the work of Stanislavsky's actors, the intricate living room sets that are so central a feature of modern realist dramaturgy cannot be said to be strictly 'real' – or even ideal – after all. They serve multiple conceptual and practical functions – including spurring actors' creative work, operating as physical cues for cast and crew, and working symbolically and imaginatively for spectators – in addition to signifying some literal version of home for characters in the moment of performance. As Sandberg remarks of Ibsen's houses, they remain incomplete, temporary constructs designed to serve their narrative plot as well as their social function:

they need to be able to be packed up and trucked away on tour. Meanwhile, with the imaginative work of actors on their characters in the mix, the idea of the house they serve grows larger than can ever be captured in concrete stage space: '[r]adical changes in consciousness, even retrospective insight, make Ibsen's houses too small for his protagonists. When such individuals become 'unhoused', they live an in-between existence, becoming travelers outside depictable space'.[33] The Stanislavskian practitioner, like the Ibsenite or Chekhovian character, cannot – in fact was never intended to – be contained by the doll's house set: when the performer playing Nora projects herself beyond the doors of her flat and moves towards the outer reaches of the stage, or when the actor embodying Hedda presses through the door *within* her living room only to fire a property gun and then emerge on the other side, for the curtain call, as both herself and someone else entirely, the power of Diamond's double optic as an alternative trope for modelling modern theatrical dwelling comes squarely into view.

YOUR HOME IN THIS BIG WORLD: LONDON'S YOUNG VIC

There are, as we have argued, many ways to be 'at home' at the modern theatre. Some of these home-ways are troubled, while others are welcoming and productive of subjectivity, community – even citizenship. Many contemporary theatre companies have taken their marketing cue from such a notion, building databases of subscribers and sending regular email blasts to 'members' of their 'families': we can be part of a theatrical home simply by signing up online for newsfeeds or mail-outs. Of course there is something cynical about this: it is designed to get us to buy tickets, attend the theatre in person, and spend money on extras like food, alcohol, and programmes while there (see Chapter 2 for the 'social functions' of theatrical extras). Everywhere the contradictions of the double optic are at play: welcome to our home! Please spend extravagantly.

Can a theatre today offer a 'home' that is *not* driven by an underlying economic imperative? London's Young Vic argues it can – and must. The Young Vic (YV) is one of London's premiere Off-West-End venues, situated in the heart of the South Bank, just blocks from major tourist attractions including the National Theatre, Shakespeare's Globe, the London Eye and the Tate Modern (see Figures 4.1 and 4.2). The YV was established in the 1970s as a place where young directors and designers could develop and hone their craft, working counter-culturally in the spirit of 1960s Marxism; in the early twenty-first century it maintains its directors' development programme and retains its reputation as a space for bold experimentation and forceful political drama. Even more significant, for our purposes, is the YV's firm commitment to its

FIGURE 4.1: The interior lobby and bar area of the Young Vic theatre on the South Bank, London. Photo copyright: Ellie Kurtz.

FIGURE 4.2: Exterior of the Young Vic theatre, London. Photo copyright: Ellie Kurtz.

immediate demographic area. The theatre sits literally on the border between two of London's poorest boroughs, Lambeth and Southwark, and via its 'Two Boroughs' programme it offers free tickets to all productions for local residents, produces two community shows each year, and provides regular opportunities to locals for internships, workshops, special events, and more. In large part because of the theatre's founding community commitment the YV has long been supported by the Arts Council of England (ACE), and it remains an ACE priority-funding recipient even in times of increasing funding cuts to the arts across the UK.[34]

The Young Vic's location in the middle of the South Bank's cultural marketplace, combined with its longstanding practice of intensive community engagement, means that it feels like a genuinely *public* place planted within increasingly privatized, globalized London. And yet, the YV is also a not-for-profit business within the purview of London's 'creative industries'. The theatre's motto, 'It's a big world in here', matches the space we have just described, but it also resonates troublingly with the 'Big Society' initiative adopted by David Cameron's Conservative coalition government in 2010. This happy-sounding umbrella term was designed to obscure a painful austerity agenda: it describes a series of measures the coalition government (2010–2015) attempted to put in place in order to empower communities to take charge of basic social services, from libraries to schools and housing projects, thus allowing the government to cut corporate taxes (which would normally help pay for public goods and services like libraries and schools) and create a 'business friendly' environment across Britain. The Big Society Network fell far short of its initial goals in 2014,[35] yet, failure or not, the logic behind the 'Big Society' – that social services should return 'home' to the community, that human needs are not a government's 'business' – had by then taken firm hold in the British public's imagination.

Like all publicly funded cultural organizations in Britain, the YV occupies an awkward position between its own ideology ('It's a big world in here', with room for everyone to learn and grow) and that of the government in power ('big society' means taking responsibility for oneself while government takes care of the business sector). For the theatre's managers, negotiating that position has meant making sometimes-contradictory choices in order to keep all stakeholders happy: local visitors, middle-class subscribers, tourists, government funders, and private sponsors. Though it is a socially minded, not-for-profit company the YV boasts a board of directors composed primarily of lawyers, media executives, and finance workers. Financial services agency IHS Markit supports its funded ticket scheme for low-income locals. The YV's community projects are also made possible through ticket revenues, something that has an impact on the choice of plays the theatre produces each season. Between 2012 and 2014, for example, the theatre staged a string of modern realist classics in its largest house, the majority of which transferred first to the West End and then to Broadway. Among these were its 2012 production of *A Doll's House*, two Chekhov plays, another Ibsen (*An Enemy of the People,* entitled *Public Enemy*), as well as Tennessee Williams's *A Streetcar Named Desire*, starring Gillian Anderson, and Arthur Miller's *A View From The Bridge*, directed by European auteur Ivo Van Hove.

These plays (like much twentieth-century narrative drama) are bankable: known by many different kinds of audience members, saleable to teachers and school groups, they draw sell-out crowds and make transfers to larger theatre venues likely. They also all focus, to varying degrees, on the loss or destruction of home, conforming perfectly to Chaudhuri's geopathological model. Given their bankability it is no surprise that the YV might programme them; given their shared focus on the trouble with home, however, their appearances on its main stage immediately conjure the double optic. After all, the YV's aim is to be a creative, productive, expansive home, a safe and welcoming space for both artists and spectators. What happens when these plays' claustrophobic, even traumatizing home-ways intersect with the YV's much rosier image of a happy, healthy, thriving theatrical world?

At its best, such a collision may produce a welcome critique of the ways in which 'home' remains a fetish for twenty-first-century British neoliberalism – including for those running a theatre like the Young Vic, as it tries to negotiate the fallout from austerity and create a utopic haven in the increasing absence of other material support for needy local residents. The two Chekhov productions the YV staged in 2012 and 2014 (Benedict Andrews's version of *Three Sisters* [Figure 4.3], and Katie Mitchell's take on *The Cherry Orchard*) put pressure on 'home' as a kind of 'big society' in spectacular ways. In the third act of *Three Sisters* the wealthy sisters at the centre of the drama attends to survivors from a fire in their community, provisioning them and offering them shelter. In Andrews's production, however, this narrative action was framed by the literal dismantling of the stage around the sisters as they huddled, increasingly isolated, on what was left of the ground beneath their feet. The dismantling was the work of stagehands 'playing' soldiers from the nearby army encampment in the play; labouring stone-faced, they rang a bell periodically to signal the ongoing emergency. In Brechtian fashion, the loud, alarming clang continuously interrupted the sisters' talk and drew audience attention to the 'offstage' action of the workers. Indeed, the front-and-centre labour of the soldiers (representatives of the Tsar, and through him the nation) made the work of dismantling a community literally central to this scene.

Meanwhile, in Mitchell's production of *The Cherry Orchard*, the brittle comedy Chekhov uses to tell the story of Liubov losing her childhood home was transformed into dark, grim irony. In one startling moment, a 'wanderer' walked into the parlour, interrupting the characters as they reminisced about

FIGURE 4.3: Tuzenbach (Sam Troughton) and Masha (Vanessa Kirby) in *Three Sisters*, directed by Benedict Andrews at the Young Vic, London, 2012. Photo by Simon Annand.

the past. Slightly drunk, but still hyper-aware of the social stakes involved in his invasion of the family's private space, he said bluntly: 'You should see some of the places I've been through coming here. If you had a clue what it was like out there you wouldn't look at me like that. You got any money?'[36] Huddled together stage right, facing in horror the unkempt man standing across from them, the other characters seemed to register that the stranger had entered 'their' house *because he could*, because he saw their home as also, potentially, his – their *Heim*, perhaps, but *Heimat* knows no such bounds. Liubov and Gayev might clutch the house tightly in their memories, but it could not for long keep out the homeless and starving on its margins.

AND WHILE LONDON BURNS: AT HOME IN THE GLOBAL CITY

The house on stage is a sign for domestic space that also stands in for the larger society; staging performances *in* homes moves this trope beyond traditional theatre venues like the Young Vic, and often makes the resulting artwork all the more socially impactful. *Tamara*, John Krizanc's 1981 production about the artist Tamara de Lempicka, took place in Toronto's historic Strachan House. Action occurred in a number of rooms in the house simultaneously; audience members decided which part(s) of the narrative(s) to follow as they moved around the house. Similarly, Paul Davies's 1986 *Living Rooms* occupied Linden, a Victorian mansion (later a boarding house and then a cultural centre) in St Kilda, Melbourne. *Living Rooms* developed its narrative from the material history of the house itself: its fictional inhabitants spanned the Boer War to the 1980s, and the shifting fortunes of their families were its primary subject. Still other examples of modern, site-specific theatre have extended their explorations of *Unheimlichkeit* to a much more specific political environment. Griselda Gambaro's *Information for Foreigners* (1971) responded to escalating state oppression in Argentina and prefigured the horrors of that nation's Dirty War (1976–1983) by imagining a falling-down mansion as a series of secret torture chambers, through which audience members were escorted by guides whose job was to keep them from witnessing too much of the political repression taking place inside. The play enacts what Diana Taylor calls 'percepticide': spectators had to choose if they truly believed in the terrors they (almost) witnessed, and if so to decide if they were willing to take action to stop them.[37] (For more on percepticide and theatrical measures countering it, see Chapter 6.) The play was not performed in Argentina before the war, nor did Gambaro permit it to be published there until 1987; in exile herself, she recognized its colliding of 'safe' domesticity directly with state terror as a radical and dangerous political act.

As Gambaro's work suggests, using a real home as a performance space does much more than merely intensify the *idea* of home at the theatre: it places spectators directly within the realm of the *Unheimlich* and asks us to think carefully about the consequences of trying neatly to separate private and public realms at the theatre – and in the world beyond. Many site-specific performance works stake their claims on exactly this ground: what might be the social and political consequences of bringing *Heimlichkeit* out of the private, domestic sphere and onto the street? Undercurrents of site-specificity's history can be found in modernist theatre through the work of the actor and theatre manager, William Poel, who in the first decade of the twentieth century rethought stage space and theatricality in relation to early modern performance. Site-specificity's more recent origins are often associated with 1960s happenings, made famous through the worlds of visual and performance art (see Chapter 9). While it is commonplace for performance today to occupy spaces beyond conventional theatres, it is worth investigating the ways in which the effects of *Heimlichkeit* continue to resonate through works that move beyond the architectural and psychological spaces of 'home', yet remain invested in the issues those spaces raise.

And While London Burns (*AWLB*) is an audio-walk around the streets of the square mile of London, from Bank tube station (at the heart of European finance capital) to Sir Christopher Wren's Monument (which commemorates the 1666 Great Fire of London). It focuses closely on the failed romance of two financial-sector workers, and broadly on the catastrophic environmental consequences of globalized capitalism's deep-seated dependence on the oil and gas industries. Produced in 2006 by Platform, written and directed by John Jordan and James Marriott, and funded by the Arts Council of England, *AWLB* telescopes the 'public' view of London (gleaned from history, maps, and glossy images designed primarily for tourist and overseas-investment markets) through the much more personal act of walking its streets. This telescoping produces a double-optic map of the city that merges the domestic with the socio-political: *AWLB* argues that street-level London remains an important 'home' – a shared dwelling-place for millions of human beings in urgent need of protection – even for those who do not literally reside within its borders.

Less a history lesson than an action plan for the future, *AWLB* continues to be available as a free audio recording downloadable onto any MP3-enabled device.[38] Its domestic narrative is told against the material effects of global warming on London (and by extension, other cities) as the walk 'track[s] the scent' of 'BP – British Petroleum' through its various stakeholders. Ironically, the further away in time from the production's origins that spectators take the walk, the more the rabid infrastructural development of central London compromises one's ability to complete it. In Act One, for example, one narrator instructs walkers to head for the ruins of the Temple of Mithras, across the road from Morley Financial Services, one of BP's major investors. The contrast of Roman-age temple ruin with multinational investment firm is meant to push the impact of contemporary finance capital into sharp perspective; in 2015, however, spectators would have found that Mithras had been relocated, replaced by scaffolding around a fresh building site.

'Home' in *AWLB* is located first through the voice of an unnamed male narrator, a trader who works at Morley. His relationship with Lucy, his colleague and romantic partner, has been seismically shaken by what the production calls the 'carbon web' that blankets financial London. Lucy has left her job and their relationship, no longer interested in being part of the web and the coming catastrophe. This story begins, in a sense, where Nora Helmer's ends: it stages the reckoning after the door slams. As spectators follow the prompts and walk the City's streets, *AWLB* points out not its most notable landmarks but rather the houses – office towers, windows, cafés, and doorways – belonging to the oil and gas companies and related industries (banks, fund management firms, recruiting agencies, and so on) who help form the invisible carbon web. The narrative asks us to re-imagine home as a fragile, shared entity in imminent danger, towards which we all bear responsibility and over which we still have some control. For London itself, the trader explains, climate change will one day mean the flooding of the Thames, leaving large portions of the existing city underwater and displacing millions of human and animal residents. The scale of this event will compare with the devastation wrought by the 1666 fire that frames the walk. The trader asks us to move towards the 'line of water', the border of the river's expected flooding; it lies a surprising distance away from the current river's edge. Between the two are countless flats, homes we must imagine flooded. The trader leads us up Wren's Monument to survey the huge tracts of the City south of the Thames that will be destroyed.

And While London Burns makes climate change an urgent matter of 'home' for all who do the walk: the production makes clear that this impending disaster *can* be averted, but it leaves participants to decide whether to implement change at a local level and/or how to contribute to larger actions designed to help prevent environmental catastrophe worldwide. To drive this urgency home the production deploys theatre's double optic in a unique way: by merging actor and audience member *physically* as well as *imaginatively*. *AWLB*'s performer is located not on the stage in front of us, but between our ears. At first there is a clear distinction between the trader and participant – he tells listeners where to go – but as the seventy-minute production proceeds the aural immersion alters our perspective on our actions in and on the environment we share. The overwhelming effect is uncanniness, as the narrative invades participants' brains.[39] *AWLB* requires that we hold the doubleness of modern spatial experience front and centre: the physical and the imagined, the world we feel beneath our feet, see with our eyes, and also imagine *beyond* them (beyond this time and place) become one. And the stakes, in this case, are high: the differences between the concrete places we see in 'real time' and the past and future spaces we conjure via our guides' voices make a material as well as an imaginative claim on us, and on our shared human futures. The walk returns us not to Nora's drawing room, but nevertheless to the alarm of physical entrapment that was so central to Ibsen and his contemporaries at the beginning of the modern era. And it returns us to the scene of neoliberal globalization: who owns the air, the ground, the water? Who is privileged to have a home to go to, and for whom is permanent exile all too real?

CONCLUSION

In this chapter we have traced theatrical modernism's investments in *Unheimlichkeit*, and modern theatre criticism's parallel commitment to geopathology, in order to nuance the longstanding claim that theatre's 'home' in the modern age is a place of illness, stress, and violence alone. Diamond's double optic, Tuan's mythic space, and Bachelard's topoanalysis all draw on the contradictory impulses (towards 'modernity at full throttle' on one hand, and the urge to stop time and retreat into ideal space on the other) that dot the material histories of modern culture in order to theorize the profound role human imagination played in shaping the material home-worlds of Euro-American modernity. Our case studies demonstrate the ways in which imaginative engagements with home on the stage continue to break down binary relations between public and private space, often in the service of shaping a fairer dwelling place for all humans on our planet. The Young Vic theatre seeks, within doors, new ways to engage with the spatial politics of classical modernist texts, while also looking outward at Lambeth and Southwark, the communities towards which it feels a local duty of care. *And While London Burns* demonstrates how integrated the public and private spheres are when both face destruction through climate change. In the early twenty-first century, modern theatre's environmental consciousness occupies a social context in which 'home' is less a haven against the world and more a *Heimat* – a community of participants charged, for better or for worse, with surviving Earth's future together. This environmental consciousness acknowledges the presence of the uncanny, and takes that uncanniness as a marker of shared political responsibility. If early modernist homes onstage were meant to function as metonyms of our own imperfect dwellings, 'home' at the theatre at the beginning of the twenty-first century signals a much broader, though no less urgent, agenda.

CHAPTER FIVE

Circulations

Visual Sovereignty, Transmotion, and Tribalography

JILL CARTER, HEATHER DAVIS-FISCH,
AND RIC KNOWLES

> Native people created narratives that were histories and stories with the power to transform. I call this rhetorical space 'tribalography'.
>
> – LeAnne Howe[1]

Indigenous scholars and performers have diverse understandings of what constitutes performance and its history, and of how performances circulate across time and space. Their many approaches to the performances of the past are linked, however, by a rejection of dominant narratives of the global circulation of theatre in the modern period, which tend to emphasize the physical movement of performances between imperial centres and colonial spaces, and to naturalize Western, hegemonic understandings of space and time through which such circulations occur. For example, early twentieth-century touring productions belatedly brought 'the latest' theatre products to settler colonies like Canada, the United States, and Australia, imposing European imaginings of theatrical space onto landscapes considered to be culturally empty and open to colonialist inscriptions. Ethnographic displays followed the opposite spatial trajectory, bringing Indigenous performers from the world's so-called peripheries to its cultural centres as fairground exotica. Meanwhile, theatrical modernists and postmodernists raided the world's Indigenous cultures for raw material, incorporating Indigenous content into performance forms deemed to be 'intercultural'. In these dominant-culture narratives of theatrical circulation, time is understood to be linear, progressive and singular, while space is static, knowable, and ownable. These imperial teleologies have been widely critiqued, not only by Indigenous scholars but also by many postcolonial, postmodern, and poststructuralist scholars. As Margaret Werry argues, however, Euro-American critics have been slow to present compelling alternatives.[2] In this chapter we contend that, by examining how Indigenous performance circulations work to preserve Indigenous survivance and realize Indigenous sovereignty, scholars can expose how most Western forms of theatrical touring and exposition function as technologies of colonization, occupation or capitalist modernity: bringing products to the colonies, and mining those colonies for the raw materials of 'authentic' performance culture, rather than negotiating, trading, collaborating, or sharing. The alternative historiography we share here is designed to genuinely query Hegelian teleologies and the circulatory practices they enable, and can be applied to Indigenous performance practices far beyond North America's borders.

Choctaw scholar LeAnne Howe's concept of tribalography raises significant questions for theatre and performance historians: How does tribalography differ from history? What difference would it make if scholars saw the circulation of theatre and performance in the modern period through an Indigenous lens, recognizing and articulating tribalographies instead of writing theatre histories? This chapter examines how circulation has been understood, practiced, and lived by Indigenous performers as part of and apart from their negotiation with modernity. In circulating across space and time, Indigenous performances transform Indigenous and settler understandings of identity and create space in which political, juridical, and spiritual sovereignty – which we define as the inherent right of both individuals and collectives to seek out and discover the purposes for which they have been placed on this earth, the responsibilities with which they have been invested, and the mechanics of maintaining the relationships into which they were born – is recognized and enacted.

Tribalography, which we approach as both the 'rhetorical space' Howe suggests and as a historiographical paradigm, reflects Indigenous understandings of temporality, spatiality, and story, which, in turn, generate specific patterns of cultural circulation. Indigenous understandings of time and space are specific to individual Indigenous Nations, but some of these might productively be considered 'pan-Indigenous'. Arapaho scholar Michael Marker suggests that for many Indigenous peoples 'history . . . is not a linear progression of people and ideas in time [. . .] but rather a spiralling of events and themes that appear and reappear within circles of seasons'. This history is 'identified in oral traditions',[3] and centres on an orbicular cosmology that sees 'new shapes of reality' emerge based on 'returning versions of both ancestors and ideas'.[4] Marker's comments are drawn from his understanding of history as both an oral and a socially constructed form of knowledge about the past; this understanding of history, in turn, has special affinity to both performance histories, and to the idea, current in modern performance studies, that performance itself is a form of history-making.

Performances of the past, the traces of their circulation over time, and their embodied and material remains in the present underline the idea that Indigenous sovereignty has always existed and continues to exist within and across traditional territories, surviving in the face of colonization. The Mississauga Chief Maungwudaus, for instance, mobilized a group of Anishinaabe performers to tour Europe and the United States in 1843. In the written account of his travels, Maungwudaus makes it apparent that even as his European and Euro-American audiences diverted themselves with (what they surely regarded as) a colourfully embodied spectacle of exotic primitivism, he, for one, was similarly captivated by the spectacle they produced: for Maungwudaus and his compatriots, these foreign audiences performed as exotic Others, affecting their Anishinaabe visitors with fascination, amusement, and revulsion. Queen Victoria, he reported, presented herself to his eye merely as a 'small woman' – not his Sovereign, nor his 'mother'. Her 'warriors [. . .] look[ed to be] fierce and savage like our American dogs when carrying black squirrels in their mouths'.[5] Maungwudaus, it seems, gazed upon this foreign pageant with equal portions of interest and disgust, commenting upon the plight of the tens of thousands of sex workers in England and France[6]; the violence perpetrated by European men on their women; and peculiarities of 'zhaagaanosh' (English) landscaping, fashion, and table manners. Anishinaabe identity insistently asserts itself throughout Maungwudaus's travel diary – an account that he has crafted in accordance with the language and narrative framework utilized by the educated Englishman. Maungwudaus may have written in English for a foreign audience, but with his own compatriots, he spoke Anishinaabemowin.[7] His diary appreciatively documents instances of kindness and humanity exhibited by his more sympathetic hosts and audiences. And, in a similar vein, honest admiration for the beauty he encountered during the troupe's progress is duly noted. Always, however, the reader of Maungwudaus's travel account sees through Maungwudaus's eyes as he watched those who had come to watch him, assessing the European exotic in accordance with Anishinaabe value systems. And while Maungwudaus wrote also of crushing losses (for example, the deaths of his wife and three of their children) his report does not linger on these personal tragedies: his treatment of these is cursory and unemotional.[8] There is no plea for sympathy, no solicitation of condolence; rather, this work holds up a mirror and invites Europe to view itself through the eyes and understanding of a nation outside of itself, soliciting from its readers affective response to the spectacle produced by their own reflections.

Here, then, in a material trace left for us by George Caitlin's 'Paris Ojibwe', we encounter 'an active sense of [Indigenous] presence [which renounces] dominance, tragedy and victimry'.⁹ It is an account of some survival strategies of this Anishinaabe troupe and of their resistance to colonialism. It is an account of what Anishinaabe scholar Gerald Vizenor terms 'survivance' that insists on its author's sovereignty. Vizenor uses this term to blend Indigenous practices of survival and resistance; he characterizes survivance as 'an active sense of presence, the continuance of Native stories', and 'renunciations of dominance, tragedy, and victimry'.¹⁰ In this chapter, we will consider three specific patterns of performance circulation through which survivance emerges for Indigenous peoples in the modern period: visual sovereignty, transmotion, and tribalography.

Seneca film scholar Michelle Raheja defines 'visual sovereignty' as 'a reading practice for thinking about the space between resistance [to] and compliance [with]' dominant cultural practices. Indigenous artists 'revisit, contribute to, borrow from, critique, and reconfigure' performance conventions inherited from – or imposed by – Western theatrical cultures.¹¹ Transmotion, according to Anishinaabe scholar Leanne Simpson, describes a 'reciprocal use of nature' between Indigenous artist, the land, and its resources, rather than a 'monotheistic, territorial sovereignty' in which the performer instrumentalizes (and dominates) the natural landscape.¹² Transmotion involves movement across physical borders and categories, but also movement beyond the physical realm. Finally, tribalographies, as described by LeAnne Howe, are stories or performance interventions that hold the power to recreate the world. Through the act of circulating tribal histories, tribalographies connect Indigenous pasts, present, and futures, people, land, and animals. These three modes of circulation allow Indigenous sovereignty in our modern, colonial present to emerge through performances that real-ize and re-present (make real, and make present *again*) Indigenous stories of survivance; we use them in this chapter in order to position Indigenous historiographical principles – rather than Western modes of history-telling – as central to our analysis.

VISUAL SOVEREIGNTY

Visual sovereignty concerns itself largely with the circulation of Indigenous performances over time. Through much of the modern period in what are now the United States and Canada, Indigenous dance and ceremonial practices were made illegal by colonial governments, and one of the major modern technologies for their preservation, circulation, re-presentation, and recreation over time was film. The moving camera might be considered the objectifying gaze of modernity, but Indigenous peoples were present as agents as well as objects of the filmic gaze from the outset. The first time Native performers appeared on film, in Thomas Edison's sixteen-second 1894 Kinetograph *Buffalo Dance*,¹³ one of the three Lakota performers from Buffalo Bill's Wild West Show – Last Horse, Parts His Hair, and Hair Coat – could barely keep his eyes off the camera. 'Turning and twisting to keep his gaze unbroken and, at one point, brandishing his stick directly at the lens',[14] he confronts the non-Native gaze, possibly in defiance of federal forces that had forbidden the dance, and winks knowingly to Indigenous audiences with whom he is communicating across space and time.

How have Indigenous peoples regarded historical performances of their cultures, particularly when seeing those performances through modern technologies of production and circulation like film? Can performances created and controlled by non-Indigenous peoples in the service of the colonial project be reclaimed in the name of survivance?[15] Raheja's theorization of visual sovereignty suggests that viewing colonial performances in this way (as potential tools of survivance) offers 'the possibility of engaging and deconstructing white-generated representations of Indigenous people'. It also offers a chance to 'intervene in larger discussions of Native American sovereignty'[16] in a way that exceeds legalistic definitions of 'sovereignty' imposed by settler society. Such representations, particularly those that employ audio-visual technologies to archive performances of the past, preserve not only the colonial assumptions of their creators but also traces of Indigenous resistance and more complex collaborative processes between Indigenous and non-Indigenous creators. The interplay of live and technologically mediated performances allows artists and audiences in the present new forms of access to the past. Visual sovereignty is most politically potent through ongoing reclamations and repatriations and through the abilities of performances to call for future action.

Many early pseudo-ethnographic films are documentary in quite a literal sense: they document, intentionally or not, Indigenous peoples' early negotiations with modernity. Robert Flaherty's 1922 film *Nanook of the North* claims to record an Inuit family's pre-contact existence, and the film has been widely criticized for popularizing and circulating the 'happy Eskimo' stereotype. (Flaherty carefully orchestrated his shots to generate the narrative and representations he hoped to include.) Flaherty's film is well known, but Harold Wyckoff and Bill Derr's 1920 *Romance of the Far Fur Country* predates *Nanook* by two years; it was filmed to commemorate the 250th anniversary of the Hudson's Bay Company (HBC). In July 1919, the Hudson's Bay Company Motion Picture Expedition set off from Montreal, and over the course of six months the filmmakers traced the trade routes of the HBC, travelling by steamship, canoe, train and dog team and encountering diverse Indigenous peoples, notably Inuit, Cree, Dene, Métis, and Kwakwaka'wakw. In 1920, the film was screened as part of the HBC's anniversary celebrations at its posts across Canada. After the celebrations concluded, the film, unlike *Nanook of the North*, stopped circulating: no original print of the two-hour feature survives,[17] while the original film canisters ended up at the British Film Institute (BFI) in London, retracing the path taken by the HBC's trade goods. In the 1990s, Peter Geller 'rediscovered' the *Romance* canisters and led an effort to return them to the HBC archives in Canada and reconstruct the original film. As part of this process Geller's team visited many Indigenous communities whose members participated in the original film, organizing public screenings and discussions. The 2014 documentary *On the Trail of the Far Fur Country* traces the original filmmakers' journey and includes footage documenting reactions of Indigenous viewers – often descendants of performers in the original film – to the 1919 material.

Although both *Romance* and *Nanook of the North* frequently primitivise their Indigenous subjects and popularize racist stereotypes, both films also preserve moments of Indigenous survivance. As Anna Grimshaw argues:

> Far from being duped or coerced by Flaherty, the evidence of the film suggests ... that Nanook [played by Inuk performer Allakariallak] and his fellow actors knowingly craft themselves into the kind of stock characters typical of the turn of the 20th century popular culture. In so doing, they can barely contain their hilarity as they perform the 'happy-go-lucky Eskimo', a satire on the Western fantasy of Arctic peoples.[18]

One infamous example of this practice occurs in a scene during which Nanook, pretending not to understand southern technology, bites a trader's gramophone record. In relation to this scene, Raheja raises the important question of Inuit reception: Nanook's response to the record 'might register one thing to his non-Inuit audience and quite another to members of an Inuit community who recognize the cultural code[s]' at work in, for example, his smile at the camera.[19]

Films such as *Nanook* (Figure 5.1) and *Romance*, when viewed by Indigenous audiences today, activate 'moving' encounters with ancestors onscreen, generating pride in their strength and perseverance. Indeed, the films exemplify a form of repatriation, returning ancestors 'captured' on film to their home territories and descendants. In *Romance*, this is particularly notable in audience responses to a sequence entitled 'Reminiscences: The Life Story of an Eskimo'. The sequence, which was imagined and partially scripted before Wyckoff arrived at Baffin Island, uses many of the racist tropes Flaherty would popularize with *Nanook*, including the representation of young Inuit men as physically bumbling in overly bulky clothing, or the almost-asexual representation of marital relations between Inuit couples. (Both of these tropes have contributed to longstanding representations of Inuit as child-like.) However, the nostalgic qualities of the narrative in this sequence – which includes contemplative shots of an older man to indicate 'flashbacks' to his supposed wedding – are juxtaposed in *Romance* to footage of the 'modern' fur trade and the arrival of a supply ship, which locates the sequence within, rather than outside of, early twentieth-century modernity. In the 2014 *On the Trail* documentary, Inuk film producer

FIGURE 5.1: Production still from *Nanook of the North*. Image courtesty of Flaherty Study Center.

Aletheia Arnaquq-Baril (Figure 5.2) identifies the older man featured in the sequence as Ingmilayuk, her great, great, great grandfather; he thereby becomes an individual living in a specific time and space and a member of a community that continues in the present. She comments, 'You read about these times and you see photographs of these times and it's really something to see moving footage of it. [. . .] [I]t's like having a family photo that's been on your wall for years suddenly moving [. . .]. I didn't expect to be taken by surprise, the emotion was just unexpected [. . .].' Not only is Ingmilayuk given back his specific identity, but the medium of film also creates space for Arnaquq-Baril to connect emotionally with the past. Arnaquq-Baril also notes the film's ability to allow Inuit viewers to feel proud of their culture's past; despite the film's 'sometimes racist undertones', she argues, 'it's important to know that history and that's why these things were filmed in the way they were and why they said the things they did cause it explains the struggle and the journey we've gone through as a people'.

Inuk singer Tanya Tagaq, who since 2012 has been performing alongside screenings of *Nanook* across Canada and elsewhere, echoes Arnaquq-Baril in

FIGURE 5.2: Aletheia Arnaquq-Baril interviewed in Iqaluit, Nunavut. Five Door Films, 2014.

her feelings about *Nanook*'s mix of racist representation and moving power. When she first saw the film, Tagaq was 'embarrassed'[20] at its representation of Inuit; however, she also believes that the film 'portrays what life was like, the struggle'. She concludes that she experiences the film 'with a mixture of pride, pride in my ancestors, and anger, the anger of seeing their life through 1922 glasses'.[21] The films are, then, at once artefacts of colonial racism and testaments to the history of the Inuit, their strength, and their endurance.

The contemporary Indigenous viewers whose spectatorial experiences are included in *On the Trail* consistently note how *Romance of the Far Fur Country* preserves examples of Indigenous resistance, particularly in two moments: a sequence shot at Alert Bay, British Columbia, depicting Kwakwaka'wakw in Potlatch regalia, and a sequence shot at Fort Chipewyan, Alberta, in which a Dene elder 'sends a message to the King'. The Potlatch scenes are possibly the most transgressive in the film because the ceremonies – traditional celebrations that used gift-giving (a pre-contact mode of circulation) to mark relationships between communities and community members – had been outlawed in 1885 revisions to the Dominion of Canada's Indian Act. This prohibition was harshly enforced in Alert Bay in 1921, just two years after the footage was shot, when many community members were jailed for participating in the ceremonies. In this short sequence, the intertitle 'Finery donned for the Potlatch ceremony' (Figure 5.3) appears, and four young men emerge from the woods and move down a path towards the camera. The next shot shows one young man posing to show off his regalia, displaying it from multiple angles.

FIGURE 5.3: Costumes used at Potlatch Ceremony, 1919. HBCA 2012/1/102. Hudson's Bay Company Archives, Archives of Manitoba.

Viewers of the *On the Trail* documentary are then attuned to the cultural value of this footage in the present, when a Kwakwaka'wakw man comments that he had never seen a mask carved like the one in the footage. Because many of the material artefacts associated with Potlatch ceremonies were destroyed during the peak of Indian Act restrictions, which outlawed many traditional Indigenous social and cultural practices in the name of assimilation, the footage preserves vital visual information about the past (Figure 5.4). The original footage is then linked to cultural resurgence by a contemporary Kwakwaka'wakw woman whose grandparents were among those arrested in 1921 for participating in potlatching. She comments that although the film documents a dark time, 'We can't stay in that place anymore. We have to move on. And we have all the things here to allow us to move on'.

The resistant nature of the Potlatch scenes in *Romance* might have remained implicit for viewers unfamiliar with Canada's Indian Act, but the cultural and political resistance captured in the scene at Fort Chipewyan is explicit. The scene's intertitle reads 'The Chief of the Chipewyans sends a message to the King by way of the camera'; spectators then see the man smoking and wearing skin clothing. The next intertitle reads, 'He says that the White Man is breaking

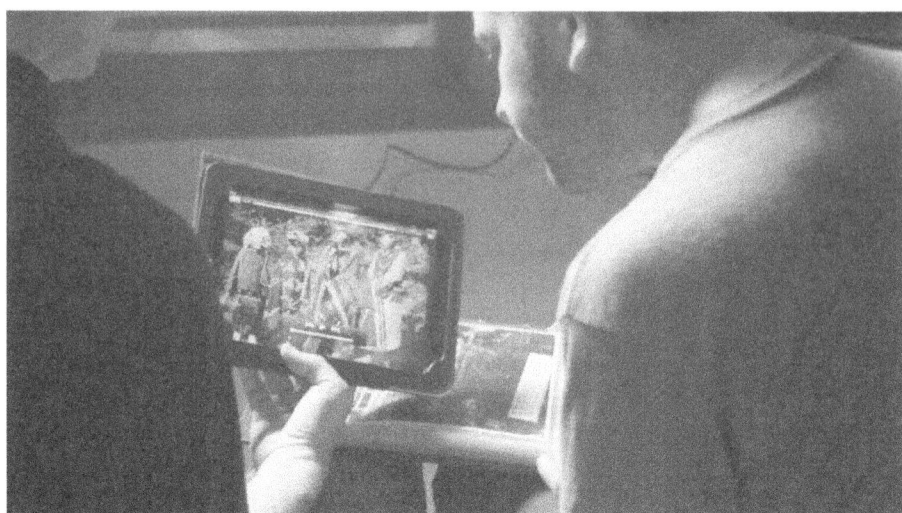

FIGURE 5.4: Filmmaker Kevin Nikkel watches footage from *The Romance of the Far Fur Country* with Trevor Issac, at the U'mista Cultural Centre, Alert Bay, British Columbia. Five Door Films, 2014.

his treaty and that for the Indian there should never be any "close season" on game'. The DVD commentary identifies the man as, probably, Dene Chief Alexander LaViolette. Geller is clear that LaViolette was consciously using modern technology to circulate his 'assertion of Aboriginal right and title' to far-away viewers, including the settler population of early twentieth-century Canada. Film technology also allows LaViolette's message to circulate across time to viewers today. Reactions to this scene in the documentary include strong expressions of frustration, anger, and pride. Arnaquq-Baril comments, 'When I saw this shot, I thought, well isn't it about time, you know? [. . .] When people, leaders like this are saying the same thing for so long, you know they're not being unreasonable, there's something really unfair here'.

If *Romance* generates space for recognizing Indigenous resistance in the past and uses this resistance to reinforce claims for sovereignty in the present and future, Tanya Tagaq's work with *Nanook* takes a more radical approach. Since 2012, Tagaq, with percussionist Jean Martin and violinist Jesse Zubot, has been performing alongside screenings of the film in venues ranging from the Luminato Festival in Toronto to the Dublin Fringe Festival. Tagaq grew up in Cambridge Bay, Nunavut, and then attended residential school[22] in Yellowknife before, as a student at the Nova Scotia College of Art and Design in the 1990s, being exposed to tape recordings of throat singing, a traditional Inuit musical form characterized by short, rhythmic, voiced and unvoiced sounds, typically performed as a friendly competition between two women. Because of the impact of residential schools on Indigenous populations in Canada, Tagaq notes that 'Not a lot of people spoke, or still speak, Inuinnaqtun, and there was no throat singing. . . . People thought it was cool to be white. And I can kind of understand it; that's how colonialism works'.[23] Her performance style is a contemporary re-interpretation of traditional throat singing, not only because she departs from its conventions by, for instance, performing solo, but also because she overtly politicizes the form.

Tagaq's performance alongside *Nanook* is most obviously resistant and viscerally powerful during the scene in which Nanook discovers and tries to bite the trader's gramophone record. In virtually all performances reviewed by critics, the only English word in Tagaq's live, improvised soundtrack is 'colonizer', and she repeats it during this infamous scene. Janet Rogers notes that Tagaq here 'exacts her revenge' on the offending trader and Flaherty's representation of him, 'delivering a gravely, equally offensive reply' to both. Tagaq is clear that she understands her performances alongside *Nanook* as reclamations of the film and its Inuit subjects, commenting that what she loves about the performance is that she can 'kill two birds with one stone. I get to make a commentary on the racist outlook toward such an amazing culture that was so technologically advanced to be able to survive in that hearty environment. I also get to be part of my ancestors'.[24] Tagaq's performances also highlight a significant circulatory power in the film and others like it. *Nanook* testifies to the ability of film to do the work of colonialism while also preserving and re-circulating Indigenous cultural traditions and technologies of survival that Canadian colonial policies deliberately attempted to destroy. By engaging with the film both from within its problematic assumptions about Indigenous identity and from the perspective of her contemporary, critical position outside of it, Tagaq reclaims Nanook's performance as one with cultural and political significance in the present, for both Indigenous and settler audiences.

TRANSMOTION

Contemporary re-performances of *Romance* and *Nanook* are concerned primarily with temporal circulations that work quite differently from traditional theatrical or filmic 'revivals' in which the past is nostalgically revisited or re-invented as if it were a foreign country. Indigenous performers, however, circulate their work in space in ways that instantiate worldviews quite different from those underlying modern, imperial forms of theatrical touring. Anthropologist Keith Basso asserts that for the Western Apache, 'Wisdom Sits in Places'[25]; this statement describes the central role of 'place' in cultural production for many Indigenous nations, particularly as it is carried through story. By way of example, Anishinaabe scholar Christine Lenze describes the tour of Anishinaabe playwright Ian Ross's *fareWell* to reserves in northern Manitoba in 1998. The play opened at Prairie Theatre Exchange, a formal theatre space in an upscale mall in downtown Winnipeg where it was read and consumed *as a play* – a representation – for largely non-Indigenous audiences. When it toured to community-based performance spaces on Indigenous reserves in the north, however, audiences interacted with it as *story* – as an act of re-presenting (that is, of making something *present again*). Relocated, it required of its audience 'a sense of response-ability to the performance in which the story is not only told but it is listened to'.[26] This anecdote raises specific questions about the circulation of Indigenous work within home territories, in 'trans-Indigenous' settings beyond those territories,[27] and in non-Indigenous settings: what does it mean for Indigenous people, whose very identity *as* Indigenous is tied to the land, to 'tour'?

Transmotion, a concept coined by Vizenor and applied by Simpson, allows for a complex consideration of the interrelation between traditional and post-contact patterns of circulation, territory, identity, and – ultimately – sovereignty, particularly through its emphasis on Indigenous patterns of circulation in space. Simpson writes: '[i]n Precolonial daily life of Nishnaabeg people, movement, change and fluidity were a reality',[28] while territorial 'boundaries' constituted relationships and instituted negotiations. Simpson argues that the circulations of traditional Anishinaabe did not consist of wandering, or moving from place to place, but of moving outward from a territorial centre to a place of encounter, 'where one needs to practice good relations with neighboring nations'.[29] Anishinaabe understandings of territory were thus defined not by physical borders but by language, philosophy, way of life, and political structure; their understandings of the earth as mother were and are inextricably tied to their identities and to all of their relationships with their surroundings, human and non-human alike. Simpson's understanding of 'transmotion' as a series of spatial negotiations carried out by human and other practitioners of the land can be seen in the work of two very different contemporary Indigenous groups: A Tribe Called Red (ATCR), and the Mother Earth Water Walkers, led by Anishinaabe Elder Josephine Mandamin. These performers circulate in ways that are fundamentally, ontologically different, on one hand, from the colonial replications of European performance spaces, practices, and modes of spectatorship in occupied territory in the late nineteenth and early twentieth centuries; and, on the other, from the 'globalization' of certain kinds of cultural performances that have become the norm at large, internationally renowned theatre festivals in post-war Edinburgh, Avignon, and beyond.

ATCR consists of three Indigenous men: DJ NDN (Ian Campeau, Anishinaabe from Nippissing First Nation), Bear Witness (from Cayuga First Nation), and 2oolman (Tim Hill, Mohawk, from Six Nations of the Grand River),[30] who together have created 'electronic pow wow' – music that 'throbs in your subwoofers with a chill-inducing message of empowerment'.[31]

ATCR has become an international sensation for their energetic layering of cutting-edge electronic music with traditional Indigenous drumming and pow wow vocables, backed by videographer Bear Witness's visual mashups of pop-culture representations of and by Indigenous peoples. Their performances have been read as a 'form of repatriation, a challenge to western concepts of copyright' and a new brand of Indigenous modernism that is embedded in Native traditions but also in conversation with like-minded work at the edge of their musical and cultural territories.[32] According to one critic, 'the group has revamped and honored their culture, contemporized an often forgotten and forsaken segment of society, and catapulted their concern and care for their people into the mainstream'.[33] ATCR have toured extensively in Canada, the United States, and Europe, but they have also created and maintained an urban Indigenous space on the club scene in their adopted home of Ottawa, Ontario, where they throw monthly Electric Pow Wow parties that ground them and their urban Indigenous community in a centre and territory from which they move outward, as Simpson says, establishing relationships and alliances with diverse cultural communities. According to Bear Witness, the Electric Pow Wow in Ottawa is 'our hometown show. [It's about] creating a base for aboriginal people in the city'.[34]

ATCR's reclamation and 'decolonizing'[35] of racist imagery in their shows, their reconnection with traditional, formerly outlawed and suppressed Indigenous music and dance traditions, and, perhaps especially, their reclaiming of urban space as Indigenous territory, all work together to engender a new, Indigenous modernism.[36] (As ATCR's producer DJ BuddaBlaze says, 'See? We can be modern too'.[37]) When touring, too, they resist the modernist model of occupying 'empty' space or mining other cultures' materials, choosing instead a mindful moving-outward as they establish reciprocal relationships with other artists working on similar terrain. On tour they perform at festivals and universities, in clubs and hotels, and on reserves and reservations, and they collaborate across difference with the 'global bass' diaspora of musicians who are working to politicize and decolonize world music and whom they consider to be 'allies'.[38] They have engaged in collaborations with Indigenous individuals and groups, but also with a wide range of non-Indigenous artists from a variety of marginalized communities internationally, performing a kind of ambassadorial function not unlike the Indigenous travellers who circulated within Jace Weaver's *Red Atlantic*, contributing centrally, as Weaver's subtitle insists, to 'the making of the modern world'.[39] It is perhaps with this in mind that, still grounded in their created home territory, they titled their second album *Nation II Nation*.

Josephine Mandamin is, like Simpson, Anishinaabekwe. In 2000, Edward Benton-Banai, presiding Grand Chief of the Three Fires Midewiwin Lodge in Wisconsin, told Mandamin that by 2030 an ounce of water would cost its weight in gold bullion 'if we continue our negligence'.[40] When Benton-Banai finished his prophecy he asked Mandamin what she intended to do to forestall the crisis. In Spring 2003, three elderly women began the first of the water walks, undertaking a journey of 1,500 miles around Lake Superior. They carried a copper bucket filled with Lake Superior Water and an Eagle Staff. They did not rehearse, nor did they solicit human audiences, monies, or government permissions for a peripatetic 'performance' crafted to re-right a fraught relationship between humans and the non-human world.

Between 2003 and 2008 Mandamin and her fellow walkers completed journeys around each of the five Great Lakes, of which the Anishinaabeg are the traditional caretakers. Then, in 2009, they traversed the territory between those lakes and the mouth of the St Lawrence River, arriving at the land the Anishinaabeg occupied before the Great Migration.[41] If these first six walks could be understood in part as solidifying relations within traditional Anishinaabe territories, in 2011 a 'Four Directions Walk' was held that moved well beyond those territories to enable broader encounters at those places 'where one needs to practice good relations with neighboring nations'. The Four Directions Walk consisted of four walks held concurrently: south from Hudson's Bay, north from the Gulf of Mexico, west from the Atlantic, and east from the Pacific, all converging at Three Fires Midwiwin Lodge in Wisconsin where the walks had begun and where the salt waters carried from each walk's source were united, simultaneously poured into the fresh waters of Lake Superior in a Midewahnikwe water ceremony.

The walks are ceremony – women's ceremony – and are carried out with solemn observances for an audience of one (Figure 5.5). Mandamin and the women who walk with her always wear long skirts, regardless of terrain or weather conditions.[42] While they do permit themselves to stop and rest, they do so mindfully and only when it is imperative: water must keep moving during the day, and as carriers, the walkers must keep moving with it.[43] When they must stop, they perform ceremony first to set the water at rest and then to pick it up and begin the journey again. The 'audience' to whom Mandamin directed her songs and prayers and for whom she choreographed this precise and repeatable physical score was the water itself – her relative and her 'director'. The movement outward from traditional territories that Simpson describes and that the Mother Earth Water Walks model culminates in what Mandamin calls 'collecting consciousness', 'the collecting of thoughts' and minds so that 'the minds, hopefully, will be of one, sometime'.[44] The Water Walks have been undertaken by walkers from many Indigenous nations and supported by many Indigenous and non-Indigenous people, who have come together to intervene on behalf of the water on which we all rely for life on earth. Most recently as we write, on the 'Sacred Water Walk on the 22nd of June, 2015, there was a

FIGURE 5.5: This is ceremony – woman's ceremony. Image copyright: Sylvia Plain.

reunion with the eastern clans of Anishinaabe Aski: Pasmaquaddy, Abenaki/Wabanaki, Micmac, Ojibways and all other clans to tell stories of the Great Migration and share the history of our people. Pipes, Tobacco, and Drums emerge[d] as our sacred stories [we]re shared.'[45] The Great Migration story was then re-enacted, as the walkers journeyed westward again.

Mandamin and other walkers have visited numerous communities, both settler and Indigenous, recounting the creation stories and reminding women of their responsibility to carry and speak for the water. And they have inspired Anishinaabe men to pick up the Eagle Staff and protect the women on the walk.[46] Now, actors from other communities have begun to remember and circulate their own teachings. In 2014, Trent University in Peterborough, Ontario, on Anishinaabe territory, hosted a Sacred Water Gathering at which Indigenous representatives from across the Americas were in attendance. Inspired by the remembered 'story' animated by Mandamin and the Water Walkers, Sahtu Dene, Hopi, Lakota Sioux, Kogi, and Cusco teachers came together to share their creation stories and cultural teachings, bringing ancient knowledge systems into the present in an attempt to inspire the reformation of human behaviour and the transformation of the dystopian, thirsty future that seems imminent.[47] Settler sensibilities have also been transformed through the Water Walks: politicians, scientists, activists, artists, reporters, writers, and homemakers have joined the walks and stood up to defend the water. The circulation of an Anishinaabe origin story has captured the North American imaginary, and people for whom water was once a necessary tool to help them to 'do life' now 'do it for the water'.

The Mother Earth Water Walkers enact Indigenous transmotion for a world in peril; each walker performs a rigorous physical score – circulating and re-presenting the original instructions set down for the Anishinaabeg in the earliest Midewewin texts – to facilitate the cleansing and healing of the land's blood (Figure 5.6).

In a reciprocal gesture, the land has 'performed' its acceptance of these ministrations, revealing those instructions scripted on rock in red medicine (the pictographs) by those who foresaw the European invasion and undertook the Great Migration to ensure Anishinaabe survivance.[48] The sharing and re-enactment of original instructions constitute performative embodiments of what Howe calls 'tribalography', bringing space and time together and speaking back to the excesses of modernity in a truly interactive performance that 'lift[s] the burden of colonialism by visioning new realities'.[49]

FIGURE 5.6: Indigenous transmotion for a world in peril. Image copyright: Sylvia Plain.

TRIBALOGRAPHY

Tribalographies are creation stories that carry the imagination of the Indigenous self and of the relationship between that self and creation. When tribalographies are carried through time and across space, they recreate and transform each new generation; indeed they recreate Indigenous Nations in each moment and every place they are uttered. The past is not remembered in tribalographies; *it is brought into and acted upon in the present* regardless of the relocations tribal people may have endured, the degradation of their biotas as a result of industrialization, the racist and colonialist re-education programmes to which they have been subjected, and the suppression of their languages and ceremonies. (Together with the social systems that contain them, these oppressive practices are all technologies of colonization governments deployed as preconditions for Indigenous entry into European brands of modernity.) And, as Howe has demonstrated, Indigenous creation stories have, from time to time, also worked to instruct and transform the strangers whose coming had been prophesied.[50]

Howe posits that America (as nation, as story) is itself a tribalography, a creation story authored during Longhouse orations witnessed by settler dignitaries who eventually engineered the unification of four colonies and wrote the constitution of the United States.[51] The Haudenosaunee[52] orations that precede all Longhouse events are performed speech acts that remember the creation of life on earth and that re-story the transformation of five warring nations into a unified body-politic governed by The Great Law of Peace – the Constitution of the Haudenosaunee people. So powerful were these performances that they birthed a new tribalography for the eighteenth-century Europeans who founded the United States of America.[53] 'Touring' to the Longhouses of the Haudenosaunee, settler dignitaries who had run from centuries of warfare in Europe as well as from internal division in their 'mother countries' (religious, economic, social) encountered embodied performances of an Indigenous creation story that worked itself upon the imaginations of America's founding fathers 'to create an image so powerful in [their] minds [. . .] that they believed if savages could unite they ought to be able to do the same thing'.[54] Benjamin Franklin, who visited the Longhouse often, was deeply moved by the profound willingness of each speaker to fully *receive* the other: 'How different this is from the conduct of a polite British House of Commons, where scarce a day passes without some confusion, that makes the Speaker hoarse in calling *to order*'.[55] The performances of seventeenth-century Longhouse orators must have been very potent indeed to have cut through the clamorous struggle for settler dominance – between 'seven rival white colonial governments on the Hudson [River]'[56] – to convince Old World rivals to put aside their differences and come together as one nation.[57] 'Native stories', Howe asserts, 'are power. They create people. They author tribes'.[58]

The Cherokee Nation is one of the so-called 'Five Civilized Tribes' that, on order of United States President Andrew Jackson in 1830, were forcibly marched over 900 miles of rough terrain from their traditional territories to the lands that are now known as Oklahoma. This journey, on which many died, has come to be known as 'the Trail of Tears'. The Cherokee are relatives of the Haudenosaunee; they remember their connections to the Confederacy in their cosmogonies, in their migration stories, and in their Iroquoian language. They too are subjects of the Great Law of Peace, and the (hi)stories that were recounted under the boughs of the Great White Pine, planted by Deganawidah, are part of the tribalography that has created, re-created, and sustained them. Out of this Nation, as a response to crisis, came a story with so unique a structure and so powerfully distinctive an aesthetic that it would profoundly affect the works of Rodgers and Hammerstein, two of America's most influential theatre workers. Ultimately, their adaptation of Cherokee and Appalachian playwright Lynn Riggs's *Green Grow the Lilacs* (1930) would re-invent the American musical, transforming the American storyway, American identity, American relations with the lands within their borders, and, perhaps, even their relations with peoples from lands outside their borders. Truly, the roots of the Tree of Peace stretch far and invite all. Riggs was born in 1899 in Indian Territory (in what is now Oklahoma), several years before statehood. *Green Grow the Lilacs* and its musical incarnation might be read as a celebration of 'the American way of life', but beneath the popular discourse of white Americana, Riggs tells another story. At once an account of the origins of the forty-sixth State of the Union and a (re) creation story of the Cherokee Nation, Riggs's play has circulated globally and literally transformed the dramaturgical praxis of North America.[59]

The opening stage directions of *Green Grow the Lilacs*, reproduced by Hammerstein for the book of *Oklahoma!*,[60] are reminiscent of a creation story:

> It is a radiant summer morning several years ago, the kind of morning, which enveloping the shapes of earth – men, cattle in a meadow, blades of the young corn, streams – makes them seem to exist now for the first time, their images giving off a visible golden emanation that is partly true and partly a trick of the imagination focusing to keep alive a loveliness that may pass away.[61]

On the title page Riggs tells us that this play (published in 1931) takes place in 1900 – seven years before the Indian and Oklahoma territories became a State of the Union. But as the play begins, we are invited into a space where all times are one: this 'radiant' dawn takes place, in ceremonial time, '*several years ago*', and readers in all times are invited to imagine it so. The rich imagery and lush syntax of these stage directions go unheard by the audience in the theatre. They may evoke nostalgia for a bygone era for those who read the play, but they invoke an actual creation for those who come to see and hear. They seized the imaginations of Rodgers, Hammerstein, and choreographer Agnes De Mille.[62] This radiant dawn has already been witnessed by countless audiences of the original and of the 2,243 performances of the Broadway production of *Oklahoma!*, by audiences in 150 cities during *Oklahoma!*'s ten-year tour, by the Second World War troops who viewed the United Services Organizations (USO) production, and by Drury Lane audiences when it opened in London in 1947, enjoying the longest run of any show that had been produced in the 287-year history of that theatre.[63] The luminosity evoked by these stage directions also lives on for those who may have never attended a live performance: the opening scene of the filmed version of *Oklahoma!* (1955) bathes the spectator in a brilliant blue-green wash stretching endlessly in seven directions.[64] And the overwhelming image here is one of the endless fields of green corn (for cattle and for human consumption), which stretch upwards towards the sun.

Critics who dubbed Hammerstein's opening musical celebration of the tall corn as a 'city boy's gaffe', revealing his ignorance of the fact that Oklahoma was not part of the corn belt,[65] failed to perceive that his compositions emerged from the image that is the necessary consequence of Riggs's invocation. What New York critic would have known that as the Cherokee travelled westward over the Trail of Tears they carried corn from their traditional lands with which to seed their new home? Could the critics have known that Oklahoma is the traditional territory of the Creek and Seminole Nations? For these Nations (as for the Cherokee), the most important observance of the year is the Green Corn Ceremony in late July or early August, which marks the New Year – a time of renewal.[66]

It is no accident that Riggs begins his account of the birthing pangs of a soon-to-be State of the Union with a song that arises out of the green corn and precedes the communal 'play party' of *Green Grow the Lilacs* or 'box social' of *Oklahoma!*. The singer is Curly, a model of white, freewheeling machismo. *His new dawn will herald in a new era of colonization on both personal and political fronts.*[67] He is about to propose to Laurey; self-governance in Indian Territory will soon be replaced by adherence to the American legal system; and he will have to trade in his horse, saddle, gun, and independence to become a good husband, farmer, and solid American citizen. This romantic hero and his ingénue will survive and endure skirmishes between individual and institution, but they will not be allowed to forget an originary conflict:

Laurey Er I wish't I lived in Virginia or Californie. In Californie, they's oranges growin', and snow fallin' at the same time. I seen a pitcher of it. In the Verdigree bottom the other day, a man found thirty-three arrow heads – thirty-three – whur they'd been an Indian battle[68] –
Aunt Eller Whut's that got to do with the White House and livin' in Californie?[69]

What do the arrowheads have to do with California or with Washington? Why does Laurey, several lines later, reiterate that she lives in Indian Territory? Riggs's invocation of American Indigenous history throbs like a heartbeat throughout the play *and* the musical, reminding us that beneath the history of disorderly conquest lies another story rooted in eternity, a story that, like the people about and for whom it is told, will endure: 'That's the way life is – cradle to grave. And you c'n stand it. They's one way. You got to be hearty. You got to be'.[70] Aunt Eller (Elder?) speaks these lines to her niece in Riggs's original play, and this call to Cherokee endurance itself endures, increasing in force and urgency until it realizes itself as a choral speech act that performs into being the survivance of a people. Within this rugged, patriarchal social construct, it is to the matriarch that the community looks for guidance and direction, and it is she who provides both. In Riggs's world, this makes perfect sense: the female is the property owner (and prime caretaker), just as she is in the Cherokee nation and in the Six Nations of the Haudenosaunee.

Curly is arrested for his part in the accidental death of Jeeter. Although it is reasonable to expect that he will eventually be found not guilty on the grounds of self-defence, it is by no means certain. Curly then breaks out of jail, not to escape, but to consummate his marriage – an act undertaken to ensure the continuance of his line. When a group of male community members comes to retrieve him and return him to prison, Aunt Eller challenges the group's authority and calls upon its members to identify themselves.

> **Aunt Eller** Why, the way you're sidin' with the federal marshal, you'd think us people out here lived in the United States! Why, we're territory folks – we ort to hang together. I don't mean *hang* – I mean *stick*. Whut's the United States? It's jist a furrin country to me. And *you* supportin' it! Jist dirty ole furriners, ever last one of you!
> **Voices** *(outside, grumbling, protesting)* Now, Aunt Eller, we hain't furriners. My pappy and mammy was *both* borned in Indian Territory! Why I'm plumb full of Indian blood myself.
> Me, too! And I c'n prove it![71]

Here, a voice (cloaked in whiteface) asserts itself against a foreign invader. And while the assertion of a Cherokee pedigree was (and is today) a tactical manoeuvre used by wealthy landholders to justify their misappropriation of traditional Cherokee lands, it is, in Riggs's world, a speech act through which the individual asserts his identity and, in so doing, embraces a set of communal responsibilities without which that identity would have no meaning. In *Oklahoma!* Eller suggests that they 'bend the law', and Curly is tried and exonerated on the spot by the community. Rodgers and Hammerstein have tried to echo Riggs's subversive message, but their adaptation dilutes its power somewhat. Unlike the musical, Riggs's play does not promise the people a perfect world with perfect justice. Curly may not be freed. Curly may, in fact, be hanged for murder. Riggs offers no promises of survival – his or ours. As Curly reminds us, 'Cain't count on a thing'.[72] What he does offer us is a vision of survivance that has resonated throughout the decades: he has crafted a tribalography that continues to re-create nations as it reformats imaginings of self and community. And perhaps we can learn to be hearty enough to 'stand' whatever hardships come.

For good or ill, the reach of Riggs's play extends beyond the generation in which it was written. Continuing the legacy of the Longhouse orations performed by his Haudenosaunee cousins centuries before the Trail of Tears, long before his birth and long before his decision to write for theatre, the most famous of Riggs's 'Oklahoma plays' has exerted its subtle influence on the idea that is 'America', shaping America's fortunes in the mid-twentieth century. When the United States entered the Second World War after the bombing of Pearl Harbor, free tickets to *Oklahoma!* were made available to soldiers who were preparing to ship out from New York City. According to Agnes De Mille, these young men were not simply entertained by a novel spectacle; they were deeply affected by it. As they sat weeping in the last three rows of the theatre, each was acutely aware of the role he had been selected to play in the ongoing creation story of America: 'It reminded them', De Mille says, 'of what they were fighting for'.[73] They had been affected by the musical's 'naïve lyricism' and felt deeply connected to the land and lifeway for which they had been called to sacrifice their lives. Such nostalgic reminiscences may suggest, for some, that the central message of *Green Grow the Lilacs* was ultimately distorted in the popular musical adaptation, transforming it into a medium of propaganda for the colonial state. It is, however, important to remember that many Indigenous people from Turtle Island (North America) saw active duty in both world wars. These warriors fought to protect the land – their living relative. And while their American settler counterparts may not have been fighting in exactly the same spirit, it seems that they were fighting to preserve something of that 'naïve lyricism' that spoke to them of the land that nurtures all and of all the life forms that sustain us.

CONCLUSION

As we have demonstrated here, to approach the topic of theatre and performance's circulation in the modern period through Indigenous understandings of time, space, and tribalography is not simply to resist the colonizing role of Western theatre histories and the stories of 'mainstream' circulation they tell. It is also to carve out a space of negotiation between resistance and compliance for contemporary Indigenous peoples living under the long shadow of nineteenth-century colonialism, a space that might allow for the emergence of an Indigenous sovereignty that can exceed the narrow, legalistic definitions of that term imposed by settler/colonialist societies all over the world. It might also model a way of invoking the theatrical past that provides a way forward, not just for Indigenous peoples, but for all.

CHAPTER SIX

Interpretations

The Stakes of Audience Interpretation in Twentieth-Century Political Theatre

DASSIA N. POSNER

ATHLETES OF THE MIND

In the period between 1926 and 1933, Bertolt Brecht and his collaborators wrote their most innovative and most overtly Communist works. One of Brecht's criticisms of the society of his day was that so many viewed labour as productivity free of pleasure – and theatre as pleasure free of productivity.[1] He set out to address this through what he called 'learning plays'. These 'Lehrstücke' aimed at inciting social transformation by effecting 'a total abolition of the division between performance and audience'.[2] (See also Chapter 2.) Actor-spectators would both perform a play and reflect on it. This simultaneous inside-outside perspective, what Brecht called being 'both inside and above the stream',[3] was meant to reveal theatre as a place not of 'unquestioning acceptance' but of 'critical intervention' and society as 'changeable and changing'.[4]

One of these learning plays was *The Yes-Sayer* (*Der Jasager*, 1930), a 'school opera' performed by children, composed by Kurt Weill, and adapted by Brecht from Elizabeth Hauptmann's translation of a Japanese *noh* play. The opera relates the story of a young boy who consents to be left to die when his weakness threatens the expedition that will save his village. The work's formal innovations, some loosely drawn from *noh* (a poetic journey, use of symbolic objects), others from Brecht's notes on epic theatre ('montage', 'man as a process'),[5] written that same year, are designed to incite critical thinking. As Katz reports, although

The Yes-Sayer's Berlin premiere 'provoked just the kind of heated debate its creators had hoped for',[6] some reviews misinterpreted it as promoting unquestioning compliance. Brecht's response was to write a new version, *The No-Sayer* (*Der Neinsager*), in which the boy opposes uncritical adherence to tradition. In the spirit of the Marxist dialectics to which Brecht was so committed, these contrasting works were to be performed together, creating another dissonant simultaneity with which to grapple. The Lehrstücke did not *teach* a perspective, then; they were designed as a tool for *learning* to interpret the world, 'physical exercises meant for the kind of athletes of the mind that good dialecticians should be'.[7]

While, as Mueller notes, the Lehrstücke's 'focus on audience reception, the insistence that the audience develop an altogether different attitude, is at the core of Brechtian theory',[8] these works also illustrate a broader phenomenon. All the arts in the modern era have shown a fascination with perspective and reception. As Russian formalist writer Viktor Shklovsky famously wrote, 'Art exists that one may recover the sensation of life; it exists to make one feel things, to make the stone *stony* ... The technique of art is to make objects "unfamiliar", ... to increase the difficulty and length of perception'.[9] In painting, cubism presented the world from multiple points of view simultaneously, while expressionism revealed a deeper subjectivity. Music was redefined through unprecedented dissonance and even silence, in works ranging from Stravinsky's *Rite of Spring* to John Cage's *4'33'*. In the latter part of the twentieth century, postmodernism in all the arts effected startling new collisions of media, sound, image, geography, and time.

Although theatre has, of course, always sought to engage its audiences, a defining characteristic of theatre in the modern era has been its unprecedented attention to the spectator's interpretive role and, therefore, to formal innovations that prompt audiences to become active co-creators of meaning. Many of the twentieth century's examples of theatre for political and social change in particular respond to the audience-centred formal innovations of Brecht, Piscator, Eisenstein, Meyerhold, and their contemporaries. Joan Littlewood and Theatre Workshop undermined heroic mythologies about the First World War in *Oh! What a Lovely War* via a mix of Meyerholdian juxtaposition and Brechtian irony. Augusto Boal's Theatre of the Oppressed developed a more radical version of the learning play by turning spectators into actors ('spect-actors') who intervene in the actions they watch on stage, improvising new material as a 'rehearsal for the revolution'.[10] (See also Chapter 2.) And at the turn of the twenty-first century, verbatim practices juxtaposed the real words and even vocal and gestural intonations of interview subjects with rigorously defined theatrical form to create performances that pondered local issues with larger ethical resonance (*The Laramie Project*, 2000; *The Exonerated*, 2003).

This chapter investigates this modern-era phenomenon of pairing audience co-creation in the theatre with a re-invention of the world outside it, focusing on productions that use juxtaposition and plural perspective to prompt audiences to mentally grapple with dissonance in both theatre and life. Though it exists in many variations, such 'theatricalist' theatre has several recurring traits. In response against fourth-wall, psychologically driven theatre, it overtly comments on life rather than being a mirror that reflects it; it assumes that actors and audiences cannot create together if they cannot interact; and it presents colliding perceptual planes and coexisting, contradictory truths for interpretation by the theatre's 'athletes of the mind'.[11]

This chapter analyses two productions, one from early in the century, the other from the end, in which a re-imagining of society coincided with a revolution in the theatre. In each case, I provide cultural context before turning to a detailed discussion of the production's relationship between formal innovation and audience interpretation. Vsevelod Meyerhold's productions of Vladimir Mayakovsky's *Mystery-Bouffe* (1918, 1921) marked the birth of modern political theatre, defined in this instance as performance that uses theatricalist devices to activate spectators as co-creators of meaning in conjunction with a proposed remaking of society. William Kentridge and Handspring Puppet Company's production of Jane Taylor's *Ubu and the Truth Commission* (1997, 2014[12]) offered a different definition of political theatre, one that invited viewers to process the unresolvable dissonances of oppression and amnesty that South Africa's Truth and Reconciliation Commission raised as part of the country's post-apartheid journey towards reconciliation.

Both productions understood spectators not as receivers, but as makers of meaning. Both aimed to give voice to the voiceless by centring on long-oppressed populations. As their artists discovered, theatre that bares the process of its making and presents conflicting perspectives prompts audiences to engage in a process of polyphonic meaning-making. Via this redefinition of theatre's structure and aims, audiences were not to be instructed in the value of a correct interpretation; they were to be awakened to the possibilities of generating new paradigms in life and art. Within the larger context of modern-era theatre, these productions reveal the stakes, difficulty, and distinct value of preserving nuance and coexisting interpretations – and, by extension, multiple truths – in opposition to theatre that is dogmatic or coercive or that passively reinforces, in Taylor's words, fixed 'habits of thought'.[13] At the start of the century, *Mystery-Bouffe*'s artists held the utopian belief that proletarian audiences would naturally embrace the socialist revolution, not realizing that the plural perspective that defined their theatre could be co-opted to indoctrinate rather than invigorate. At the century's other end, *Ubu*'s creators came to view nuanced, flexible, open interpretation not only as something to be protected, but as a necessary ethical act.

THE FIRST SOVIET PLAY

Mayakovsky's *Mystery-Bouffe* was 'the first Soviet play', that is, the first by a Soviet playwright to be dedicated thematically – and literally – to the 1917 October Revolution. Fevralsky calls it 'probably the first play in world literature to express the age-old aspiration of the people . . . for the overthrow of the power of exploiters, for the liberation of human consciousness from the vestiges of slavery, and for the creation of a communist society comprised of workers'.[14] Meyerhold staged the play twice, mounting the world premiere in 1918 to commemorate the first anniversary of October and directing a second production, which I analyse in more detail, in 1921. The discussion that follows traces *Mystery-Bouffe*'s cultural milieu, its audience-centred innovations, and interpretations of the productions in the context of debates over the function of theatre in Soviet society.

The Russian serfs were freed in 1861, two years before the slaves were emancipated in the United States, but, as in the US, freedom did not mean equality. The driving impulse behind the October Revolution fifty-six years later was to replace the inequitable class structure with a 'dictatorship of the proletariat', a society in which workers and peasants were to be 'enlightened' (the Russian word *prosveshchenie* means both education and enlightenment) out of the backwardness to which they had been subject for centuries. In 1918 four-fifths of the Russian population remained illiterate; Lenin called Russia 'an uncivilized country . . . in which the masses have been *robbed* of so much in the sense of education, enlightenment and knowledge'.[15] The new Bolshevik government therefore placed immense value on practical and political education. Theatre, an oral and visual art form long understood in Russia as 'a powerful instrument of education', became uniquely valuable to this effort.[16]

In the wake of October, there was an explosion of national interest in theatre. The hundreds of amateur groups of Proletkult, a sprawling, state-funded proletarian cultural organization, provided newly egalitarian opportunities for all to make theatre. Soviet artists enthusiastically subverted the former imperial suspicion of large crowds by drawing audiences of thousands to massive outdoor spectacles on revolutionary holidays, the most famous being 'The Storming of the Winter Palace' (1920; see also Chapter 7). Mobile troupes on 'agit-trains' performed *agitprop* (an amalgam of the Russian words for political agitation and propaganda) throughout the countryside. Beginning in autumn 1918, many theatre workers were drafted into Red Army 'front-line theatre units' that performed 'a mixture of contemporary and classical plays and short propaganda pieces on topical issues (*agitki*)' with pro-Bolshevik themes.[17] Audience composition at established theatres also changed significantly. Post-revolutionary audiences of workers, peasants, and soldiers, many of whom previously had never attended the theatre, revelled in an artistic form that now was addressed to them. In

Rudnitsky's words, 'Time and again performances reached the pitch of mass meetings'.[18]

The emphasis the Bolsheviks placed on enlightenment through theatre is clear from their first actions after seizing power. Less than twenty-four hours after the Storming of the Winter Palace (25 October 1917; 7 November new style), Lenin became President of the Council of People's Commissars – and Anatoly Lunacharsky was appointed Commissar of Enlightenment, a position with the massive charge of regulating all of Soviet education and the arts.[19] The primary task of the Theatrical Division (TEO) of Narkompros (the Commissariat of Enlightenment) was 'to create a new theatre connected with the rebuilding of the state and society on the principles of socialism'.[20] How to do this was not immediately clear. Lunacharsky was steadfast in the belief that all perspectives on art must be allowed to develop – with the assumption that theatres eventually would embrace revolutionary content on their own.[21] He often served as a shield between theatres and would-be repressors of artistic pluralism – Lenin, for instance, who preferred classics to the avant-garde and was eager to wield theatre as a Bolshevik hammer.

The battle over theatre in the RSFSR[22] became a battle over who had the right to interpret; civil war raged on both political and artistic fronts. Established theatres were suspicious that Bolshevik control would, in the opinion of one Imperial Theatre worker, 'destroy the theatre and permit it to be put to some use that was base . . .'.[23] Many protested the Bolsheviks by refusing to review, act in, or relinquish stage space to revolutionary productions. Of those that supported the Revolution, most hoped the new order would provide creative freedom in a country that always before had had censorship; Stanislavsky wrote, for instance, 'it is impossible with impunity to transfer art into the other plane of politics or practical life, which is alien to it by nature'.[24] Such was the position of much of the theatrical 'right' (within which there was much variation): that theatre must remain separate from politics to avoid being debased by it.

Those on the self-proclaimed 'left' applied the radical formal innovations of pre-Revolutionary artistic movements (cubism, futurism, suprematism) to productions with revolutionary content. For many leftist artists, simply infusing naturalistic plays with revolutionary themes was no better than, in Shterenberg's words, 'pouring new wine into old, tattered wine-skins'.[25] Mayakovsky, one of the first artists to support the Bolsheviks, proclaimed, 'Only the eruption of the Spirit of Revolution will rid us of the rags of antiquated art'.[26] *Mystery-Bouffe* was his first major attempt to do just this.

MYSTERY-BOUFFE, 1918, 1921

Mystery-Bouffe is a reinterpretation of the Biblical story of Noah's flood. Here, though, it is the red flood of Revolution that is sweeping the world. The sole survivors are seven pairs of 'the Unclean' – representatives of the noble proletariat – and seven pairs of 'the Clean' – base aristocrats of international origin. Two by two they find the only remaining dry land: the North Pole. The Clean, who refuse to work, persuade the Unclean to build an ark. Once they set sail, the Unclean throw overboard first their new tsar (a reference to the February Revolution), then the Clean (a nod to the October Revolution). The Unclean journey through both Hell and a dissatisfying Heaven, finally returning to inherit the Earth: a self-made paradise in which work grows sweet when aided by 'Comrade Things'. Many scenes 'tilt'[27] episodes from medieval mystery (Corpus Christi) plays and the Bible; examples include the Harrowing of Hell and irreverent rewritings of the Sermon on the Mount. The play also captured the jubilant energy and rapid change of the times. Mayakovsky described its dissonant forms and impressions:

> *Mystery-Bouffe* . . . is our great revolution condensed into poetry and theatrical action. The mystery is what is great in the revolution, the bouffe is what is comical in it. The poetry of *Mystery-Bouffe* is the slogans of rallies, shouts from the streets, the language of newspapers. The action of *Mystery-Bouffe* is the movement of crowds, the clashes between classes, the struggle of ideas – the world in miniature within the walls of the circus.[28]

Mystery-Bouffe, co-directed by Meyerhold and Mayakovsky and designed by Kazimir Malevich, played at the Petrograd Musical Drama Theatre (to that theatre's undisguised dismay) on 7 and 8 November 1918. The production's greatest virtue, developed as it was with little time, few resources, and considerable controversy, was that it embraced the audience as a co-creator. For over a decade, Meyerhold's pre-Revolutionary theatrical experiments had centred on developing new forms that mentally ignited the spectator. It was a short step to broaden his artistic revolution to include the political one. If the October Revolution was a freeing of the oppressed classes, Meyerhold's theatrical revolution was intended to free the oppressed imagination – the right to subjective interpretation. He mined popular entertainments for audience engagement techniques. Before the Revolution, like many theatrical modernists, he drew from temporally or geographically distant forms: *commedia dell'arte, kabuki*, fairground performance. Beginning with *Mystery-Bouffe*, he used contemporary, working-class forms: circus, film, variety theatre. In the production's most beloved circus act, Mayakovsky as 'Simply Man' entered by soaring through the air on a cable.[29]

Most reviewers of the 1918 production protested it loudly with utter silence. Only two articles framed it for a reading public. In an essay published before the premiere, Lunacharsky called the play 'original, strong, and beautiful', but cautioned of the production,

Futurism has one wonderful quality: it is a young and brave movement. And since its best representatives are in accord with the communist revolution, they can more easily than others become the virtuoso drummers of our Red culture. But at the same time they are a product of the well-known aesthetic excesses of the old world.[30]

In the only review, Levinson questioned the aims of this new theatre, writing 'The very claim of Futurism – to become the official art of the awakening masses – seems to me coercive'.[31] In hindsight, he glimpsed something Mayakovsky and Meyerhold did not yet recognize: that once theatre offered itself up as a 'virtuoso drummer' of 'Red culture', it was all too easily co-opted for political aims, especially in a society that had already begun to view mental pluralism with suspicion.

Meyerhold took his audience activation experiments further in the second *Mystery-Bouffe,* which opened – despite myriad obstacles – at his new Theatre RSFSR 1 on 1 May 1921. As Aksenov recalls, 'A prolonged and cutthroat campaign preceded this production'.[32] Many were outraged 'that a man with the reputation of Mayakovsky dared touch on so tender and fragile a thing as the proletarian revolution'.[33] Ironically, given later Soviet anti-religious campaigns, the censor banned the play for being sacrilegious (May Day, the international workers' holiday, fell that year on Russian Orthodox Easter). Mayakovsky made some hasty rewrites – the Unclean no longer smashed up Heaven or chased out God – and the play was passed.[34]

Prior to these enforced changes, Mayakovsky had already significantly rewritten the play, adding topical content and a new act in the 'land of wreckage' (a reference to post-Civil War reconstruction). Just before the premiere, he penned a new prologue that introduced the production's audience-centred conventions.[35] The Moscow Art Theatre, the 'House of Chekhov', became a specific target:

> For other theatres | how the show is presented is not important: | for them | the stage is | a keyhole. | Sit, be quiet, pay attention . . . | and look at a piece of someone else's life. | Look and you will see- | droning at each other on the sofa, | Aunt Manyas | and Uncle Vanyas . . . | We will show you real life, too, | but | transformed by the theatre into spectacle most extraordinary.[36]

The prologue's invitation to engage with life (rather than to simply watch it) was the production's leitmotif. Before spectators took their seats, the playbill informed them they could 'enter the auditorium even during the show. Expressions of approval (applause) and protest (whistles) are permitted. Actors respond to [curtain] calls both after each scene and throughout the course of the performance'.[37] Upon entering the theatre, audiences encountered a set that was as much a manifesto as the prologue. Rather than representing life, it spilled into life. There were no footlights, curtain, or masking. The front rows of seats were removed to accommodate 'an enormous semi-sphere',[38] of marked 'earth', that jutted into the audience. The final act's 'Comrade Things' occupied several audience boxes.[39] The stage floor was level with the auditorium floor, erasing divisions between stage and spectator.[40] 'Meyerhold turned the entire theatre into a stage', a critic later wrote, '. . . he is even able to convince the Russian spectators, who are not particularly theatrical by nature, to participate in the performance'.[41]

Meyerhold also cultivated active interpretation by presenting spectators with multiple perspectives. He viewed audience co-creation as a complex cognitive process to be stimulated via the 'grotesque': collisions of incongruous elements and styles. In his theatre, self-aware spectators make and unmake meaning as they encounter conflicting or incomplete images and ideas, using the imagination to mentally 'finish drawing what a given scene hints at'.[42] *Mystery-Bouffe* provoked this by presenting simultaneous perspectives in the scenic design and contrasting styles in the costumes and acting (see Figure 6.1). Inspired by medieval simultaneous settings and Russian folk forms, Lavinsky

FIGURE 6.1: Anton Lavinsky, scene design for *Mystery-Bouffe*, by Vladimir Mayakovsky, dir. Vsevolod Meyerhold and Valery Bebutov, Theatre RSFSR 1 (1921). КП 88139. © A. A. Bakhrushin State Central Theatre Museum, Moscow.

and Khrakovsky's set presented all the places of action at once: heaven, earth, and the 'land of wreckage' appeared in a single vertical structure that suggested an ark.

The 'earth' globe concealed a hell mouth; when rotated, it revealed a trap door for the entrances of devils from underneath the stage.[43] The lights remained up on the audience throughout the performance, prompting spectators to remain aware of their reality as well as that of the onstage fiction.

The production also collided performance styles. In Rudnitsky's words, 'The devices of the carnival barker ... join forces here with the devices of circus clowns and the language of mass meetings'.[44] The Unclean wore identical blue work shirts[45] and performed with 'heroic emotion and plastic monumentality'.[46] These characters were a development of Meyerhold's pre-revolutionary experiments with identically clad 'forestage servants'[47] who served as interlocutors between audience and stage. Conversely, satirical characters were individualized and highly entertaining. The Clean, Devils, and Saints wore cubist costumes in Picasso's manner.[48] Igor Ilinsky played the 'Compromiser', a Menshevik new to the second version, as a traditional Russian 'red-headed' clown.[49] These differing approaches to character reinforced three perceptual planes: the spectators' real world, that of the Unclean – allegorical versions of the proletariat audience – and that of the satirical characters whose world was being overthrown.

Meyerhold believed the audience's process of interpreting these contrasting styles and planes should be 'coactive' and joyful.[50] Multiple accounts confirm that the premiere 'swept over' the audience like 'a wave of joy'.[51] Following a collective singing of the Internationale, Fevralsky recalls,

> The spectators rushed the stage ... and literally pulled the author, directors, actors, and even the stage crew out from backstage ... For the over half century that has passed since, it is difficult to recall another production that has gripped the audience with such enthusiasm.

Similar excitement persisted in subsequent performances: 'This effect was primarily an outgrowth of something then still entirely unaccustomed: experiences and words that were poetically transformed and transferred from the life of a revolutionary country to the stage'.[52]

More than any other director of his day, Meyerhold attempted to document his spectators' responses to his productions. Following *Mystery-Bouffe* performances, paper surveys (see Figure 6.2) queried age, sex, education, social class, and profession, and sought opinions of the play, the production, the artistic elements, the RSFSR 1, and the building.[53]

Mikhail Zagorsky, who headed this process, discovered from the nearly 200 surveys he analysed that although opinions varied, spectators fell roughly into

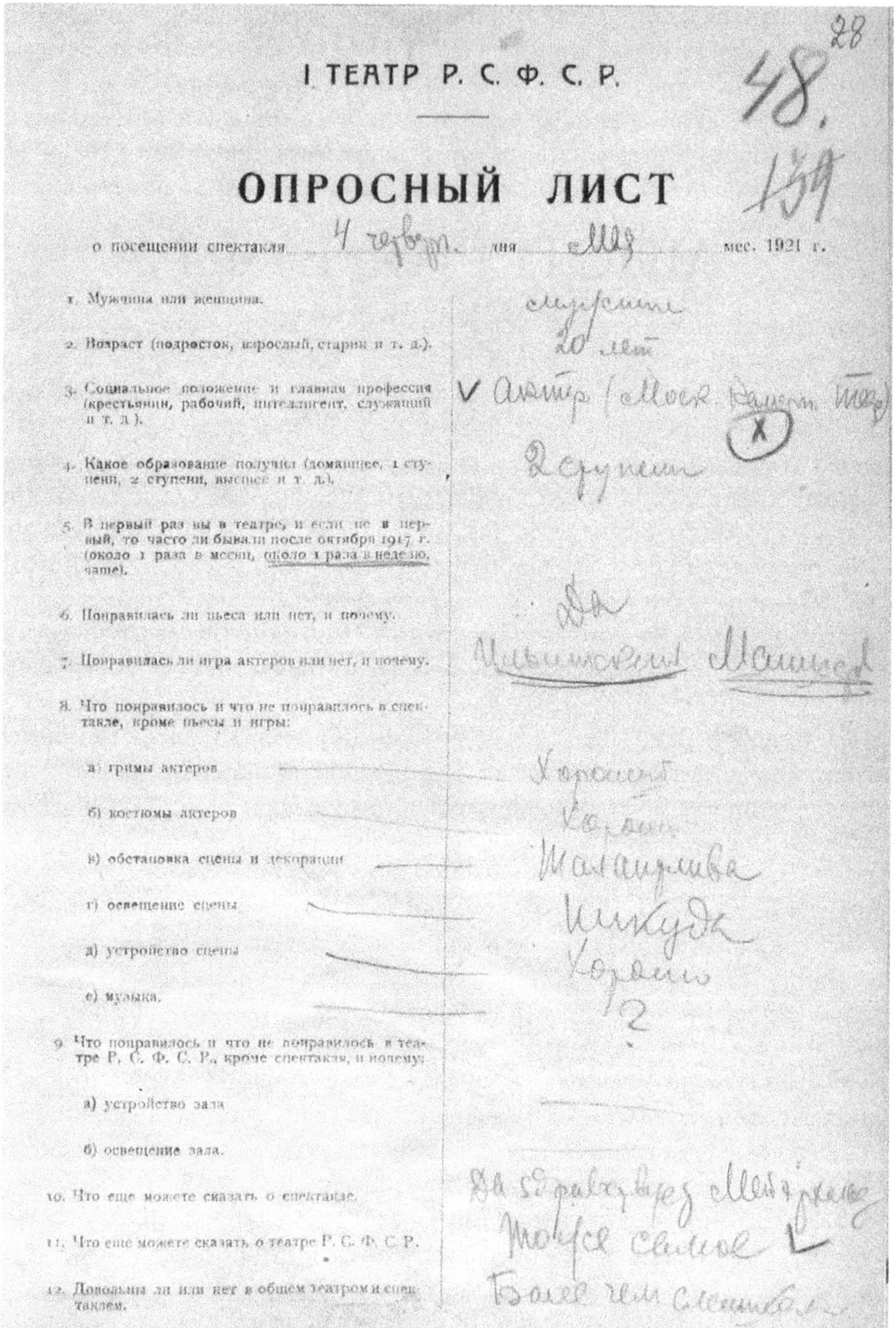

I ТЕАТР Р. С. Ф. С. Р.

ОПРОСНЫЙ ЛИСТ

о посещении спектакля ______ дня ______ мес. 1921 г.

1. Мужчина или женщина.
2. Возраст (подросток, взрослый, старик и т. д.).
3. Социальное положение и главная профессия (крестьянин, рабочий, интеллигент, служащий и т. д.).
4. Какое образование получил (домашнее, 1 ступени, 2 ступени, высшее и т. д.).
5. В первый раз вы в театре, и если не в первый, то часто ли бывали после октября 1917 г. (около 1 раза в месяц, около 1 раза в неделю, чаще).
6. Понравилась ли пьеса или нет, и почему.
7. Понравилась ли игра актеров или нет, и почему.
8. Что понравилось и что не понравилось в спектакле, кроме пьесы и игры:
   а) гримы актеров
   б) костюмы актеров
   в) обстановка сцены и декорации
   г) освещение сцены
   д) устройство сцены
   е) музыка.
9. Что понравилось и что не понравилось в театре Р. С. Ф. С. Р., кроме спектакля, и почему:
   а) устройство зала
   б) освещение зала.
10. Что еще можете сказать о спектакле.
11. Что еще можете сказать о театре Р. С. Ф. С. Р.
12. Довольны ли или нет в общем театром и спектаклем.

FIGURE 6.2: Audience questionnaire completed after a performance of *Mystery-Bouffe*, by Vladimir Mayakovsky, dir. Vsevolod Meyerhold and Valery Bebutov, Theatre RSFSR 1 (1921). КП 180171/28. © A. A. Bakhrushin State Central Theatre Museum, Moscow.

two categories. In the first were educated individuals who were so preoccupied by 'general indignation against the revolution' that their hastily scribbled comments showed 'a decrease in consciousness and in ability to analyze, and an increase in emotion, vented in crude and angry outcries directed at the author and actors'.[54] Of one such survey Zagorsky noted, 'there is no mark of any kind of analysis – it is an unremitting reproachful outcry'.[55]

While some became wholly unable to interpret the production, others felt free to do so for the first time. Many workers, peasants, and Red Army soldiers expressed excitement that the production represented an end to class exploitation; one peasant wrote, 'I liked it because it enlightened our in-the-dark class about how . . . we were deceived'.[56] Another common response was that the production captured working-class life: a train worker declared, 'Give this play to the working masses and they will tell you, this is our theatre, this is our play'.[57] It was 'our play', not because it mirrored life, however. Realism is close to life in one specific way: it resembles life as it is already known. *Mystery-Bouffe* spectators meant this differently: the production *responded* to their lives and actively solicited their critical engagement. It drew form and inspiration from their entertainments, and its frequently updated topical insertions (largely absent from the published edition) celebrated proletarian concerns.

Reviews of the production were few: most critics boycotted it.[58] The few that were published present contrasting visions of revolutionary theatre. Beskin's review radiated excitement for the production's formal innovations: 'There is no stage and no auditorium. There is a monumental platform pushed into the audience. One feels that these walls are too constraining for it. It needs a public square, a street . . . It needs a mass'.[59] He concluded that *Mystery-Bouffe*, which 'does not copy life with its swaying curtains and idyllic crickets . . . is the first powerful, green shoot of a proletarian theatre culture, the first artistic seedling of revolutionary art'.[60] Blium's review defended the production by criticizing those unable to see beyond Mayakovsky's youthful futurist days, when the latter had issued incendiary manifestos and shouted poetry in the streets. Yet Blium, who was to become the head theatre censor in 1923, to accuse Meyerhold of 'formalism' in 1926, and to condemn all satire in 1929, was, to some degree, already unable to see beyond how the production should align with party dogma; he suggested, for instance, that the Compromiser should be depicted more 'correctly'.[61]

THE TRUTH OF OUR EXISTENCE

In 1925, one of Meyerhold's close associates wrote a book about the director's first post-revolutionary productions. Although it was denied publication for being too 'subjective, biased, and unacceptably frank', Meyerhold lauded the book as 'the truth of our existence [*bytie*]'.[62]

Two Russian words, *byt* and *bytie*, sound similar, but mean very different things: *byt* refers to everyday life and *bytie* to 'existence'. Meyerhold and Mayakovsky rejected theatrical explorations of *byt* – commonplace, daily routine – and instead explored *bytie* – asking who we are as human beings and how we make sense of our existence. *Mystery-Bouffe* captured the *existence* of a society in revolution, with all its chaos, dissonance, and hope. Certainly the production had propagandistic elements. It was, after all, a manifesto for a changed world. Yet it was designed to be exhilaratingly freeing by making audiences *creators* of this new world, of their own truth, of their own existence.

In their fervent iconoclasm, Meyerhold and Mayakovsky did not anticipate the ruthlessness with which the new nation's leaders would co-opt theatre for politically conformist aims. Lenin and, to a much greater degree, Stalin interpreted theatre as a tool with which to convince peasants to relinquish grain or to build Socialism. Theirs was a theatre of *byt,* of productions with fixed doctrines and utopian visions. As the USSR reverted to authoritarianism, Stalin quashed theatre of interpretation in favour of Socialist Realism, a heroic-realistic style, mandated in 1934, that adopted a corrective and regulatory function with respect to audiences. Mayakovsky's poetic outpouring of hope was supplanted by arrests, show trials, and other repressions of individual thought. In 1930, Mayakovsky committed suicide. A decade later, Meyerhold was arrested, shot, declared 'an enemy of the people', and erased from the historical record.[63] Stalin designated Mayakovsky a national poet, effecting other lasting distortions born of politically motivated canonization.

In the wake of early twentieth-century innovations such as this, theatre in the modern era has become inherently politicized: it reasserts a status quo or seeks to change it (on a spectrum rather than in a binary), dulls an audience's interpretive freedom or activates it. How, then, does theatre cultivate interpretation rather than imposing it? How does it resist being co-opted to serve as a *vehicle* for meaning, and instead become a *maker* of meaning? 'Exquisitely pathbreaking art can serve totalitarian, conservative, fascist, or reactionary ideals', notes Kimberly Jannarone, 'and left-wing performance can easily be co-opted by such regimes, even if it started as a subversive, anti-hegemonic act'.[64] Even well intentioned activist theatre is at risk of using the coercive tactics of regimes it opposes when it mistakes conformity for unity.

INTELLECTUAL ANARCHY

In 1996, in the wake of the fall of apartheid in South Africa, director Malcolm Purkey asked similar questions of South African theatre, writing, 'As apartheid gives way to a new form of government, can theatre makers protect and increase their hard-won relative autonomy, allowing theatre to maintain its responsive and critical role . . . or will theatre be expected to be subservient to the new order of things?'⁶⁵ His questions were a reaction to *Tooth and Nail*, a 1989 production that, like *Mystery-Bouffe*, was about a flood – and premiered in a country on the brink of revolution. A racially integrated collaboration between Handspring Puppet Company and Junction Avenue Theatre Company, of which Purkey was a founding member, *Tooth and Nail* responded to the near-civil-war conditions of the late apartheid era. In it a character laments, 'Everywhere there are floods of blood . . . Noah built himself a survival craft that sailed him into the future . . . We need to build an unsinkable survival craft'.⁶⁶ Mayakovsky's play had overflowed with utopian hope. *Tooth and Nail* feared South Africa would drown.

In *Tooth and Nail*, a photographer, played simultaneously by a puppet and puppeteer (see Figure 6.3), examines 'photographs of [six revolutionary] artists who have died in various regimes' in order to try to comprehend their suppression. Significantly, two of the six are Meyerhold and Mayakovsky.⁶⁷ The same year *Tooth and Nail* premiered, the Berlin Wall fell; unsuccessful protests in China's Tiananmen Square galvanized worldwide activists against political oppression; and Poland declared independence from Soviet rule. Over a dozen countries followed, and the Soviet Union fell in 1991. Orkin explains that the end of communism in so many places offered 'a sober challenge to . . . some members of the resistance movement within South Africa, who, over the years, had committed

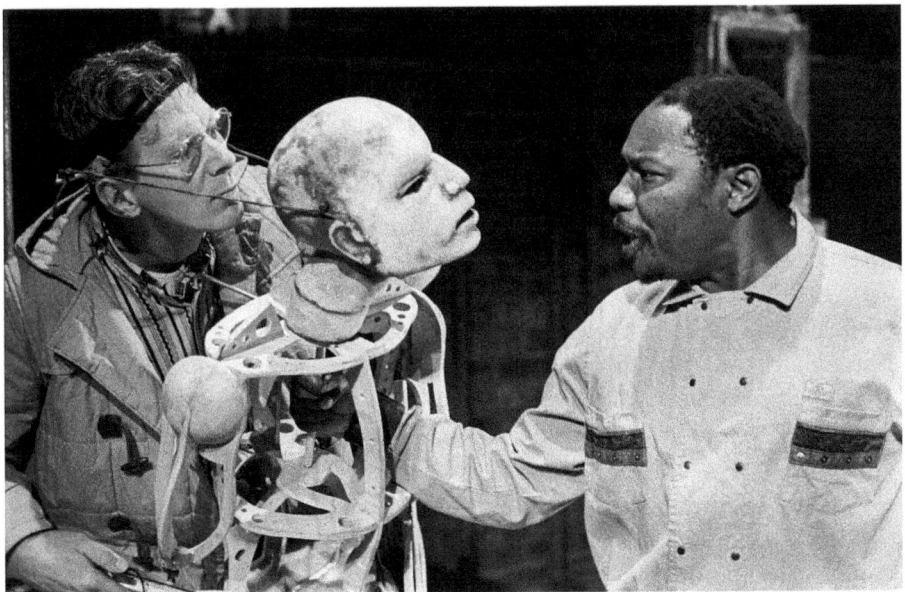

FIGURE 6.3: Production still of Saul, performed simultaneously by puppet and puppeteer (Basil Jones), in *Tooth and Nail*, created by Junction Avenue Theatre Company and Handspring Puppet Company (1989). Photo © Ruphin Coudyzer FPPSA.

themselves to Marxist, socialist, or communist modes of interpreting history'.[68] Many South African artists became preoccupied with how new theatrical forms could interpret a new South Africa. *Tooth and Nail* illuminates a vital strain of late- and post-apartheid theatre that was suspicious of glib solutions to complex problems.[69] Above all, it recognizes the stakes of preserving 'intellectual anarchy' – freedom for thought to travel in many directions – in the face of 'the dangers that anyone involved in the documentation, reportage or interpretation of history may face within climates insisting on political conformity'.[70] This investigation of what truth is, how it is made, and how its complexity can be preserved contextualizes the work of Handspring Puppet Company over the following decade, particularly in *Ubu and the Truth Commission* (1997), written by Jane Taylor and directed by William Kentridge. This was a production that generated new modes of ethically engaged audience interpretation in response to South Africa's Truth and Reconciliation Commission.

TRUTH AND RECONCILIATION

F.W. de Klerk became South Africa's president in 1989. Shortly after, he announced that he was committed to negotiations that would effect a transition to a non-racial (racially integrated) democracy, thus ending 300 years of white-minority domination. One of his first actions was to meet with Nelson Mandela in prison; Mandela was released (after twenty-seven years) a few months later. In 1994, Mandela was elected South Africa's first black president in the country's first non-racial elections. He embarked immediately on the complex task of building a unified South Africa. A critical part of this process was the Truth and Reconciliation Commission (TRC, 1996–2003).

The TRC was a product of negotiations between the outgoing Nationalist Party, which established apartheid in 1948, and the incoming African National Congress (ANC). It was the seventeenth truth commission in history,[71] but the first of its kind in structure and the first to hold public hearings[72]; these began in 1996 with Archbishop Desmond Tutu presiding. Three committees implemented two processes: in the Human Rights Violations Committee hearings, victims (the TRC's term) recounted the violence enacted upon them and family members; remuneration was then available (though inefficiently) from the Reparation and Rehabilitation Committee. The Amnesty Committee, a separate entity, allowed perpetrators of politically motivated crimes to apply for amnesty in exchange for full disclosure of truth.[73]

The TRC hearings – held across South Africa, translated into each of the nation's eleven official languages,[74] and broadcast nationwide on television and radio – became, for millions, a collective experience of grief. Given the horrific nature of the thousands of crimes committed, it became incomprehensible that such violent oppressors should escape punishment. In Kentridge's words,

'Therein lies the central irony of the Commission. As people give more and more evidence of the things they have done they get closer and closer to amnesty and it gets more and more intolerable that [they] should be given amnesty'.[75]

It was this unresolvable dissonance that made the wildly incompatible subjects of Alfred Jarry's 1896 play *Ubu Roi* and the TRC apposite partners. Disparate perceptual planes and the friction between them formed the basis for the aesthetic and political language of Handspring's *Ubu and the Truth Commission*, which premiered as South Africans were still inundated daily by media accounts of the atrocities the TRC revealed. 'Artists deal with death, suffering and loss', Taylor said. 'I felt that the arts could probe difficult terrain that the commission couldn't afford to take on while maintaining its legal brief'.[76] If the TRC's role was to document apartheid abuses, interpret culpability and victimhood, and promote reconciliation, *Ubu*'s was to provide a reflective space for interpreting the meanings of 'truth' and 'reconciliation' in the commission's wake.

PERMANENT PARABASIS AND THE PUPPET

By the beginning of the *Ubu* collaboration, Handspring Puppet Company had a lengthy history of probing such 'difficult terrain'. Founders Basil Jones and Adrian Kohler believed that they must 'respond to the South Africa around them',[77] that theatre that bares its process of creation is more honest than illusionistic theatre, and that, for audiences, navigating multiple perceptual planes can spark new interpretations of the world. In Bread and Puppet Theater founder Peter Schumann's words, 'Alienation is automatic with puppets'.[78] For example, one simultaneously sees the puppet's life *and* how that life is created. Handspring foregrounds this duality in various ways, ranging from undisguised chisel marks on a puppet's wooden face to fully visible puppeteers. They embrace puppetry as inherently an instance of 'permanent parabasis', a term first used by Frederich Schlegel to describe theatre that comments on its own making not through sporadic asides and interruptions, but constantly.[79]

Kentridge discovered in his first collaboration with Handspring, *Woyzeck on the Highveld* (1992), that permanent parabasis allows the audience to 'sustain . . . belief in agency'.[80] 'We are . . . given multiple contradictory fragments from which we will construct the world', says Kentridge. 'The bedrock of puppetry is a demonstration of how we make sense of the world'.[81] He 'promotes "trust in the contingent, the inauthentic, the whim, the practical, as strategies for *finding* meaning" rather than receiving it'.[82] This, of course, has political reverberations: truth is not a fixed and stable thing; it, too, can be 'made and remade'.[83]

Handspring prompts meaning finding for spectators by establishing multiple perceptual planes for them to negotiate. The company discovered early that audiences watch the puppet, but also watch the puppeteer watching the puppet. In Kentridge's analysis, the audience has to look at the manipulator, but then follows the manipulator's gaze . . . to the puppet and back as they become aware of themselves watching the puppet. So there's a triangulation of the process with a fourth step . . . being that every now and then you find yourself sitting in the row behind yourself, watching yourself being fooled, and enjoying that.[84]

'It is very much about impure viewing' he adds. 'You are always watching things on different planes'.[85] Constructing and deconstructing separate planes has allowed Handspring to contest apartheid's boundaries by revealing their artificiality; they challenged the racial divisions on which the apartheid system relied, for instance, by refusing to separate puppets from live actors, a common artificial division in the theatre.

UBU AND THE TRUTH COMMISSION, 1997

The collision of constructed realities imbues every aspect of *Ubu and the Truth Commission*.[86] 'The director was consciously experimenting', notes Coetzee, 'with how many of these realities could exist alongside each other in the minds of the audience, and how quickly the switches could be made from one reality to another'.[87] A crocodile becomes a paper shredder, a handbag, and a repository for incriminating evidence. Three dog heads share one body but many metaphorical meanings. A single location becomes, through different uses, geographically split. Boundaries of race are troubled; actress Busi Zokufa appears at times as Ma Ubu without makeup, at times in whiteface, and at times as a puppeteer, puppet voice, or translator.

Taylor's play is a 'productive misreading'[88] of Jarry's *Ubu Roi*, itself an impudent refraction of *Macbeth*. Jarry's Pa Ubu (Figure 6.4) embarks on a remorseless killing spree recounted through the devices of farce (*Ubu Roi* infamously begins with a mispronunciation of the French word for shit). In *Ubu and the Truth Commission,* Pa is an agent of the apartheid state who comes home late each night and washes off the blood of his victims. Ma Ubu fears his absences are due to infidelity until she discovers that he was (to her relief) 'hard at work, protecting me from the Swart Gevaar [black threat]'.[89] His fear of being found out and her public airing of his actions drive him to testify before the Amnesty Committee, a process from which he emerges unscathed. This story is punctuated with deeply moving scenes featuring TRC witnesses, who recount verbatim testimony from the Human Rights Violations Committee hearings.

Taylor's play responds to the fact that Jarry's Ubu 'apparently has no measurable effect upon those who inhabit the farcical world which he creates around himself'.[90] Taylor describes the 'disjuncture[s]' of the TRC hearings, in which it was 'chilling to note the frequency with which an act of astonishing cruelty has been undertaken, as it were, negligently, with no sense of the impact

FIGURE 6.4: Pa Ubu (Dawid Minnaar) in *Ubu and the Truth Commission*, by Jane Taylor, dir. William Kentridge, designed and performed by Handspring Puppet Company. Production playbill, Market Theatre, Johannesburg, South Africa (31 July–30 August 1997). Courtesy of Northwestern University Library.

of such actions on other human lives'. Her goal, then, was 'to take the Ubu-character out of the burlesque context, and place him within a domain in which actions do have consequences'.[91] She and her *Ubu* collaborators structured the piece around the interplay between 'Cause' (the world of the Ubus) and 'Effect' (the world of the TRC witnesses).[92] This duality prompts audiences to re-perceive the violence of apartheid's 'separate but conflicting worlds',[93] to bear witness to the testimony of apartheid victims, and to engage in interpretation as an ethical act of working out meaning.

Ubu establishes performance conventions that at first ask spectators to believe that the Ubus, played by actors, and the TRC witnesses, played by puppets, inhabit separate worlds established through the inability of characters in one world to 'see' those in the other. Yet from the start, the separateness of these worlds is troubled. As the lights first rise, a puppet is making soup. Pa's first action is to destroy her peaceful domestic setting 'with no evident sense of what he has done'.[94] In the next act, a puppet sets up a faraway shop at the centre of the Ubus' dining room table; again, they cannot see one another – yet the Ubus help themselves to the dismayed shopkeeper's goods. In Jones and Kohler's description: 'This division between the human clowns and the puppets, mirrors the era of trauma the play describes'.[95]

Over the course of the production, the puppet characters grow increasingly impossible for Pa to ignore. In the last of several witness scenes, he and a life-sized version of Jarry's Ubu form a tableau, while two witness puppets use this tableau as the floor upon which they stand to recount their testimony. As the physical proximity between these characters is erased, the audience's effort to maintain belief in the face of such obviously constructed separateness is overstrained. Spectators must reject the artistic and political conventions in which they were asked to believe just a half hour before.

The production's TRC scenes invited audiences to bear empathetic witness to the atrocities of apartheid through layers of artistic mediation. As Kentridge explains, the decision to have puppets play witnesses grew from a wish to transmit rather than impersonate:

> There seemed to be an awkwardness in getting an actor to play the witnesses – the audience being caught halfway between having to believe in the actor for the sake of the story and also not believe in the actor for the sake of the actual witness . . . There is no attempt made to make the audience think the wooden puppet or its manipulator is the actual witness. The puppet becomes a medium through which the testimony can be heard . . . It is trying to make sense of the memory rather than be the memory.[96]

The TRC scenes acknowledged the structure of the hearings without duplicating them. Two puppeteers (who recalled the professional 'comforters' real witnesses had available as they gave testimony[97]) operated each puppet, one also providing the voice. A simultaneous interpreter stood in a booth – Pa's shower stall – and translated the testimony into English in 'affectless' tones.[98] The staging of each scene marked the individual testimony as unique, preventing one account from blending into another. Puppeteers cycled through different roles, now serving as the voice, now as a translator, now as a comforter, thus watching and allowing the audience to watch scenes from different perspectives. At one point, even divisions between puppet and puppeteer were blurred. When a puppet witness, voiced by Louis Seboko, described his dead children, Seboko suddenly transformed into the witness, showing the audience the puppet that was now his murdered child, before resuming the role of puppeteer (Figure 6.5). The production thus 'circumnavigated the dangers of merely replicating testimony through verbatim theatre', Davids notes, 'allowing for gaps in testimony, for fragmentation, for silence. In this, [it] invited audiences to participate in co-authoring the un-scriptable'.[99]

These two ways of activating interpretation – foregrounding theatre's constructedness to reveal apartheid's constructedness and using artistic mediation to bear witness to real violence – merge poignantly in the final scene of *Ubu and the Truth Commission*. During Pa Ubu's testimony before the Amnesty

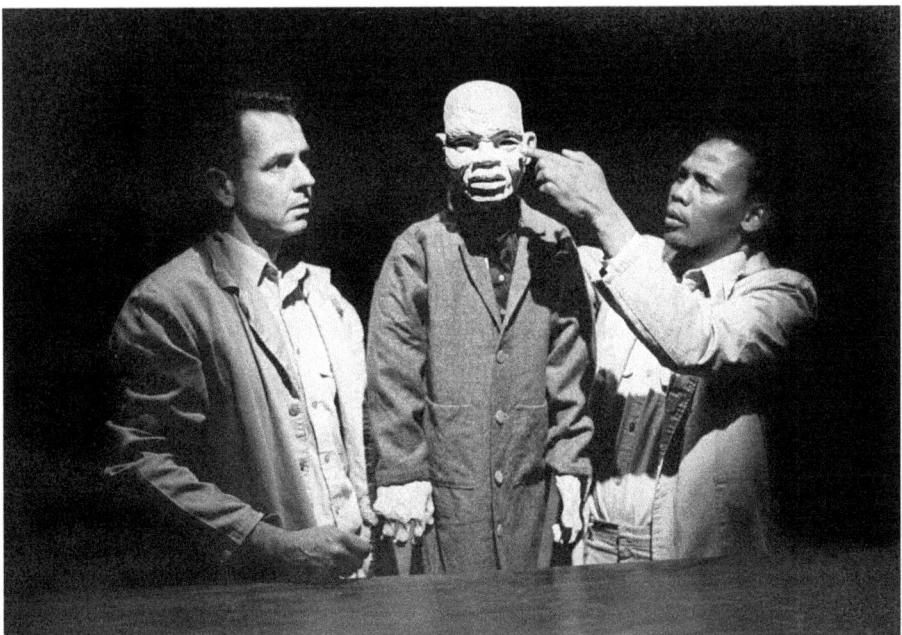

FIGURE 6.5: TRC witness puppet and puppeteers (Adrian Kohler and Louis Seboko) in *Ubu and the Truth Commission*, by Jane Taylor, dir. William Kentridge, designed and performed by Handspring Puppet Company (1997). Photo © Ruphin Coudyzer FPPSA.

Committee, he stands alone onstage behind two microphones. As he attempts to deny wrongdoing, the microphones unexpectedly recoil, reluctant to amplify his voice. When his denials grow more vehement, they protest more violently, attacking him on a long arm like a mechanical boxing glove. Though Pa and the witness puppets never interact directly, here *things* themselves rise up in defence of humanity. If even the material world is compelled to behave ethically, this scene seems to ask, can we humans claim we lack agency to make change?

Pa's desperate response is to appeal to the TRC's Christian values with a hymn about the mercy of Jesus: 'Send a flood, send a flood/ Send your blood like a flood over me', he sings. His voice is drowned out by a wave of celebration, though, as 'the fullbodied voice of a massed chorus singing "Nkosi"[100] swells and fills the auditorium'[101] and the audience watches documentary footage of South Africans celebrating the lifting of the ban on the ANC. Yet this surge of joy is tempered by a final contrasting image: Pa and Ma escape into a cartoon sunset having faced no consequences. The production ends on this note of profound emotional dissonance: audiences encounter unavoidable ethical considerations, but no concrete answers.

CONCLUSION: INTERPRETIVE REVERBERATIONS

While Meyerhold and Mayakovsky's *Mystery-Bouffe* audiences were defined by specific limiting factors – class, geographical location, political milieu – *Ubu*'s viewers span over a dozen countries and nearly two decades. The production was revived in 2014 to mark twenty years of democracy in South Africa and, as of the writing of this chapter, is still being performed internationally. Taylor notes that the first South African audiences included largely middle-class spectators, 'black commissioners, as well as artists and extended families of the performers, black and white', adding that 'In the 1990s, [it] provoked some strong emotions, particularly because Pa and Ma Ubu are seen to "get away with it" at the end of the play'.[102] South African audiences in 2014 absorbed the revival differently:

> Many audience members now were not born until the end of the Apartheid era – so this provides something of a memory project, an affective archive of a defining and deforming history. It also cultivates a sense of awe across generations, of what one generation endured on behalf of their inheritors.[103]

Ubu's resonance extends far beyond South Africa's borders, however, not only because it premiered in Germany or because Handspring's audience base is 'diverse, large and global', especially since the creation of *War Horse*.[104] *Ubu*'s creators tell numerous stories of international spectators commenting on local resonance, evidence that the work's interpretive frameworks prompt the creation of local knowledge wherever it tours.[105] 'This is not just a South African story', Taylor wrote in a 1997 programme note. 'Ours is an era of singular attention to questions of war crimes, reparations, global "peace-keeping". We are, it seems, increasingly aware of the obligation to hear testimony, while we are yet defining ways of acting upon what we have heard'.

'*Ubu* is one of those rarities', one reviewer mused in 1998, 'a piece of political theater that transcends politics'.[106] It provided a very different interpretive framework than the one Meyerhold pioneered in Soviet Russia at the beginning of the century. *Ubu* redefined political theatre by making room for, in Kentridge's words, 'ambiguity, contradiction, uncompleted gestures and uncertain endings', for 'an art (and a politics) in which optimism is kept in check and nihilism at bay'.[107] It allowed truth to be self-defined through empathetic witnessing in a world in which countering 'percepticide' – deliberate self-blinding – has become an urgent ethical necessity.[108] In *Mystery-Bouffe*, Meyerhold and Mayakovsky fostered audience engagement for specific political aims: to give proletarian spectators creative agency to remake society and theatre together. A century later, *Ubu and the Truth Commission* understood interpretation itself as political, as an active, ethical choice – and as something that can easily fall under threat.

Interpretation is a word with an array of definitions, ranging from 'proper explanation' to 'the action of translating'. Many of its definitions imply a simple transfer of meaning. This chapter's case studies have instead explored the thorniness of working out meaning at the modern theatre, and the freeing of subjectivity implicit in a different definition of interpretation: 'To give a *particular* explanation of'.[109] As the modern era has revealed, theatre that embraces audiences as potential 'athletes of the mind'[110] has the potential to foster ethical thinking by developing nuanced thinking. Such theatre becomes a maker of meaning rather than a transmitter of it, thus providing a critical space in which to grapple with uncertainty. As Oliver Sayler wrote in the years between the two *Mystery-Bouffes*, 'theatre is ... a concentration and an explanation of life. If life cannot be explained at least its inexplicability can be faced'.[111]

CHAPTER SEVEN

Communities of Production

A Materialist Reading with an Offstage View

CHRISTIN ESSIN AND MARLIS SCHWEITZER

On 7 November 1920, 8,000 performers gathered around Petrograd's city square facing the Winter Palace to recreate the revolutionary event that had occurred there three years earlier; the Bolsheviks selected this stage as the ideal symbol to celebrate their toppling of the Russian Provisional Government. The assembled community of performers included some of the same Red Army and Baltic Fleet soldiers who participated in the original military action as well as 'professional actors, pupils of the dramatic workshops, members of the proletcult clubs, [and] of the theatre societies'.[1] The huge ensemble demonstrated the strength of collective action to make historical change and write national history. Performing en masse, they crafted a spectacular reconstruction that supplanted people's memories of the actual event (Figure 7.1). Each scene, with its own director coordinating large groups of actors, depicted the Bolshevik's growing strength against the palace backdrop; crowds with red flags amassed chanting 'Lenin!' and singing the 'Internationale'; machine guns fired as combatants fought, first in the square then the palace where shadows against windows projected the Red Army's victory. According to historian James von Geldern, the performance 'distilled the Revolution to a single moment. It was the instant of transition: the moment when history began and from which the future unfolded'.[2] The performers, once usurpers but now custodians, claimed the city square as their rightful inheritance alongside 100,000 spectators.

FIGURE 7.1: *Storming of the Winter Palace*, 1920. Credit: photographer unknown, public domain.

In storming the Winter Palace, an impromptu community of soldiers, artists, and citizens defined themselves politically and historically, claiming the city and their role as protagonists within it. Through this mass spectacle a new community of production emerged, one that confronted capitalist practices and anticipated a bright future through historical re-enactment. This chapter presents a modern history of such 'communities of production', a phrase that encompasses large congregations of bodies as well as more intimate gatherings of individuals striving towards collective goals. As our opening suggests, we treat those who act *on* stage similarly to those who act behind the scenes, viewing all theatrical personnel as members of the same community. The communities considered here were bound by complementary occupations and united aims, namely producing theatre but also securing economic, political, and social rights as theatre workers. Such communities arose through writing scripts, building props, fitting costumes, staging scenes, memorizing lines, and calling cues. Whether performed in rehearsal halls or studios, studies, shops, and other far-flung work spaces, their labour collectively informed each community's perception of its identity and its objectives.

While 'putting on the show', twentieth-century communities of production formed, disbanded, readjusted, and reformed according to shifting landscapes of theatrical production and practices of theatrical labour. In some cases, as with the 1919 Actor's Equity Strike in the United States, workers drew together to confront exploitative labour conditions; in others, as with the international artists who gathered in Zurich at the Café Voltaire during the First World War, they collectively rejected industrial hierarchies and the domination of commercial production practices. Touring ensembles, from members of the Moscow Art Theatre in the early twentieth century to performers on Disney Cruise ships today, found comfort in the companionship of compatriots while simultaneously encountering economic and political circumstances that confronted their national identities. Others, like the unregulated performers who currently populate New York City's Times Square, not so much joined or fought against capitalist economies as survived them, creating audiences out of tourists in commercial theatre districts. Each production community we discuss responded to forces of modern change – urbanism, industrialism, consumerism, globalization – within their particular geopolitical circumstances and sought to support their members' livelihoods alongside their artistic vision.

This chapter also recognizes the dynamic and relational way that bodies in motion constitute space and identify place. Following Michel de Certeau's observation that 'space is a practiced place',[3] we not only trace how different sites gave rise to communities but also examine how communities *produced* sites through their interactions in, through, and across them. To that end we consider various sites, places, and locales where communities of theatrical production took shape: from city streets to neighbourhood pubs; scenic shops to fly rails; tour buses to cruise ships. By throwing a spotlight on previously overlooked, ignored, discounted, or disappeared individuals, objects, and systems that underpin artistic production, this chapter expands our understanding of 'what counts' *as* a community and *where* production labour begins. We deliberately emphasize sites where workplace activities collide or interact with the marketplace, recognizing that any analysis of production must always take into account acts of consumption and distribution,[4] and we assume that an analysis beginning with political insurgency in one city square can end with the appropriation of tourist dollars in another.

The chapter works across time and space through a series of targeted case studies focused around four sub-topics meant to exemplify the range of production communities that developed throughout the twentieth century. In 'Sites of Living/Gathering', we examine collaborative occupations of and practices within urban landscapes. 'Sites of Construction' peeks behind the often-closed doors of shops where behind-the-scenes construction activities bring together a variety of craftsmen. 'Sites of Transit' investigates production communities' interactions with (and within) modern modes of transportation. Finally, 'Sites of Consumption' explores urban locations appropriated by self-defined communities to work alongside other urban inhabitants engaged in commercial activities, including those attending their productions.

SITES OF LIVING/GATHERING

In *The Politics of Modernism* (1989), cultural historian Raymond Williams examines the influences of urban landscapes on modern arts communities, and particularly how cities brought together diverse populations and sparked rebellions against mainstream aesthetics and artistic practices.[5] As millions of immigrants and political refugees, driven by religious oppression, economic necessity, and the outbreak of war, converged in modern metropolises in the early twentieth century, artists bridged previous spatial and social boundaries, self-consciously aware of the material changes affecting their daily lives. Some temporarily abandoned the frenetic pace of urban living, finding rural sanctuaries to cultivate new ideas and work practices. The sites where they lived, gathered, and from whence they retreated produced an experiential geography that shaped the cultural identity of cities and their environs. In exploring how tensions between urban living and rural retreats gave rise to modern communities of production, this section foregrounds striking connections between theatre personnel in Russia/the Soviet Union and the United States. Despite their vastly different political contexts, these communities cohered around similar desires and actions.

The 1920 *Storming of the Winter Palace* provides spectacular evidence of a production community whose labour radically transformed the collective identity of an urban space. Part mass performance, part mass occupation, the re-enactment strategically reshaped and cemented the Soviets' historical memory of the 1917 event and transformed a site previously associated with monarchic decadence into a symbol of freedom from an oppressive government. A similar performance of labour solidarity had disrupted US theatre production only a year before when thousands of members of the Actors Equity Association (AEA) took to the streets of Manhattan to protest their oppressive treatment by the commercial theatre managers who operated collectively as the Producing Manager's Association (PMA). The AEA's complaints were many: unpaid rehearsals; broken contracts; no salary floor; requirements to purchase shoes, tights, and other costume materials; being stranded on the road after the sudden closure of a tour. Some performers feared that union participation, with its implied association with other forms of manual labour, would undermine their efforts to be perceived as respectable artists. But the AEA leadership assured members that if they projected a united front, they would force the PMA to yield to their demands.[6]

Like other US labour unions rebelling against their employers' rigid control, the AEA embraced public spectacle – parades, rallies, impromptu performances, and motorcades – to raise awareness of and sympathy for their cause. Yet as 'objects of popular fascination', the striking performers were perceived differently from other strikers. 'Their mere presence on the streets served to define their struggle with the producing managers as an entertainment experience as well as an industrial dispute', observes theatre historian Sean P. Holmes.[7] This became vividly clear when stage celebrities such as Ethel Barrymore, Lillian Russell, Marie Dressler, or Eddie Cantor spoke passionately at rallies about the inequities that they and many less fortunate performers experienced daily. But while these stars brought considerable publicity to the AEA, one of the most effective and memorable strike spectacles showcased the union's most exploited members: chorus girls.

In many respects, chorus girls were a synecdoche for the US commercial theatre industry. Although theatregoers knew few (if any) chorus girls by name, their labour was central to every Broadway musical comedy, operetta, revue, and North American commercial tour. Chorus girl bodies also featured prominently in national newspaper articles, sheet music, magazines, and promotional materials. Trained to perform en masse, these women embodied the technological rationalization of the human body in the industrial era and the allure of the cute yet voiceless 'girl'. Yet their practiced uniformity meant that they were also easily exploited; indeed, chorus girls in Lee and JJ Shubert's *The Passing Show of 1919* had rehearsed unpaid for twenty-two weeks![8] Though the AEA had previously excluded chorus girls from its membership, they soon recognized their political value and formed a special Chorus Equity unit to represent their specific complaints.

During the strike, the AEA leadership transported the collegiality of the chorus girl dressing room into the heart of New York's financial district. Every day, troops of well-coifed performers travelled down Broadway to Wall Street by automobile to distribute pamphlets. Parading from office to office in a stunning display of collectivity,[9] they persuaded bankers, lawyers, stockbrokers, and other influential businessmen to discourage their wives and servants from attending Broadway shows until the strike was over (Figure 7.2). Thus with their dazzling smiles and waving banners, 'the prettiest strikers in history' infiltrated the male-dominated space of Wall Street,[10] transforming New York's financial district into a site of female-driven labour activism (and creating a template for much later performative protests against capitalist greed, including 2011's Occupy Wall Street). After a month of these and other spectacular urban protests, the PMA capitulated to the AEA's demands, and chorus girls returned to their lines with higher wages and the guarantee that their rehearsal labour would no longer go unpaid.

Downtown in Greenwich Village, other communities formed in opposition to New York's commercial entertainment industry, not through union organizing but with the establishment of non-profit endeavors. The 'Village', known previously as the '9th Ward' by Italian immigrant residents, took shape in the early twentieth century with the arrival of artists attracted by low rents that freed them from market pressures.[11] Although few identified as theatre professionals, many used theatrical activity to explore progressive ideas about feminism, racial equality, homosexuality, Freudian psychology, and trade unionism. Taking their cue from Europe's independent theatres, Villagers established alternatives to Broadway's 'escapist' fare. Both the Washington

FIGURE 7.2: Striking chorus girls turn Manhattan sidewalks into sites of spectacular protest, 1919. Billy Rose Theatre Division, The New York Public Library for the Performing Arts, Astor, Lenox and Tilden Foundations.

Square Players and Provincetown Players emerged from neighbourhood activities, establishing production practices that suited their needs before ultimately influencing the development of little theatres and university theatre programmes across the US.

Locations around Washington Square became crucial gathering sites: the Brevoort Hotel bar and Polly Holiday's restaurant for eating, drinking, and mingling; socialite Mable Dodge's apartment for salon events; the Liberal Club and Boni Brothers' bookstore for in-depth discussions about art and culture. The Villagers forged their modern identity from this neighbourhood crucible and their artistry increasingly advertised the neighbourhood as a bohemian enclave. Susan Glaspell, a founder of the Provincetown Players, critiqued outsiders' perceptions of their lifestyle: 'Every once in a while, in the Sunday paper, I read of Greenwich Village. It is a wicked place, it seems, and worse than wicked, it is silly'. She experienced it, however, as 'a neighborhood where people were working, where you knew just which street to take for a good talk when you wanted it, or could bolt your door and work all day long'.[12] Pursuits that appeared unusual or frivolous to outsiders were the serious work of inhabitants traversing neighborhood streets and intersecting at key locations.

Taking their name from the neighbourhood's civic hub, the Washington Square Players surfaced from Liberal Club members' attempt to give energetic form to their intellectual discussions.[13] In 1914, a young Robert Edmond Jones, soon to find fame as a New Stagecraft designer, placed a platform in the Boni's bookstore for a staging of Lord Dunsany's *The Glittering Gate*, a play first produced by Dublin's Abbey Theatre in 1908 and the type of serious, modern drama neglected by New York's commercial theatres.[14] They continued to perform dramas from Europeans like William Butler Yeats, George Bernard Shaw, and Maurice Maeterlinck, hoping to inspire American writers to consider the stage as a space for serious artistry. The Provincetown Players, formed by Liberal Club members who vacationed at Cape Cod, Massachusetts, were invested more in developing native playwrights. They used their summer escape from the city heat to experiment with modern dramatic structures and narratives. Because their production practices were minimal, they easily shifted from their use of summer cottages as impromptu stages to the small ground-floor room below Polly's when they took up residence in the Village in 1916 (see Figure 7.3). By that time, the Washington Square Players had left the neighbourhood, moving uptown in 1915 to the Bandbox Theatre on 57th Street to expand their audience; in 1918, some of its members founded the Theatre Guild, an organization that continued to produce modern plays and develop an audience for 'serious' drama uptown.

FIGURE 7.3: Provincetown Players setting the stage for *Bound East for Cardiff* at 139 Macdougal St, New York, 1916. Courtesy of Jeffrey Kennedy.

The Group Theatre's retreat from the city fifteen years later was more of an intentional act of community formation than the Provincetowners' summer escapes. In 1931, a faction from the Theatre Guild – 'the group', as they called themselves – retreated to Brookfield Center, Connecticut, an hour-long drive from New York. They were inspired by the strong ensemble acting of the Moscow Art Theatre (MAT), whose founders Konstantin Stanislavsky and Vladimir Nemirovich-Danchenko set a precedent for sequestering artists in a pastoral setting for an intense period of work without distractions from the modern world. During the summer of 1897, the MAT group left Moscow for the village of Pushkino, using an old stone warehouse for rehearsals and living in lodgings that typically housed factory workers.[15] To create, in the words of Stanislavsky, this new 'people's theatre ... to bring light into the dark lives of the poorer classes, to give them joyful aesthetic moments amidst the gloom which envelops them', they needed to escape Moscow and connect authentically with one another.[16] Thirty years later, the Group Theatre, guided by their interpretations of Stanislavsky's acting theories, hoped to replicate the MAT's cohesive ensemble spirit, retreating to solidify their own ensemble identity.

Cheryl Crawford, who managed the company alongside Harold Clurman and Lee Strasberg, described Brookfield Center as a 'country enclave'; they used a large barn for rehearsals and five houses served as the residences for the three directors and twenty-eight actors (plus some wives and children).[17] The company spent twelve weeks in acting workshops and rehearsals for Paul Green's *The House of Connelly*; they received no salaries, but funding from benefactors provided their 'meals, living quarters, and laundry expense'.[18] 'Our chief problem the first summer', wrote Clurman in *The Fervent Years*, 'was the unification of our people', using their uninterrupted time together to establish 'a common artistic ideal, a common search for a way of life'.[19] Like the MAT ensemble, they returned to their city with a shared artistic vision to share with other urban dwellers and a collective practice to produce that vision. Back on the streets of Moscow and New York, the members of these two companies continued to deepen their connections, making a significant impact on their respective national theatre practices. Their artistry, formed and sustained as ensembles within and outside cities, is emblematic of the attempts of many modern production communities to elevate theatre as a medium to engage citizens in meaningful dialogues. Whether fighting for higher wages and better working conditions or retreating from the imperatives of commercial theatre production, these communities built sustainable homes for their artistry and, in so doing, they paved the way for today's urban artists who continue to use urban spaces and city resources to forge community identities.

SITES OF CONSTRUCTION

While many modern artists powerfully demonstrated that theatre could engage audiences without elaborate sets and costumes, the workshop spaces where craftspeople build sets and costumes have remained important sites for the socio-political formation of modern theatrical communities. Although generally valued by the industry, labourers who work in construction sites at a distance from rehearsal rooms and performance venues often remain overlooked by spectators and unnamed by historians.[20] Commercial entertainments tend to generate the most labour for shop workers who build and paint scenery and properties; repair, maintain, and rent lighting and sound equipment; construct, bead, and paint costumes. Their tools and skills changed rapidly with the advent of new technologies during the twentieth century, yet time-honoured, proven abilities in hand craftsmanship are still necessary to the industry, and continue to transfer from one generation to the next through apprenticeships. As a result, shop spaces in the modern period continued to bring together a wide range of skilled artists and labourers, working adjacently and in direct collaboration, sharing meals and socializing on breaks. However, the increasing mobility and international migrations of theatre workers during the twentieth century (see next section) significantly affected and diversified shop communities, including where they live, how they interact, and how they relate to the theatrical products they have a hand in crafting.

In 1911, Austrian architect and designer Joseph Urban emigrated to the US to work for the Boston Opera, bringing his former staff with him: business manager Rudolf Adler, scenic painters Karl Koeck, Otto Weber, Max Kamerzell, and their wives.[21] The following year, he formally established a shop in Swampscott, Massachusetts with quick train access to Boston. A journalist covering the company's coup in recruiting Urban away from his Austrian state sponsorship illustrated the setting: 'Hidden from the street by a few apple trees and workingmen's house, lies the scenic studio of the Boston Opera Company . . . No passerby suspects that here is the greatest factory of illusions of our country, that here men work carrying out with sure purpose a part of the intentions of the greatest musical geniuses of all ages'.[22] The 'men' referenced remain anonymous, as do their wives whose upholstery and curtain sewing skills were equally necessary to Urban's elegant, Art Nouveau-inspired settings. Urban's technique for creating scenic backdrops by stretching and painting canvas on the floor with multiple, layered colours created seemingly magical effects, transitioning from dawn to dusk with the fading of theatrical lights. The results, especially for Florenz Ziegfeld's 1915 *Follies* revue (shipped by train to New York), were spectacular; Broadway audiences flocked to the New Amsterdam Theatre to see Urban's settings, as well as the British fashion designer Lucile's sumptuous costumes.[23]

In 1917, Urban moved his shop to Yonkers, New York to be closer to his commissions on Broadway and at the Metropolitan Opera. At the conclusion of the First World War, Urban continued to recruit from Vienna; workers in the largely immigrant shop adapted to the US while still sharing Austrian traditions. Urban's daughter Gretl fondly remembered visiting the annexed kitchen where the crew 'had a delicious big meal every day with Viennese cooking: goulash, Wiener schnitzel, and pastries, and always a little wine'.[24] Americans also joined the mix; young New Stagecraft designers like Norman Bel Geddes apprenticed themselves to the shop to learn Urban's modern techniques. This transmigration of shop skills, learned within the close-knit community, made a significant impact on modern scenic painting practices not only in the US but in the countries where trained apprentices travelled to set up their own shops.

A scenic shop even larger than Urban's continues to operate in Yonkers today, with a diverse population of craftspeople practicing the same techniques perfected by Koeck's crew as well as many more skills in carpentry, steel work, and computer automation. Hudson Scenic Studios operates in a 120,000 square foot facility with the floor space to paint multiple backdrops; located within walking distance from the Metro North Ludlow train stop, the shop is a convenient commute for many employees who live in the city. Scenic painter Midge Lucas (Figure 7.4) commutes from Queens; he grew up and trained as a

FIGURE 7.4: Midge Lucas working in the Hudson Scenic paint shop. Photo: Christin Essin.

weaver in London, then moved to the US and trained in New York with painters who connected him to a genealogy of craftsmanship reaching back to Urban's Viennese immigrants. Lucas could work in shops closer to his home, but he likes Hudson's community and scenic charge, Pat Bases, who assigns work not only according to people's specialized skills but also to give them creative challenges.[25] The paint shop's break room, in addition to a refrigerator and microwave for prepping meals, features a mélange of old decorations from past birthday parties. Hudson's scenic painters travel greater distances than their predecessors who lived in shop-adjacent houses with apple trees, but they similarly build working relationships and social connections around shared meals, celebrations, and a collaborative understanding of how their skills shape the theatre industry and their professional identities.

While established craftspeople have opportunities to travel and migrate from job to job, familial bonds and privileged social statuses kept the profession largely closed to minority populations during the twentieth century; strict gender codes also determined placement in shops and accessibility to apprenticeships. One US art theatre, the Neighborhood Playhouse, challenged this system by offering craft training to disadvantaged immigrants, women, and minorities as part of their mission. In 1915, wealthy sisters Alice and Irene Lewisohn opened the theatre at 466 Grand Street after years of volunteering at the Henry Street Settlement House in New York's Lower East Side. They recruited other women – Aline Bernstein, Agnes Morgan, Helen Arthur, and Alice Beer – to serve on the executive board. Many of the Henry Street volunteers had come from long-standing German Jewish families with a desire to help assimilate and find work for the recently immigrated Eastern European Jews who lived in the neighbourhood's squalid, overcrowded tenements. The company tended to produce modern texts, dance as well as drama, and increasingly gained a reputation for quality, experimental artistry. In 1926, a *New York Times* reporter described the difficulty of uptowners finding the venue through a 'maze of trucks' supplying the neighbourhood's commerce and crowds of children in the streets, a daily journey for many 'actors, students, stagehands, and other members of this semi-professional group'.[26] The influx of New Yorkers from outside the neighbourhood brought attention to the challenges facing its largely impoverished residents and the city's neglect of its regulatory responsibilities over living conditions.

The Neighborhood Playhouse expanded the settlement house's training programmes, especially in 1917 when it annexed a building on Pitt Street for additional construction space and storage. Without using commercial shops, they crafted their own production materials out of their workshop classes, thus becoming one of the first self-supporting theatres and a model for other non-profit organizations.[27] They recruited some professionals to lead workshops, but the producing staff taught the majority of classes in carpentry, scenic painting, sewing, dying, wig making, and crafting masks with the intent to 'prepare the way for professional work'.[28] Increasingly, more than just neighbourhood residents sought these apprenticeships, bypassing the union-controlled, patriarchal father-to-son traditions of occupational instruction that regularly excluded women and minorities. As a high-visibility endeavour operating within a politically progressive social movement, the theatre altered the neighbourhood's landscape, identifying it as a place of possibilities. Although the shop annex no longer exists, the playhouse (now part of the Abrons Art Center) and backstage construction space still remain, used by many downtown artists in the early stages of their careers as they augment their training and build their resumes.

The Neighborhood Playhouse example points to the importance of shop environments for building and sustaining local communities over time. Elsewhere, shop activities have supported the creation of transnational communities bound not by culture, nation, or geographic location but by collective engagement in large-scale theatrical productions. The Cape Town-based Handspring Puppet Company offers an excellent example of this shift from the locally situated shop to the globally dispersed organization in the late twentieth century. (See Chapter 6 for further discussion of the Handspring Puppet Company.)

For Handspring's four founding members, finding a location to build puppets and make t-shirts and toys to sell to audiences was an important first step in the company's development. In late autumn 1980, company member Jill Joubert discovered an ideal, albeit grim, building for the company's premises: a former funeral parlour with the off-putting name of Human and Pitt. 'Thousands of corpses had passed through those doors', founding member Basil Jones recalled, 'and we were forced to wonder whether our newborn baby would survive such inauspicious surroundings'.[29] It did. The spacious building afforded enough room for several studios, a workshop, an office space, 'a small storeroom with tiled walls (where the undertakers used to wash the bodies)', and a rehearsal hall.[30] Breathing life into puppets of all shapes and sizes, the company radically transformed the former funeral parlour into a site of dynamic creation. From there, Handspring toured South Africa in a 'cramped truck, surrounded by sets and boxes', playing to approximately 200 schools as they moved from their shop/studio spaces onto impromptu stages.[31] But in the mid-1980s heightened racial violence and the declaration of a State of Emergency forced Handspring to rethink its identity as a touring company. In May 1986 it relocated from Cape Town to Johannesburg to pursue opportunities in television. There, the company moved into a custom-made workshop, studio, and office, and transformed Adrian Kohler and Basil Jones's home into office space for the newly formed NGO The Handspring Trust for Puppetry and Education.[32] Surrounded by wires, computers, and new staff members, Handspring's founders found themselves in an enlarged production community dedicated to children's education.

The end of apartheid brought further changes to Handspring and its production processes; these included collaborations within South Africa as well as a growing number of commissions from outside the country. These new relationships required shifts in production processes, spaces, and schedules. For example, when Handspring began working with a Malayan puppet company on the production of *Ubu and the Truth Commission* (discussed in detail in Chapter 6), they noticed striking discrepancies in crew hierarchies and wage structures, both for those working in the shop and for those performing on stage. Whereas the standard Handspring contract guaranteed higher than average wages and equity to all touring company members, the Malayan company worked from a more hierarchal model and tended to offer its members payment in kind.[33]

Handspring's collaborations also have required extensive planning across borders and time zones and the involvement of continually expanding production communities. For *War Horse* (2007), produced in collaboration with The National Theatre in London, Handspring's puppet designers attended initial workshop rehearsals at the National Theatre Studio, where they worked with properties master Alan Edwards to make 'quick mockups of horse heads and necks out of torn cardboard and shredded newspaper'.[34] The Handspring crew then returned to their studio in Cape Town where Adrian Kohler began working on a cardboard scale model from which the company would develop a prototype design. For four months, Kohler worked with a growing community

FIGURE 7.5: Scene from the Australian production of *War Horse*, 2013. Photo: Corbis Images.

of welders, puppeteers, designers, and other technically skilled assistants to complete the prototype, which was then loaded into a special crate and shipped by boat to London.[35] Back again a month later at the National Theatre Studio, Handspring worked with another team of puppeteers, actors, and the production's directors Marianne Elliott and Tom Morris to perfect the design.[36] This included working with an occupational therapist who recommended several changes to the position of controls and the overall design of the horses to prevent the puppeteers from succumbing to repetitive strain injuries.[37] Thus, while Handspring was responsible for the initial design and construction of the *War Horse* puppets, the puppets that ultimately trotted across the National Theatre stage owed their existence to the collaborative efforts of an international production community working across time and distance and between shop space and rehearsal space (see Figure 7.5). Indeed, Handspring's process spotlights the porousness of the border between shop and stage, crew and cast, prompting audiences to ask not just '*how* did they do that?' but '*who* did that?'

SITES OF TRANSIT

Life lived 'on the road' makes and breaks communities by bringing individuals into close, constant contact; crammed into small state rooms or cabins, performers and crew members have to learn to live with or at least tolerate one another. It is hardly surprising to find lengthy accounts of travel (the good, the bad, the ugly) in the memoirs of actors, dancers, producers, writers, and other theatrical personnel.[38] Nor is it surprising that Hollywood musicals of the 1930s, 1940s, and 1950s celebrated the itinerant lifestyle of theatrical professionals; recall Bing Crosby and Danny Kaye singing about snow in the diner car in *White Christmas* or Fred Astaire dancing on the ceiling of his steamer cabin in *Royal Wedding*. Such films point to the importance of trains, ships, aeroplanes, buses, automobiles, and other forms of modern transportation as sites of performance – 'practiced places' where companies rehearse lines, rewrite scenes, share meals, and pose for photographs, marking their mobility as well as their formation *as* a community. Turning now to sites of transit, this section borrows from the 'new mobility paradigm' within sociology and cultural geography to emphasize how movement defined theatrical communities of production in the modern period. As sociologist John Urry writes, a focus on mobility calls attention to 'different forms of travel, transport and communications with the multiple ways in which economic and social life is performed and organized through time and across various spaces'.[39]

In the nineteenth and early twentieth centuries, innovations in steam travel and the expansion of railroad networks throughout Europe, North America, Asia, and Australia facilitated the rapid, transnational circulation of theatre companies. Although actors and managers had embarked upon world tours from the mid-nineteenth century on, technological advances in transportation fueled by international business rivalries meant that it was increasingly feasible, both economically and logistically, for managers to coordinate national and international travel for an entire theatre company, complete with crewmembers, sets, props, and costumes.[40]

The Moscow Art Theatre's tours across Europe and the US exemplified the impact of mobility on an ensemble's ability to maintain (or increase) their cohesive working relationships while simultaneously expanding their spectatorship and international impact on other production communities. In 1906, at some of the first signs of revolution and a general strike, the MAT embarked on its first European tour with directors Stanislavsky and Nemirovich-Danchenko, twenty-seven actors, and eighty-five support staff members to produce sixty-two performances in eleven cities. The company's American tours in 1923 and 1924 significantly influenced the emergence of the Group Theatre and acting practices of other performers captivated by the ensemble's realistic style.[41] In a letter to Nemirovich-Danchenko written during the 1923 tour, during which the company travelled to Chicago, Philadelphia, and Boston performing a repertory of *Tzar Fiodor*, *Lower Depths*, *Cherry Orchard*, and *Three Sisters*, Stanislavsky communicates some difficulties they encountered. He mentions not the practicalities of moving large numbers of people and equipment in unfamiliar geographies, but rather the divisive nationalist politics that followed them: 'Here we are attacked by both Russians and Americans for using our theatre to glorify present-day Russia. In Moscow they are slinging mud at US because we are preserving the tradition of bourgeois theatre. . . . Believe me it is not for my own pleasure that I am spending almost two years going from place to place, from city to city with absolutely no time for the things I love and dream about . . .' Stanislavsky's frustration indicates the degree to which international touring drew focus to concerns of national identity in interpretation of their work. In an expression of national allegiance, geographic isolation, or both, he closes by saying that he 'yearn[s] with all my heart for Russia'.[42]

While Stanislavksy and the MAT faced criticism for (supposedly) mixing art and politics, later touring companies made little effort to disguise their political aims. During the height of the Cold War, North American governments enlisted theatre and dance companies to promote democratic ideals in Communist countries or Communist-influenced regions. For example, in 1973, the Ontario-based Stratford Festival undertook a lengthy European tour that included stops in Poland and the Soviet Union, where they performed key pieces from the company's classical repertoire.[43] Travelling one year after the Canadian national hockey team had triumphed over the Soviet Union in the 'Summit Series', the Stratford company was tasked with representing Canada's cultural achievements in the home of Stanislavsky.[44] The US government similarly used performing communities of production to advance its anti-Communist agenda. As cultural historian Penny M. Von Eschen details, Cold War tensions encouraged the US government to sponsor the world travels of jazz musicians and other influential performers. Playing to audiences in Africa, Asia, and the Middle East, African American performers like Louis Armstrong and Paul Robeson pushed against their intended role as representatives of American freedom and instead offered more complex counter-narratives; Robeson's revised interpretation of the Broadway classic 'Old Man River', for example, simultaneously conveyed the violent history of US race relations and his star power to critique them. In *On The Performance Front,* Charlotte Canning interrogates the 'second class at home, but first class abroad' status of performers with the state-sponsored international tour of *Porgy and Bess* (1952–1956), arguing that the performers' agency as cultural diplomats materially impacted their status as a community of production. By forging close ties with international audiences living in the shadow of colonialism, these performers supported the development of much larger communities bound by shared social and political goals.[45]

Life lived on the road or at sea likewise encouraged the geographic expansion of theatrical communities and the formation of new transnational networks. In 1910, US theatre manager Charles Frohman staged the full-length play *The Climax* on board the transatlantic ocean liner SS *Mauretania* as his New York-based company travelled to London to mount the show there. Unfortunately, rough seas and a seasick leading lady prevented the performance from opening, but Frohman's venture nevertheless demonstrated the potential for bringing theatre to ocean-bound audiences.[46] Today most luxury cruise ships offer a range of employment opportunities for actors, dancers, singers, and musicians. These floating communities bring the sounds of Broadway or the West End to tourists travelling the Caribbean or Mediterranean, with entertainment options ranging from scaled-down versions of hit musicals to more intimate cabaret performances and revues. As perpetually mobile subjects, cast and crew enjoy opportunities to travel, encounter new cultures, broaden career possibilities, and compare their working conditions with those experienced by local performers hired at ports of call.

But life at sea can be difficult. Many cruise ship performers are recent graduates of performing arts programmes, and therefore eager to accept less-than-ideal working conditions. While large companies like Disney respect equity rules for rehearsals and employments, they are not obligated to do so because union regulations do not apply in international waters. As a result, performers are not only vulnerable to exploitation during employment but also leave the job without an equity card.[47] They work long hours and live in close quarters, with few days away from the ship and, in the case of Disney cruises, are often expected to work as greeters even when they are not performing. More troublingly, the obligation to present a continuously cheerful, flirty front for the benefit of the consumer-passengers can result in undesired sexual advances from passengers who fail to interpret the cheerful front as a form of forced entertainment.[48]

Working at sea, however, teaches performers skills in versatility and concentration that are unique to their mobile environment. 'We had to learn how to dance and move on a stage when it's rocking', one former Disney cruise ship entertainer recalled. 'If you're doing a jump, the ship could list while you're in the air and the floor is never where you expect it to be. It took concentration to make the turns and the pirouettes. You learn how to hold your center so you can land and stay stable'.[49] Overcoming such challenges fosters strong feelings of community among the cast and crew, who come together to form a surrogate family that offers support, friendship, and a sense of stability that defies the rocking of the waves.

SITES OF CONSUMPTION

Cruise ships give rise to new communities of production *and* consumption by fueling the global circulation of entertainment products. Taking a cue from these floating sites, our final section examines locations of selling and consuming, paying particular attention to urban spaces where theatrical workers seek recreation and rejuvenation as well as those sites where unregulated performers come into contact with tourists and other entertainment consumers. Continuing to expand traditional notions of production communities and question the industry's labour hierarchies, we return to urban spaces and its citizens claiming their 'rights to the city', specifically through their occupation of spaces marked for the exchange of goods and services related to theatre and performance.

Bars and restaurants, for example, bring business owners, industry professionals, and paying spectators/diners together to sustain the city's cultural economy. Before artists like Hugo Ball, Marcel Janco, and Tristan Tzara used the Café Voltaire to stage their evenings of Dada entertainment, the Zurich establishment was known only as a rowdy bar on the Spiegelgasse in the city's old quarter. Zurich was a destination for many Europeans – German, French, Romanian – evading or protesting the war. In February 1916, the Dadaists adopted the café in a run-down corner of the city to stage their discontent with the war, old world values, and the cultural products of past generations: 'Art cannot have any respect for the existing view of the world unless it renounces itself', Ball proclaimed.[50] They produced variety performances with multiple media to pronounce the death of reason and worthlessness of art with any claim to coherence. 'Painters, students, revolutionaries, tourists, international crooks, psychiatrists, the demimonde, sculptors, and police spies on the lookout for information, all hobnobbed with one another', wrote artist Marcel Janco.[51] As a public place of consumption, the café accommodated multiple communities, each searching to escape through debauchery or, in the words of Ball, to 'fight against the death-throes and death-drunkenness of his time'.⁵² After the war, Dadaist art and artists moved to a range of venues in other European cities, but the Café Voltaire remains in the forefront of the movement's history, a stage for discontent and rebellion appropriated from urban commercial space.

Restaurants in commercial theatre districts provide production communities with convenient spaces to take meals, conduct business, and celebrate accomplishments; in exchange, the establishments gain prestige as the watering holes of famous or would-be famous performers. Around the corner from New York's Times Square on West 44th Street, Sardi's has hosted industry insiders since its 1927 opening. It gained renown in the 1940s and 1950s as a celebrity haunt in Walter Winchell's nationally syndicated newspaper column 'On Broadway'. Vincent Sardi Jr. described the restaurant's many functions as a 'club, mess hall, lounge, post office, saloon and marketplace of the American theater'.⁵³ But the rotating and evolving collection of Broadway caricatures that grace its walls has also made Sardi's a tourist destination and continues to identify Broadway theatre as a celebrity-making enterprise. Joe Allen's restaurant on West 46th Street became a gathering spot for many performers after its opening in 1965. A 1988 dining review labels it 'as much a fixture of the New York theater scene as "The Fantasticks"', yet the posters of Broadway flops that adorn its walls remind insiders and pre-show diners alike of the commercial industry's volatility and unreliability.⁵⁴ Stagehands tend to frequent their own bars, with McHales on the northeast corner of 8th Avenue and 46th Street being a favourite until it closed in 2006. These and other businesses around Times Square are vital not only as impromptu work sites for Broadway production communities but also as 'home' sites grounding individual members in a familiar neighbourhood milieu, alleviating feelings of placelessness that can result from the itinerant lifestyles of theatre workers.

Gift shops, theme restaurants, toy stores, and other tourist-orientated sites are likewise central to the production of Times Square, but the community that labours on behalf of tourists is often quite distinct from the community that labours on behalf of Broadway productions. The so-called 'revitalization' or 'Disneyfication' of the Times Square theatre district in the 1990s saw the swift removal of the strip clubs, X-rated cinemas, and other adult-orientated businesses that had defined the district for much of the 1970s and 1980s. In their place sprang up a host of 'family-friendly' stores and restaurants run by huge multi-national corporations, often with connections to the corporations producing Broadway musicals. By the millennium, a family leaving Disney's production of *The Lion King* at the famed New Amsterdam Theatre (where Joseph Urban had once mounted his impressive *Follies* designs) could take their hungry brood to Bubba Gump's Shrimp Co. at 1501 Broadway, inspired by the 1994 Academy Award-winning film, *Forrest Gump,* produced by Disney's rival, Paramount Pictures. To get there, though, the family would first have to pass through *The*

Lion King gift shop in the New Amsterdam lobby, and the array of cute stuffed animals and t-shirts representing the musical's main characters.

In her scathing critique of the Disneyfication of Times Square, Maurya Wickstrom points to the troubling way that *The Lion King* gift shop (among others) invites theatregoers, especially children, to labour on behalf of the Disney brand through their consumptive acts. When they purchase a Simba doll or wear a t-shirt emblazoned with the image of Mickey Mouse, tourists become part of an entertainment corporation's consumer army and come to resemble the commodities they desire, hold, or wear. Through consumption, Wickstrom writes, 'The human is woven into the thing, and ultimately the thing appears the more lifelike of the two, as the fact of its dependency upon the human fades into view'.[55] The labour involved in such acts of consumption, however, is often obscured, and the consumer embracing her Simba doll is typically unaware of (or unconcerned with) her role within a vast community of production that services multi-national corporations.

In recent years, this interweaving of human and thing has manifested in performers dressed as larger-than-life Disney characters, video game avatars, Sesame Street monsters, Marvel superheroes, and other globally recognizable (trademarked) toy mascots who occupy the Times Square district where they pose for photos for a fee. Uninformed tourists often assume that the plush corporate mascots have ties to nearby Broadway productions and have been sent into the streets for promotional purposes. Trained in the repertoire of consumer performance, these tourists take photos just as they would at Disneyland or other themed commercial environments: with the understanding that the mascots exist to service them for free. But most of the mascots who populate the hyper-commercial district are underemployed, many of them new immigrants who have rented (often shabby and generally unlicensed) costumes in the hope of attracting a few tourist dollars. Not surprisingly, violent confrontations have erupted between costumed labourers and frustrated tourists. In February 2013, a man wearing a Spider-Man costume allegedly punched a woman in the face when she refused to pay him for posing for a photo with her children.[56] Two months later, a man costumed as the Sesame Street character Cookie Monster allegedly pushed a two-year-old child when his mother refused to pay him two dollars for the photo she had taken. He was later charged with assault and endangering the welfare of a child.[57]

Aware that such confrontations have jeopardized their livelihood, some mascots have joined forces to lobby for improved working conditions. In August 2014, a group of mascots convened a news conference in Manhattan where they announced the formation of New York Artists United for a Smile, a non-union alliance that they hoped would 'create a culture of respect'.[58] For these labourers, the issue was not simply the few 'bad apples' antagonizing tourists but also the laws stipulating that performers can only request tips for their services. Political leaders have proposed alternative solutions, including 'legislation that would require all street performers who disguise themselves to register and go through a licensing process that would require them to wear ID cards'.[59] But mascot advocates have objected to such policing measures. As Sean Basinski, director of the Street Vendors Project, which also aims to support and protect New York street performers, observed, 'The city created a new Times Square for tourists, and when the tourists come, people come to do business here. Now that they're here, the city doesn't like them anymore. The city created a Disneyland here, and now they're upset that it's Disneyland'.[60] Basinski's words offer an eerie gloss on Lefebvre's notion of the 'right to the city', which stresses the rights of individuals to reshape the city through collective efforts. Through their costumed labour, the mascots 'logically' extend the Disneyfication of Times Square to street commerce. In so doing, they expose the hollowness of the American Dream, or indeed any corporate-sponsored dream that promises life and vitality through consumptive labour.

As a policed community of production occupying civic space and beginning to find strength through organization, Times Square mascots evoke the ghosts of the 8,000 men and women who gathered outside the Winter Palace in 1920, demanding that their voices be heard. Although it is unlikely that pseudo-Hello Kitty and Spider-man will storm the 'provisional government' of corporatized Times Square, their actions draw strength from earlier protest repertoires. Like the chorus girls who invaded Wall Street a century ago, the mascot's work location also gives them an incredibly colourful and well-lit stage from which to speak (or revolt). Halfway around the world, the Palace Square in Petrograd, now St Petersburg, still functions as a stage for public events, although many of these are decidedly un-revolutionary, embedded as they are within systems of Western capitalism. Citizens and tourists alike attend concerts in the square, including some spectacular events with superstar performers like Paul McCartney (2004), The Rolling Stones and Elton John (2007), Madonna and Duran Duran (2009), and Sting (2011). While some might be tempted to dismiss the production communities that cohere around these performers as politically inconsequential, it is worth recalling that the labour of individuals working collectively to bring a production to life is always fraught with revolutionary potential. Yesterday's hammer and sickle recognized the power of workers' demanding their rights by wielding the tools of their trade; those who work today with power drills, makeup brushes, and mascot costumes gain strength from their alignment with industry peers, particularly when they see themselves as compatriots.

CHAPTER EIGHT

Genres and Repertoires

Redressing the Nation in Ireland and Japan

MICHELLE LIU CARRIGER AND AOIFE MONKS

INTRODUCTION: FROM A LITERARY FRAMEWORK TO A PERFORMANCE STUDIES MODEL

The words 'genre' and 'repertoire' have typically been understood as a means of organizing information taxonomically about dramatic performance. Historically, 'repertoire' names the collection of plays that an actor or theatre company is capable of performing, and 'genre' describes different types and styles of theatre, beginning with Aristotle's division of theatre into tragedy, comedy, and satyr play and going on to distinguish popular from 'high' culture theatre, musical forms from spoken forms, and so on. In a wider sense, however, genre can be understood as a system in which the features of a (usually literary) art object are made sensible through their distinctiveness within a broader classification of artistic forms. As John Frow argues in his book *Genre*, genres are thus '*productive* of meaning', not merely ways of classifying meanings.[1]

Just as Frow expands typical definitions of 'genre', Diana Taylor redefines and expands the use of the word 'repertoire' in her book *The Archive and the Repertoire* to draw attention to the ways in which embodied performances can maintain and transmit cultural meanings. Through the live, embodied aspects of performance, the repertoire preserves social memories (or, indeed, theatrical ones) that may not have been captured by the more 'official' methods of documentation that rest in the archive. Both Taylor's and Frow's interventions into the terms 'genre' and 'repertoire' will underwrite our thinking in this chapter, particularly as we pay attention to how theatrical performance necessitates approaches that expand well past the usual literary connotations of these terms to encompass not just texts, but auditory and visual presentation, material objects, and even political and cultural ideas and ideals.

In this chapter, we examine 'genre' and 'repertoire' in the modern age as intertwined concepts. That is, we explore how both of these concepts are *embodied* in the modern theatre, how they overlap and mutually determine one another, and indeed how they ultimately become productive of modern bodies themselves on the modern stage. An instructive example of 'embodiment' as a generic, classificatory practice can be found in the ways that *costume* functions, on the stage but also beyond it, as it encodes ways of being and doing the body that align with modern politics, and especially with the politics of nationalism during the twentieth century.

As Anne Hollander suggests, costumes are the expression of bodily codes that pre-exist performers and individual play texts; they represent a case where repertoire precedes and then manifests genre in performance. As she argues of ritual performances, 'the costumes are the drama, the characters are known by what they wear and any accompanying words support the clothes instead of the other way round'.[2] The popular genres of variety theatre sketched out in the previous volume in this series emphasize how generic categorization exceeds the level of text, since the shared codes of that stage are contained primarily in performed behaviours and stage effects. Costume's role in shaping genre is further evident in Tracy C. Davis's claim that the costumes worn by nineteenth-century actresses mapped directly onto the hierarchies of classification in the period: 'while black velvet and white lace were the marks of artistry, gauze and spangles were the key to mass appeal and commercial success'.[3] Davis's study suggests that nineteenth-century actresses' costumes not only indicated the generic status of a performance, they actually constituted genre on the stage, fixing character types within specific styles of performance and enabling audiences to decode the visual rules of the form. The costumes that actresses were required to supply for their own performances correlated to different, standardized theatrical genres in the nineteenth century, allowing performers to render themselves intelligible within various repertoires and simultaneously to ensure that audience members could situate their experience within the correct set of theatrical conventions. Contemporary dramas and comedies were even known as 'modern dress plays' in contrast to classical tragedies, which were played in stylized period costumes.

In this way, costume might be understood to recognize the particular status of genre in the theatre, which becomes a means of classifying, and comprehending, *a repertoire of embodied practices* enabled by costumes, while costumes in performance in turn make meaning in relation to generic classifications already evident on the stage. Theatre costume thus does not function as merely 'surface' decoration within a performance but rather works to constitute the point of interdependence between genre and repertoire, creating, as Frow argues, 'effects of reality and truth, authority and plausibility' on (and beyond) the stage.[4]

MODERN THEATRE AND THE POLITICS OF DRESS

Modern theatre, like 'modernity' in a wider sense, can be characterized by the attempts of a range of artists to break down old generic divisions and invent new theatrical forms that would better reflect the tumultuous experiences of modern life, which seemed to its participants to be moving and changing ever more quickly through revolutions in technology, the rapid expansion of cities, shifting morals and societal norms, and shattering new forms of warfare. In response to the psychic disorientation that these changes induced, modern avant-garde theatre-makers proposed to overcome the old bourgeois theatre's fixed dramatic genres – characterized by drawing room comedies, well made plays, and sensational melodrama; the folk displays and orientalist spectacles characteristic of ballet and opera; as well as Shakespeare productions costumed in modern dress – accusing these genres of being inadequate for the theatrical depiction of a shocking, new, modern world. For example, in his 1880 essay 'Naturalism in the Theatre', the playwright and novelist Émile Zola demanded a more scientific and socially aware theatre that used psychology to portray gritty, urban, 'true life' stories rather than providing aspirational and consumerist spectacles of upper middle class life.[5] His writing chimed with George Bernard Shaw's joking dismissal of bourgeois drama's aesthetics, which he described as 'a tailor's advertisement in the middle of an upholsterer's and decorator's advertisement'.[6]

Artists at the turn of the twentieth century proposed to restore the stage to its imagined role in depicting the world authentically. Movements that re-imagined theatrical genres included naturalism and realism in the late nineteenth century, Symbolism around the turn of the twentieth century, Expressionism, Futurism, Dadaism, and Absurdism through the two world wars, as well as the specific practices of various individual theatre theorists and makers: Antonin Artaud's Theatre of Cruelty, Bertolt Brecht's Epic Theatre, and Jerzy Grotowski's Poor Theatre, for example. The politicized exploration of genre carried on, after the mid-century, into postmodern performances that sought to systematically deconstruct the unity and coherence of the theatre-going experience by scrutinizing text, scenography, temporality, and even audience pleasure for aesthetic or political ends. Genre in the modern age might be described ultimately as having been atomized into smaller and smaller units.

As part of these theatrical experiments, artists routinely renegotiated the meanings of stage costume, and this concern with costume was in turn driven by an intensive theatrical focus on the status of *the body* in modernity. That body was often imagined by artists and cultural critics to be deformed, exhausted, unhygienic, unwell, inauthentic, and in need of revival. (For more on the modern theatre's overarching interest in embodiment, see Chapter 9.) The modernist drive towards a critique of human embodiment at the theatre mirrors other approaches to the body in the early twentieth century. Various dress-reform movements across Europe sought to restore the body to its imagined natural, unpolluted state: the Italian Futurist Giacomo Balla's claim that modern dress was responsible for 'the negation of the muscular life' was typical.[7] As Russian costume and dress designer Nadezhda Lamanova wrote in 1923, 'if [. . .] we gain comfortable, harmonious and functional clothing, we will achieve at the same time an enrichment of our daily life, and we will wipe out the prejudice of fashion [. . .]. The new dress will suit the new life – active, dynamic and conscious'.[8] To change clothes was, for these writers, to restore the body to a healthier state, making it capable of greater dynamism and action on the stage and in the street. The changing nature of stage costume thus became a key front in the battle to rehabilitate the human body in the modern public sphere.

These approaches to dress reform sometimes sought to produce the idea of a 'pure' body, uncontaminated by fast-paced modern life; however, modern life itself complicated this impulse as technological advances in travel and communication brought the countries of the world into ever-closer contact, with mixed results. Through the nineteenth and twentieth centuries the theatre registered the complexities and pleasures of imperialism and globalization through the transnational circulation of popular forms: acrobats from China and Japan toured Europe, Britain, and the US; amateur and professional theatre companies toured European and English-speaking outposts around the globe; 'freak shows' and museum exhibits brought 'specimens' from around the world together into pseudo-educational displays; and the dissemination of dominant cultural products (like Shakespeare) was aggressively pursued in colonial territories. Yet, even as international exchange became a regular and inextricable part of daily life, many nations became powerfully concerned with articulating specific national identities through the management of the body and its dress. Cultural nationalists across Europe, for example, drew on the fantasy of a pure identity lost to globalizing modernity in order to advocate for an embodied return to an imagined, pre-modern state through folk costume and performance. International exchange and the emergence of nationhood as a political concept thus worked in concert, resulting in new, hybrid forms of embodiment that were paradoxically imagined as nationally 'pure' even as they rested for their recognition upon cross-cultural repertoires of performance and dress.

Taking costume as the central focus of this chapter enables us to consider its role in helping to shape key social, political, and aesthetic debates as those manifested on and in the bodies displayed on the modern stage (and in the modern street). Understanding genre and repertoire at the theatre as channelled primarily through the body, we explore some of the ways in which theatrical modernism used the organization and classification of bodies through costume to articulate powerful new forms of national, and transnational, subjectivity. The next section of this chapter, 'Inventions', tracks the politicized rejection of historical theatrical genres through the development of new forms of national costume in Ireland and Japan in the early part of the twentieth century. The following section, 'Interventions', investigates how the new genres created through that process were then reframed and once more rejected via the costuming of postmodern, transnationally hybrid bodies in both countries at the end of the twentieth century. We conclude with an example that brings the two national contexts together: Yeats's *At The Hawk's Well* demonstrates how the collision of a Japanese body, a pan-European dance practice, and the work of an Irish playwright exemplifies the contradictions and tensions embedded in the orientalist borrowing and transnational circulation of repertoires and genres during the modern period.

Our case studies come from Ireland and Japan because they are two countries whose national contexts are sometimes treated as implicitly marginal in Anglophone theatre studies, and yet their histories may simultaneously be seen as paradigmatic to global modernism. By focusing on Irish and Japanese theatre costume, we demonstrate how experimentation with genre through costume at these cultural 'margins' can reveal new insights into stage practices in so-called theatrical 'centres'. (See Chapter 5 in this volume for a similar approach to theatrical circulation in the modern period.) The period we explore includes the violent emergence of the new Irish state in the early twentieth century, as well as the massive cultural upheavals wrought by the modernization campaign of Japan's Meiji era from 1868 to 1912 (and beyond into the twentieth century). Tracking Irish and Japanese theatre costumes alongside the expression of national senses of self and cultural concepts of public space helps us to see how competing claims for modern, national bodies were dialectically intertwined with existing cultural conditions, as well as with the renovation of extant artistic repertoires. Throughout the chapter we use examples from Irish and Japanese theatre, dance, and street performance to sketch out two, contrasting strategies of national embodiment: a recourse to ancient ideals, untouched by the 'polluting' effects of modernity; and a determined re-imagining of national identity as fundamentally contingent on transnational negotiation.

INVENTIONS

Red Shawls and Petticoats

Modern Irish theatre is famous for its riots, and quite a number of these riots have centred on the question of costume. From the opening of the Abbey Theatre in 1904, the stage was a site of contestation and debate over how the nation should be understood in the midst of the nationalist struggle for independence and how the new Irish state should be articulated after a bloody civil war in 1922. At the heart of these struggles were the questions of how Irish bodies should be rendered intelligible on stage, and of the ways in which old repertoires of stage dress, such as those of nineteenth-century melodrama and stage-Irishness, should be reformed and rejected in the service of modern Irish subjectivities. From its inception in 1899 as the Irish Literary Theatre, the Abbey's founding artists set out a reforming manifesto, characterized by Lady Augusta Gregory's statement that 'we will show that Ireland is not the home of buffoonery and of easy sentiment, as it has been represented, but the home of an ancient idealism'.[9] The Abbey set itself most forcefully against the genre of Stage-Irish melodrama, inherited from the popular theatres of the British Empire, which featured powerfully in the plays of the great Irish impresario Dion Boucicault. Theatre artists such as Sean O'Casey, W.B. Yeats, and J.M. Synge responded to this challenge by offering new models of the Irish body through an experimental modernism, and by utilising old forms of costume explicitly in order to reject them (see Figure 8.1).

The popular nineteenth-century stereotype of Irishness on stage depicted Irish men as drunken, violent, inarticulate, and irrational, maintaining a British colonial fantasy of Ireland as an infantilized and uncivilized place in need of imperial rule. Of course this stereotype was made instantly recognizable through the generic encoding of the Stage-Irishman's costume: his (usually green) ragged clothes, his stovepipe hat, and his ever-present shillelagh (a walking stick also used as a weapon) all served to encode the character as an instantly recognizable type. The female counterpart to the Stage-Irishman was the innocent young peasant girl, who was known by her costume of red shawl, petticoat, or bodice. These red costumes were enshrined in performance by Dion Boucicault's 1860 melodrama, *The Colleen Bawn*, setting off a souvenir trade and fashion trend among the female spectators of the London bourgeoisie who bought them as souvenirs and wore them to the theatre.[10] Red shawls also featured in nineteenth-century paintings of Irish peasant women such as Frederic William Burton's *The Aran Fisherman's Drowned Child* (1841), Augustus Nicholas Burke's *A Connemara Girl* (1865), and Ford Maddox Brown's *The Irish Girl* (1860), and were displayed in folk spectacles such as the Columbian Exhibition in Chicago in 1893 and the Imperial International Exhibition in London in 1909. Synge himself described them in his depiction of the Irish peasant women he observed on his many anthropological trips to the Aran Islands: 'their red bodices and white tapering legs make them as beautiful as tropical sea birds'.[11] Through the nineteenth century, then, red costumes functioned as the insignia for a generic and sentimentalized version of Irish femininity on the stage and in paintings, rendering any woman wearing them as instantly 'Irish' in a simplified, melodramatic form. Irish peasant women were depicted by theatre artists such

FIGURE 8.1: Example of Stage-Irishman costume, in an image by Samuel De Wilde of Mr Rock as the Irishman. Image courtesy of the Victoria and Albert Museum.

as Boucicault in the 1860s as uncouth and naïve but also pure of heart, standing in for a nostalgic depiction of innocent pre-modern femininity. This stereotype combined with that of 'Hibernia' or Mother Ireland in nationalist iconography in the period, too, as Barbara O'Connor has pointed out.[12]

In attempting to offer a counter-image to this inherited tradition of generic characters and costumed repertoires, which they saw as the debased, colonial misrepresentation of Irish identity, playwrights including Yeats, Gregory, Synge, and O'Casey experimented openly with the meanings of costume in their work, influenced by the dress-reform movements and the modernist theatrical experimentation taking place across Europe that we note above. This experimentation approached the meanings of inherited costume traditions through the adoption of a radically new repertoire of performance styles that undid the extant generic codes governing the relationship between performers and their costumes (for example, red petticoat as signifier for sentimental Irish melodrama). A particularly influential manifestation of this project can be seen in J.M. Synge's *The Playboy of the Western World*, which mixed conventional 'Stage-Irish' costumes with a stylized, even satirical form of realism. Set in a rural community in the west of Ireland, *Playboy* tells the story of Christy Mahon, whose claim to have murdered his father turns him into a local celebrity and sex symbol; he is then attacked by the community once he is exposed as a fraud. Central to the play's social critique is not only Mahon's tall tale of brutality, but the community's own hypocrisy in condemning him for it. The play caused huge controversy in its opening performances in Dublin in 1907, and was greeted by riots and protest.

Synge framed the *Playboy* as a modernist rejection of the languages of the popular bourgeois melodrama of the late nineteenth century. The power of the performance was located in the ways in which it relied upon the inherited visual repertoires of the Stage-Irish genre, most particularly in the use of red shawls, petticoats, and bodices to costume the female actors. However, when Synge deployed these generically encoded visual repertoires in his work, it was with the desire to upend a sentimental portrait of Irish poverty and to reveal the dark complexities and contradictions of Irish peasant life. When Pegeen Mike, the female protagonist of the play, appeared as 'a wild looking but fine girl [. . .] dressed in the usual peasant dress'[13] at the start of the play, it was clear that the visual world of the play relied upon a set of familiar generic codes that the performance set out to critique. It was not so much that Synge offered an alternative image to the popular colonial versions of Irishness, but rather that he orientalized them, estranging the familiar tropes so that they became 'tropical' for their modern Dublin audiences, a suggestion also contained in the play's title that invoked 'The Western World' as a distant and exotic space of otherness for bourgeois metropolitan spectators. Synge's use of red petticoats and shawls relied on his audience's intimate familiarity with the genre of Stage-

Irishness in order to make female Irish bodies intelligible onstage; it then estranged that familiar image in order to produce the crucial modernist experience of shock, depicting an inherited, colonial representation of Irish culture to modern Irish audiences as corrupt and hypocritical rather than safely and sentimentally comical. In essence, the characters wore the clothes from a theatre form that they no longer fit, to provocative political effect.

In fact, the controversy that ensued over *Playboy* emerged not only around female dress, but specifically around female underwear – the 'shift' or chemise invoked by Christy's line, 'it's Pegeen I'm seeking only, and what'd I care if you brought me a drift of chosen females, standing in their shifts itself maybe, from this place to the eastern world?'.[14] On this line during the play's premiere, pandemonium ensued in the auditorium, as Gregory put it in a telegram to Yeats: 'Audience broke up in disorder at the word shift'.[15] As Nicholas Grene explains, the word 'shift' had become taboo in London and Dublin, and uttering the term was seen to pollute a version of Irish womanhood held to be sacred by nationalists.[16] While the image of the Irish *colleen* produced by Boucicault had characterized the Irish peasant girls Eily O'Conor or Arrah na Pogue through their innocence and purity of heart, here, scandalously, Synge invoked what might be going on 'underneath' the costumes. The reaction of the *Freeman's Journal* was typical, describing the play as an 'unmitigated, protracted libel upon Irish peasant men, and, worse still, upon Irish peasant girlhood. . . . The worst specimen of Stage-Irishman of the past is a refined, acceptable fellow compared with that imagined by Mr. Synge'.[17] To invoke a sexualized image of womanhood with lines spoken from within costumes that resembled the powerful iconography of a sentimentalized melodrama was to upturn the meanings of these repertoires of dress and the political identities they encoded.

The source of the *Playboy* controversy can be pinned to Synge's 'leaky' employment of the generic image of Irish womanhood: notably, he did not overthrow that image, but reconfigured it so that the stage conventions usually produced by red shawls and petticoats were re-inscribed and reframed within a 'not this, but also this' logic that echoed the later work of Bertolt Brecht. Synge's production of shock relied directly upon the well-known generic codes of Stage-Irishness, the repertoire of costumes that produced it on stage, and the colonial vision of Irish bodies that it attempted to reject; the result of his remixing of repertoire (Stage-Irish dress) and genre (switching a sentimental, melodramatic framework for a critical, realist one) was upheaval inside the theatre, and a pointed political intervention beyond it.

The Emperor's New Costume

In Japan, modernity was first experienced as a great shock from abroad during the second half of the nineteenth century. After more than two hundred years of isolationist foreign policy, which had cut off the vast majority of Japanese people from the rest of the world and vice versa, the United States spearheaded a campaign, beginning in 1853, to force Japan to trade freely with them and other imperial powers. By 1868, the domestic turmoil surrounding Japan's forced re-calibration of international relations led to a regime change known as the Meiji Restoration. Although the new government gained power with the slogan *Sonnō jōi* (尊皇攘夷, 'Revere the emperor, expel the barbarian'), that refrain quickly changed to 'Civilisation and Enlightenment' (文明開化, or *bunmei kaika*). *Bunmei kaika* came to describe an all-encompassing cultural project of adopting and adapting Western practices in Japan in hopes of avoiding colonization and competing with Western nations for imperial supremacy on the global stage. This cultural project operated on both a macro level, with major changes to government (introducing a constitution and democratic legislative assembly), the military, and national infrastructure, as well as on a micro level, at which the government took an intimate interest in remaking the individual bodies of citizens, advocating and even coercing changes in diet, hairstyles, and clothing (for example, moving from kimono to Western dress).

Theatre in Japan during this time both obeyed the injunction to 'civilize and enlighten' and demonstrated the promises and perils of Japan's cultural makeover project. The long-established indigenous forms of theatre – principally *noh*, *bunraku*, and *kabuki* – were immediately relegated to 'backward' status within the paradigm of *bunmei kaika*. While *noh* is a high-status form, using slow and mysterious dancing and chanting to recount tales of mythological and supernatural happenings, and *kabuki* is famous for swashbuckling, sprawling narratives of valour, daring, or forbidden love, emerging theatre artists in Japan during the modern period drew primarily on European dramatists like Ibsen as inspiration for a new theatre form that would emphasize text over live performance elements and realistic acting and scenography over highly stylized, indigenous ones.

The project of Westernization in Japan went hand in hand with the project of modernization, and, just as in our Irish example, in Japan changing generic codes at the theatre reflected and supported these projects in large part through the re-styling of Japanese bodies on the stage. Costumes are a key mode by which bodies are interpellated into a social milieu; where *noh* and *kabuki* costumes are gorgeous, elaborate, and richly symbolic confections that render the actor's body monumentally impressive on stage, the new genres of *shinpa* (新派, 'New School') and *shingeki* (新劇, 'New Drama'), both modelled on European realism, favoured realistic costumes meant to be indistinguishable from everyday clothing. In some early performances of foreign plays in Japan, actors even donned blond wigs and fake noses to approximate those characters' European appearances.[18]

Such literal costuming may seem laughable now, but these experiments in cultural mimesis vividly materialize the deep crisis the *bunmei kaika* policy posed to Japanese subjectivity near the beginning of the twentieth century. In the theatre, the limits of cultural borrowing were tested and debated: what indeed is necessary to evoke 'modernity' in Japan? Is blond hair on a head a prerequisite for Western ideas inside that head? To what extent is the preoccupation with precise imitation of a model a hallmark of naturalism and realism? (For example, André Antoine, naturalist pioneer, famously hung real sides of beef in his slaughterhouse set for *The Butchers* in 1888.) What is most 'natural' to a play onstage – that artifice be used to make the actor resemble the character portrayed, or that an actor appears as indistinguishable from a 'real' person on the street as possible? Performing foreign plays with Japanese bodies forced a reckoning of how imported ideas could best be assimilated, and thus of how *bunmei kaika* could best be carried out by domestic bodies outside the theatre.

Experiments with foreign, realistic-looking costumes extended beyond the stage as they also shaped the struggle to define a new Japanese citizenry. Just as a director might use a character's choice of suit or kimono to declare something about that character's attitude toward policies of Westernization and modernization, so ordinary men and women in Japan used their personal appearance to situate themselves in shifting social contexts. For example, in the early twentieth century, the term *hai-kara* (ハイカラー) became a popular way to describe very modern and cosmopolitan, urbane young people – the term is a transliteration of the 'high collar' on their Western-style shirts. Although the term refers to men's shirts worn with ties, *hai-kara* could refer to men or women – what was important was less the specific item of clothing than the modern attitude such clothing denoted. *Hai-kara* people employed the performative power of clothing to present themselves as exemplary citizens of a modern, cosmopolitan Japan; in effect, they inhabited *bunmei kaika* as social genre on the stage of everyday life.

Perhaps the most 'realistic' change introduced via the adoption of the genres of *shinpa* and *shingeki*, however, was the return of women performers to a sex-desegregated stage. While some *bunmei kaika* changes had been fairly simple to make, others contradicted deeply held Japanese attitudes. Such was the case with women and mixed-gender performances: Japan's performing arts had been rigidly gender-segregated for generations, with *kabuki*, *bunraku*, and *noh* performed officially by men only beginning in the seventeenth century. (This despite the fact that the invention of *kabuki* is attributed to a woman named Okuni in 1603.) Meanwhile, women performed as *geisha* ('arts people') in tea houses and private parties, singing, dancing, and playing music in modes quite similar to those men pursued in *kabuki* and *bunraku*. Some critics made arguments against allowing women to take the stage on aesthetic grounds, arguing that women playing female characters would bring no artistry to the portrayal, that they would be merely themselves (women) rather than the idealized Woman that an *onnagata* could allegedly portray. In practice, early *shinpa* did feature both *onnagata* (male performers of female roles in *kabuki*) and actresses until the 1910s (and the traditional genres of *noh*, *kabuki*, *bunraku*, and *kyogen* at the professional level remain gender-segregated to this day).

The controversy about allowing women to perform on the modern stage exemplified other offstage issues regarding the role of women in the reorganized nation, particularly in regard to women's visibility. Indeed, their appearance on the stage might be considered a quintessential example of women's status as public individuals in modernizing Japan. Despite the fact that female characters had always appeared on stage, biological women, especially respectable wives and mothers, rarely made public appearances. In the Meiji period, at the same time that *shinpa* was negotiating the appearance of women as stage actresses, the wives and daughters of nobles and politicians were so unused to social appearances that many balls and banquets for the social elite were attended instead by hired *geisha* – 'public' women who were accustomed to mingling and entertaining and therefore more emboldened to play at the dancing and conversation-making required of European-style society interactions.[19] The appearance of female performers on the stage thus mirrored the rising visibility of women on the street, who increasingly took newly created jobs like those of elevator girls and shop assistants and attended new schools for women.[20] Modern girls were such a phenomenon that they even gained their own neologism: *moga*, a portmanteau of 'modern' and 'girl' (モダンガール: *modan ga-ru*).

Shinpa and *shingeki* experiments with both costumes and female performers baldly demonstrated the juxtaposition between inherited representations of the ideal Japanese body and Japanese conceptions of the (ideal) Western body, performing before audiences the collision of foreign and indigenous definitions of modernity. Attempting to forge a modernity recognizable to and approved by foreign powers lent a sense of self-conscious theatricality to the Japanese modernization project, what scholar Morris Low calls 'exhibitory modernity'[21]; yet, these imported ideas were subjected to a process of 'domestication' to Japan's unique situation.[22] In this way, Japanese citizens on and off the stage worked together to negotiate new, embodied practices that could instantiate a shared genre of Japanese modernity, enabling both economic trade and cultural exchange with the West that Japan sought to emulate. Direct generic borrowing from the Western stage reflected but also refracted clothing practices at street level; meanwhile, performances of self on the street were transformed by new uses of costume, dress, and the appearance of female bodies on the stage. As in the example of Synge's *Playboy*, an inherited genre (in this case, that of European realism) blended with culturally hybridized repertoires of dress and its embodied performance (wigs, high collars, and other trappings of Western style, practiced in estranging fashion on Japanese bodies both on and off stage) to generate both new, modern subjectivities (the *moga*, like the Irish colleen clad only in her shift) and a fresh national politics. As in the case of Irish nationalism, however, Japanese *bunmei kaika* could also not be practiced in a straightforward fashion. The generic codes deployed by authorities in the service of normalizing a hoped-for, modern national identity collided with quotidian practices on and off the stage as repertoires of dress challenged linear progress narratives and transformed performers' bodies into peculiar cultural hybrids.

INTERVENTIONS

Modern Girls Will Be Boys?

Japan's most wildly successful modern theatre domestication project appeared not from amongst the intelligentsia practicing *shingeki* and *shinpa*, but in a small town outside Osaka in 1914: Takarazuka, the all-female musical revue, was dreamed up by Kobayashi Ichizo, the owner of the private Hankyu rail line, as a tourism ploy. Expressly modelled on contemporary Parisian showgirl extravaganzas, but with a fierce emphasis on clean, family entertainment, the Takarazuka Revue featured actresses acting, singing, and dancing in both men's and women's roles. 'Takarasiennes' were advertised as good girls from upstanding families whose performances brought an exciting international flair to central Japan during the heyday of modernization. In this sense, Kobayashi's theatre appeared to be an exemplary *bunmei kaika* project, but in fact it was a hybrid undertaking, catering to the expectations of its domestic audiences with a deliberate appeal to exotic novelty. The gender segregation of the Revue cleverly inverted the generic performance codes of traditional Japanese all-male troupes while also relying on other, more traditional theatre practices such as *oshiroi* (the makeup used for white-face performance). Chosen for their height, beauty and foreign(esque) features, yet admonished to embody 'Japanese' values like modesty and filial loyalty, many Takarasiennes became celebrities, and emblematic of the *moga*. Takarasiennes, *shinpa* and *shingeki* actresses, and their off-stage counterpart the *moga*, together reflected the domestication of imported Western standards and instantiated new, hybridized repertoires of Japanese personal identity, fundamentally informed by the ongoing encounter with the West (see Figure 8.2).

In the early twenty-first century, the Takarazuka company remains arguably the most popular theatre in Japan, performing about a thousand shows a year and reaching 2.5 million audience members. While the majority of Takarazuka's repertoire remains the performance of stories set in far off places and times

FIGURE 8.2: Tokyo, Japan: Yuri Shirahane (L) as Queen Marie-Antoinette, Wataru Kozuki (C) as Swedish Count Hans Axel von Fersen, and Kei Aran (R) as female captain of the royal guard Oscar François de Jarjayes wave in the grand finale during the Takarazuka theatre's *The Rose of Versailles* final rehearsal in Tokyo, 17 February 2006. TOSHIFUMI KITAMURA/AFP/Getty Images.

(including adaptations of popular American musicals like *Guys and Dolls*, *West Side Story*, and *Gone with the Wind*), the company also presents stories and plays set in a fantastical, historical Japan. For example, the 2011 Cosmos troupe production, *A Beautiful Life – Ishida Mitsunari, His Eternal Love and Loyalty*, is set in the sixteenth century and tells the story of a noble samurai and his exploits. Although the plot features classic *kabuki* twists such as the forbidden love between a samurai and a concubine, it also includes Americanized song and dance numbers (like a jitterbug performed in front of Osaka castle), as well as handsome male characters played by women in very distinctive costumes that signify the features of the character alongside high-heeled shoes, fluffy dyed pompadours, and elaborate eye makeup. Like every Takarazuka show, this one ends with a spectacular curtain call, during which each star performer wears a glittering finale costume featuring large feather fans.

Takarazuka's well-honed formula retains its obvious relation to certain generic features of the Western musical revue, such as Las Vegas or Parisian showgirl feathers and Broadway or West End song and dance, but to the regular European or American audience member much of Takarazuka also seems quite bizarre. Beyond the unexpected mix of melodramatic storylines and requisite glitzy curtain call, what tends to be shocking is not so much that women are playing both the female and male roles but that in Takarazuka male characters present a highly stylized and (many fans would say) idealized portrayal of a man. Takarazuka features a very specific repertoire of gendered performance that offers up to the audience fantastical, exotic bodies performing virtuosic feats of artistry. While the wildly dressed, heavily made up, gender-bending Takarasienne is certainly not commonly thought of as an example provided for contemporary people to emulate, nevertheless she presents an exemplary postmodern Japanese body – carefully calibrated in terms of appearance, combining influences from around the globe into a uniquely Japanese model of virtuosic ability and virtuous offstage lifestyle.

In the Takarazuka version of traditional Japanese stories, even Japan's own history is exoticized as a timeless, romantic fantasy. This sense of all history 'universally available but equally emptied of meaning'[23] to be redeployed as pastiche is often considered fundamental to the 'postmodern condition' and yet in Takarazuka these detached signifiers of other times and places are consistently re-harnessed to contemporary concerns about what it means to embody Japanese values and represent oneself as a member of the national culture. In the early twentieth century the *moga*-Takarasienne helped to establish new norms for Japanese women: more publicly visible, with shorter hair, but still dutifully attached to hierarchical institutions and domestic moral virtues. Today, performance at Takarazuka continues to stage the ideal national body as a hybrid of traditional Japanese behaviours matched to generic practices from the US, Japan, and beyond; in its incredible popularity with Japanese audiences, the revue celebrates hybridity as essential to Japanese identity while also demonstrating practically the power of embodied repertoires to reconfigure completely the historical genres (Hollywood musical melodrama, stock *kabuki* narrative) on which Takarazuka's very currency relies.

Dancing Bodies

The eclecticism of national bodies seen in Takarazuka is also echoed in the codification of the Irish dance costume that emerged as a hybrid form in the early twentieth century. Unlike the costumes of Takarazuka, however, modern Irish dance costume was presented as if it were untouched by modernity. With the formation of the nationalist Gaelic League in Ireland in 1893, a growing interest in reclaiming Irish identity was expressed through the desire to 'purify' the Irish dance form's techniques, codes, and dress. As Nellie O'Brien put it: 'the man who has the Irish language on his lips will wish also to have Irish clothes on his back'.[24] Dance costumes were envisioned as not just a form of national dress – Irishness as something to be worn and performed, particularly by women – but as an embodiment of the new, independent, post-colonial nation more broadly. By 1901, the Gaelic League 'directed that no prize be awarded to a competitor in an *Oireachtas* (an Irish cultural festival) unless the competitor was dressed in clothes of Irish manufacture'.[25]

The first national dance dresses were inspired by the genre of Stage-Irishness and named 'colleen bawns' (due to the red skirts and white petticoats that resembled those of Boucicault's peasant women); this design was soon replaced, however, by a style of dress drawn from Eugene O'Curry's 1873 book, *On the Manners and Customs of the Ancient Irish*. The style was based on ancient Celtic designs, but it was also influenced by the Arts and Crafts aesthetic, designed as supposedly Celtic tunics but imagined along neo-classical lines, embroidered with motifs drawn from the medieval manuscript the *Book of Kells* and decorated with Tara brooches. Over time, these 'nationalist' costumes absorbed transnational influences, codifying the national Irish body as theatrical and hyperbolically feminine. By the 1980s, influenced by North American beauty pageant culture, the costume featured day-glo colours, lurid embroidery, and enormous curly wigs.

Then, in 1994, a ten-minute segment of the Eurovision Song Contest (a pan-European competition broadcast live on television and hosted in Dublin that year) changed the face (and body) of Stage-Irishness once more. *Riverdance* was choreographed and performed by the Chicago-born Michael Flatley, along with the New York-born Jean Butler and a chorus of Irish dancers. The piece radically transformed the ways in which the Irish national body was understood in Ireland and globally. Emerging as a two-hour stage show in the following year, the production has since toured to forty countries in four continents, and has been seen live by 20 million spectators (Figure 8.3).

Riverdance is notable for the way it transformed the visual and embodied vocabularies of the Irish dancing body, and this transformation was accomplished primarily through costume. Like Yeats, Synge, Gregory, and the other Irish nationalist playwrights we discuss above, *Riverdance* borrowed from older generic codes in order to renew them for a postmodern moment. *Riverdance*

FIGURE 8.3: Jean Butler and Colin Dunne in *Riverdance*, 1996. Photograph by Jack Hartin, by kind permission of Abhann Productions.

drew on an imagined, ancient Irish past, but mixed it deliberately with a globalized cosmopolitanism in order to invent a post-national Irish body.

In *Riverdance* female performers wore dresses that retained the silhouette of traditional Irish dance dress but were entirely black, with matte embroidery; the female dancers also wore their hair straight rather than curly. Flatley, as the lead virtuoso, marked his star status by donning a blue silk matador shirt, which reorganized his dance vocabulary: the shirt allowed him to move his arms, breaking the Irish dance convention of a rigid upper torso. Flatley's virtuosity was further established through his mastery of the vocabularies of other dance styles: even as his feet engaged in the steps of Irish dancing, he drew from Flamenco by elevating his torso and arms, from Salsa in the mobility of his hips, and he invoked the Broadway musical in his smile. Flatley and *Riverdance* therefore presented a theatricalized 'Irishness' as the organizing genre for a diasporic repertoire of dance forms. (This became most evident in the two-hour stage version of the show, which featured dancers from Spain, Russia, and the US, who performed their 'authentic' forms of folk dance as part of the spectacle.) *Riverdance* sold 'Irishness' as at once pure *and* globalized by styling Irish dance as rooted in local authenticity and yet fully internationalized, available for the enjoyment of audiences worldwide.

In the cultural reception of *Riverdance* the earlier, nationalist project of Yeats and Synge was framed as both exhausted and inauthentic. *Riverdance* continues to seek to restore the Irish body to its pre-State vitality, liberating it from the framework of the nationalist project through a modern form of dress and a global movement vocabulary. Yet, even as *Riverdance* lays claim to inventing a new, (post)modern Irish body through new versions of costume and bodily conduct, it relies on similar approaches to those employed by the Abbey artists: it essentializes other dance forms and performers as 'authentic' with the ultimate aim of revitalizing and re-inventing Irish dance for contemporary audiences.

ORIENTALIST CROSSINGS: IRISH *NOH*

We have seen how the conditions of globalization that gathered steam throughout the twentieth century produced modern national bodies in both Ireland and Japan; in each case, the invention and re-invention of the genres of 'national' costume on stage supported the development of new, modern bodily repertoires in the theatre and beyond. Two contrasting strategies supported this process: Westernized modernization in Japan, and the 'invention' of tradition in Ireland. However, both strategies relied heavily for their potency on European orientalism – a transnational aesthetic practice that played a major role in the development of theatrical modernism worldwide. In this section, we consider an example of how the Irish re-invention of national dress drew on a fantasy of an ancient Japanese culture that was simultaneously being renegotiated and revalued in Japan itself.

At the same time that Japanese *shimpa* and *shingeki* artists were imitating Western stage realism in concert with the policy of *bunmei kaika* and Kobayashi was mining Parisian musical revues to turn Takarazuka into a theatrical mecca, European avant-garde artists were looking to Asia for artistic inspirations in order to re-invigorate and revolutionize their practices. Antonin Artaud, for example, praised the Balinese dancers he saw at the Paris Colonial Exhibition in 1931 for seeming to him like 'animated hieroglyphs',[26] while Bertolt Brecht was inspired to model his epic acting techniques after the stylized, estranging performances of Mei Lan Fang, the Chinese opera star. As these examples suggest, many artists calling upon Asian forms were doing so to find ways of breaking with realist genres – just at the moment when avant-garde *shingeki* artists were advocating for Japanese theatre to adopt the tenets of realism. It is important to emphasize that these alternating currents of transnational 'borrowing' operated within very different political contexts – this was not an equal exchange. The revolutionizing of Japanese through realism was not simply something that Japanese theatre makers wanted to do; after decades of the *bunmei kaika* policy, they were operating in a society that had collectively agreed to believe that Western models were better and more civilized than Japanese ones, and that try as they might to invent new forms, indigenous ones would never measure up. By contrast, European artists' appropriation of Asian repertoires was characterized by their freedom to pick and choose, freely altering and re-imagining their sources to suit their artistic purposes. This privilege – to borrow from within a national repertoire, rather than being pressed to adopt the tenets of an entire stage genre – can be characterized by Edward Said's term 'orientalism', a powerful example of which emerges in a play written by W.B. Yeats and first performed in 1916.

Based on a *noh* play by Zeami, *At The Hawk's Well* concerns the mythical Irish warrior Cuchulain, who seeks to drink from the waters of an ancient well, having learned of its promises of immortality. Cuchulain is seduced by the mesmerizing dance of the female hawk spirit, who lures him into a confrontation with his enemy, the warrior queen, Aoife. Yeats collaborated on the production with the Japanese dancer Michio Ito, who choreographed the performance and also played the female hawk spirit, wearing a stylized costume designed by the French illustrator Edmund Dulac (Figure 8.4). From the beginning, then, the performance was a highly cosmopolitan affair, heightened by the fact that, as Aoife McGrath points out, Ito's dance practice was in turn strongly influenced by the techniques of modern artists such as Vaslav Nijinsky in Russia, Isadora Duncan in America, and Émile Jaques-Dalcroze in France.[27]

FIGURE 8.4: Michio Ito in costume as the Hawk Spirit in *At The Hawk's Well*, 1916. Digital positive from nitrate roll film negative. Image courtesy of the Coburn collection at the George Eastman House.

Despite the fact that he had had extensive European modern dance training in a range of forms and little if any training in *noh* – a form that performers are usually born into and trained in from childhood – Ito was cast by Yeats as the embodiment of ancient Japanese dance and culture. Ito complained: 'because I was billed as the Japanese Dancer, I had to create a Japanese atmosphere . . . My dancing is not Japanese'.[28] In Ito's frustrations we can hear some of the tensions that undergirded the project of inventing new bodily repertoires for the modern stage. In their hunger to revitalize the modern body and overthrow the exhausted practices of the nineteenth century, artists like Yeats sought out forms of performance that were imagined to predate their immediate European inheritance, reaching for models drawn from ancient cultures and rituals – Ancient Greece, mythical Ireland, and traditional Japanese performance, among others. In the process, Yeats essentialized and decontextualized those other practices, presenting Ito to audiences as an 'authentic' Japanese performer – as if authenticity could only be located in the past or in the east, guaranteed not by training or experience, but by Ito's Japanese body itself.

In his codification of the performer's body through stylised masks and ritualized costume, Yeats attempted in *At the Hawk's Well* to shape a revitalized, timeless Irish body. Like many other modernist experimenters, Yeats sought to counteract inherited and simplistic theatrical stereotypes of Stage-Irishness by offering a richly complex model of Irish identity through a renewed theatrical vocabulary, borrowed from abroad. And yet, even as Yeats did so, his orientalism also served, paradoxically, to oversimplify the identity of the Japanese dancer who performed in his plays, and the Japanese cultural practices that he had borrowed to restore his own Irish ones.

CONCLUSION

Our examples of experimentation with costume from Ireland and Japan show how theatres in an increasingly globalizing world nevertheless continued to emphasize the importance of national identity and the harnessing of citizens' bodies to the great work of embodying the nation, ideologies that would be carried to their most terrifying extreme in the Second World War. Our case studies in this chapter have come from Japan and Ireland, but the combination of striving towards a global modern future and borrowing from an imagined past has informed theatrical projects around the world throughout the twentieth century. In Soviet Russia, Futurist artists such as Vladimir Mayakovsky and Vsevolod Meyerhold intertwined popular and folk performance forms with a technologically utopian vision of a liberated worker's body clad in overalls and working like a machine. (See Chapter 6 for more on Mayakovsky and Meyerhold.) In the 1930s and 1940s, the Nazi German nationalist fervour that fuelled the Second World War was fed by mythologizing about folk culture in tandem with the drive to eugenically purify the national body. By contrast, since the 1970s feminist artists like Sandra Ogel, Bobby Baker, and Lois Weaver have turned to traditional craft and feminine folkways in order to re-imagine and revalue domestic work, developing a politicized repertoire of feminist performances in the process. Meanwhile, even as modern theatre forms such as those we have surveyed here depended increasingly on borrowed practices, actors travelled the globe with both costumes and their repertoires in tow, carrying new fashions with them – and with those fashions new models for embodying modern subjectivity on the streets of emerging global centres.[29]

Costume inserts the body into its social and cultural contexts – as we have seen in Japan and Ireland, the challenges of creating a 'national' body in a rapidly globalizing world have been persistently worked out through theatre and performance costume practices throughout the twentieth century. Repertoires of costume establish and refine how national identities appear, or are believed to appear, *as genre* both on stage and in the world beyond the theatre; even as these repertoires were increasingly constituted through intercultural exchange during the twentieth century, national identity remained an overriding preoccupation of the age. In pointing out the theatrical fantasies required to establish any identity as pure or authentic, we begin to realize that national identity may be a fiction that can only ever be realized within the frame of performance. This realization, too, is a legacy of the generic evolutions and revolutions of the modern age.

CHAPTER NINE

Technologies of Performance

Machinic Staging and Corporeal Choreographies

ASHLEY FERRO-MURRAY AND TIMOTHY MURRAY

> Contradictions are our only hope!
> – Brecht, 'The Film, The Novel, and Epic Theatre'

The past century witnessed a series of technological revolutions that deeply impacted the social relations and cultural productions of their time. In this chapter, we review technological production from 1900 to the present to consider how playwrights, directors, and performers capitalized on the availability of new theatrical machinery to shape their works. The chapter tracks performance's incorporation of and commentary on technologies across three technological periods: the mechanical age, the televisual age, and the age of the Internet. Within each technological era we explore various approaches to technology that establish trends in theatrical experimentation, while also exposing contradictions in approaches to technology in performance. The role of the performing body will emerge as a central focus as we examine the marriage of theatre and technology during all three periods. Theatre, as an art form predicated on the liveness of bodies on stage, had a distinct opportunity to comment on the relationship between bodies and their identities in twentieth- and early twenty-first-century cultural productions of technology. Consideration of the body's conception *as a technology* in the modern age will be important to understanding the cultural implications of technology in the theatre and in culture more broadly, especially in relation to class, gender, sexuality, and race.

We begin with the Industrial Era in the late nineteenth and early twentieth centuries and the concurrent invention of assembly line machinery and cinema. In this era, machines had a major impact on theatrical production, from the mechanization of body movement in Vsevolod Meyerhold's acting techniques to the integration of emerging theatre technologies by the Futurists, who go so far as to ponder performance without bodies in which technology itself becomes the actor. The theatrical exploration of the relationship between the body and technology emerges as a pattern in performance during this time. In the mid-twentieth century, popular culture technologies, from television to video, enlivened the debate about the importance of live, non-recorded performance that first surfaced at the turn of the century with cinema. The increasing ubiquity of screen culture peaked in the late twentieth century with the development of personal computers, the Internet, and, eventually, mobile devices. We consider how hybrid body-technology approaches have helped to shape political performances that incorporate identity critique in this later period.

Performers from the 1960s onward specifically acknowledged the influence of the technological experimentations of the century's earlier directors and theoreticians, especially Antonin Artaud and Bertolt Brecht. Before turning to the important technological legacies of Artaud and Brecht, we provide an historical overview of theatrical approaches to technology at the turn of the twentieth century, with the arrival of industrialization and cinema. The chapter's second section, 'Gestures of Contradiction: Legacies of Artaud and Brecht', then traces the proliferation of post-war technologies across the rise of avant-garde theatre, performance art, and political theatre from the 1950s to the 1970s. In our final section, 'Technogestures and Virtuality', we discuss theatrical approaches to the digital technologies that promised, by the end of the twentieth century, to substitute the presence of the live, acting body with the virtuality of cyborgs and teleportic machineries. We will show how feminist performance, work about HIV/AIDS culture, and the exploration of racial identity was central to late twentieth-century imaginings of the interrelationship between theatre and technology.

Responding to Brecht's proclamation, 'contradictions are our only hope!', we seek throughout the chapter to illustrate the many paradoxes that arise when charting the history of body-technology relationships brought about by innovations in performance. Conceiving of the body as a technology of theatre and performance in its own right, we dialogue with the artists whose work we discuss in order to imagine how bodies and technologies oppose, limit, or even extend one another in the theatre of the twentieth and early twenty-first centuries. As we shall see, bodies and technology operate in a constant feedback loop throughout the so-called 'modern age'.

THE MECHANICAL AGE: THE RISE OF MACHINE CULTURE IN PERFORMANCE

The rise of machine culture in the late nineteenth and early twentieth centuries impacted modern notions of humans, their bodies, and their emotions. Most pronounced were the effects of the scientific management of Taylorism on both industrial and artistic life. Robert Winslow Taylor's philosophy of economic efficiency and labour productivity prompted assembly line work models, and promoted an aesthetic of mechanization, efficiency, and uniformity. In the aftermath of the Industrial Revolution, the everyday human actor became harmonized with the industrial machine and equated with motorization. Anson Rabinbach chronicles principles of Taylorism whereby the human body is to 'conserve, deploy, and expand the energies of the laboring body' in order to eliminate the final obstacle of efficient progress: 'the stubborn resistance to perpetual work that distinguished the human body from the machine'.[1] The movements of assembly line workers, for example, aesthetically mimicked the movements of the machines on which they worked. Each worker had a distinct job that required repetitive physical performance, and each body became yet another gear in the factory machine, completing one task so the entire machine could run smoothly and, most importantly, efficiently. The incorporation of bodies into mechanical rhythm and uniformity stripped individual workers of their identities and equated them with the disembodied parts of a machine. Their labour energies were thus equivalent to the motorized energy driving production.

This industrialization of the body left an indelible mark on the aesthetics of performance throughout the twentieth century. One of the most famous popular performances of this uniform machine aesthetic was the chorus line dance performed by the Tiller Girls. John Tiller established The Tiller Girls dance group in Manchester, England, in 1890 in response to his sense that a lack of discipline diminished the effect of the chorus line in theatre. Tiller extracted the chorus line from the theatrical performance, isolating it in order to perfect the precision of the girls' movements. The Tiller Girls would perform mass chorus line numbers in the manner of the Rockettes of the later twentieth century: the dancers hooked arms and rotated en masse, all while performing kick-line movements with the utmost precision. Together, the performers' movements resembled patterns that one might see in a kaleidoscope. In his famous 1923 essay, 'The Mass Ornament', Siegfried Kracauer associates the precision of Tiller performances with machine aesthetics, labelling the Tiller girl the agent of industrial capitalism. Kracauer argues that Tiller's chorus line is no longer made up of individual girls, but of 'indissoluble girl clusters' that are 'composed of thousands of bodies, sexless bodies in bathing suits'.[2] Moving seamlessly from lines to circular formations to create intricate shapes, which Kracauer calls 'ornaments', the chorus line positions its female dancers as one cohesive unit in motion. Kracauer explains, 'The bearer of the ornaments is the mass and not the people [Volk]' as it exhibits only 'remnants of the complex of man that enter into the mass ornament'.[3] Participants of the ornament, 'The Tiller Girls can no longer be reassembled into human beings after the fact'.[4] Instead, the performers' ability to fade into the ornament demonstrates a technical virtuosity that parallels mastery over human motor efficiency, which was exemplary in industrial projects. As Kracauer poetically puts it, 'The hands in the factory correspond to the legs of the Tiller Girls'.[5]

This early imprint of industrialization on performance carried over into emergent theories of the theatre. To Edward Gordon Craig, actors should no longer serve as the active agents of realistic interpretations of dramatic character but should be relegated to the function of symbolic marionettes. Redefining theatre away from dramatic author, actor, character, realism, and historical verisimilitude, Craig emphasized the machinic inventions of design as well as the centrality of the director ('the true artist of the theatre'). In his influential essay, 'The Art of the Theatre' (1905), he argued that directorial vision should be artistic rather than representational. To facilitate directorial control over the vision of performance, Craig introduced to the stage the use of mobile, hinged screens. He provided these mobile units to the Abbey Theatre in Ireland to enhance the symbolist aesthetic of William Butler Yeats, and he also employed them in his co-production with Stanislavsky of *Hamlet* at the Moscow Art Theatre in 1912. Following something of an industrial model, Craig outlined his scheme in a 1910 patent application. He likewise re-invented the conventions of lighting, moving the theatre away from bright frontal footlights that enriched spectatorial appreciation of actors' facial expressions and towards ceiling lighting, which rendered a rich palette for backgrounds, enveloping the actors in emotive veils of colour. Indeed, Craig's innovations in colour and design served the effect of rendering the actors as cogs, tools in his overall emphasis on theatre's production value. Adolphe Appia also adapted such an emphasis on light and dramatic space for his productions of Richard Wagner's operas. Encouraging his actors to frame their movements with forceful symbolic gestures, he carried on the tradition of 'machine aesthetics' by synchronizing theatrical space, light and performance gesture with the rhythms of Wagner's music.

It is no surprise, then, that the strong cultural shift towards early twentieth-century mechanization and efficiency would also influence the theatre, which had previously been a space for narrative-based drama and a haven for naturalist expressions of human emotion – the antithesis of efficient labour and mechanical designs of gesture and set. Known for the incorporation of machine philosophy into his formal approach to theatre, Russian constructivist director and producer Vsevolod Meyerhold developed a method for acting that he called 'biomechanics'. While distinct from promoting a mechanized body devoid of emotional expression, biomechanics likened the 'actor of the future' to the productive industrial worker. Meyerhold's explicitly Taylorist approach to acting influenced several aspects of his theatre. First and foremost the actor's body was to be centred on gravity, focused on rhythm, and was to drive the physical efficiency of his acting. Meyerhold explained that the actor 'will be working in a society where labour is no longer regarded as a curse, but as a joyful, vital necessity'.[6] Biomechanics promoted the complete integration of art into working life such that art, which Meyerhold otherwise associated with rest, developed a 'vital' function. Theatre should synchronize the economies of movement and time. The actor must use his time 'as economically as possible'.[7] Meyerhold embraced the contradictions of what this might entail in the context of traditional staging. He costumed his actors in overalls, an outfit that could move seamlessly from art to work. Brockett, Mitchell, and Hardberger emphasize his belief that to create exuberant joy, 'it may be more efficient for the actor to plummet down a slide or to swing on a trapeze than to restrict himself to normal human behavior'.[8] Rather than emphasize internal emotional motivations, biomechanics relied on external apparati and kinetic experience to produce emotions in actors.[9] Emotion in Meyerhold's constructivist theatre, then, became not a characteristic of human behaviour, but, instead, a mechanical response to kinetic acts.

While the machine aesthetics of the early twentieth century had conceptual and aesthetic consequences for theatrical practice, the machines themselves also had a profound impact on the mechanics of theatrical spectacle. Italian Futurism, the first twentieth-century avant-garde movement, manipulated revolutionary technological effects such as coloured gases, artillery and aeroplanes to inspire innovations in stage design and theatrical effects. Like Meyerhold's constructivist theatre, the Futurists also abandoned the emotionally driven narrative. By 1925, the Futurist theatre had displaced the role of the actor altogether. Enrico Prampolini's 'Futurist Scenic Atmosphere' manifesto placed all of the focus on design, rendering the human actors no more than '"luminous plastic elements" floating through an "electro-dynamic polydimensional" stage'.[10]

One consequential effect of the actor's relative effacement in the electronic nexus is a corollary indifference to issues pertaining to what we appreciate today as the politics of performer identity. This does not mean, however, that Italian Futurism lacked identity politics per se. Steve Dixon has explored how the first Futurist manifesto 'reads like the posturing taunts of drunken men spoiling for a fight, full of youthful machismo'.[11] Given this macho drive of the technologies of Futurism, it is not surprising that playwright Mina Loy, after writing several feminist Futurist plays, left the movement and attacked its misogyny in her satirical play *The Pamperers* (1916).[12] The increasing mechanization of the theatrical actor, set, stage, and narrative in the early twentieth century and the subsequent uniformity and dehumanization of performers often precluded any opening to the kinds of progressive perspectives (such as feminism) that might account for some notion of personal difference in performance. As Kracauer observed of the Tiller Girls, machine aesthetics produced the appearance of 'sexless bodies in bathing suits'.[13]

But the incorporation of machine technology into early modernist performance also did not guarantee the eradication of the gendered body under the regime of theatrical futures. Loïe Fuller, an American pioneer in stage lighting and modern dance working in the 1890s in France, became famous for a performance style she developed called the serpentine dance (see Figure 9.1). The dance relied on a large silk skirt, which she twirled and swirled around her body as she danced. Fuller worked wooden dowels to extend the reach of her arm, and thereby signalled the fluid dynamism of the corporeal that would thrust fabric into space. Fuller illuminated the silk fabric with revolutionary, multi-coloured lights, creating the illusion that the movements of her body and skirt propelled the movement of colour. While some argue that Fuller's performance technique turned the body into an anthropomorphic figure of fabric and lighting, Fuller's technologized stage performance can be appreciated, on the contrary, for its foregrounding of the performer herself.[14] Fuller's physically strenuous movements enabled her to explore the impact of her moving body in time and space. Even more, the artist's scientific development of lighting technologies coupled with her choreography and gesture performed an early feminist appropriation of performance technologies. As a woman manipulating the power positions of choreographer and lighting designer, Fuller turned modern dance – a naturalist performance of femininity that historically opposed the primitive body to the modern machine – into an early performative exploration of how female bodies and technologies could powerfully interface with one another.

GESTURES OF CONTRADICTION: LEGACIES OF ARTAUD AND BRECHT

Early twentieth-century artists embraced Fuller's performances for their promising formalism, and pioneering filmmakers the Lumière Brothers restaged the dazzle of her 'Serpentine Dance' for film in 1896. To do so, they freeze-framed the swirling motions of Fuller's dance in order to laboriously hand-tint each frame, thus rendering Fuller a product of their own aesthetic imaginary. The art nouveau sculptor, François-Raoul Larche, similarly encased the flow of Fuller's performances in the fixed form of sculpture. But it was just this sort of formalist encasement of the performing body, transforming it into an aestheticized object, which raised the ire of Antonin Artaud in the later 1920s. Rather than champion a design aesthetic based on corporeal control and predictably mechanized form, Artaud's Futurist embrace of a theatre of 'Becoming' aimed to be unpredictably anarchical in movement, gesture, design, and time. Arguing that theatre should abandon the dramatic 'culture through words' for a 'culture through gestures', Artaud proposed an anarchist aesthetic that would challenge

FIGURE 9.1: Loïe Fuller in *La Danse Blanche*. Photograph by Tabor Prang Art Co. Courtesy of The Jerome Robbins Dance Division, New York Public Library for the Performing Arts.

'all object to object relations and the signification of form'.[15] He insisted, very energetically, that theatre 'should break from actuality so that its object is not to resolve social or psychological conflicts, is not to serve as a battleground for moral passions, but to express objectively secret truths, to bring to light by active gestures that aspect of truth hidden in the forms of their encounters with Becoming'.[16] His embrace of the potential of theatre stemmed from his disappointing encounter with the mechanical and industrial qualities of film, in which he had expressed early hopes. Stymied by the conventions and politics of the early French film industry, he then put all of his efforts into liberating performance from the culture of capital and bourgeois identification that linked theatrical realism to the burgeoning culture of cinema. Artaud became enamoured, instead, by the magical realism of Mexico and the mysteries of Balinese puppet theatre (an interest his critics would later problematize for its colonial taint). This anarchical prophet of the theatre nevertheless recommended a combination of very 'concrete and spatial' revolutions on the stage by surrounding the audience with the action and by pummelling safely distanced spectators with the confusing energies of unbridled spectacle. By championing the technical extremes of movement, lighting, sound, and design whose 'language of gesture [is] designed to evolve in space',[17] Artaud dismissed the culture of the 'detached art' of bourgeois decadence and entertainment that he perceived both on the narrative realist stage and in the modern cinema to permit the dramatic creation of a 'passionate equation between Man [l'Homme], Society, Nature, and Objects'.[18]

We cannot overstate the broad cultural implications of Artaud's artistic reaction to the 'detached art' of the performing body. His foregrounding of the technologies of *affective* performance has had a pivotal influence on the theatre across the modern age: from performative gesture to violent cry, from piercing light to deafening sound, from surround-space to uncontrolled action. He championed the human body as *the* primary theatrical technology in the service of a theatre that wishes to wake up the masses and prompt a cultural revolution. He believed that these mass publics would embrace performance technologies that provided access to 'the human skin of things'.[19] His 'theatre of cruelty' was designed for those excluded from the cultural order by the theatrical boredoms of the proscenium stage, with its focus on dramatic character and bourgeois virtue, those dramatic conventions of 'the literary chefs-d'oeuvre' from Strindberg to Chekhov.[20] Although Artaud is not featured prominently in histories of theatre and technology, his emphasis on the cultural shifts made possible by technological performance, as well as his articulation of the body as an unpredictable theatrical technology in itself, became key, as we shall later discuss, to the evolution of performance's relationship to technology in the latter half of the twentieth century.

This anarchical approach to performance technology in response to the perceived cultural malaise of realist and bourgeois theatre worked differently for German Bauhaus and epic theatre. László Moholy-Nagy first articulated the Bauhaus concept of 'Total Theatre' in 1925: it would shape all disparate artistic and architectural elements of a performance into a harmonious whole. Particularly important was his emphasis on technology within this paradigm. As Brockett, Mitchell, and Harberger argue, Moholy-Nagy championed 'the amplification of voices and inner thoughts, close-up images of faces and gestures, recordings and films. He advocated directional sound and multiple projections and suggested that artists . . . had not yet begun to realize the potential of light'.[21] Very much in tune with Craig and Meyerhold, the Bauhaus approach to 'total theatre' emphasized mechanics over character, and machineries of performance over deliveries of emotion. But it was Erwin Piscator who profited from the Bauhaus project to shift the aesthetics of 'total theatre' to the more culturally oriented context of what he called 'political theatre'. Sharing the contempt of both Moholy-Nagy and Artaud for the bourgeois address of realist theatre's distancing proscenium, Piscator's commitments were even more decidedly social and political. Deeply influenced by the cultural traumas of the First World War and the Russian Revolution, Piscator turned to stage technology to awaken the political consciousness of the public.[22] Regarding his 1927 production of Rasputin by Leo Tolstoy at the Berlin Theatre am Nollendorfplatz, which portrays the subjection of the monk, *Rasputin*, to the power of the Russian royal family, Piscator stressed the politics of world history rather than melodrama, using technological experimentation to deliver political commentary while undermining the emotional identifications typical of melodrama. This shift hinged on a set shaped like a globe that opened up segmented acting platforms and turned on a rotating platform. The globe's white exterior surface doubled as a projection screen for imagery culled from 6,000 feet of archival film. Noting the use of three projectors, Piscator's wife, Maria Ley-Piscator, adds that 'another screen was hung above the globe, while a narrow filmstrip, a kind of "calendar", on one side of the stage kept a multitude of events rolling, giving dates and marginal footnotes'.[23] Proclaiming the beginning of a new dramaturgy that combined film-based media and theatre, Ley-Piscator boasted how 'the film accompanied the action, clarified it, and sometimes even anticipated it'.[24]

Bertolt Brecht described Piscator's technological dramaturgy as 'causing theatrical chaos' in the name of politics.[25] Known for his early exchanges with Piscator and his embrace of Marxist epic theatre, Brecht ironically lamented that Piscator's 'aesthetic considerations were completely political'.[26] Brecht thought that the cinematic and technological heaviness of Piscator's apparatus foregrounded audience instruction at the expense of entertainment – a politically naïve move. Similar to Artaud, but with a fierce commitment to Marxism, Brecht embraced technologies of gesture as a means of returning both the pleasurable attraction and the critical power of aesthetics into the dramatic mix. Like Artaud, Brecht understood the acting body as a fundamental technology of performance. But rather than work to overwhelm the spectator with erratic movement and forceful facial contortions, Brecht worked to develop micro- and macro-movements that would remove the 'fourth wall' of illusion and remind the audience of their critical distance from the spectacle and its fable. For example, in the 1950 Berliner Ensemble production of *Mother*

Courage and Her Children, after Courage's daughter Kattrin is shot by Catholic soldiers, one simple gesture disrupted Courage's mourning over Kattrin's death. While gathering money for her daughter's funeral, Courage (Helena Weigel) paused to put some of the coins back into her purse, saving them to purchase more goods to sell for profit to the soldiers of war. In this single, epic 'gestus', Courage's display of the greed of business within the depths of war worked to interrupt any spectatorial identification with her grief.

In his plays, Brecht consistently frames the actor's epic gestures with simple yet effective technologies. He became infamous for shining a bright light on the stage to violate the conventions of the soft illusions of muted lighting. Describing his lighting choices for the 1949 Berlin production of *Mother Courage*, Brecht writes that brilliant light 'enabled us to get rid of any remnants of "atmosphere" such as would have given the incidents a slightly romantic flavor'.[27] He also typically bared the stage wings to reveal the technological supports that were traditionally hidden to enhance a set's magical illusions. For the same production of *Mother Courage*, Brecht utilized a burlap cyclorama behind a completely empty stage. He expressed satisfaction with how the illusion of 'a flat landscape with a huge sky' served both the beginning and ending of this play by reflecting the continuous devastations of war. It permitted the actors to suggest 'at the start that there is a wide horizon lying open to the business enterprise of the small family and their canteen, then at the end that the exhausted seeker after happiness is faced by a measureless devastation'.[28] Brecht staged the social contradictions of his plays in a way that dismantled the illusionistic theatrical apparatus, from corporeal figure to architectural form, in order to boost the audience's ability to demystify the dramatic principles of imitation as well as the cultural principles of capital.

In elaborating on his 'gestic principle', which would instill in the spectator a critical view of the cultures of capitalism, Brecht argued that his approach permitted a complete revolution in stage design. 'A representation that alienates', Brecht argued in 'A Short Organum for the Theatre', 'is one which allows us to recognize its subject, but at the same time makes it seem unfamiliar'.[29] What became known as Brecht's Alienation-effect (A-effect), or what has been translated more recently as the 'Distancing-effect', relies on uncanny techniques of distancing to separate the spectators critically from illusionistic identification. Everything depends on the strategic application and portrayal of *Gestus*. In further contrast to Piscator's theatre, which Brecht admired but found far too heavy-handed in its political aesthetics, a crucial element of Brecht's gestural principle is what he called its parsimony. Supplementing his imperative of the economies of acting technique, music, and choreography, Brecht aligns his many technologies of the stage around the simplicity of the 'poor' gesture.[30] The stark gestures of his epic theatre, performed simply by human actors, extended across the 'epic' performance apparatus, moving alongside its sparse use of placards, projections, open platforms, indexical costume, acting style, and choreography. Human and machine technologies worked in counterpoint to provoke a theatrical politics. (See Chapter 6 for a discussion of Brecht and Meyerhold in relation to audience agency.)

THE TELEVISUAL AGE: POST-WAR PERFORMANCE

While it is generally recognized that no major innovations in technology significantly altered the terrain of performance in the first two decades after the Second World War, the legacies of Artaud and Brecht continued to impact this period's nexus of technology, performance, and theory. In this section, we will elaborate on two contrasting, if not contradictory, directions: (1) related developments in the poor theatre, The Living Theatre, and The Performance Group; (2) expansive inclusion in performance of the newer electronic technologies of television, satellites, and computing, a televisual interface that would flourish from the 1970s onward.

The legacy of Brecht's emphases on simplicity and the enhancement of critical distance by making staging 'poor' is nowhere more apparent than in Jerzy Grotowski's (1933–1999) articulation of 'a poor theatre'. The Polish director decried the tradition of total or 'rich theatre' since it 'depends on artistic kleptomania, drawing from other disciplines, constructing hybrid-spectacles, conglomerates without backbone or integrity, yet presented as an organic artwork'.[31] Grotowski turned his focus to the technologies of performance interaction. He created minimal and flexible stage spaces that permitted movement and interaction between the actors and spectators. He forsook elaborate lighting and cinematic projection to allow for stationary light-sources with which the actor could experiment with shadows and bright spots, permitting the spectators to 'become visible' in an illuminated zone and thereby 'play a part in the performance'.[32] Returning to the simpler precedents of acting theory, Grotowski believed that the technology of lighting actually inhered in the actors themselves, who 'can "illuminate" through personal technique, becoming a source of "spiritual light"'.[33]

This shift from technology's literal electronics to technology as a complex interaction between actor and spectator crossed the Atlantic at the mid-century. Blending the legacies of Brecht and Artaud, it was best typified by the influential performances of Judith Malina and Julian Beck's The Living Theatre. For its performances, which were informed by protests against the war in Vietnam and related cultures of non-violence and anarchism, The Living Theatre elected to include no scenery or traditional stage space. This permitted the actors of its infamous *Paradise Now* (1968) to marshal a kind of Artaudian and Grotowskian 'illumination', directly assaulting (assumed) middle-class spectators with obscenities and invectives. This abandonment of the fourth wall for the direct involvement of spectators also typified the 'environmental theatre' of Richard

Schechner's The Performance Group. Its controversial New York production, *Dionysus in '69* (1969), shocked the theatre world with its performers' nude and sexual contact with each other and audience members. An adaptation of Euripides' *The Bacchae*, Schechner's performance capitalized on the multilevel in-the-round space provided by the Performing Garage in New York City. Surrounded by and in close proximity to the audience, Schechner's troupe 'would by turns chant, or dance, make love, plot murder, whisper to the audience, or among themselves hold group therapy sessions'.[34] The bare life of these emotions spilled over into live physical and sexual interactions with audience members. Technology here essentially was rendered bare, in all senses of the term.

In sharp contrast to Schechner's minimalist, spatially interpersonal performance, influenced more by the holistic magic of Artaud than by the critical distance of Brecht, we can plot the parallel development of an early tradition that brought the televisual into performance. The Wooster Group emerged from Schechner's ensemble. Its founders, Elizabeth LeCompte and Spalding Gray, created a multivalent environment of performance that frequently combined mixed-media and traditional theatre technologies. Similarly, Richard Foreman's Ontological Hysteric Theatre combined the traditions of Artaud and Brecht in its strategic use of blinding spotlights and deafening sound.

A prior cultural excitement over the new apparati of television and satellite transmission in the 1950s and 1960s gave rise to theatrical experiments that openly dialogued with such post-war developments in technology and that carved the path for the digital multimedia platforms of the 1970s onward. Josef Svoboda (1920–2002) extended the legacies of Moholy-Nagy, Meyerhold, and Piscator as the principal designer at the Czech National Theatre where he developed the 'kinetic stage' by combining a wide range of mechanical and electrical devices with film projection, hydraulics, and even three-dimensional pillars of light.[35] His electronic installations for Expo '58 in Brussels left a particularly strong imprint on the future of technological performance. The dazzling piece, *Laterna Magika*, set the precedent for the kinds of large-scale multimedia installations now common in the age of global biennales. Eight mobile screens were arranged in the stage space with directional reflective surfaces that could move, fold, rotate, rise, and fall in rhythm with the actors. Multi-speaker stereophonic sound accompanied the polymorphous projects of three film and two slide projectors, to which actors responded live.[36] Svoboda later extended these techniques for his productions of Wagner across Europe. His 1974 staging of *The Ring* at Covent Garden featured a mirrored surface on the bottom of the stage platform that permitted audiences to view scenes enacted below stage level, just as giant lenses magnified characters and simulated movie close-ups to emphasize the power relationships in Wagner's opera.[37]

French designer Jacques Polieri (1928–2011) embraced the new media of the post-war years even more boldly. What Salter calls Polieri's 'electronic image scenography' blended reality with electronic visualizations and extended to the development of huge outdoor projection screens that simulcast live video feeds. The impact of his interest in 'the mobility and three-dimensionality of the emission and reception of acoustic and visual data'[38] can be tracked along two parallel lines that flow into the video and digital multimedia performance traditions of the 1970s onward. In one direction, Polieri's experimentation with large-scale electronic spectacles that merged concrete space and visual tableau led to the work of Robert Wilson, Laurie Anderson, and Ping Chong, whose live performers were dwarfed on stage by colossal electronic visuals and sounds that shaped the conceptual content of their works. Their theatre has been aligned with what Stefan Brecht coined the 'theatre of visions' as it privileges the visual as significantly independent of 'verbal, intellectual, or discursive analysis'.[39] These large-scale spectacles opened the door for later multimedia performances that incorporated the complexities of computing. Notable among many others are the collaborations between the conceptual director, Herbert Blau, and electronic artists Woody and Steina Vasulka, in their restaging of *Jacob's Room* by Morton Subotnick at the American Music Theatre in 1993, or William Forsythe's complex multimedia choreographies performed by his company based in Frankfurt, Germany, from the 1990s until 2015.

In another under-explored direction, and which we would like to foreground as being crucial to the history of modern performance and technology, Polieri's openness to spatial and televisual technologies was compatible with international developments in conceptual art in the 1950s and 1960s. The French conceptual artist, Yves Klein, acknowledged the vision of Polieri, with whom he worked while exhibiting at the 1956 Festival d'Avant-Garde in Marseille (which Polieri co-directed with the French architect Le Corbusier).[40] One can hear the compatibility of their visions in Klein's lecture to the Sorbonne on 'immateriality' in art when he urged artists to embrace the emergent technologies of space and to expand the artistic toolbox to include the immaterial forces of electronics, fire, and performance.[41] Such openness to technics in the broadest sense continues to impact today's global art scene, from the pyrotechnic and digital installations of Chinese artists Cai Guo-Chiang and Xu Bing, to Joan Jonas's multimedia performance in the US Pavilion at the 2015 Venice Biennale, whose installation spans the history of her choreographic media performances since the 1970s.

Multimedia work by these contemporary performance artists from East and West is deeply indebted to earlier, pioneering experiments that blended performance and video art. For example, feminist performance artist Charlotte Moorman collaborated with video artist Nam June Paik on a series of pieces that incorporated miniature video monitors and experimental electronic imagery into the extemporaneous scene of performance.[42] Making an indelible mark on video performance in the late 1960s and 1970s, Moorman became especially well known for performing her cello topless in many Paik pieces. In the most infamous performance, 'TV Bra for Living Sculpture' (1969), she covered her nude torso with video 'bras', which Paik had constructed out of miniature television screens to broadcast audiovisual collages appropriated from TV imagery. She also performed her cello for 'TV Bed' (1972) while lying on top of an assemblage of video monitors in a way that contrasted her active performing body with the objectification of women in post-war televisual culture.[43] This combination of high and low cultural references foregrounded the historical representation of woman as generally marginal in musical and performance history, and as objectified sexually in art history. In contrast to these traditions, Moorman stood proud as a female performer whose televisual underwear brought her into critical dialogue with the patriarchs of mainstream TV and classical music composition and performance.[44]

Argentinian artist and FLUXUS member Marta Minujín, meanwhile, took televisual performance to an even higher level. Moving away from staging herself on video and towards artistic experimentation with transmission itself, she collaborated as early as 1966 with another FLUXUS member, Wolf Vostell of Germany, and American artist Allan Kaprow, to take performance work literally into space. For their collaborative piece, 'Simultaneity in Simultaneity', which Minujín called an 'environment signal' event, the artists simulcast on radio, TV, telephone, and telegraph their performance happenings in Buenos Aires, Berlin, and New York.

THE COMPUTER AGE: TECHNOGESTURES AND VIRTUALITY

Similar new medial technologies introduced by engineering and computing generated the legendary 1966 experiment, *9 Evenings: Theatre and Engineering*. Although situated outside of the theatre, *9 Evenings* capitalized on earlier trends in theatre technology while opening the door to new relationships among technology, choreography, and performance. Led by Bell Labs engineer Billy Klüver and artist Robert Rauschenberg, the evenings featured large-scale, multifaceted collaborations between ten well-known avant-garde artists and forty prominent engineers from Bell Labs.[45] Choreographers Yvonne Rainer, Deborah Hay, Steve Paxton, and Lucinda Childs, sound artists John Cage and David Tudor, director Robert Whitman, and visual artists Robert Rauschenberg, Alex Hay, and Oyvind Fahlstrom each paired up with engineers who would construct technical systems and devices to realize the artists' goals. *9 Evenings* happened at the spacious 69th Street Armory in New York City, where participants experimented in a huge black box environment with emergent technologies including remote-control robots, Doppler sensors, wireless AM/FM transmitters, closed circuit television, and projection.

Initial inspiration for *9 Evenings* lay in its potential for social impact, once again placing pressure on the power of intermedial performance to foreground, and intervene in, dominant-culture trends in an era of increasing technological dependence. In addition to gesturing to the increasing media presence in popular culture, these artists and technicians acknowledged that the United States was in the middle of the global arms race and that technology played a critical role in its political and cultural capital worldwide. Reversing the theatrical tradition of profiting from emergent technological developments, such as the impact of assembly line technology on early twentieth-century theatrical practice or the import of cinematic apparati into epic theatre, Klüver felt that the arts could play an active role in bettering the 'human and social consequences resulting from technological change'.[46] In stark contrast to early twentieth-century Taylorism, *9 Evenings*' engineer Herbert Schneider expressed hope that the experiments might illustrate how engineers are not solely interested in 'immediate profits'.[47] Recalling the ideals of Brecht, the *9 Evenings* artists staged their experimental technical events in front of a live audience with the expectation that such performances would blend pedagogy and entertainment. Ironically, the *9 Evenings* technologies often failed, thus distracting artists, performers, and audience members from artistic activities on the stage. In a popular image, Alex Hay sits in the middle of his performance, *Grass Field*, with engineers attending to the failed technology that sits in a pack on his back (Figure 9.2). Nevertheless, engineer Seymour Schweber saw the glitch as having a positive effect. As if forecasting the development of 1980s

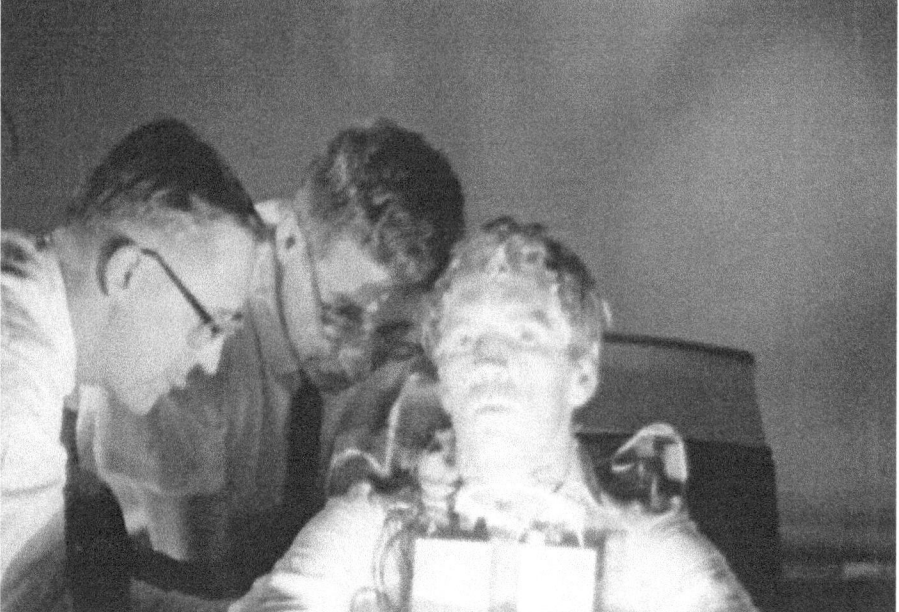

FIGURE 9.2: Alex Hay, *Grass Field*. Still from the factual footage shot in 16 mm by Alfons Schilling. The Daniel Langlois Foundation for Art, Science, and Technology, *9 Evenings: Theatre and Engineering* fonds. Permissions Julie Martin.

and 1990s digital 'glitch aesthetics', he proclaimed: 'I liked the fact that not everything worked . . . Half of the audience was completely bewildered because not knowing what was happening they were in a state of shock.'[48]

In addition to the technological innovations enabled by these performances – from the artistic appropriation of military technology to the unanticipated rise of glitch aesthetics – *9 Evenings* stands as a particularly important feminist moment in the history of theatre and technology. Although the engineers involved in the project were all male, as was indicative of the engineering demography of the period, Childs, Hay, and Rainer each maintained artistic and directorial control of their pieces. While they did not engineer the technologies that they helped to conceive, they did develop the systems in which they functioned. When Childs's air-propelled boxes failed, for example, she choreographed a solution to the technical problem by staging a human dancer to move the box. In contrast to staged mechanization, recalling the Tiller Girls, these choreographers included many female performers as active participants in their critically engaged interventions in techno-capital. Echoing Fuller's early interventions in performance technology and Moorman's work with Paik in this same period (the 1960s), these women's technical artistry and their central presence 'at the table' in *9 Evenings* staged an interrogation of the relationship between the female body and technological devices as the machine age gave way to the digital future.

The blending of media technology with the ideologies of gender and sexuality in *9 Evenings* gave emphatic voice to the emergent discourses of feminism, critical race theory, and queer activism in visual, installation, and performance art, all of which continue to inform fusions of technology and performance today. Especially notable is the use of intermedial techniques by black female artists, who often rely on them for their contradictory abilities to entertain but also to produce forceful ideological critique. Robbie McCauley, for example, ponders the complexity of her mixed-race heritage in her feminist solo performance, *Indian Blood* (1989). Reflecting on her grandfather's violence against Native Americans when he murdered his own blood relatives while a member of the black American Tenth Cavalry, McCauley frames her autobiographical performance with Brechtian exaggerated movement, syncopated speech, and media presentation. She surrounds the stage with multimedia imagery of historical newspaper accounts, and frames herself with two black-and-white video monitors that contrast her moving gestures with the static image of a televisual 'talking head' lecturing on the revisionist history of Occidental imperialism.[49] McCauley thus stages the contradictions inherent in the technologies she uses on stage: they objectify black populations through racialized media coverage, but are then subsequently re-appropriated by her live, gestural performance as she 'talks back' to the mediatized images surrounding her.

In the late twentieth and early twenty-first centuries, live performance has consistently invoked the political histories shaping (and shaped by) media representations, as McCauley does in *Indian Blood*; this practice has become increasingly prevalent in performances that take up queer and feminist disputes over access to reproductive (and other health-related) technologies. The cross-disciplinary choreographic performance work *[OR]* (1997) by the Japanese collective Dumb Type reflected on the AIDS-related death of the group's director, Teiji Furuhashi. The collective staged a larger-than-life concave projection screen as the backdrop to an ensemble dance revolving around a medical gurney. A high-pitched beep reminiscent of a heart rate monitor or IV machine accompanied the visual projection, and stark and sterile strobe lighting invoked the look and feel of a hospital room. The medicalized set of *[OR]* placed the work's live choreography in direct conversation with the audiovisual spectacle as the work staged the biomedical struggle surrounding the HIV/AIDS epidemic. Extending the reach of this queer commentary on the biopolitics of AIDS culture, the subRosa collective has staged since the 1990s mock-performances of scientific experiments that blend the discourses of genetic coding and reproductive rights. subRosa critiques the social pressure 'to exceed the embodied self through novel gadgets, pseudo techno-sociality, useless technologies, and distracting techno-spectacle'.[50] When performing, they adopt the costumes of scientists and trade show representatives to stage mocu-tisements involving audiences. In 'Expose EmmaGenics', for example, they staged a 'fantasy "woman-friendly" trade show' that offered their participants 'complete reproductive choice and control'.[51] This collective of interdisciplinary feminist artists thus combine performance art, social activism, media representations, and politics to explore and critique the impact biotechnologies have on women's bodies, lives, and work in the digital age.[52]

In 1991 cyber-theorist Donna Haraway proclaimed that humans and technologies are 'bound in a spiral dance'[53]; indeed, the rise of the Internet at the end of the twentieth century paradoxically re-introduced the dichotomous relationship between actor and technology to more traditional forms of theatre and performance. Rather than mechanize the live actor, or replace that actor with machine technologies, as was the case in the Industrial era and in Constructivist and Futurist aesthetics, the normalization of the Internet provoked a shift from live to virtual presence on stage, as well as an extension of the 'real' stage to include virtual, online spaces. Technologies such as mobile devices, computer animation, and motion capture made it possible for pre-recorded, streamed, or even live virtual actors to be projected onto a stage in place of or alongside physically live performers. Illuminating the cultural potential of technological effects for live performance, the theatre group Elevator Repair Service collaborated with digital artists and programmers Ben Rubin and Mark Hansen to stage a 'mash-up' performance in which the company read aloud *The Great Gatsby*, *The Sound and the Fury*, and *The Sun Also Rises* simultaneously (2011). As the audience wandered around the New

York Public Library reading room to interact with the performers, the actors read bits of algorithmed text from all three books. Their scripts were delivered in real time via handheld devices embedded in the books (held by the actors or on tablets and projection screens viewable to all participants). Technologies of reading and performance were staged as being *literally* embodied in the hands of the reading actors and in the movements of spectators who roamed from device to device for better access to the actors.

Elsewhere, groups such as the Builder's Association, led by former Wooster Group dramaturge Marianne Weems, have exhaustively explored the potential for implementing live video conferencing alongside actors physically present on stage,[54] while German collective Rimini Protokoll's 'mobile phone theatre' *Call Cutta* (2005) consists of a one-person audience but no live actors in the physical presence of that audience. The audience member in Berlin, Germany, picks up a ringing telephone to have a conversation with a call centre operator in Kolkata, India, who leads the audience member on a personal tour through the streets of Berlin. The video trailer for *Call Cutta* calls the project a unique theatre experience, with the city as the stage and a call-centre operator as the actor: or, it asks, 'are you', the spectator, 'the actor?'[55] Recalling Brecht's essay 'The Street Scene',[56] as well as the tradition of early twentieth-century agit-prop theatre, *Call Cutta* modernizes street theatre for the twenty-first century by commenting on the performative politics of capitalism's dependence on call-centre technologies in our digital, global age. In so doing, the performance also interrogates what 'distance' means in such an age by staging an intimate exchange between two people who remain physically far apart from one another even as they communicate over, and with, digital media.

In *technésexual* (2009), performers Micha Cárdenas and Elle Mehrmand took live acting to an even more distinctly 'virtual' platform as they performed sexual acts on stage (Figure 9.3). The cultural significance of this performance relates to the play on words in the title 'technésexual', which puns on Cárdenas's identity as a transwoman of colour. Sensors attached to the performers' bodies during the live performance of *technésexual* communicated their pulses and heart rates directly to the virtual avatars of Cárdenas and Mehrmand in the performance's simultaneous online space. This virtual world was projected on a screen upstage of the performers; spectators watched the live performing bodies being mirrored by their avatars in a way that confused the primary source of performance data – were the avatars acting on the 'live' bodies or was it the other way around? Cárdenas and Mehrmand not only merged onstage presence with virtual reality but also imposed the materiality of their bodies directly, and passionately, upon the virtual realm.

As artistic media traditionally predicated on the live, physical presence of actors' bodies, theatre and performance have provided paradoxical sites for the interrogation of the modern age's cultural shift from liveness to virtuality.[57] In

FIGURE 9.3: Micha Cárdenas and Elle Mehrmand, *technésexual*. Hemispheric Institute Encuentro, Bogotá, Colombia, 2009. Photo by Cristhian Ávila.

the cases we have discussed, however, the ontological question that technology begs of performance centres not necessarily on liveness – since a virtual avatar can perform live on stage – but might be better said to revolve around questions of presence. Does theatre necessitate the presence of a live actor or can virtual actors take over the role of the live actor altogether? How might the answer to this question reflect a wider cultural reality outside the theatre in the twentieth and early twenty-first centuries?

Rabih Mroué and Lina Saneh's *33rpm and a few seconds* (2012) revels in a 'theatre without actors'.[58] Further exaggerating the conceit driving *Call Cutta*, *33rpm and a few seconds* relies on screens and audio to tell a story loosely based on the death of a Lebanese activist. Information on the dead activist's Facebook page as well as voicemails and other now-everyday technologies are central to the narrative development of *33rpm*. While acknowledging the central role that social media plays in international activisms in the digital age, Mroué and Saneh ironically develop their theatre without actors to critique the now-ubiquitous cultural centrality of social media as it has come to replace in-person, human-to-human communication.

In the tradition of the early twentieth century innovations we discussed earlier in this chapter, virtual technologies are increasingly subject to critique by theatre and performance artists for the ways they facilitate and mediate communication and presence in contemporary culture. The artist collective

Critical Art Ensemble (CAE) has gone so far as to criticize virtual theatre for reinforcing 'the worst elements of the disembodiment of the technocratic class for the sake of greater instrumentality'.[59] Yet, as our discussion of the historical precedents in theatre and performance technology amply suggests, we can trace the affirmative material effects of new media on both stage technologies and actors' bodies – in the tradition of Artaud or even Brecht – rather than conceiving of them as simply instrumental replacements for stages or bodies altogether. In its critique of virtual theatre, CAE paradoxically opens the door to our thinking about digital theatre affirmatively:

> For the most part, virtual theatre lacks all the redeeming characteristics of theatrical practice, whether they are resistant functions or just pleasurable social functions. The short answer to this problem is simply to argue that the body is still the key building block of theatre, and that if performers are to drift into virtuality, they should find the means to develop feedback loops between the electronic and the organic.[60]

When the body itself is conceived as a theatrical technology – as happened frequently and consistently in the twentieth-century experimentations we have discussed in this chapter – the general technological trends in performance always reflect what CAE calls a 'feedback loop'. We need not lament the disappearance of the presence of the body as theatrical technologies expand and shift our cultural landscapes; an alternative narrative that foregrounds the contradictory powers of human *Gestus* alongside mediated stage technologies presents a more complex, nuanced picture of the twentieth-century history of performance and its recent virtual extensions.

Our readings of recent performance works also return us to the early twentieth-century trend of utilizing theatrical technology for political pedagogy. While performances by DumbType and subRosa metaphorically reference the gender and sexual politics of biomedicine, works by The Builder's Association, Elevator Repair Service and Rabih Mroué explicitly bring technological systems onto the stage in order to interrogate the cultural impact of digital objects and technologized bodies. Rather than merely dazzle and entertain spectators with the stunning effects of digital technologies, virtual theatre artists of the new millennium follow the early lead of Brecht and the later example of post-war artists by raising core questions about the cultural effects of medialization. Going a step further, artists such as Cárdenas, Mehrmand, and subRosa experiment with performative technologies for culturally recombinant purposes, remixing the digital technologies of theatre with sustaining blends of art and politics. Perhaps the many contradictions introduced to the modern theatre by Artaud, Brecht, and their technological forbears have now morphed successfully into the feedback loops of virtual theatre and digital performance.

CHAPTER TEN

Knowledge Transmission

Media and Memory

SARAH BAY-CHENG

INTRODUCTION

Philip K. Dick's short story, 'The Preserving Machine', describes the efforts of Doc Labyrinth to preserve music for future generations. Confronting a future in which warfare threatens to destroy all remnants of civilization, Labyrinth works with an unnamed American university to create 'the preserving machine'. His device is designed to serve as an archival tool by turning musical scores into living creatures with better survival skills than the paper copies of the music he loves. After watching oddly formed critters emerge from the machine (some with more obvious endurance abilities than others), Labyrinth and the unidentified narrator put one of the misshapen insects – a 'bach beetle' – back into the machine to test the accuracy of its documentation. The result is disappointing: 'I listened to the music. It was hideous.'[1] As Labyrinth and the narrator discover, the process of documentation distorts what it originally sought to preserve.

First published in 1953, Dick's story reflects the anxieties of the mid-twentieth century. In the wake of two devastating world wars and under the threat of global nuclear annihilation, 'the brutalization of beautiful things'[2] was a reality for most of post-war Europe and Japan. At the same time, Dick's notion of a preserving machine for art both reflects the changes created along with the development of recorded media and prefigures the ways in which cultural archives, particularly in the performing arts, would transform throughout the latter half of the twentieth century. The inventions of modern media – first photography, then gramophone and radio, and later cinema, television, and digital media – all revised modern theatre practices while also introducing entirely new archival practices for performance. Although the future of art and culture might seem pale in comparison with the consequences of the Second World War's mechanized warfare and systematic genocide, Dick's story speaks to the instability of performance recordings, including not only of music but also of theatre and dance as they responded to new media emerging throughout the twentieth century. The modern performing arts were shaped by new technologies that were themselves shaped by modern warfare, such as the advancement of the radio in the First World War and the development of computers for code-breaking in the Second World War. This chapter traces the impact of recording technologies on modern theatre and performance; it focuses on the ways in which the seismic shift from experiences of co-presence (live events witnessed by audiences as they unfold in real time on the stage) to increasingly mediated forms of spectatorship profoundly altered the transmission of cultural memory at the theatre, and transformed the processes of performance documentation and historiography in the process. Like Dick's dystopian fantasy, the ensuing debate between modern drama and media often focused on questions of fidelity, re-enactment, and the potentially distorting impact of new media technologies on existing theatre practices. Long before the so-called 'liveness' debate at the turn of the twenty-first century, modern theatre artists responded to and entered into dialogue with the influence of emergent recording technologies on art and aesthetic representation.

Some modernists responded positively to new technologies. Photographer and filmmaker László Moholy-Nagy, for example, believed that the invention of photography and film 'enable us to fulfill representational purposes incomparably more completely than painting', leaving painters free to embrace abstract representation.[3] Moreover, he saw the machine as the essence of the modern age: 'The reality of our century is technology: the invention, construction, and maintenance of machines. To be a user of machines is to be of the spirit of this century. Machines have replaced the transcendental spiritualism of past eras'.[4] German theorist Walter Benjamin had a more ambivalent response. While the invention of mass media recordings, most especially cinema, might productively democratize art and enable political transformation through media, such technologies also threatened to empower charismatic dictators and alienate the stage actor from his own likeness on screen. Quoting Rudolf Arnheim, Benjamin contends that at its worst the cinema treats 'the actor as a stage prop chosen for its characteristics'.[5]

Playwrights, directors, designers, and performers embraced new technologies in ways that influenced everything from dramatic form and structure to staging and acting styles. Techniques enabled by the cinema – editing cuts, simultaneity, repetition, and camera tricks – were manifested in plays by avant-garde artists on stage as well as in their films. Jean Cocteau, for example, put phonographs on stage as characters in his play *The Wedding on the Eiffel Tower* (1922), itself a tribute to the world's largest radio antenna, and Gertrude Stein drew connections between theatre and cinema in her lecture 'Plays' (1934), where she wrote that, 'the cinema undoubtedly had a new way of understanding sight and sound in relation to emotion and time'.[6] But new technologies did not only manifest among the avant-gardes; photography proved a significant influence on naturalists August Strindberg and Émile Zola, among others. Zola, for instance, described theatre itself as a screen: 'Any work of art is like an open window on creation; there is, encased by the frame of the window, a kind of transparent screen [*écran*], through which you can see the objects more or less distorted'.[7] Later, Lee Strasberg used audio tape recorders extensively in his development of Method acting training, a critical foundation for American realism.[8]

Even as theatre artists of the early twentieth century were quick to absorb and integrate new techniques like the record player and movie screen into their dramaturgy, anxieties quickly arose regarding media's ontological connection to theatre and live performance. Distributing theatre recordings through radio and cinema meant that theatrical performances could be heard and seen by larger audiences at great geographical distances from the live event; modernist theatre artists and filmmakers alike worried that audiences would confuse theatre and film for each other. Late nineteenth- and early twentieth-century comparisons of recorded media and live performance thus sought to make clear and compelling distinctions between the two forms, but the language of rivalry between media would shape the debate throughout the twentieth century. Film theorist Erwin Pudovkin argued that 'the first attempts to relate cinematography to the world of art were naturally bound up with the Theatre', but that film would never become art until it ceased to simply photograph 'the art of the actor'.[9] Susan Sontag felt compelled to ask, 'Is cinema the successor, the rival, or the reviver of the theatre?'[10]

As the century wore on, cinema, video, and eventually digital media came to be seen both as a threat to theatre's very existence and, paradoxically, as the means that would sustain it in the future. Playwrights adopted recording technologies as both material and metaphor for their works, reflecting a world in which live representations of human beings could not do without reflections on the effects of technological expansion on what it meant to experience and remember the world. They also began writing, increasingly, for film, television, and radio, working across media and thus inevitably promoting intermedial practices as a new norm on the stage. Further, even as media technologies seemed to displace theatrical performance for consumers and (some) producers, media records steadily populated performance archives. As recording technologies expanded from radio and cinema to television and digital media, theatre performances gradually circulated outside of theatrical spaces and their historical traces could be found in more than scripts, scores, and other textual documents.

The rise of television after the Second World War drew heavily on theatrical forms, including not only televised plays, but also the practice of using a live audience for taping. This 'live' audience was recorded along with the performance, creating a sense of temporal immediacy for the television viewer. In particular, Hollywood situation comedies and game shows used their live audiences to create a sense of presence for the subsequent TV-viewing audience, even though the shows were taped well in advance. (A week's worth of game shows, for instance, are regularly recorded on the same day to limit production costs.) Televised plays were common on public television in the United States, the UK and Europe from the 1970s until the 1990s. These sorts of advances gradually redefined the modern theatrical audience from one of immediate (that is, *unmediated*) proximity and co-presence to one constituted through networks of media reproductions. The transmission of cultural knowledge at, and about, the theatre in the modern period was thus part of an ongoing intermedial negotiation, bound to both the threat and the promise recording technologies held for the theatre's future. This tension emerges at the beginning of the period of theatrical modernism, and it shaped debates about both theatrical and archival practices throughout the twentieth century and into the twenty-first.

MEDIA IN THE MODERN THEATRE

In one of his extensive histories of modern technological transformation, historian and architecture critic Lewis Mumford argued that transformations in technology and culture were mutually dependent upon one another. As he wrote in 1930, 'Behind all the great material inventions of the last century and a half was not merely a long internal development of technics: there was also a change of mind. Before the new industrial processes could take hold on a great scale, a reorientation of wishes, habits, ideas, and goals was necessary'.[11] At the theatre, we see this change of mind emerging not only in new technical inventions, but also in late nineteenth-century dramaturgy as playwrights incorporated emerging media – first photography and the gramophone, and later radio and film – directly into their stage works. In her compelling study, *Art, Vision, and Nineteenth-Century Realist Drama: Acts of Seeing*, Amy Strahler Holzapfel traces the influence of optical technologies on late nineteenth-century realist drama. Like Mumford, Holzapfel notes that the shift in theatrical communication represented by realism was in part a reaction to emerging technologies, particularly photography. She argues that the intersection of photography and drama was not simply evidence of a new technology creating new practical options or inspiring new ideas; it demonstrated *how* modern audiences looked at the world and at themselves: 'If nineteenth-century realist theatre invites comparison to photography, it is not because both media sought exact transcriptions of life, but because both mediums favored the singularity of their observers' embodied, hence unique, points of view.'[12] In Strindberg's drama, for instance, Holzapfel finds characterizations influenced by nineteenth-century composite photography. Noting Strindberg's own experimental photography, she contends that 'the subjective act of seeing does not simply represent the self, it *makes* the self'.[13]

Like photography, early cinema was also changing perceptions of daily life and culture at large. The Lumière brothers' early films, for example *Workers Leaving the Lumière Factory* (1895) (Figure 10.1) and *The Arrival of a Train at a Station* (1895), gave audiences the opportunity to see themselves en masse and on screen. As Arthur Knight described it, the Lumière's films 'were a revelation ... everything could be seen larger than life and, curiously, even more real'.[14]

Early cinema was characterized by two complementary but distinct trends, both of which sought to distinguish the emerging art form from the dominant

FIGURE 10.1: Film still from *Workers Leaving the Lumière Factory in Lyon* (*La Sortie de l'Usine Lumière à Lyon*), 1895.

theatrical narratives of the period; these trends were representational verisimilitude, and imagery that defied theatre's temporal continuity. However, following the Lumières's style, cinema was characterized by its authenticity, the ability to show things as they actually happened. Films such as *Baby's Dinner* (1895) display exactly what their titles suggest without narrative, actors, or overt manipulation. At the same time, the mechanics of cinema and the camera offered new creative possibilities for repeated actions, simultaneous projections, and composite images. Fernand Léger's *Mechanical Ballet* (1924) introduced several of these early techniques, including clever composite images and repeated actions that demonstrated cinema's ability to control time and space. Russian filmmakers Sergei Eisenstein and Lev Kuleshov developed new approaches to meaning in cinematic construction based on non-linear editing and radical juxtapositions of images. Fellow Soviet Dziga Vertov similarly began experimenting with what he called the 'Kino-eye', his term for the unique vision of the camera that superseded the limitations of human vision. Though formally radical, Vertov's films intended to convey the 'truth' of life in the early twentieth century and he was particularly fond of juxtaposing the mechanical gestures of factory workers with the machines they operated as in *Man with a Movie Camera* (1929). For Vertov, early twentieth-century life was itself a mechanical existence and thus its truth could only be realized fully in the cinema.[15]

Such ideas were not unique to communist filmmakers. In her 1928 expressionist play, *Machinal*, American journalist and playwright Sophie Treadwell makes similar observations when she describes the experience of modern life – including work, love, marriage, and sex – as various forms of mechanized labour. Treadwell's play followed other American playwrights who experimented with technological influences in expressionist plays such as Eugene O'Neill's *The Hairy Ape* (1922) and Elmer Rice's *The Adding Machine* (1923). Much like the Russian filmmakers, American playwrights used repetition and juxtaposition in their texts alongside skewed stage design, mechanical sound effects, and acting styles that de-personalized individual characters. O'Neill's use of masks in *The Hairy Ape* is particularly relevant, but the creation of performing, undifferentiated masses and the threat of the industrialized urban space they convey recurs throughout modernist drama and cinema.

The collision of recording technologies with theatrical performance resulted from the effects of the industrial revolution, but was accelerated by the experiences of the First World War (1914–1918). The mechanized violence of that war inspired a range of artistic innovators, including the leftist revolutionaries of Dada who responded to the horrors of war by embracing cinema's fragmentation and simultaneity. Although influenced by many of the emerging media technologies of the early twentieth century, Dada artists did not simply adapt recording technologies into performance. On the contrary, even as they adopted recording techniques, their work specifically laboured against the representational verisimilitude of photography and cinema and they drew on the more non-realistic aspects of cinema in manipulations of theatrical time.

Hugo Ball, one of Dada's founding members, volunteered to fight in the First World War on behalf of Germany. Declared unfit for duty, he nevertheless travelled to the front lines with the intention of independently joining the ranks of the German forces. There, on the battlefields of France, he discovered horrors that would send him to neutral Switzerland and prompt the creation of the Dada movement as an artistic and political response to the absurdity and brutal losses of modern warfare. In his diary, *Flight Out of Time*, Ball connects his perspective on the war to his changing ideas about art in general and the realist theatre in particular. 'I am beginning to understand the theatre', he wrote in 1915. 'It is a tyranny that furthers the development of acting talents. The importance of the theatre is always inversely proportionate to the importance of social morality and civil freedom'.[16] Looking for alternative modes of performance outside realism and the well-made play, Ball and others established the Cabaret Voltaire in Zurich as the founding site of Dada. The purpose of Dada was not to reject the theatre per se, but to re-envision it in entirely new terms suited to the novel experiences of modernity. As Ball wrote in his 1916 'Dada Manifesto':

> I shall be reading poems that are meant to dispense with conventional language, no less, and to have done with it. Dada . . . I don't want words that other people have invented. All the words are other people's inventions. I want my own stuff, my own rhythm, and vowels and consonants too, matching the rhythm and all my own.[17]

In place of literary prose and logical descriptions, Ball's new, explicitly anti-war language resonates with mechanical repetitions and sounds that suggest the deep imbrication of mechanization within the avant-garde. In particular, his poems are filled with non-linear, irrational structures modelled both in the violent chaos of mechanized war and realized in the cinema. Written as performance texts, Ball's poems and his performance of them, complete with costumes, props, and designed settings, embodied the new technologies. His iconic performance of 'Gadji Beri Bimba', for example, exhibits a heavy staccato rhythm in the language much like the repetitious clicking of film projectors.

Other artists similarly recognized these qualities. In his 1924 essay, 'Theatre, Circus, Variety', Moholy-Nagy noted that in avant-garde 'literature it was not the logical-intellectual content which belonged in the foreground, but the effects which arose from the word-sound relationships'.[18] The next stage, for Moholy-Nagy, was what he called, 'the mechanized eccentric', a form of highly controlled human movement that would allow for a completely mechanized form of performance. While not dismissing the role of the human performer entirely, as Edward Gordon Craig proposed in his *Übermarionnette*, Moholy-Nagy wanted the function of the actor to become another technical element 'employed ON AN EQUAL FOOTING WITH THE OTHER FORMATIVE MEDIA' (original emphasis)[19] like the lights, sets, or costumes in a performance. In the photographic and film documentation of Bauhaus work, its elaborate, abstract costumes continually work both with and against the human figures inhabiting and animating them; large sculptural figures might reveal a single bare leg, or the performer's head might poke out of a large box.

We see perhaps the epitome of mechanized prose and bodily performance in Tristan Tzara's play *The Gas Heart* (1921–1923). Written shortly after the end of the First World War, Tzara incorporates anti-war sentiments within a dramatic structure and style that echoes cinematic techniques such as montage; he also anticipates Moholy-Nagy's mechanized human performer (1924). Following the philosophy espoused in Ball's first Dada Manifesto (1916), the play begins with the character of Eye reciting a series of random words. Written and performed in French in 1923, the English translation reads as:

> Statues jewels roasts
> statues jewels roasts
> statues jewels roasts
> statues jewels roasts
> statues jewels roasts
> and the wind open to mathematical allusions[20]

Other lines of dialogue include repetitions of 'cigar pimple nose', declarations of a diplomat's wife Clytemnestra's beauty (although no such character exists), and a typographical illustration of a man falling from a funnel in the ceiling onto a table.[21] Throughout, *The Gas Heart* tests the limits of performance. Written to be performed (and staged at a Dada soirée in 1923), the play presents numerous challenges in its realization. The six characters – Eye, Mouth, Nose, Ear, Neck, and Eyebrow – are not only difficult to conceptualize, but they further engage in a series of nonsensical and repetitive conversations that include observations both bizarre and banal. For example, Eye suddenly states, 'Upon the ear the vaccine of serious pearl flattened to mimosa'. To which Ear and Mouth reply, 'Eye: Don't you think it's getting rather warm? / Mouth (*who has just come in again*): It gets warm in the summer'.[22]

Stanton Garner has suggested that the character names and the nonsensical dialogue refer to the violence of the war, which saw disfigured and dismembered soldiers survive in unprecedented numbers. Citing evidence of new techniques in plastic surgery and facial reconstruction, Garner offers a reading of the play and its character names as a response to the bodily fragmentation of war, which in turn causes him to see 'the reparatory elements of Tzara's dramaturgy.

Indeed, the very principles of dislocation, non-sequitur, and bizarre juxtaposition that drive the play's staging and dialogue create a fantastic world of new bodily combinations'.[23] But while the play may well reflect the physical realities of soldiers disfigured by the war, Tzara's stage representation of bodily dismemberment also owes a debt to cinema. The repetition of language on the page reads much like the series of frames in a film strip. His manipulations of words as images transform the printed stage into a dynamic surface on which the letters and words dance, much like the fragmented figure of the mechanical Charlie Chaplin in Léger's subsequent film *Mechanical Ballet* (1924). These techniques can be found throughout the work of the avant-garde, suggesting the pervasive influence of cinema across its practice in the early twentieth century. Although Tzara certainly responds to the violence and aftermath of modern warfare, his stage techniques also incorporate and echo the disruptive, even violent, cutting and splicing practices of the film edit, demonstrating the extent to which Dada's use of cinematic modes helped it to transmit the fracture of post-war experience to its live audiences.

Although the experiences of the First World War profoundly shaped modernist theatre and culture in the first half of the twentieth century, the experiences of the Second World War (1939–1945), the European Holocaust, and post-war civil rights battles in the United States were perhaps even more profound in their effects on the modern theatrical imagination and prompted further intermedial innovations. In the wake of the Nazi occupation in France and England's long, draining war against the Axis powers, post-war drama throughout Europe reeled in the aftermath of conflict. Most European countries were deeply in debt, sparking what would become more than two decades of social unrest, culminating in the social protests of 1968. In the wake of a brutally mechanized conflict and set against the rise of radio and television as venues for social and political engagement, post-war drama from the late 1940s through the 1970s drew overwhelmingly on other media and technology. Many of the playwrights in what Martin Esslin termed the 'theatre of the absurd' extended the experiments of the avant-garde to explore and describe conditions in Europe after the war. Eugene Ionesco, for example, drew upon mechanized metaphors to analyse the moral capitulations he witnessed during the Nazi occupation of France. Playwrights such as Harold Pinter, Caryl Churchill, and Adrienne Kennedy incorporated contemporary media into their works as a way to articulate the changing political landscapes of the 1960s and 1970s. Pinter and Churchill both wrote radio drama and Pinter continued to write screenplays throughout his stage career. As Gay Gibson Cima argues, 'With *Old Times* Pinter forg[ed] a new theatrical form, borrowing from cinematic art to revolutionize the stage' and, thus, radically revised the role of the stage actor in the second half of the twentieth century. Instead of creating a logical sequence of actions based on clear causes and effects, Pinter juxtaposed events or statements without clearly causal effects.

Much like the earlier avant-gardes, Pinter composed according to the logic of the film cut: as with Kuleshov's experiments in non-linear editing, his plays rely on the viewer to make sense of the resulting juxtapositions. For Cima, Pinter's 'incorporation of film techniques into his creative process challeng[ed] actors to respond in kind, to fashion an approach to performance which center[ed] on movement instead of the Stanslavski-based "spine"'.[24] (Later, Philip Auslander would make a similar observation in response to his interview with Willem Dafoe. There, Dafoe noted the similarities in non-linear performing techniques between avant-garde theatre that avoided causal narratives, and cinema where scenes are routinely recorded out of order to save costs.[25]) Churchill meanwhile engaged technological metaphors in plays such as *Not Not Not Not Not Enough Oxygen* (1971) and *Love and Information* (2012), the latter of which uses networks of digital information exchange as the framing allegory for contemporary relationships. Kennedy's *A Movie Star Has to Star in Black and White* (1967) locates racism and lack of agency and power within the familiar tropes of popular films that serve to constrain both non-whites and women. These theatrical visions not only articulated the horrors of mechanized war, the Holocaust, the atomic bomb, and simmering racial tensions but also spoke to the future of theatrical knowledge transmission through other modern media.

Samuel Beckett's *Krapp's Last Tape* offers a compelling example of these post-war theatrical developments, including experiments with language and struggles with representing historical memory; most importantly, however, it offers an early but insightful reflection on the role of technology in crafting theatrical histories of the future during the modern age. From even a cursory reading, it is clear that *Krapp's Last Tape* is about memory. What is remarkable about the play, however, is that Beckett is among the first (*the* first?) to stage the problem of *mechanically recorded memory*. Within Krapp's recordings Beckett captures not only the anxiety of post-war Europe, the implications of a technologically-driven society, and the effects of cinema on the stage, but he also projects his ideas into the future. Although rarely discussed as such, *Krapp's Last Tape* (1958) is fundamentally a Futurist play: it is simultaneously about the past and future of technology, history, and memories of the self. As such, the play illustrates a quintessential moment in the theatre's cultural history in post-war Europe as it negotiates the weight of recent history, painful memories, and an anxious future.

In his biography of Beckett, Anthony Cronin identifies what he calls the 'oddity' of the play's timeline.[26] Cronin notes that the tape recorder that Krapp uses (see Figure 10.2) had not been widely available prior to 1958, and would not have been in existence on either of the recorded birthdays that Krapp recalls during the play. These earlier birthdays occur thirty years and forty-two years prior to the birthday on which we encounter Krapp in the play. It would appear that Cronin overlooks (or does not take seriously) the first line in the play, which clearly states that the short play is set in '*A late evening in the*

FIGURE 10.2: Patrick Magee in Samuel Beckett's *Krapp's Last Tape*, 1959. Photograph by Ida Kar. Reprinted by permission of the National Portrait Gallery, London.

future'.[27] The question, of course, is how far in the future. According to the evidence of his biographers, Beckett first got the idea of the tape recorder from his work with the BBC on the radio play *After the Fall* in 1957.[28] As Donald McWhinnie, director of the play's premiere at the Royal Court in 1958, recounts, 'magnetic tape only came into use in the middle 'fifties. When Sam wrote *Krapp's Last Tape*, I don't think he knew for a minute how the mechanics of the thing worked'.[29] Beckett's text notes that on his sixty-ninth birthday, Krapp has made forty-five annual recordings. Imagining that Krapp acquired the tape recorder in approximately 1955 ('the middle 'fifties'), the subsequent recordings would take place in 1970 (age 39) and 2000 (age 69), the future years in which the play is set. For all of its other ideas, Beckett's play is fundamentally about the future of memory and the role of technology in documenting human experience.

Beckett was not alone in imagining the world at the end of the second millennium. Throughout the 1950s, scientists and science fiction writers alike often speculated on life in the year 2000. For example, in 1951 *Time Magazine* excerpted remarks from James Bryant Conant, chemist and president of Harvard, to the American Chemical Society. Looking into his crystal ('plastic') ball, Conant made a series of rosy predictions about life in the year 2000, including the aversion of atomic warfare, the end of fossil fuels as dominant energy sources, and an end to overpopulation, among others.[30] Not surprisingly, Beckett's vision of the future is less optimistic than those of mid-century Futurists. There is nothing in the play to suggest that the world's problems have been solved; indeed, there is very little of the outside world at all in the play, except for oblique references to a lack of other people and Krapp's speculation on his thirty-ninth birthday that, 'The earth might be uninhabited'.[31] This vision of a world in a permanent state of darkness and isolation was not unrealistic for those living under the threat of nuclear war in 1958, a theme Beckett had recently explored in *Endgame* (1957).[32] Beckett's vision is much closer to French philosopher Jacques Ellul's in *The Technological Society*, where he worries about a world in which humanity becomes so mechanized as to become less human. First published as *La Technique ou l'enjeu du siècle* ('the stake of the century') in 1954, Ellul's book argued that, 'Technology cannot put up with intuitions and "literature". It must necessarily don mathematical vestments. Everything in human life that does not lend itself to mathematical treatment must be excluded . . . and left to the sphere of dreams'.[33]

I have no evidence that Beckett read Ellul, but Krapp points to a future tension that Ellul clearly anticipates.[34] In the recording from his thirty-ninth birthday, Krapp accounts for his sexual encounters – a most intimate human experience – in the form of statistics. Indeed, through his near obsessive attention to the tape recorder, Krapp has transformed himself and his life into mathematical coordinates: box three, spool five. His memories are numbered and catalogued and he relies on the machine to remember what he cannot. For example, Krapp's hand-written note for one recording, listed as 'Equinox, memorable equinox', is not memorable at all. After reading his own note aloud, the stage directions dictate, '*He raises his head, stares blankly front. Puzzled*'.[35] This ironic pun of a memorable equinox, now forgotten, fits within the larger wordplay of Beckett's work. As others have noted, every word in the title and subtitle is a pun and the play's text repeats alternating images of light and dark: the white dog with the black ball, the 'dark nurse' in the white uniform, etc. The equinox, of course, is one of two days annually when day and night (light and dark) take up the same length of time. The word derives from the Latin *aequus* (equal) and *nox* (night) and suggests a day of balance between the contradictory forces of the universe. In the play, there is neither balance nor memory, only the *recording* of a memory, and the distinction between 'real' memory and its recorded trace is difficult to determine and definitely not in balance.

Other elements support a reading of Beckett's play as a rumination on mediated memory and history. The interplay of light and dark suggests not only the many oppositions in Beckett's writing – spirit and flesh, life and death – but also the flicker of cinematic images. The descriptions of Krapp's appearance as a figure in shades of grey recalls images of actors in black and white film, and his relationship to his own recorded self similarly echoes the emotional experience of early cinema. In his review of the London premiere, Roy Walker connected Krapp's alienation from his previous self to the experience of making a recording. 'Anyone who has made a BBC recording', he writes, 'may emerge feeling that he can no longer call himself his own'.[36] Italian playwright Luigi Pirandello said much the same about the film actor in his novel *Si Gira*, or *Shoot!* (1916): 'The film actor feels as if in exile – exiled not only from the stage but from himself'.[37] The very idea of the play emerged from Beckett's experience of listening to actor Patrick Magee (the first Krapp) on the radio and his experience with tape-recorded versions of his radio play, *All That Fall* (1957). Attempting to create an experience of a disembodied humanity, Beckett inserts a machine, a device to recall memories of the self but also to reflect the self, as a substitute for actual human connection with others. In this sense, Beckett is the most prescient of the mid-century Futurists: Krapp seems to embody the kind of social alienation that Sherry Turkle describes in her Internet-age book *Alone Together: Why We Expect More from Technology and Less from Each Other* (2012). Analysing the role of technology in twenty-first-century daily life, Turkle darkly notes, 'we love our objects, but enchantment comes with a price'.[38] It is a statement that chimes with Krapp's relationship to technology, or as Donald Davis (who played Krapp in the US premiere) observed, 'Alan [Schneider, director] and I both agreed that the tape-machine had a rather more special place in Krapp's life than it has in most of our lives . . . It was as though the machine had become an extension of his living with people and without people'.[39]

Krapp's Last Tape is not overtly about human relation to the technologies of the future any more than it is about mid-century politics, though evidence of both may be found within its spare language. Like other post-war dramatists, Beckett reflects an age in transition, a time in which the pain of the past can be neither fully recalled nor forgotten, and in which the future threatens to play out on an unalterable and lonely trajectory, subjective experience mediated out of existence. In 1948, Norbert Wiener introduced the idea of 'cybernetics', the study of closed-loop systems and self-regulating mechanisms. Whether Beckett knew of Wiener's work or not, he ingeniously depicted a single closed-loop feedback system for the stage, one that compresses the past and future together, even while it suspends the present precariously in time. *Krapp's Last Tape* offers us the image of someone who is lonely and desperate, yet alienated from humanity and from himself, emotionally and physically connected only to a device that stores his memories and former selves. Beckett articulates a poignant image of life in the wake of unimaginable horror, facing a lonely future.

Thinking of his work in conjunction with contemporary 'social media' (an oxymoron that he surely would have appreciated), we can recognize Beckett as not the most optimistic of Futurists, but as perhaps among the most accurate. Krapp's last tape was the world's first 'selfie'.

KNOWLEDGE TRANSMISSION IN MEDIA

Just as recording technologies affected the way modern theatre artists represented the modern subject's lived experience on stage, new media also shaped the evolution of theatre archives and historiography in the twentieth century, directly affecting the way those stagings passed into historical memory. In the wake of the first experiments in photography and cinema, and later in video and digital archiving, the transmission of theatre events and histories shifted from predominantly textual narratives to the documentation and dissemination of performance first in separate sound and images and later in mediated forms that integrated sound, image, and movement. Of course, such records were not isolated from the evolution of theatre practices. In an essay from 1997, Laurence Senelick ponders the potentially reciprocal relation between new archival technologies and modes of performance. He compares the mechanics of nineteenth-century photography to the dominant acting styles of the same period. As he notes, early photography required relatively long exposure times so that enough light could enter the camera's iris to make a clear image on a photo-sensitive plate. To avoid blurring or otherwise distorting the final image, the photographic subject needed to remain as still as possible for the duration of the exposure. (This is one reason why people in photographs before 1900 are never depicted smiling.) Senelick compares these long exposure times to pre-modern acting styles such as melodrama, in which actors enacted and often held a series of poses to create a particular impression. Tracing subsequent photographic innovations and their parallels in theatrical style, he notes that the progression of photographic techniques that attempted to capture movement (i.e., stop-action) followed similar shifts towards naturalism in the theatre. Senelick's interleaving of photography and theatre practices prompts his question, 'did the technology arise to meet the need or was the need confected from an awareness of the technology?'[40] His query recalls both Mumford's theory regarding the change of mind that enabled modern machine culture, and Cima's argument about the responsiveness of acting styles to new media formats in Pinter's work.

Indeed, developments in recording technologies corresponded to changes in theatre practices throughout the twentieth century, and we can trace the influence of recording technologies on theatrical communication and preservation back to the earliest attempts to document theatre in the mid-nineteenth century. Prior to the use of photography, theatres relied on lithographs, engravings and graphical illustrations in printed plays to serve as remnants of theatrical moments. Even after the invention of photography, it took some time for photos to emerge as a desirable means to capture and circulate theatrical performance. Examining the collections available in theatre archives today, one finds that the earliest photographic images are most often either exterior shots of prominent theatre buildings, or photographic portraits of actors. Many of the earliest theatrical photographs are cabinet cards, a form of portraiture initially intended to advertise the services and abilities of a professional photographer rather than to promote the actor depicted or their most recent play. However, as those images became popular as collectables, actors realized that they could prove useful in promoting their own careers. As David Mayer argues, 'By the final two decades of the [nineteenth] century, actors sent booking agents cabinet photographs with printed résumés of their touring successes'.[41] Yet even as actors worked to promote themselves through photographs, these images were composed largely in photographers' studios and conveyed little of the productions in which their subjects performed. Further, even with the advent of the daguerreotype, the quickest exposure time was still at least fifteen minutes and lighting posed a consistent problem for photography on the actual stage. However, developments in lighting technology quickly created new possibilities for photographic documentation in the modern theatre. As David S. Shields has documented, Charles Brush's electric carbon-arc lamp allowed photographers to capture images in spaces previously devoid of the requisite light (for example, theatre interiors) and by the early twentieth century photographs of stage performances had become a standard part of theatrical documentation.[42]

By the mid-twentieth century, photography had become nimble enough to accommodate 'action' shots of theatrical performances. Chantal Meyer-Plantureux argues that stage photography changed fundamentally in 1945, contemporaneously with theatre practice's shift in emphasis from the work of the actor to that of the director and the crafting of a *mise-en-scène*. She locates the change particularly in the work of Roger Pic, who photographed theatre without either additional lighting or a privileged viewing position. By photographing more of the stage and capturing its events in action, Pic could document the dynamism of performance beyond the presence of a single actor. Whereas earlier photography was posed for the camera with only a few actors, now the entirety of the space crafted by the director could be visible. Photography in this era began to capture not only the visuality of the theatre, but also its temporality and gesture, suggesting a larger coordinating presence at work beyond any of the actors. Earlier, stage tableaux were constructed for and directed artificially at the photographer, but Pic's camera became, according to Joel Anderson, 'just one spectator of the show (albeit one apparently not confined to a seat), unable (and unwilling) to control or order the fleeting events of the stage'.⁴³ Anderson argues that these developments led directly to the emergence of photography as a tool for theatrical documentation, introducing a new form of performance dissemination in the latter half of the twentieth century. Certainly, the plethora of post-1950 photographic materials in theatre and performance archives support his claims. The rise in performance photography also foreshadowed the use of film and video as tools of theatrical documentation in subsequent decades.

Modern media technologies were not just for inspiration and documentation, however; beginning in the early twentieth century, theatre and dance makers actively used film as vehicles for performance. Stage magician George Méliès was perhaps the first to recognize the creative potential of film as a tool for magical effects in performance. Carefully recreating the stage proscenium in accordance with the screen frame, Méliès designed his early films to appear as theatre, thus enhancing the effect of his magic. In his *Wonderful Living Fan* (1904), for instance, he used dissolves and edits to make the women on screen appear and disappear as if by magic. For Méliès, the screen was simply another theatrical space, one enabled by the technology of the camera. Although he had little interest in the documentary uses of film deployed by the Lumières, Méliès's theatrical performances endure precisely because they have been so thoroughly preserved in his cinema.

Although avant-garde artists did not use film to document live performances, many were enamoured of the new medium and began staging works for camera that incorporated elements of live performances. Man Ray, for instance, introduced performance scenarios into films such as *L'Etoile de Mer* (1928) and *The Mysteries of the Chateau of Dice* (1929). Theatre was also fodder for early film scenarios; D.W. Griffith based many of his early short films on plays and theatrical scenarios (for example *A Drunkard's Reformation* [1909], a short metatheatrical melodrama about the redemptive power of love witnessed on stage). As David Mayer writes, much of Griffith's early film work was adapted from the stage: 'Nearly half of his most admired films are adaptations of stage dramas and are heavily reliant on theatrical practices for their effectiveness'.⁴⁴ Because of the need for material, early film served as a perhaps unintentional theatrical archive and distribution centre. But the economics of these relations quickly shifted as film theorists and artists called for cinema to break its reliance on theatre (a comparatively traditional medium). By 1905 nickelodeon movie theatres in the US were taking over vaudeville houses and music halls that had been the primary sources of mass entertainment throughout the nineteenth century. The first nickelodeon was built in 1905, and by 1910 there were more than 10,000 in the US alone. According to Russell Merritt, by 1910 more than twenty-six million Americans, nearly 20 per cent of the population, attended nickelodeons every week.⁴⁵ Increasingly when audiences saw performance, they saw it on screen.

By the mid-twentieth century both audio recordings and photography had been eclipsed by filmic documentation of theatre. Since 1970, the New York Public Library for the Performing Arts has maintained the Theatre on Film and Tape Archive, one of the largest collections of stage recordings in existence. Although the collection includes a number of works recorded on film, the majority of the collection was recorded on magnetic videotape, a format that would dominate from the 1980s until the advent of digital video in the late 1990s. Invented in the early 1950s, videotapes facilitated recording, editing, and broadcast. The first videotapes were introduced in 1956 and CBS Television used them for a delayed broadcast that same year. As videotape technologies became more affordable in the 1980s, individual artists and companies began documenting their own work. Performance artists and companies often recorded performances on film, usually in collaboration with filmmakers. Merce Cunningham, Yvonne Rainer, and Pina Bausch were only a few of those who collaboratively created dance performance for film. *Dionysis in 69*, directed in 1970 by Brian de Palma from the stage work by Richard Schechner and the Performance Group, remains an iconic example of theatre on film. Such endeavours were costly; video allowed theatre artists to record and disseminate performances much more quickly, and it permitted television stations to broadcast stage plays. Throughout the 1970s and 1980s, theatre broadcasts increased on television. Perhaps the most ambitious and widely watched of these was the 1982 mini-series *The Life and Adventures of Nicholas Nickelby*, filmed from the stage version at the Old Vic in London and broadcast by Channel 4 in the UK. (It was re-broadcast in the United States in 1983.)

As recording technologies became more accessible in the late twentieth century and video became a dominant mode of theatrical transmission, such changes prompted important debates about the use of media documentation to produce historical artefacts of theatrical performance. These debates were ontological in nature – that is, they were concerned with the things that defined live performance's identity in an age of cinematic and digital representations – and they continued through the 1990s and into the twenty-first century. Among the most cited texts in this debate is American performance theorist Peggy Phelan's *Unmarked* (1993), which defined performance as that which 'cannot be saved, recorded, documented, or otherwise participate in the circulation of representations *of* representations'.[46] French scholar Patrice Pavis similarly argued that it was the 'living archive' of performance that was the most significant: 'it is this living memory of theatre that is much the most precious, a treasure that escapes mediated recordings'.[47] Pavis further cites director Eugenio Barba's characterization of theatre as 'living memory'.[48] And yet, Pavis also acknowledges video as a useful resource for performance analysis. 'Video', he writes, 'reproduces the real time and general movement of a performance. It constitutes the most complete medium [for documentation and transmission of live performance] on the level of bringing together the greatest amount of information'.[49] By the end of the twentieth century, media recordings were no longer only supplements to theatrical performances, but threatened to surpass the live event as the primary mode of viewing those performances. In *Liveness: Performance in a Mediatized Culture* (1999), American theorist Philip Auslander challenged Phelan's assertion that performance was that which could not be recorded. He reframed her polarized distinction between recorded work and live performance, arguing that both media (the recorded and the live event) needed to be defined in relationship to audiences' daily experiences, where the live and the mediatized increasingly blurred into one another (in, for example, the viewing of 'live-to-air' television specials, or the popularity of Broadway musicals based on Disney movies). In 2005, he followed this work with an analysis of the 2004 National Endowment for the Arts (NEA) report on American arts participation. There he reported that 'even though the percentage of adults who attended live theatre at least once in 2002 is higher than the percentage that viewed theatre in mediatized forms, the theatre is being consumed in mediatized forms two to three times more often than it is attended live'.[50]

In the years after Auslander's influential publications, the availability of mediated performance through digital networks and digital media expanded further, with new venues for performance and its documentation emerging online. Performing arts archives that had proliferated in the 1990s increasingly turned to digital and streaming video. England's National Theatre Live launched in June 2009 and since then has broadcast over twenty productions to 3.5 million people worldwide; New York's Metropolitan Opera Live in HD programme began in 2006 and broadcasts live opera performances to movie theatres throughout North America.[51] The TOFT (Theatre on Film and Tape) video collection at the New York Public Library is digitizing its collection, while the Jerome Robbins Dance Division Audio and Moving Image Archive launched a streaming website in 2014. The Hemispheric Institute Digital Video Library at New York University offers more than 600 hours of performance recordings, and On the Boards in Seattle, WA (US) documents contemporary theatre and dance for viewing through its online video service, ontheboards.tv. In the early twenty-first century, publishers similarly began investing in digital content that includes video documentation of live performance, and new archives and collections are constantly expanding.[52] Less formal peer-to-peer networks of performance documentation have emerged as well, such as The Contemporary Performance Network and Dance-Tech.net. Throughout the 1990s and early 2000s, scholars debated the validity of mediated documents for use in theatre history and analysis, but as the inevitable influence of digital technologies took hold, scholarly organizations such as the American Society for Theatre Research launched the American Theatre Archive Project to support theatre companies as they developed their own archival materials.

Of course, not all performance archives are so formally constituted. As dance and performance scholar Maaike Bleeker has observed, YouTube videos have afforded the current generation of dance-makers the most comprehensive knowledge of dance history ever available.⁵³ Today theatre, digital culture and cultural memory converge online, simultaneously turning many of us into voracious archivists of our own daily experiences (in, for example, social media postings of daily life: food, pets, and children, among many other things) even as we outsource our individual memory functions to our digital devices. Thanks to digital technologies, many of the world's history museums increasingly operate like theatres themselves, with interactive displays and role-playing built into the design of collections. Theatre historian Scott Magelssen has documented the proliferation of performance in history museums and the international conference MuseumNext regularly includes workshops and sessions dedicated to fostering visitor engagement through theatrical installations. (For example, the UK-based immersive theatre company Punchdrunk produced a site-specific interactive performance for the Royal Maritime Museum in London, and the George W. Bush Presidential Center and Library features an interactive history game, Decision Points Theater, at the centre of its exhibits.) Meanwhile, traditional dramatic forms continue to experiment with new media platforms, both in the development of genres such as Twitter plays and more subtly and symbolically, as in Anne Washburn's play *Mr. Burns: A Post-Electric Play* (2014), which imagines a future society without electricity reconstructing its culture by restaging popular television shows. Plays like Washburn's, increasingly popular in the digital age as a reflection of an e-hungry culture, hark directly back to the Dadaists and other avant-garde modernists in their urge simultaneously to document and to critique the modern subject's core reliance on recording technologies as a source of identity and memory, as well as a means of preserving the modern experience for posterity.

CONCLUSION

As we approach the middle decades of the twenty-first century, digital technologies have become quotidian, their incursions into our daily lives the subject of continual cultural commentary. Few commentators remark, however, on the extent to which these technologies create *theatrical* experiences of our lives even as they archive them. More common is the oft-expressed concern that the theatre is 'dying', as audiences experience performance in a wide range of mediated forms instead. But perhaps we should view the changing status of theatre differently. Thanks to the inherent performativity of digital media, theatre no longer needs to happen exclusively within conventional theatre spaces but may embed itself within new social modes, from museums to Facebook to Twitter plays and beyond. Throughout the twentieth century, theatre steadily moved from the exclusive domain of live enactments to increasingly mediated ones distributed across new technological platforms; the resulting hybrid practices documented and preserved the theatre event, but also altered modern theatre's ontology in the process. That we often do not see these mediated practices as forms of theatre recalls the ultimate lesson of Dick's preserving machine, with which this chapter opened. Perhaps theatre has found a way to survive amid the various media of the modern age, but like the deformed 'bach beetle' fed back to the machine, we no longer recognize it as what it once was.

NOTES

Introduction: The Impossible Modern Age

1. See Austin 1975 [1962], Butler 1990.
2. Arguably, all historical eras are performative; 'History' as a discipline does the work of speaking history-as-era into being. The modern is a limit case for this practice, in part because it describes multiple eras at once (thus demonstrating the impossibility of its existing *except* as a function of discourse), and in part because we continue, in the moment of my writing and your reading, to live in a moment broadly construed as modern – and to naturalize our modernity as a natural state of human affairs.
3. Scholars generally use the term 'early modern' to describe moments in European history beginning in the fifteenth century and ending roughly at the industrial revolution; for some the early modern does not begin before the Enlightenment, while for others it begins long before the birth of Shakespeare. 'Late modern' as a historiographical marker tends to coincide with the use of the term 'late capital' – the latter signifying the shift into first a technologically-driven manufacturing economy (Fordism), and then a financial-services-driven economy based on immaterial labour (see Lazzarato 1996). Hobsbawm (1988, 1975) locates the 'age of capital' between 1848 and 1875, recognizing the fundamental imbrication of capitalism and modernity during the industrial revolution. Jameson (1991) theorizes relationships among the modern, the so-called postmodern, and neoliberal marketization. McKinnie discusses modern theatre's imbrication with late finance capitalism extensively in Chapter 1.
4. Albanese 1996, 2. See also De Certeau 1988.
5. Singer 2001, 19.
6. On modern theatre and memory see Gluhovic 2013; Rayner 2006; on theatrical memories and the politics of recording them, see Phelan 1993.
7. This is not to suggest Anglo-European modernity is unique in this regard; modernity practiced in other geographical and cultural locales looks and feels differently, and

enacts space and time differently. For an influential discussion of 'multiple modernities', see Eisenstadt 2000. For an instructive example from the Japanese perspective, see Chapter 8.

8. This founding division enabled the cultural genocides that shaped modernity in settler-colonial nations such as Canada, where Indigenous populations were forced into residential schooling throughout the twentieth century or 'scooped' form their parents through the 1960s, and South Africa, where racial segregation used space as a tool to hierarchize bodies until the official end of apartheid in 1994.
9. Brief examples might include: Ferdinand de Saussure's conception of the linguistic sign as tripartite; Jacques Lacan's split between the eye and the gaze as the psychoanalytic subject struggles but fails to see himself directly; Julia Kristeva's articulation of abjection as a psychosomatic paradigm, in which the world is fractured into that which is 'self' and that which cannot be admitted into the self (but which shapes and defines the self nevertheless).
10. For examples that discuss modern theatre in this way, see the essays collected in Ackerman and Puchner 2006 and Knowles et al. 2003; Diamond 1997, 3–41; Ridout 2006, 35–69.
11. See Diamond 2003, 11.
12. See Dolan 1988, 1, for a clear articulation of this critical commonplace. For an exploration of naturalism's ethics in relation to modernity's social promises, see Williams 2006.
13. Solnit 2003, 1–24.
14. Solnit briefly touches upon the invention of time zones nationally and transnationally in order to aid rapid human and goods movement; for an expanded and nuanced discussion of temporal coordination, see Ogle 2015.
15. Ibid., 11–12.
16. In 1914 the assassination of Archduke Franz Ferdinand and his wife, Sophie, of Austria precipitated the first major events of the First World War; the Berlin Olympics of 1936 offered a spectacle of growing Nazi power on a grand scale; the assassination of Martin Luther King, Jr. in 1968 changed the face of the American civil rights movement; student pro-democracy protestors were brutally slaughtered during the Tiananmen Square Massacre of 1989.
17. The Napoleonic Wars offer an instructive antecedent here; twentieth- and twenty-first-century global warfare normalizes what Napoleon's ambition inaugurated in the early nineteenth century.
18. See Aston 2013.
19. See Hobsbawm 1975, 270–93.
20. As feminist architecture critics have recently argued, the invention of the modern home by the premiere male architects and designers of the period relied heavily on invisible female labour; see Colomina 2007 and Friedman 2007 for just two examples.
21. De Certeau 1983, 91–110.
22. Diamond would call this 'the time of the other' (2003, 7).
23. Davis 2010, 148.
24. See Abel 2003, vi.
25. See Oltermann 2014.

Chapter One: Institutional Frameworks: Theatre, State, and Market in Modern Urban Performance

1. I wish to thank Franco Boni and Tiana Roebuck at The Theatre Centre for their assistance in the preparation of this chapter.
2. Although I do not discuss The Theatre Centre, I address the ideology of a 'permanent home' and the history of Toronto's theatrical and urban development in McKinnie 2007.
3. Among other things, these incentives include: tax regimes that treat capital gains more favourably than earned income; long-term wage stagnation, which encourages seeking out other sources of income or credit (for instance, by investing in property or borrowing against equity held in property); and cuts to private and public pensions (which intensify the hope that the value of a property might be monetized at a future date and replace income that would otherwise have been provided by a pension).
4. See Polanyi 2002, and Polanyi 1957.
5. Agnew 1988, 2.
6. Burawoy 2013, 38.
7. Polanyi 2002, 76.
8. To a lesser degree this antagonism has been directed towards the market, though modern theatre's history as a predominantly bourgeois institution makes disavowal of the market a rather more complicated, and ontologically troubling, endeavour.
9. Other countries that could be said to occupy this middle position are the United Kingdom, Australia, Ireland, and New Zealand. This is perhaps not surprising, given that many of them, including Canada, modelled their own arts funding bodies on the Arts Council of Great Britain to greater and lesser degrees. There are, of course, many variations and nuances within this general typology (including within Canada itself – Quebec subsidizes the arts to a greater extent than other provinces in Canada) but I would contend that they do not disrupt a broadly accurate larger picture.
10. Agnew 1988, 6.
11. Balme 2014, 41–2.
12. Ibid., 42.
13. Ibid., 43.
14. For a discussion of these legal developments and some of their contemporary implications, see Woolf 2009, 18–19.
15. This disposition is reinforced by the fact that part of the operation of an institution must be devoted to the reproduction of the institution itself, usually along already existing lines.
16. Sellars 2003, 133.
17. Jackson 2011, 16.
18. In some cases there may also be a complete overlap between institutions and organizations. One prominent example of this, as Balme notes, is a national theatre designated by statute. A national theatre is an institution insofar as it is a category established by law but an organization in that it is realized through the creation of a particular theatre company.

19. Balme 2014, 43.
20. Postlewait 2009, 80.
21. Ibid., 64. The corollary to the shock trope is the crisis. The crisis may arise within theatre itself, where some sort of action is implored to remedy a proclaimed malaise or impasse (as with Peter Brook's 'Deadly Theatre'), or it may arise in society at large, and therefore theatre is compelled to intervene (as Sellars argues). The formulation of some sort of 'manifesto' is often a key first step either way.
22. Pilkington 2001, 60.
23. Ibid.
24. Ibid., 61.
25. Melanson 2013. For relevant statistics on Toronto's development boom, and its geographical distribution, see City Planning Division 2015.
26. For statistics on high-rise construction across the globe, see http://skyscraperpage.com/cities/?s=1&c=4&p=0&r=50&10=0 (a high-rise is defined as a building twelve storeys or higher). The City of Toronto's Economic Development Committee began regularly tracking such projects in 2011, and each year Toronto has outpaced any other North American city for buildings under construction. For the most recent comparative data see Economic Development Committee 2016, 16–17.
27. Carlson 1989, 72–97.
28. See Ouzounian 2014; Ouzounian 2013; 'Queen West Gains Arts Hub' 2014; Nestruck 2014; The Theatre Centre n.d.
29. Of course, the history of the building's sponsorship illustrates some of the rather more complicated relationships that the apparent altruism of such civic institutions can tend to efface. Carnegie's philanthropy, for example, was made possible by some fairly controversial business practices including his involvement in the Johnstown Flood in Pennsylvania 1889, which killed over 2,000 people, and his ruthless suppression of the Homestead Strike in 1892.
30. Toronto Arts Council 2014, 16.
31. The formal BMR policy was first adopted in 2002, though the practice of providing low-cost tenancies to organizations that helped achieve municipal aims predates this. It should be noted that the BMR agreement relating to 16 Ryerson Avenue, the home of Theatre Passe Muraille, is between the City and Artscape, a non-profit cultural property manager that operates a number of arts facilities and housing projects in Toronto. Theatre Passe Muraille is Artspace's sub-tenant.
32. Deputy City Manager and Chief Financial Officer 2014, 13.
33. Ibid.
34. *Planning Act* 1990.
35. These are only some of the problems that arise from Section 37 agreements. Their complications are coming under increasing scrutiny, including from the City itself. See Gladki Planning Associates 2014; Moore 2013.
36. In a number of cases, it has also resulted in new theatres and arts facilities not only being financed by condominium developments but also housed within them. For example, Crow's Theatre is situated within a condominium development in Riverdale, a neighbourhood in the east end of downtown Toronto. Supported by Streetcar Developments, the new Crow's facility has been named after its sponsor: 'Streetcar Crowsnest'.

Chapter Two: Social Functions: Consumers and Producers

1. Partha Chatterjee 1997, 204.
2. Ridout 2006, 40.
3. Habermas 1981.
4. Adorno and Horkheimer 1997, 137.
5. Adorno 2013, 309.
6. Bharucha 1983, 9.
7. Sudipto Chatterjee 2007, 11.
8. Da Costa 2010, 45.
9. Bharucha 1983, xv.
10. Bhatia 2004, 76–94.
11. Da Costa 2010, 52.
12. Ibid., 54.
13. Bharucha 1983, 185.
14. See for example Deshpande 2002.
15. Boal's *Theatre of the Oppressed* was published in English in 1979.
16. Babbage 2004, 20.
17. Ganguly 2010, 73–4 and 87–9.
18. Da Costa 2010, 8–9.
19. Ibid., 69, 70.
20. Ibid., 71.
21. Martin 2004, x.
22. Brecht 2015b, 193.
23. Ibid., 227.
24. Brecht 2015a, 61–71.
25. Goehr 2008.
26. Adorno 2009, 199.
27. Adorno 2013, 26.
28. Adorno 2009, 196.

Chapter Three: Sexuality and Gender: New Stories and New Spaces on the Modern Stage

1. Thanks to Kim Solga, who was instrumental to formulating this chapter's argument and carefully revised the text and supported me throughout the process.
2. Schnitzler 1982, xi.
3. Ziolkowski 2009, 99.
4. Though the play had been produced on Broadway as early as 1955 (running simultaneously with *Cat on a Hot Tin Roof*), several adaptations were produced on and off-Broadway and in London in the late 1980s through to the 2010s. This wave of adaptation and translatation may have been because the embargo on German-language productions was lifted in 1982, but seems most likely to be traced to the ways in which the play's critique of meaningless sex and hints of syphillis were newly relevant in the AIDS-affected continental and North American theatre.
5. Haydon 2009.

6. Richards 1994.
7. Martinez 1998.
8. Brantley 2011.
9. Foucault 1978, 18.
10. 'Before and After the Wolfenden Report' n.d.
11. Bordman 1999, 283.
12. Quoted in Louvish 2007, 120.
13. Historians and biographers have variously reported the number of *Sex*'s performances as 339, 356, 375 and 385.
14. Quoted in Schlissel 1997, 15.
15. Quoted in Schlissel 1997, 10.
16. Critics also compared *Sex* to a disease, co-opting familiar tropes about venereal disease and prostitution in their reviews. For example, on 30 April 1926 the *New York Daily Mirror* railed that '[t]his production is not fit for the police. It comes rather in the province of our Health Department. It is a sore spot in the midst of city that needs disinfecting'; on 8 May 1926 the *New Yorker* complained that the audience was left as sick as they might be near 'anything indescribably filthy'. The theatre became a place where one might become diseased rather than a space for entertainment and leisure activity; West had to be removed in order to 'clean up' the theatre itself.
17. Hamilton 1997, 43.
18. Borsodi 1929, 7.
19. Ibid., 1.
20. For more on US burlesque in the period, see Pullen 2002 and Shteir 2005, especially 49–91 and 143–77. For European burlsque, see Gay 2001, Gordon 2015, and Walkowitz 2012.
21. Though both the post-Second World War Kinsey Reports and Masters' and Johnson's 1960s and 1970s research established that homosexuality and sexual promiscuity were more common than previously believed, I use 'mainstream' here to refer to the ideological belief, still powerful through the later twentieth century in Amerian and some European contexts, that sexual activity was only permissible between heterosexual, married couples.
22. Wollman 2008, 8.
23. Rich 1989.
24. Wollman 2013, 3.
25. Ibid., 5.
26. Bair 1990, 640.
27. Tynan et al. 1969, 9.
28. Ibid., 122–3.
29. Zarhy-Levo 2008, 230.
30. Funke 1969, 54.
31. Barnes 1969.
32. Sova 2004, 194.
33. 'Naked and Uncensored' 1970, 14.
34. Saunders 2015.
35. Wollman 2013, 13.
36. Taubman 1963, 125.
37. Kauffman 1966, 93.

38. May 1988, 82.
39. Bottoms 2003, 177.
40. Ibid., 178.
41. Bottoms 2009, 12.
42. Ibid., 232.
43. Argelander 1974, 82.
44. Ibid., 86.
45. Ibid., 86.
46. McNulty 1992, 68–9.
47. Gerard 1987.
48. Kaufman 2002, 119.
49. Ludlam 2001, 269.
50. Ibid., 271.
51. Bottoms 2009, 274. For more on the history of La MaMa and its pre-eminence in New York City's theatre community, see pages 272–4.
52. Ibid., 326.
53. Gussow 1970, 57.
54. Ibid.
55. Quoted in Kaufman 2002, 122.
56. Ibid.
57. Ibid., 123–4.
58. Ibid., 124–5.
59. Ludlam's work anticipates the queer feminist troupe, Split Britches, founded in 1980 by Peggy Shaw, Lois Weaver, and Deborah Margolin. Split Britches began performing their own pastiche of classic film, the theatrical canon, and narratives of alternative sexuality at the WOW Café, a feminist performance space. For more on Split Britches see Case, *Split Britches: Lesbian Practice/Feminist Performance*.
60. Atkinson 1955a.
61. Atkinson 1955b, 18.
62. Ibid.
63. Price 1955, 8.
64. Pappus 1955.
65. Robert Anderson's *Tea and Sympathy* (1953) tells the story of a prep school boy suspected of being gay by his classmates; he prefers music to sports and enjoys reading. His housemaster's wife, frustrated in her marriage, flirts with him in order to bolster his confidence. Real affection grows between the two; she leaves her husband and eventually marries and lives happily ever after.
66. McNamara 2001, 127.
67. 'M-G-M Buys 'Cat' . . .' 1955.
68. Palmer and Bray 2009, 172.

Chapter Four: The Environment of Theatre: 'Home' in the Modern Age

1. For more on the global influence of this play, see Holledge 2008, and Bollen and Holledge 2011. For more on Ibsen and architecture, particularly in the context of his work illustrating 'the concept of a true home [. . .] to be nothing but a copy and a shell', see Sandberg 2015.

2. Some of the many critics who address this issue include Chaudhuri 1995, Grene 2014, and Sandberg 2001. For books that extend the topic, see Hill 2011, Mani 2012, Magnarelli 2008, and Rokem 1986.
3. For a collection of articles on the state of the arts under the social and economic constraints of neoliberal austerity following the 2008 market crunch, see Ridout and Schneider 2012.
4. As we write this chapter in 2015, news feeds in the UK and Europe are dominated by stories of the movement of economic migrants and peoples displaced by war from Libya, Syria, and North Africa, to locations throughout Europe; and by stories of profound daily suffering from Greece as that nation struggles to hold onto its status as a Eurozone member.
5. This project has echoes with Grene, who argues for 'the double story: of the mutations of the naturalist interior as imagined by successive playwrights through the modern period and of the shifting theatrical realisation of that iconic form, home on the stage and its staging' (2014, 13). He also argues that directors and playwrights still seek 'to find the right images to release the range of meanings immanent within the still fraught, still compelling idea of home on the stage' (2014, 206). Chaudhuri also deploys a doubled image in her analysis of staging place in modern drama, that of the 'incessant dialogue between belonging and exile, home and homelessness' (1995, 15). Our use of the term 'double optic', however, derives from Elin Diamond, and focuses on the animating contradictions within the modern notion of home as both scourge and sanctuary, concrete and imaginary (2003, 11).
6. Chaudhuri 1995, 15.
7. For the relationships among theatre-going, shopping, and gendered consumer patterns at the turn of the twentieth century, see Schweitzer 2009.
8. Morley 2000, 16.
9. See Burnett (1978, 95) on the range of homes that were developed for this market, and on the rise of the middle class as a group that placed great store in the type of home they inhabited.
10. Burnett 1978, 193. On the gendered dimensions of the modern bourgeois home, see Colomina 2007 and Friedman 2007.
11. Morley 2000, 7.
12. Short 1999, x.
13. Hobsbawm quoted in Morley 2000, 4.
14. Chaudhuri 1995, xii.
15. Ibid., 8.
16. Ibid., 53.
17. Ibid., xiii.
18. Ibid., 212.
19. Diamond 2003, 19.
20. Ibid., 2003, 11.
21. Freud 1919, 4; emphasis and lower case in original. Keane observes that the second meaning of *Heimlich* is 'concealment'; thus '*heimlich* contains *unheimlich*, because to conceal is the exact opposite of making familiar' (lower case in original). Likewise, Bammer explains that home 'has always been *unheimlich*: not just the utopian place of safety and shelter for which we supposedly yearn, but also the place of dark

secrets, of fear and danger, that we can only inhabit furtively' (Keane and Bammer quoted in Morley 2000, 80, 79). For the uncanny in the context of domestic architecture, see Vidler 1992.
22. Tuan 1977, 100.
23. Ibid., 99.
24. Ibid., 86.
25. Allain and Harvie 2006, 62.
26. Tuan 1977, 88.
27. Ibid., 47.
28. Bachelard has been critiqued for romanticizing domestic life and disregarding darker aspects of uncanny experience; see Morley 2000, 19 and 56.
29. Bachelard 1969, xxxvi.
30. Ibid., 4.
31. Ibid., 203.
32. See Carnicke 2014 for a full explanation of 'experiencing' in Stanislavsky's framework for actors.
33. Sandberg 2001, 43–4.
34. In 2012–2015 the Young Vic received just over £5.2 million in public support through the Arts Council of England's Grant-in-Aid programme, and from 2015 to 2018 it is projected to receive slightly more (Arts Council of England 2015).
35. Wright 2014.
36. Chekhov 2014, 39.
37. Taylor 1997, 115–38.
38. The only cost associated with *AWLB* is the £3 fee to climb the Wren Monument at tour's end.
39. Janet Cardiff produces comparable work. See for instance *The Missing Voice: Case Study B* (Cardiff 1999).

Chapter Five: Circulations: Visual Sovereignty, Transmotion, and Tribalography

1. Howe 1999, 117.
2. See Werry 2014, 100.
3. Marker 2011, 100.
4. Ibid., 101
5. Maungwudaus 1848, 4.
6. Ibid., 5–7.
7. Ibid., 6
8. See ibid., 8–9.
9. Vizenor 1994, vii.
10. Ibid.
11. Raheja 2010, 193.
12. Simpson 2011, 88, quoting Vizenor 1998, 15.
13. *Buffalo Dance*, Library of Congress n.d.
14. Bold 2015, 225.
15. It is important to note that not all filmic representations of Indigenous peoples *were* controlled by non-Indigenous producers. The earliest silent-film westerns, while

continuing to draw on pre-cinematic 'Indian' stereotypes, relied heavily on Native talent, often under Indigenous cinematic control, and often going 'energetically against the stereotypical grain'. See Bold 2015, 228.
16. Raheja 2010, 193–4.
17. Nikkel 2014, 19.
18. Grimshaw 2014, 432–3.
19. Ibid., 192.
20. Tagaq, quoted in Falk 2014.
21. Tagaq, quoted in Nicholls 2014.
22. Beginning in the mid-nineteenth century, Aboriginal children were removed from their families and sent to government-funded, church-run schools, which had the effect of severing children's connections to their families, languages, and cultures. Over 150,000 children attended these schools. The last residential school in Canada closed in 1996.
23. Tagaq, quoted in Dickie n.d.
24. Tagaq, quoted in Buzzalino 2015.
25. Basso 2010.
26. Lenze 2009, 80.
27. See Allen 2012.
28. Simpson 2011, 89.
29. Ibid.
30. 2oolman replaced DJ Shub as producer in Summer 2014.
31. Bondy 2013.
32. Colhoun 2015.
33. Benevides 2012.
34. Bear Witness, quoted in Bondy 2013.
35. DJ NDN, quoted in Werman 2012.
36. Drawing upon new modernist studies, we understand 'modernisms' to refer to artistic responses to modernity that have taken different forms as they have emerged at different times among different cultures in different parts of the world. See Mao and Walkowitz 2008.
37. DJ BuddaBlaze, quoted in Colhoun 2015.
38. 'Global bass' refers to a global movement in which usually working class, colonized musicians blend politicized hip-hop, dance music, and electronic music, always bass-driven. Bear Witness told journalist Halley Bondy in 2012, 'we've become *allies* with the global bass community' (emphasis added).
39. Weaver 2014. Weaver's book re-reads the history and literature of the Atlantic to find Indigenous peoples at the centre, as cosmopolitan agents of international change and exchange.
40. Mandamin et al. 2012, 14.
41. Prior to contact, the Anishinaabeg lived near the Atlantic, but after it was prophesied that a light-skinned race would come to those shores bringing death and destruction, the people began to travel westward towards the Great Lakes – the Great Migration – as a protection against the coming colonizers.
42. Trudging up an unplowed mountain road in freezing rain with the sodden material of one's skirt wrapping itself around one's legs is no easy feat, but it is what is

required for the enactment of ancient ceremonial responsibilities. Water is, for Mandamin, a living relative with whom she communicates. Every action during these walks is undertaken for a vast audience of one: this 'performance' is '[only] for the water'. ('I will do it for the water' is the widely circulated slogan of the Water Walks. See Mandamin et al. 2012, 1.)
43. Ibid., 15.
44. Mandamin, quoted in Ashawasegai 2011.
45. Quoted in Mother Earth Water Walks n.d.
46. Ibid., 17.
47. See Higgs 2014.
48. See Mandamin et al. 2012, 16.
49. Simpson 2011, 34.
50. Howe 1999, 118.
51. Ibid., 118–20.
52. 'Haudenosaunee' means the Longhouse People. The Six Nations who came together, entering into a confederacy that has endured over 1,000 years, under the Great Tree of Peace, are the Onondaga, Mohawk, Seneca, Oneida, Cayuga, and Tuscarora nations.
53. Howe 1999, 122–3.
54. Ibid.
55. Franklin 1784, 30 (emphasis in original).
56. Howe 1999, 121.
57. Ibid., 120.
58. Ibid., 118.
59. The significance of Riggs's play cannot be overstated: one of the most powerful and evocative imaginings of the colonizing experience in the American canon, it engendered the transformation of 'the [American] musical from the smart, worldly wise musical comedy', as Robert Emmet Long has argued, 'to operetta that was set close to nature and celebrated ordinary American lives with a naïve lyricism'. See Long 2001, 37–8.
60. Sears 2008.
61. Riggs 1961, 132.
62. In 1931, Theresa Helburn produced *Green Grow the Lilacs* at New York City's Theatre Guild. It received good reviews and attracted good-sized audiences for the several weeks it played there, despite the new economic realities of the Great Depression. Afterwards, the Guild formed a road company and took the production across the United States. A decade later, America was facing a new crisis: it had just entered the war against Germany and Japan. It was at this time that Helburn happened to attend an amateur production of Riggs's play and was inspired to convince Rodgers and Hammerstein to adapt it into the musical that ultimately transformed Broadway. See Morrow 2014.
63. Hischak 2007, 73.
64. For many Indigenous peoples these are the four cardinal directions, plus up, down, and 'here'.
65. See Long 2001, 38.
66. See Womack 1999, 43.

67. See Riggs 1961, 156.
68. This refers to the final battle between the Osage and the Cherokee. When the Cherokee were forcibly relocated to the traditional territories of other nations, competition for shrinking resources became violent. Here and elsewhere Riggs is preoccupied with the violence that Indigenous people perpetrate on one another as learned behaviour imposed by the agents of colonization.
69. Riggs 1961, 138.
70. Ibid., 163.
71. Ibid., 167.
72. Ibid., 165.
73. *Broadway* 2004.

Chapter Six: Interpretations: The Stakes of Audience Interpretation in Twentieth-Century Political Theatre

* Translations from Russian are my own unless cited from secondary sources in English. Russian transliterations are based on common spellings in the text and on a simplified Library of Congress system for references cited in the endnotes.
1. Mueller 2006, 102.
2. Ibid., 105.
3. Brooker 2006, 215.
4. Fischer 1988, 372.
5. Willett 1964, 37.
6. Katz 2015, 300.
7. Mueller 2006, 107.
8. Ibid., 102.
9. Shklovskij 1998, 16.
10. Boal 2009, 137.
11. Mueller 2006, 107.
12. The 2014 revival was directed by Janni Younge.
13. Taylor 2009, 11.
14. Fevral'skii 1971, 22.
15. Lenin 1958–1965, 127, quoted in Rudnitsky 1988, 41.
16. Borovsky 1999, 12.
17. Russell 1990, 150.
18. Rudnitsky 1988, 41.
19. Fitzpatrick 1970, 1.
20. Tasks of the Theater Section, in *Sbornik dekretov i postanovlenii po narodnomu obrazovaniiu* (1919) 1: 140–3, in Senelick and Ostrovsky 2014, 61.
21. Fitzpatrick 1970, 157.
22. Russian Soviet Federative Socialist Republic.
23. Lunacharsky, 'Three Meetings', quoted in Fitzpatrick 1970, 141.
24. *Vestnik teatra* no. 48 (13–19 January 1920), quoted in Fitzpatrick 1970, 140.
25. Fitzpatrick 1970, 123n35.
26. Mayakovsky 1918, in Senelick and Ostrovsky 2014, 56.
27. Payne 1995, 10.

NOTES

28. Maiakovskii 1956, 359.
29. Fevral'skii 1971, 73. His books reproduce primary sources, many of them unpublished, from his personal archive. My analysis of the *Mystery-Bouffe* productions is based primarily on his books and these sources.
30. Lunacharskii 1918, in Lunacharskii 1964, 39.
31. Levinson 1918, in Lanina 1997, 384.
32. Aksenov [1926], in Fel'dman and Panfilova 2014, 30.
33. Ibid., 35.
34. Ibid., 35–6.
35. Fevral'skii 1976, 57.
36. Maiakovskii 1956, 248.
37. Rudnitsky 1988, 64.
38. Fevral'skii 1976, 59.
39. Ibid., 62–3.
40. Ibid., 61–2.
41. Erenburg 1922, 14, in Fel'dman and Panfilova 2014, 140.
42. Meierkhol'd 1968, 164, quoted in Posner 2015, 365.
43. Fevral'skii 1976, 62.
44. Rudnitsky 1988, 42.
45. Fevral'skii 1976, 62.
46. Vladimir Solov'ev, 'One of my Remembrances of Mayakovsky', in Senelick and Ostrovsky 2014, 58.
47. Sometimes translated as 'proscenium servants'.
48. Fevral'skii 1976, 62.
49. Braun 1995, 166.
50. Senelick and Ostrovsky 2014, 119.
51. Fel'dman 2014, 248.
52. Fevral'skii 1976, 64.
53. Daruze 1990, 81–2.
54. Zagorskii 1922, 111–12.
55. Ibid., 107–8.
56. Ibid., 109.
57. Ibid., 108.
58. Braun 1995, 168.
59. Beskin 1921, in Lanina 2000, 19.
60. Ibid., 19–20.
61. Sadko [Vladimir Blium] 1921, in Lanina 2000, 23.
62. This book was first published (in a journal) only in the 1990s and again, recently, in Fel'dman and Panfilova 2014.
63. Meyerhold was shot as an 'enemy of the people' on 2 February 1940. He was entirely erased from books, photographs, and mentions in daily life. His sentence was not overturned until 26 November 1955. Braun 2002, 159.
64. Jannarone 2015, 13.
65. Purkey 1996, 155–6. Sincere thanks to Malcolm Purkey for generously discussing this production with me.
66. Junction Avenue Theatre Company 2001, 256–7.

67. Ibid., 279.
68. Orkin 2001, 226.
69. Purkey 2015.
70. Orkin 2001, 230.
71. Cole 2010, xii.
72. Ibid., 5.
73. Lee 2001. Of the roughly 7,000 applicants, about 10 per cent were granted amnesty.
74. A TRC hearing typically provided onsite oral interpreters for four languages. See Cole 2010, 67–71.
75. Taylor 2010, viii.
76. McNeil 1997.
77. Kohler 2009b, 58.
78. Brown et al. 1968, 70.
79. Marx 2009, 240.
80. Kentridge 2009, 179.
81. Ibid., 198.
82. Jamal 2003, 56.
83. Ibid., 55.
84. Kentridge 2009, 193.
85. Ibid., 197.
86. The production premiered at the Kunstfest Weimar, Germany, on 17 June 1997 after a workshop production at Johannesburg's Market Theatre. It returned to the Market for a month-long run that August before embarking on an international tour. My analysis is based on Taylor 2010, the playbill, and a filmed performance from the 1997 Market run, plus photographs, reviews, articles, and interviews.
87. Coetzee 1998, 42.
88. Purkey 1997, 13.
89. Taylor 2010, 45.
90. Ibid., iii.
91. Ibid., iv.
92. Taylor 2007, n.p.
93. Taylor 2010, 24.
94. Ibid., 1.
95. Jones and Kohler 2010, xvii.
96. Coetzee 1998, 48.
97. Jones and Kohler 2010, xvii.
98. Cole 2010, 12.
99. Davids 2014, 23.
100. A Xhosa freedom hymn incorporated into the South African national anthem in 1994.
101. Taylor 2010, 69.
102. Taylor 2015.
103. Ibid.
104. Davids 2014, 22.
105. Taylor 2010, xv.
106. Triplett 1998.

107. Glueck 2001.
108. D. Taylor 1997, 123.
109. Definitions of 'interpret' and 'interpretation' are from the Oxford English Dictionary. Italics added.
110. Mueller 2006, 107.
111. Sayler 1920, 7–8.

Chapter Seven: Communities of Production: A Materialist Reading with an Offstage View

1. Carter 1929, 145. Translated from the firsthand observations of German artist and publicist, Arthur Holitscher.
2. Von Geldern 1993, 199.
3. De Certeau 1983, 117.
4. For this reason, we deliberately discuss consumption in this chapter alongside more 'traditional' analyses of production.
5. Williams 1989, 31–2.
6. For more on the AEA strike see Glenn 2000 and Holmes 2013.
7. Holmes 2013, 73.
8. Glenn 2000, 203.
9. Stufft uses the term 'chorus girl collective' to describe the collective nature of chorus girl performance, onstage, in dressing rooms, and in boarding houses (2011).
10. Quoted in Glenn 2000, 207. See also Holmes 2013, 71, 74.
11. Chauncey 1994, 228.
12. Glaspell 2005 [1926], 200.
13. Stansell 2000, 88.
14. Folpe 2002, 260.
15. Syssoyeva 2013, 49, and Worrall 1996, 21. According to Worrall, Stanislavsky stayed nearby on his parents' country estate and arrived to rehearsal every morning on horseback (42). He and Vsevolod Meyerhold used the same property in 1905 as a retreat to form a new company, the Theatre-Studio, which never opened.
16. Stanislavsky 1954–1961: vol. 5, 175; translated and quoted in Worrall 1996, 43.
17. Crawford 1977, 54.
18. Clurman 1945, 36.
19. Ibid., 51.
20. White (2014) addresses this neglect in the US commercial industry.
21. Carter and Cole 1992, 45; the wives' names are unknown.
22. Adalbert Albrecht, 'The Opera Factory of Illusions', *Evening Transcript* 25 September 1912. Cited in Carter and Cole 1992, 54.
23. For more on Lucile's designs for the *Follies* see Schweitzer 2009, especially chapter 5. For more on Urban's *Follies* settings, see Essin 2013, chapter 4.
24. Cited in Carter and Cole 1992, 103.
25. Lucas 2015.
26. 'One Day in Grand Street' 1926, 2.
27. For more details on designer Aline Bernstein's contributions to the Neighborhood Playhouse, see Essin 2013, chapter 3.

28. Neighborhood Playhouse season brochure, 1925–6.
29. Jones 2008, 1.
30. Ibid., 2.
31. Ibid., 4.
32. Ibid., 8.
33. Ibid., 11.
34. Kohler, Jones, and Luther 2009, 347.
35. Ibid., 347–50.
36. Ibid., 351.
37. Kohler 2009a, 26–32.
38. See, for example, Jones 2008, 4; Shapiro 1993.
39. Urry 2007, 6, 18. See also Cresswell 2006. For theatre and performance studies responses to the new mobility paradigm, see Wilkie 2014; Haenni 2008; Schweitzer 2015.
40. See Schweitzer 2015, chapter 1; Balme 2015; Davis 2000; Gillette 2015.
41. For more specific dates and tours, see Worrall 1996, 4, 77. Also see Poliakova 1992, 32–72.
42. Benedetti 1991, 320.
43. Stratford Festival 2015.
44. The following year, while in Toronto as part of a Canadian tour with the Kirov Ballet, the celebrated Russian dancer Mikhail Baryshnikov defected from the Soviet Union and found political asylum in Canada.
45. Von Eschen 2006.
46. See Schweitzer 2015, chapter 1.
47. Cooperstein 2014.
48. Crow 2014.
49. Cooperstein 2014.
50. Elderfield 1974, 101.
51. Quoted in Erickson 1984, 5.
52. Motherwell and Arp 1981, 51.
53. Sardi and West 1991, 5.
54. Miller 1988.
55. Wickstrom 2006, 79. For more on the transformation of Times Square see Wollman 2002.
56. Celona and Cusma 2013.
57. Kavanaugh 2013.
58. Schlossberg 2014.
59. Ibid.
60. Basinski, quoted in Schlossberg 2014.

Chapter Eight: Genres and Repertoires: Redressing the Nation in Ireland and Japan

1. Frow 2006, 10 (emphasis added).
2. Hollander 1978, 238.
3. Davis 1991, 111.

NOTES 237

4. Frow 2006, 2.
5. Zola 1974, 718.
6. Quoted in Kaplan and Stowell 1994, 11.
7. Balla 2004, 158.
8. Lamanova 2004, 176.
9. Gregory 1913, 9.
10. See Daly 2009, 61.
11. Synge quoted in Grene 2000, 83.
12. O'Connor 2009, 146.
13. Synge 1961, 41.
14. Ibid., 106.
15. Gregory 1913, 112.
16. Grene 2000, 82.
17. *Freeman's Journal* 1907, n.p.
18. Wetmore et al. 2014, 18.
19. Meech-Pekarik 1986, 187.
20. Freedman et al. 2013.
21. Low 2012, 1.
22. Tobin 1994, 4.
23. Smith 1996, 6.
24. O'Brien 1911, 7.
25. Quoted in Robb 1998, 14.
26. Artaud 1958, 54.
27. McGrath 2013, 44.
28. Quoted in McGrath 2013, 44.
29. See Kaplan and Stowell 1994, Schweitzer 2009.

Chapter Nine: Technologies of Performance: Machinic Staging and Corporeal Choreographies

1. Rabinbach 1990, 2.
2. Kracauer 1995, 76.
3. Ibid., 76, 83.
4. Ibid., 78.
5. Ibid., 79.
6. Meyerhold 1978.
7. Ibid.
8. Brockett et al. 2010, 270.
9. Meyerhold 1978.
10. Gordon 1995, 19.
11. Dixon 2007, 48.
12. Ibid.
13. Kracauer 1995, 76.
14. Ann Cooper Albright follows this counter argument by focusing on Fuller's dancing in Cooper Albright 2007, 2.
15. Artaud 1964, 62.

16. Ibid., 105.
17. Ibid., 92.
18. Ibid., 123.
19. Artaud 1988, 151.
20. Ibid., 115.
21. Brockett et al. 2010, 281.
22. Innes 1972, 185.
23. Ibid., 85. See the discussion of this piece by Brockett et al. 2010, 277.
24. Ibid.
25. Brecht 1978, 130. John Willett discusses interactions between Piscator and Brecht in Willett 1998, 102–20.
26. Ibid.
27. Brecht 1978, 218.
28. Ibid., 219.
29. Ibid., 192.
30. It is fitting that the French translation of 'Writings on Scene Architecture and Theatre Music' renders Brecht's phrase: 'elle fait pauvre'. Brecht 1972, 435.
31. Grotowski 2002, 19.
32. Ibid., 20
33. Ibid.
34. Greenspun 1970, n.p.
35. Burian 1970, 124.
36. Ibid., 134.
37. Brockett et al. 2010, 294.
38. Quoted in Salter 2010, 53
39. Brecht 1978, 9, quoted in Dixon 2007, 58.
40. O'Neill 2012, 122.
41. Klein 2006.
42. Philip Auslander understands the relation between US television and theatre 'as an allegory for the general relationship of live to mediatized forms within our cultural economy'. He also suggests that theatre influenced the desire to tape television shows in front of a 'live' studio audience. Auslander 2008, 10, 20–4.
43. Experimental Television Center n.d.
44. Reminiscent of Fuller's legacy, Moorman's feminist appropriation of technology for performance could be argued to have given rise to the genre of narcissistic video performance (for example, in the manner of Vito Acconci).
45. Bell Labs was a leader in developing technology for high-profile government projects at a moment in American history when technology directly impacted national and international politics. In the 1960s, for example, Bell Labs was involved in the arms race through the government's Apollo programme.
46. Klüver n.d.
47. Schneider 1972.
48. Schweber 1973.
49. Murray situates the discourse of *Indian Blood* in relation to the emergent discourse of critical race studies in Murray 1997, 169–88.

NOTES   239

50. subRosa 2014.
51. Jordan-Young 2010, n.p.
52. Fernandez et al. 2003.
53. Haraway 1991.
54. Jackson et al. 2015.
55. Rimini Protokoll 2012.
56. In Brecht 1978.
57. Peggy Phelan locates performance in an expression of liveness that evades representation and is contingent upon the presence of the body. Even more, she explains, 'Performance's independence from mass reproduction, technologically, economically, and linguistically is its greatest strength'. Phelan 1993, 149.
58. Vartanian 2014.
59. Critical Art Ensemble 2001, 104–5.
60. Ibid.,108.

Chapter Ten: Knowledge Transmission: Media and Memory

1. Dick 1969, 9.
2. Ibid., 6.
3. L. Moholy-Nagy 1987, 15.
4. S. Moholy-Nagy 1950, 19.
5. Benjamin 1968, 232.
6. Stein 1935, 104.
7. Quoted and translated in Holzapfel 2013, 52.
8. Gallagher-Ross 2015, 294.
9. Pudovkin et al. 1949, 52.
10. Sontag 1966, 24.
11. Mumford and Winner 2010, 3.
12. Holzapfel 2013, 5–6.
13. Ibid., 122.
14. Knight 1971, 14.
15. Vertov 1984, 42.
16. Ball 1974, 15.
17. Ibid., 221.
18. Gropius and Wensinger 1996, 26. See also Trimingham 2012.
19. Ibid., 34.
20. Benedikt 1964, 133.
21. For a more detailed consideration of the typographical illustrations, see Bay-Cheng 2007.
22. Benedikt 1964, 135.
23. Garner 2007, 510.
24. Cima 1984, 55.
25. Auslander 1994, 44.
26. Cronin 1999, 485.
27. Beckett 1960, 9 (emphasis added).

28. See Esslin 1975.
29. Knowlson 1980, 46–7.
30. See 'Science: Plastic Ball' 1951. Jacques Ellul's *The Technological Society* (1954; trans. 1964) includes similar speculations from an article in the Paris weekly *l'Express* in 1960. This essay included predictions from American and Russian scientists, who, according to Ellul, predicted frequent voyages to the moon, resolution of energy productions, and the accumulation of all human knowledge in '"electronic banks" and transmitted directly to the human nervous system by means of coded electronic messages'. See Ellul 1964, 432.
31. Ibid., 22.
32. Knowlson 1980, 28.
33. Ellul 1964, 431.
34. There is, for instance, no mention of Ellul or his book in Dirk Van Hulle and Mark Nixon's *Samuel Beckett's Library* (2013).
35. Beckett 1960, 13.
36. Roy Walker, 'Love, Chess and Death', in Knowlson 1980, 49.
37. Benjamin 1968, 229.
38. Turkle 2012, 283.
39. Knowlson, 'An Interview with Donald Davis', in Knowlson 1980, 62.
40. Senelick 1997, 262.
41. Mayer 2002, 229.
42. Shields 2014.
43. Anderson 2015, 53.
44. Mayer 2009, 5.
45. Merritt 2002.
46. Phelan 1993, 146.
47. Pavis 2003, 45.
48. Barba 2003, 36.
49. Pavis 2003, 43.
50. Auslander 2005, 7.
51. See Steichen 2009.
52. See for example the Routledge Performance Archive (www.routledgeperformancearchive.com), and the Digital Theatre Archive (www.digitaltheatrearchive.com).
53. Bleeker 2012.

BIBLIOGRAPHY

Abel, Lionel. 1963. *Metatheatre: A New View of Dramatic Form*. New York: Hill and Wang.
Abel, Lionel. 2003. *Tragedy and Metatheatre: Essays on Dramatic Form*. New York: Holmes & Meier.
Ackerman, Alan, and Martin Puchner, eds. 2006. *Against Theatre: Creative Destructions on the Modernist Stage*. Basingstoke: Palgrave.
Adorno, Theodor. 2009. *Night Music: Essays on Music 1928–1962*. London, New York and Calcutta: Seagull Books.
Adorno, Theodor. 2013. *Aesthetic Theory*. London: Bloomsbury.
Adorno, Theodor, and Max Horkheimer. 1997. *Dialectic of Enlightenment*. London and New York: Verso.
Agnew, Jean-Christophe. 1988. *Worlds Apart: The Market and the Theater in Anglo-American Thought, 1550–1750*. Cambridge: Cambridge University Press.
Aksenov, Ivan. [1926]. 'Piat' let Teatra im. Vs. Meierkhol'da'. In Fel'dman and Panfilova 2014, 21–208.
Albanese, Denise. 1996. *New Science, New World*. Durham, NC: Duke University Press.
Allain, Paul, and Jen Harvie. 2006. *The Routledge Companion to Theatre and Performance*. London: Routledge.
Allen, Chadwick. 2012. *Trans-Indigenous: Methodologies for Global Native Literary Studies*. Minneapolis: University of Minnesota Press.
Anderson, Joel. 2015. *Theatre and Photography*. London: Palgrave.
Andrews, Benedict, dir. 2012. *Three Sisters*. The Young Vic, London. Performance.
Argelander, Ronald. 1974. 'Charles Ludlam's Ridiculous Theatrical Co'. *TDR* 18 (2): 81–6.
Artaud, Antonin. 1958. *The Theatre and Its Double*, trans. Mary Caroline Richards. New York: The Grove Press.
Artaud, Antonin. 1964. *Le Théâtre et son double*. Paris: Gallimard.
Artaud, Antonin. 1988. *Selected Writings*, ed. Susan Sontag. Berkeley and Los Angeles: University of California Press.
Arts Council of England. 2015. 'National Portfolio, 2015–18'. Artscouncil.org.uk. Web.

Ashawasegai, Jennifer. 2011. 'Grandmother Walks to Protect Water'. *Windspeaker*. Web, 6 August 2015.
Aston, Elaine. 2013. 'But not that: Caryl Churchill's Political Shape Shifting at the Turn of the Millennium'. *Modern Drama* 56 (2): 145–64.
Atkinson, Brooks. 1955a. 'Theatre: Tennessee Williams' "Cat": Writer Depicts Some Restless Delta Folk'. *New York Times*, 3 April.
Atkinson, Brooks. 1955b. 'Theatre: Tennessee Williams' "Cat on a Hot Tin Roof"'. *New York Times*, 25 March.
Auslander, Philip. 1994. *From Acting to Performance: Essays in Modernism and Postmodernism*. New York and London: Routledge.
Auslander, Philip. 2005. 'No-Shows: The Head Count from the NEA'. *TDR* 49 (1). Web.
Auslander, Philip. 2008 [1999]. *Liveness: Performance in a Mediatized Culture*. Second Edition. New York and London: Routledge.
Austin, J.L. 1975 [1962]. *How To Do Things With Words*. Cambridge, MA: Harvard University Press.
Babbage, Frances. 2004. *Augusto Boal*. London and New York: Routledge.
Bachelard, Gaston. 1969 [1958]. *The Poetics of Space*, trans. Maria Jolas. Boston: Beacon.
Bair, D. 1990. *Samuel Beckett: A Biography*. London: Vintage.
Ball, Hugo. 1974. *Flight Out of Time: A Dada Diary*. Berkeley, CA: University of California Press.
Balla, Giacomo. 2004. 'The Antineutral Dress, A Futurist Manifesto'. In *Against Fashion: Clothing as Art, 1850–1930*, ed. Radu Stern, 157–9. Cambridge: MIT Press.
Balme, Christopher B. 2014. *The Theatrical Public Sphere*. Cambridge: Cambridge University Press.
Balme, Christopher B. 2015. 'The Bandmann Circuit: Theatrical Networks in the First Age of Globalization'. *Theatre Research International* 40 (1): 19–36.
Barba, Eugenio. 2003. *The Paper Canoe: A Guide to Theatre Anthropology*. London: Routledge.
Barnes, Clive. 1969. 'Theater: "Oh, Calcutta!" a Most Innocent Dirty Show'. *New York Times*, 18 June.
Basso, Keith. 2010. *Wisdom Sits in Places: Landscape and Language Among the Western Apache*. Albuquerque, NM: University of New Mexico Press.
Bay-Cheng, Sarah. 2007. 'Translation, Typography, and the Avant-Garde's Impossible Text'. *Theatre Journal* 59 (3): 467–83.
Beckett, Samuel. 1960. *Krapp's Last Tape And Other Dramatic Pieces*. New York: Grove.
'Before and After the Wolfenden Report'. N.d. *The Cabinet Papers 1915–1988*. Nationalarchives.gov.uk. Web.
Benedetti, Jean, ed. 1991. *The Moscow Art Theatre Letters*. New York: Routledge.
Benedikt, Michael. 1964. *Modern French Theatre: The Avant-Garde, Dada, and Surrealism: an Anthology of Plays*, ed. and trans. Michael Benedikt and George E. Wellwarth. New York: Dutton.
Benevides, Jose Luis. 2012. 'Album Review: A Tribe Called Red – Free Download'. *Gozamos*, 27 March. Web, 7 August 2015.
Benjamin, Walter. 1968. 'The Work of Art in the Age of Mechanical Reproduction'. In *Illuminations: Essays and Reflections*, ed. Hannah Arendt, trans. Harry Zohn. New York: Schocken.

Benjamin, Walter. 1999. *The Arcades Project*, trans. Howard Eiland and Kevin McLaughlin. Boston: Harvard University Press/Belknap.

Beskin, E. 1921. 'Revoliutsiia i teatr. *Misteriia-buff* Maiakovskogo'. *Vestnik rabotnikov iskusstv* 7–9. In Lanina 2000, 19–20.

Bharucha, Rustom. 1983. *Rehearsals of Revolution: The Political Theater of Bengal*. Honolulu: University of Hawaii Press.

Bhatia, Nandi. 2004. *Acts of Authority / Acts of Resistance: Theatre and Politics and Colonial and Postcolonial India*. Ann Arbor: University of Michigan Press.

Bleeker, Maaike A. 2012. '(Un)Covering Artistic Thought Unfolding'. *Dance Research Journal* 44 (2): 13–25.

Blium, Vladimir [pseud: Sadko]. 1921. 'Misteriia-buff'. *Vestnik teatra* 91–92. In Lanina 2000, 21–5.

Boal, Augusto. 1979. *The Theatre of the Oppressed*. London: Pluto Press.

Boal, Augusto. 2009. 'Theatre of the Oppressed'. In *Applied Theatre Reader*, ed. Tim Prentki and Sheila Preston, 130–7. London: Routledge.

Bold, Christine. 2005. 'Early Cinematic Westerns'. In *A History of Western American Literature*, ed. Susan Kollin, 225–41. Cambridge: Cambridge University Press.

Bollen, Jonathan, and Julie Holledge. 2011. 'Hidden Dramas: Cartographic Revelations in the World of Theatre Studies'. *The Cartographic Journal* 48 (4): 226–36.

Bondy, Halley. 2013. 'A Tribe Called Red Continues to Conquer: A Native DJ Trio from Ottawa Has Risen Amidst a New Civil Rights Movement'. *MTV Iggy*, 14 March. Web, 7 August 2015.

Bordman, Gerald. 1999. *American Theatre: A Chronicle of Comedy and Drama 1914–1930*. Oxford: Oxford University Press.

Borovsky, Victor. 1999. 'Russian Theatre in Russian Culture'. In *A History of Russian Theatre*, ed. Robert Leach and Victor Borovsky, 6–17. Cambridge: Cambridge University Press.

Borsodi, Ralph. 1929. *This Ugly Civilization*. New York: Simon and Schuster.

Bottoms, Stephen. 2003. 'The Efficacy/Effeminacy Braid: Unpacking the Performance Studies/Theatre Studies Dichotomy'. *Theatre Topics* 13 (2): 173–87.

Bottoms, Stephen. 2009. *Playing Underground: A Critical History of the 1960s Off-Off Broadway Movement*. Ann Arbor: University of Michigan Press.

Brantley, Ben. 2011. 'Web of Love, Explicitly Woven in Shades of Anguish.' *The New York Times*, 20 March. Web.

Braun, Edward. 1995. *Meyerhold: A Revolution in Theatre*. Iowa City: University of Iowa Press.

Braun, Edward. 2002. 'Vsevolod Meyerhold: The Final Act'. In *Enemies of the People: The Destruction of Soviet Literary, Theater, and Film Arts in the 1930s*, ed. Katherine Bliss Eaton, 145–62. Evanston: Northwestern University Press.

Brecht, Bertolt. 1972. *Ecrits sur le theater 1*, trans. Jean Tailleur et al. Paris: L'arche.

Brecht, Bertolt. 1978. *Brecht on Theatre: The Development of an Aesthetic*, trans. John Willett. London: Methuen.

Brecht, Bertolt. 2015a [1978]. *Brecht on Theatre: The Development of an Aesthetic*, trans. John Willett. London: Bloomsbury.

Brecht, Bertolt. 2015b. *Collected Plays: Two*. London: Bloomsbury.

Broadway: The American Musical. 2004. Prod. and dir. Michael Kantor. PBS Andorra. DVD.

Brockett, Oscar G., Margaret Mitchell and Linda Hardberger. 2010. *Making the Scene: A History of Stage Design and Technology in Europe and the United States*. Austin, TX: University of Texas Press.

Brook, Peter. 2008. *The Empty Space*. London: Penguin.
Brooker, Peter. 2006. 'Key Words in Brecht's Theory and Practice of Theatre'. In *The Cambridge Companion to Brecht*, ed. Peter Thomson and Glendyr Sacks, 209–24. Second ed. Cambridge: Cambridge University Press.
Brown, Helen, Jane Seitz, Peter Schumann, Kelly Morris and Richard Schechner. 1968. 'With the Bread and Puppet Theatre: An Interview with Peter Schumann (1968)'. *TDR* 12 (2): 62–73.
Buffalo Dance. N.d. Archive video. Library of Congress. Web, 11 December 2015.
Burawoy, Michael. 2013. 'Marxism After Polanyi'. In *Marxisms in the 21st Century*, 34–52. Johannesburg: Witts University Press.
Burian, Jarka M. 1970. 'Josef Svoboda: Theatre Artists in an Age of Science'. *Educational Review* 22 (2): 123–45.
Burnett, John. 1978. *A Social History of Housing 1815–1970*. London: Methuen.
Butler, Judith. 1990. *Gender Trouble: Feminism and the Subversion of Identity*. London: Routledge.
Buzzalino, Sebastian. 2015. 'High Performance Rodeo 2015: Tanya Tagaq'. *Beatroute*, 7 January. Web, 13 July 2015.
Canning, Charlotte. 2015. *On The Performance Front: US Theatre and Internationalism*. New York: Palgrave.
Cardiff, Janet. 1999. *The Missing Voice: Case Study B*. Audio-walk. Cardiffmiller. com. Web.
Carlson, Marvin. 1989. *Places of Performance: The Semiotics of Theatre Architecture*. Ithaca: Cornell University Press.
Carlson, Marvin. 2003. *The Haunted Stage: Theatre as Memory Machine*. Ann Arbor: University of Michigan Press.
Carnicke, Sharon M. 2014. *Stanislavsky in Focus: An Acting Master for the Twenty-First Century*. Second ed. New York: Routledge.
Carter, Huntley. 1929. *The New Spirit in the Russian Theatre*, trans. Arthur Holitscher. London: Brentano's.
Carter, Randolph, and Robert Reed Cole. 1992. *Joseph Urban: Architecture, Theatre, Opera, Film*. New York: Abbeville.
Case, Sue-Ellen. 1996. *Split Britches: Lesbian Practice/Feminist Performance*. New York and London: Routledge.
Celona, Larry, and Kathryn Cusma. 2013. 'Times Sq. Spidey Hits ma'. *New York Post*, 11 February. Web.
Chatterjee, Partha. 1997. *The Present History of West Bengal*. Oxford: Oxford University Press.
Chatterjee, Sudipto. 2007. *The Colonial Staged: Theatre in Colonial Calcutta*. London, New York and Calcutta: Seagull Books.
Chaudhuri, Una. 1995. *Staging Place: The Geography of Modern Drama*. Ann Arbor: University of Michigan Press.
Chauncey, George. 1994. *Gay New York: Gender, Urban Culture, and the Making of a Gale Male World 1890–1940*. New York: Basic.
Chekhov, Anton. 2014. *The Cherry Orchard*, adapted by Simon Stephens. London: Bloomsbury.
Cima, Gay Gibson. 1984. 'Acting on the Cutting Edge: Pinter and the Syntax of Cinema'. *Theatre Journal* 36 (1). Web.
City Planning Division. 2015. 'How Does the City Grow?' Profile Toronto. Toronto: City of Toronto. Web.
Clurman, Harold. 1945. *The Fervent Years*. New York: Alfred A. Knopf.

Coetzee, Yvette. 1998. 'Visibly Invisible: How Shifting the Conventions of the Traditionally Invisible Puppeteer Allows for More Dimensions in Both the Puppeteer–puppet Relationship and the Creation of Theatrical Meaning in *Ubu & the Truth Commission*'. *South African Theatre Journal* 1–2: 35–51.

Cole, Catherine M. 2010. *Performing South Africa's Truth Commission: Stages of Transition*. Bloomington: Indiana University Press.

Colhoun, Damaris. 2015. 'A Tribe Called Red's Electric Powwow Puts Indigenous Culture Center Stage'. *The Guardian*, 28 July. Web, 7 August 2015.

Colomina, Beatriz. 2007. *Domesticity at War*. Boston: MIT Press.

Cooper Albright, Ann. 2007. *Traces of Light: Absence and Presence in the Work of Loïe Fuller*. Connecticut: Wesleyan University Press.

Cooperstein, Paige. 2014. 'I Got My Dream Job as an Actress on a Disney Cruise – Here's What It Was Really Like'. *Business Insider*, 4 February. Web.

Crawford, Cheryl. 1977. *One Naked Individual: My Fifty Years in the Theatre*. Indianapolis: Bobbs-Merrill.

Cresswell, Tim. 2006. *On the Move: Mobility in the Modern Western World*. New York: Routledge.

Critical Art Ensemble. 2001. *Digital Resistance: Explorations in Tactical Media*. New York: Autonomedia.

Cronin, Anthony. 1999. *Samuel Beckett: The Last Modernist*. New York: Da Capo.

Crow, Melinda. 2014. 'Confessions of Cruise Ship Entertainers: What We Really Think of You'. *Yahoo! Travel*, 12 December. Web.

Da Costa, Dia. 2010. *Development Dramas: Reimagining Rural Political Action in Eastern India*. London, New York, and New Delhi: Routledge.

Daly, Nicholas. 2009. *Sensation and Modernity in the 1860s*. Cambridge: Cambridge University Press.

Daruze, G. 1990. '*Misteriia-buff* glazami zritelei 20-kh godov'. *Teatr* 1: 81–2.

Davids, Nadia. 2014. '"It's Very Tied to the Content of the Play": Basil Jones, Adrian Kohler, Jane Taylor and Mervyn Millar of Handspring Puppet Company in Conversation with Nadia Davids'. In *Theatre and Adaptation: Return, Rewrite, Repeat*, ed. Margherita Laera, 21–34. London: Bloomsbury.

Davis, Tracy C. 1991. *Actresses as Working Women: Their Social Identity in Victorian Culture*. London and New York: Routledge.

Davis, Tracy C. 2000. *The Economics of the British Stage, 1800–1914*. Cambridge: Cambridge University Press.

Davis, Tracy C. 2010. 'Performative Time'. In *Representing the Past: Essays in the Historiography of Performance*, ed. Charlotte Canning and Thomas Postlewait, 142–67. Iowa City: University of Iowa Press.

De Certeau, Michel. 1983. *The Practice of Everyday Life,* trans. Steven Rendell. Berkeley, CA: University of California Press.

De Certeau, Michel. 1988. *The Writing of History*, trans. Tom Conley. New York: Columbia University Press.

Deputy City Manager and Chief Financial Officer. 2014. 'Annual Report on City's Loan and Loan Guarantee Portfolio'. Staff Report. Toronto: City of Toronto.

Deshpande, Sudhanva. 2002. 'Theatre of Modernity: A Celebration of Modernity?' *Theatre India* 5: 8–14.

Diamond, Elin. 1997. *Unmaking Mimesis: Essays on Feminism and Theater*. London and New York: Routledge.

Diamond, Elin. 2003. 'Modern Drama/Modernity's Drama'. In Knowles et al. 2003, 3–14.

Dick, Philip K. 1969. *The Preserving Machine*. New York: Ace Books.
Dickie, Mary. N.d. 'Tanya Tagaq Grabs the World by the Throat'. *Music Works* 118. Web, 14 July 2015.
Dixon, Steve. 2007. *Digital Performance: A History of New Media in Theater, Dance, Performance Art, and Installation*. Boston: MIT Press.
Dolan, Jill. 1988. *The Feminist Spectator as Critic*. Ann Arbor: University of Michigan Press.
Economic Development Committee. 2016. 'Economic Dashboard – Annual Summary 2015'. City of Toronto, 17 February 2016. Web.
Eisenstadt, S.N. 2000. 'Multiple Modernities'. *Daedalus* 129 (1): 1–29.
Elderfield, John, ed. 1974. *Hugo Ball, Flight Out of Time: A Dada Diary*. Berkeley, CA: University of California Press.
Ellul, Jacques. 1964. *The Technological Society*. New York: Vintage.
Erenburg, I.G. 1922. 'Zametki o novom russkom teatre'. *Teatr* 1 (3–7 October): 14. In Fel'dman and Panfilova 2014, 140.
Erickson, John D. 1984. *Dada: Performance, Poetry, and Art*. Boston: Wayne.
Essin, Christin. 2012. *Stage Designers in Early Twentieth-Century America: Artists, Activists, Cultural Critics*. Basingstoke: Palgrave.
Esslin, Martin. 1975. 'Samuel Beckett and the Art of Broadcasting'. *Encounter* 45 (3): 38–46.
Executive Director, Social Development, Finance and Administration. 2012. 'Update on the Policy for City-Owned Space Provided at Below-Market Rent'. Staff Report. Toronto: City of Toronto.
Experimental Television Center. N.d. 'Chronological History of the Center, 1969–Present'. Experimentaltvcenter.org. Web.
Falk, David. 2014. 'Review: Tanya Tagaq's Take on "Nanook of the North"'. *Sound + Noise*, 10 February. Web, 13 July 2015.
Fel'dman, O.M. 2014. 'K chitateliu'. In Fel'dman and Panfilova 2014, 7–20.
Fel'dman, O.M and N.N. Panfilova, eds. 2014. '*Pravda nashego bytiia*': *Iz arkhivov Teatra Vs. Meierkhol'da*. Moscow: Novoe izdatel'stvo.
Fernandez, Maria, Faith Wilding and Michelle M. Wright, eds. 2003. *Domain Errors! Cyberfeminist Practices*. Brooklyn, NY: Automedia.
Fevral'skii, A.V. 1971. *Pervaia sovetskaia p'esa 'Misteriia-buff' V. V. Maiakovskogo*. Moscow: Sovetskii pisatel'.
Fevral'skii, A.V. 1976. *Zapiski rovesnika veka*. Moscow: Sovetskii pisatel'.
Fischer, Gerhard. 1988. 'The *Lehrstück* Experience on a Contemporary Stage: On Brecht and the GRIPS-Theatre's *Voll auf der Rolle*'. *Modern Drama* 31 (3): 371–9.
Fitzpatrick, Sheila. 1970. *The Commissariat of Enlightenment: Soviet Organization of Education and the Arts under Lunacharsky, October 1917–1921*. Cambridge: Cambridge University Press.
Folpe, Emily Kies. 2002. *It Happened on Washington Square*. Baltimore: Johns Hopkins University Press.
Foucault, Michel. 1978. *The History of Sexuality, Volume 1*. Trans. Robert Hurley. New York: Pantheon Books.
Franklin, Benjamin. 1784. *Two tracts: Information to those who would remove to America, and, Remarks concerning the savages of North America*. London: Sabin Americana.
Freedman, Alisa, Laura Miller and Christine Reiko Yano, eds. 2013. *Modern Girls on the Go: Gender, Mobility, and Labor in Japan*. Stanford: Stanford University Press.
Freeman's Journal. 1907. Dublin. 28 January.

Freud, Sigmund. 1959. [1919.] 'The "Uncanny"'. In *Collected Papers, vol. 4*, trans. Joan Riviere, 368–407. New York: Basic.
Friedman, Alice T. 2007. *Women and the Making of the Modern House*. New Haven, CT: Yale University Press.
Frow, John. 2006. *Genre: The New Critical Idiom*. London and New York: Routledge.
Funke, Lewis. 1969. 'Tynan Plans a Stage Tribute to Eros'. *New York Times*, 9 April.
Gallagher-Ross, Jacob. 2015. 'Mediating the Method'. *Theatre Survey* 56 (3). Web.
Ganguly, Sanjoy. 2010. *Jana Sanskriti: Forum Theatre and Democracy in India*. London and New York: Routledge.
Garner, Stanton B. 2007. 'The Gas Heart: Disfigurement and the Dada Body'. *Modern Drama* 50 (4): 500–16.
Gay, Peter. 2001. *Weimar Culture: The Outsider as Insider*. New York: W.W. Norton and Company.
Geller, Peter. 2015. 'Romancing the North: The Making and Meanings of *The Romance of the Far Fur Country*'. In *Romance of the Far Fur Country*. Companion pamphlet to DVD, 12–18.
Gerard, Jeremy. 1987. 'Charles Ludlam, 44, Avant-Garde Artist of Theater, Is Dead'. *New York Times*, 20 May.
Gillette, Kyle. 2015. *Railway Travel in Modern Theatre: Transforming the Space and Time of the Stage*. Jefferson, NC: McFarland.
Gladki Planning Associates. 2014. 'Section 37 Review: Final Report'. Toronto: City of Toronto. Web.
Glaspell, Susan. 2005 [1926]. *The Road to Temple*. Jefferson, NC: McFarland.
Glenn, Susan. 2000. *Female Spectacle: The Theatrical Roots of Modern Feminism*. Cambridge, MA: Harvard University Press.
Gluhovic, Milija. 2013. *Performing European Memories: Trauma, Ethics, Politics*. Basingstoke: Palgrave.
Goehr, Lydia. 2008. 'Hardboiled Disillusionment: *Mahagonny* as the Last Culinary Opera'. *Cultural Critique* 68: 3–37.
Gordon, Mel. 1987. *Dada Performance*. New York: PAJ Publications.
Gordon, Mel. 1995. 'A History of the Theater of the Future (to 1984)'. *Theater* 26 (1–2): 12–32.
Gordon, Mel. 2015. *Horizontal Collaboration: The Erotic World of Paris, 1920–1946*. New York: Feral P.
Greenspun, Richard. 1970. '*Dionysus in 69* (1970) Screen: De Palma's "Dionysus in 69"'. *New York Times*, 23 March. Web.
Gregory, Lady Augusta. 1913. *Our Irish Theatre: A Chapter of Autobiography*. New York and London: G. P. Putnam's and The Knickerbocker Press.
Grene, Nicholas. 2000. *The Politics of Irish Drama*. Cambridge: Cambridge University Press.
Grene, Nicholas. 2014. *Home on the Stage: Domestic Spaces in Modern Drama*. Cambridge: Cambridge University Press.
Grimshaw, Anna. 2014. 'Who Has the Last Laugh? Nanook of the North and Some New Thoughts on an Old Classic'. *Visual Anthropology* 27 (5): 421–35.
Gropius, Walter, and Arthur S. Wensinger, eds. 1996. *The Theater of the Bauhaus*. Baltimore: Johns Hopkins University Press.
Grotowski, Jerzy. 2002. *Towards A Poor Theatre*. New York: Routledge.
Gussow, Mel. 1970. 'Laughs Pepper Ghoulish "Bluebeard"'. *New York Times*, 5 May.

Habermas, Jürgen. 1981. 'Modernity: An Unfinished Project'. *Critique* 37.413: 950–67.

Haenni, Sabine. 2008. *The Immigrant Scene: Ethnic Amusements in New York, 1880–1920*. Minneapolis: University of Minnesota Press.

Hamilton, Marybeth. 1997. *'When I'm Bad, I'm Better: Mae West, Sex, and American Entertainment*. Los Angeles: University of California Press.

Haraway, Donna. 1991. 'A Cyborg Manifesto'. In *Simians, Cyborgs and Women: The Reinvention of Nature*, 149–81. New York and London: Routledge.

Haydon, Andrew. 2009. '*La Ronde*: Too Risqué for the 21st Century?' *The Guardian*, 17 March. Web.

Higgs, Matt. 2014. 'Art a Part of Sacred Water Gathering'. *The Peterborough Examiner* 15 April. Web.

Hill, Anita. 2011. *Reimagining Equality: Stories of Gender, Race, and Finding Home*. New York: Beacon.

Hischak, Thomas S. 2007. *The Rodgers and Hammerstein Encyclopedia*. Westport, CT: Greenwood.

Hobsbawm, Eric. 1975. *The Age of Capital: 1848–1875*. First edn. 1996. New York: Vintage.

Hobsbawm, Eric. 1988 [1975]. *The Age of Capital, 1848–1875*. London: Abacus.

Hollander, Anne. 1978. *Seeing through Clothes*. New York: Viking.

Holledge, Julie. 2008. 'Addressing the Global Phenomenon of *A Doll's House*: An Intercultural Intervention'. *Ibsen Studies* 8 (1): 13–28.

Holmes, Sean P. 2013. *Weavers of Dreams, Unite! Actors' Unionism in Early Twentieth-Century America*. Urbana: University of Illinois Press.

Holzapfel, Amy. 2013. *Art, Vision, and Nineteenth-Century Realist Drama: Acts of Seeing*. New York: Routledge.

Howe, LeAnne. 1999. 'Tribalography: The Power of Native Stories'. *Journal of Dramatic Theory and Criticism* 14 (1): 117–25.

Innes, C.D. 1972. *Piscator's Political Theatre*. Cambridge: Cambridge University Press.

Jackson, Shannon. 2011. *Social Works?: Performing Art, Supporting Publics*. New York: Routledge.

Jackson, Shannon, Marianne Weems and Shannon Sindelar. 2015. *The Builders Association: Performance and Media in Contemporary Theater*. Boston: MIT Press.

Jamal, Ashraf. 2003. 'Faith in a Practical Epistemology: On Collective Creativity in Theatre'. *South African Theatre Journal* 17 (1): 37–64.

Jameson, Frederic. 1991. *Postmodernism, Or, The Cultural Logic of Late Capitalism*. Durham, NC: Duke University Press.

Jannarone, Kimberly. 2015. *Vanguard Performance Beyond Left and Right*. Ann Arbor: University of Michigan Press.

Jones, Basil. 2008. 'Financing Handspring Theatre Company'. In *African Theatre: 7 Companies*, ed. Martin Banhan. London: James Currey.

Jones, Basil, and Adrian Kohler. 2010. 'Puppeteers' Note'. In Taylor 2010, xvi–xvii.

Jordan, John, and James Marriott, dirs. 2006. *And While London Burns*. Audio-walk.

Jordan-Young, Rebecca. 2010. 'The subRosa Collective: Cyberfeminist Interventions'. *S&F Online* 9 (1–2). Web.

Junction Avenue Theatre Company. 2001. *Tooth and Nail*. In Orkin 2001, 237–96.

Kaplan, Joel H., and Sheila Stowell. 1994. *Theatre and Fashion: Oscar Wilde to the Suffragettes*. Cambridge: Cambridge University Press.

Katz, Pamela. 2015. *The Partnership: Brecht, Weill, Three Women, and Germany on the Brink*. New York: Nan A. Talese/Doubleday.

Kauffman, Stanley. 1966. 'Homosexual Drama and its Disguises'. *New York Times*, 23 January.
Kaufman, David. 2002. *Ridiculous! The Theatrical Life and Times of Charles Ludlam*. New York: Applause.
Kavanaugh, Shane Dixon. 2013. 'Times Square Cookie Monster jailed for Altercation with Toddler'. *New York Daily News*, 8 April. Web.
Kentridge, William, with Jane Taylor. 2009. 'In Dialogue'. In Taylor 2009, 176–209.
Kinos-Goodin, Jesse. 2011. 'A Tribe Called Red's Urban Powwow'. *National Post*, 23 August. Web, 7 August 2015.
Klein, Yves. 2006. *Vers l'immatériel: Le dépassement de la problématique de l'art, La conférence à la Sorbonne*. Paris: Editions Delicta.
Klüver, Billy. N.d. 'Remarks by Billy Klüver, President'. Experiments in Art and Technology Press Conference, New York. Jerome Robbins Dance Division, New York Public Library.
Knight, Arthur. 1971. *The Liveliest Art*. New York: Penguin.
Knowles, Ric, Joanne Tompkins and W.B. Worthen, eds. 2003. *Modern Drama: Defining the Field*. Toronto: University of Toronto Press.
Knowlson, James, ed. 1980. *Samuel Beckett, Krapp's Last Tape: A Theatre Workbook*. London: Brutus.
Kohler, Adrian. 2009a. 'Engineering Movement'. *Ingenia* 40 (September): 26–32.
Kohler, Adrian. 2009b. 'Thinking through Puppets'. In Taylor 2009, 42–147.
Kohler, Adrian, Basil Jones and Tommy Luther. 2009. 'Statement of Practice: Handspring Puppet Company'. *The Journal of Modern Craft* 2 (3): 345–54.
Kracauer, Siegfried. 1995. 'The Mass Ornament'. In *The Mass Ornament: Weimer Essays*, ed. and trans. Thomas Y. Levin, 75–88. Cambridge, MA: Harvard University Press.
Lamanova, Nadezhda. 2004. 'Concerning Contemporary Dress'. In *Against Fashion: Clothing as Art, 1850–1930*, ed. Radu Stern, 174–6. Cambridge: MIT Press.
Lanina, T.V. 1997. *Meierkhol'd v russkoi teatral'noi kritike*. 2 vols, vol. 1 (1898–1918). Moscow: Artist, Rezhisser, Teatr.
Lanina, T.V. 2000. *Meierkhol'd v russkoi teatral'noi kritike*. 2 vols, vol. 2 (1920–1938). Moscow: Artist, Rezhisser, Teatr.
Lazzarato, Maurizio. 1996. 'Immaterial Labor'. In *Radical Thought in Italy: A Potential Politics*, ed. Paulo Virno and Michael Hardt, 133–47. Minneapolis: University of Minnesota Press.
Lee, Margaret C. 2001. 'Truth and Reconciliation Commission'. In *The Oxford Companion to Politics of the World*. Oxford: Oxford University Press.
Lenin, V.I. 1958–1965. *Polnoe sobranie sochinenii*, 55 vols, vol. 26, 127. Moscow: Izdatel'stvo politicheskoi literatury. Quoted in Rudnitsky 1988, 41.
Lenze, Christine. 2009. '"The Whole Thing You're Doing is White Man's Ways": *fareWel*'s Northern Tour'. In *'Ethnic', Multicultural, and Intercultural Theatre*, ed. Ric Knowles and Ingrid Mündel, 76–82. Toronto: Playwrights Canada.
Levinson, Andrei. 1918. '*Misteriia-buff Maiakovskogo*'. *Zhizn' iskusstva* (11 November). In Lanina 1997, vol. 1, 384–5
Long, Robert Emmet. 2001. *Broadway, the Golden Years: Jerome Robbins and the Great Choreographer-Directors 1940 to the Present*. New York: Continuum.
Louvish, Simon. 2007. *Mae West: It Ain't No Sin*. New York: St Martin's Griffin.
Low, Morris. 2012. *Japan on Display: Photography and the Emperor*. London: Routledge.
Lucas, Midge. 2015. Interview conducted by Christin Essin, 29 January. Hudson Studios, New York.

Ludlam, Charles. 2001. *Bluebeard: A Melodrama in Three Acts. The Mystery of Irma Vep and Other Plays*. New York: TCG.

Lunacharskii, Anatolii. 1918. 'Kommunisticheskii spektakl'. *Petrogradskaya pravda* (5 November). In Lunacharskii 1964, vol. 3, 39–40.

Lunacharskii, A. 1964. *Sobranie sochinenii*, ed. G.I. Vladykin and U.A. Gural'nik. 8 vols. Moscow: Khudozhestvennaia literatura.

'M-G-M Buys "Cat on a Hot Tin Roof" as a Starring Vehicle for Grace Kelly'. 1955. *New York Times*, 10 July.

Magnarelli, Sharon. 2008. *Home Is Where the (He)art Is: The Family Romance in Late Twentieth-Century Mexican and Argentine Theater*. Lewisburg, PA: Bucknell University Press.

Maiakovskii, Vladimir. 1956. *Polnoe sobranie sochinenii v trinadtsati tomakh*, ed. N.V. Reformatskaia, 13 vols, vol. 2 (1917–1921). Moscow: GIKhL.

Mandamin, Josephine, Deborah McGregor and Hilary McGregor. 2012. 'N'guh izhi chigaye nibi onji: I will do it for the water'. In *Anishinaabewin Niizh: Cultural Movements, Critical Moments*, ed. Alan Corbiere, Deborah McGregor and Crystal Migwans, 13–22. M'Chigeeng, ON: Ojibwe Cultural Foundation.

Mani, Bakirathi. 2012. *Aspiring to Home: South Asians in America*. Stanford, CA: Stanford University Press.

Mao, Douglas and Rebecca L. Walkowitz. 2008. 'The New Modernist Studies'. *PMLA* 123 (3): 737–48.

Marker, Michael. 2011. 'Teaching history from an Indigenous perspective: Four winding paths up the mountain'. In *New Possibilities for the Past: Shaping History Education in Canada*, ed. Penney Clark, 97–114. Vancouver, BC: UBC Press.

Martin, Randy. 2004. *Socialist Ensembles: Theatre and State in Cuba and Nicaragua*. Minneapolis: University of Minnesota Press.

Martinez, Julio. 1998. 'Review: "Hello Again"'. *Variety*, 21 April. Web.

Marx, Gerhard. 2009. 'A Matter Of Life And Death: The Function of Malfunction in the Work of Handspring Puppet Company'. In Taylor 2009, 225–68.

Maungwudaus [aka Henry George]. 1848. *An account of the Chippewa Indians, who have been travelling among the whites, in the United States, England, Ireland, Scotland, France, and Belgium*. Rochester, NY: Privately Published. Web, 1 December 2015.

May, Elaine Tyler. 1988. *Homeward Bound: American Families in the Cold War*. New York: Basic Books.

Mayakovsky, Vladimir. 1918. 'Open Letter to the Workers'. *Gazeta futuristov*, 15 March 1918. In Senelick and Ostrovsky 2014, 55–6.

Mayer, David. 2002. '"Quote the Words to Prompt the Attitudes": The Victorian Performer, the Photographer, and the Photograph'. *Theatre Survey* 43 (2). Web.

Mayer, David. 2009. *Stagestruck: Filmmaker: D. W. Griffith and the American Theatre*. Iowa City: University of Iowa Press.

McGrath, Aoife. 2013. *Dance Theatre in Ireland: Revolutionary Moves*. Basingstoke: Palgrave.

McGregor, Deborah. 2012. 'Anishinaabe Knowledge and Water Governance in Ontario: Honouring Our Responsibilities'. In *Anishinaabewin Niizh: Cultural Movements, Critical Moments*, ed. Alan Corbierre, Deborah McGregor and Crystan Migwans, 23–37. M'Chigeeng, ON: Ojibwe Cultural Foundation.

McKinnie, Michael. 2007. *City Stages: Theatre and Urban Space in a Global City*. Cultural Spaces. Toronto: University of Toronto Press.

McNamara, Brooks. 2001. 'Broadway: A Theatre Historian's Perspective'. *TDR* 45 (4): 125–8.

McNeil, Donald G., Jr. 1997. 'Grahamstown Journal; Playwrights Are Doing an Autopsy on Apartheid'. *New York Times,* 5 August. Web.
McNeil, Donald G., Jr. 1998. 'Puppeteers With a Hand in the Apartheid Protests'. *New York Times*, 6 September. Web.
McNulty, Charles. 1992. 'The Ridiculous Theatrical Company: Still Mocking After All These Years'. *Theater* 23 (3): 68–9.
Meech-Pekarik, Julia. 1986. *The World of the Meiji Print: Impressions of a New Civilization*. New York: Weatherhill.
Meierkhol'd, Vsevelod. 1968. *Stat'i, pis'ma, rechi, besedy,* ed. A.V. Fevral'skii. 2 vols, vol. 1 (1891–1917). Moscow: Iskusstvo.
Melanson, Trevor. 2013. 'Toronto Falling from Grace? Canada's No. 1 City Is Soaring'. *Canadian Business*, 22 February.
Merritt, Russell. 2002. 'The Nickelodeon Theater, 1905–1914: Building and Audience for the Movies'. In *Exhibition, the Film Reader*, ed. Ina Rae Hark, 21–30. London: Routledge.
Meyerhold, Vsevolod. 1978. *Meyerhold on Theater: Revised Edition*, ed. and trans. Edward Braun. London: Bloomsbury.
Meyer-Plantureux, Chantal. 1972. *La photographie de théâtre, ou, La mémoire de l'éphémère*. Paris: Audiovisuel.
Miller, Bryan. 1988. 'Restaurants'. *New York Times,* 19 August. Web.
Mitchell, Katie, dir. 2014. *The Cherry Orchard*. The Young Vic, London. Performance.
Moholy-Nagy, László. 1987. *Painting, Photography, and Film*, trans. Janet Seligman. Reprint edition. Cambridge, MA: MIT Press.
Moholy Nagy, Sibyl. 1950. *Moholy Nagy: Experiment In Totality*. New York: Harper & Brothers.
Moore, Aaron A. 2013. 'Trading Density for Benefits: Section 37 Agreements in Toronto'. IMFG Perspectives. Toronto: Insitutute on Municipal Finance and Governance, Monk School of Global Affairs, University of Toronto. Web.
Morley, David. 2000. *Home Territories: Media, Mobility and Identity*. London: Routledge.
Morrow, Charles. 2014. 'Broadway's Forgotten Man'. *This Land* 5 (7). Web, 25 September 2015.
Mother Earth Water Walks. N.d. 'About Us'. Web, 6 August 2015.
Motherwell, Robert, and Jean Arp. 1981. 'Hugo Ball, *Dada Fragments (1916–1917)*: June 12, 1916'. In *The Dada Painters and Poets*, 49–54. Boston: G.K. Hall.
Mueller, Roswitha. 2006. 'Learning for a New Society: The *Lehrstück*'. *The Cambridge Companion to Brecht*, ed. Peter Thomson and Glendyr Sacks, 101–17. Second ed. Cambridge: Cambridge University Press.
Mumford, Lewis, and Langdon Winner. 2010. *Technics and Civilization*. Chicago: University of Chicago Press.
Murray, Timothy. 1997. *Drama Trauma: Specters of Race and Sexuality in Performance, Video, and Art*. London and New York: Routledge.
'Naked and Uncensored'. 1970. *Economist*, 8 August.
Nanook of the North: A Story of Life and Love in the Actual Arctic. 1998. Dir. Robert Flaherty. Criterion Collection. DVD.
Neighborhood Playhouse. 12th Season Brochure. 1925–6. Clippings Folders, Neighborhood Playhouse. Billy Rose Theatre Collection. New York Public Library for the Performing Arts, New York.
Nestruck, Kelly. 2014 'A New Development in Downtown Toronto – and This One's for Artists'. *The Globe and Mail*, 21 March. Web.

Nicholls, Liz. 2014. 'Reclaiming Nanook of the North: Tanya Tagaq lends vocals to infamous film'. *Edmonton Journal*, 28 January. Web, 13 July 2015.

Nikkel, Kevin, dir. *On the Trail of the Far Fur Country*. 2014. Five Door Films. DVD, pamphlet insert.

O'Brien, Nellie. 1911. *An Claidheamh Soluis*. 30 December.

O'Connor, Barbara. 2009. 'Colleens and Comely Maidens: Representing and Performing Irish Femininity in the Nineteenth and Twentieth Centuries'. In *Ireland in Focus: Film, Photography and Popular Culture*, ed. E. Flannery and M. Griffin, 144–65. Syracuse: Syracuse University Press.

O'Curry, Eugene. 1873. *On the Manners and Customs of the Ancient Irish*. Dublin: Williams and Norgate.

O'Neill, Rosemary. 2012. *Art and Visual Culture on the French Riviera, 1956–1971: The Ecole de Nice*. Aldershot: Ashgate.

Ogle, Vanessa. 2015. *The Global Transformation of Time, 1870–1950*. Cambridge, MA: Harvard University Press.

Oklahoma! 1955. Dir. Fred Zinneman. Twentieth Century Fox. DVD.

Oltermann, Philip. 2014. 'Katie Mitchell, British theatre's true auteur, on being embraced by Europe'. *Guardian*, 9 July. Web.

'One Day in Grand Street'. 1926. *New York Times*, 2 May: X2.

Orkin, Martin, ed. 2001. *At the Junction: Four Plays by the Junction Avenue Theatre Company*. Witwatersrand: Witwatersrand University Press.

Ouwerkerk, Jacco. 2015. 'The Real Virtuality of MuseumNext'. *IN10 Communicatie*, 8 May. Web.

Ouzounian, Richard. 2013. 'The Theatre Centre Finds New Home in Carnegie Library'. *The Toronto Star*, 6 November. Web.

Ouzounian, Richard. 2014. 'The Theatre Centre Finally Has a Home'. *The Toronto Star*, 15 March. Web.

Palmer, R. Barton, and William Robert Bray. 2009. *Hollywood's Tennessee: The Williams Films and Postwar America*. Austin: University of Texas Press.

Pappus, Fredrick. 1955. 'Against Cat'. *New York Times*, 26 June.

Pavis, Patrice. 2003. *Analyzing Performance: Theatre, Dance, and Film*, trans. A. David Williams. Ann Arbor: University of Michigan Press.

Payne, Robert. 1995. Introduction to *Mayakovsky – Plays*, trans. Guy Daniels. Evanston: Northwestern University Press.

Phelan, Peggy. 1993. *Unmarked: The Politics of Performance*. London and New York: Routledge.

Pilkington, Lionel. 2001. *Theatre and the State in Twentieth-Century Ireland: Cultivating the People*. London and New York: Routledge.

Planning Act. 1990. Government of Ontario. Web.

Polanyi, Karl. 1957. *Trade and Market in the Early Empires*. Glencoe, IL: Free Press.

Polanyi, Karl. 2002. *The Great Transformation: The Political and Economic Origins of Our Time*. Second ed. Boston: Beacon.

Poliakova, Elena. 1992. 'In Time, Out of Time: The Moscow Art Theatre's American Tours'. In *Wandering Stars: Russian Émigré Theatre, 1905–1940*, ed. Laurence Senelick, 32–72. Iowa City: University of Iowa Press.

Posner, Dassia N. 2015. 'Baring the Frame: Meyerhold's Refraction of Gozzi's *Love of Three Oranges*'. *Theatre Survey* 56 (3): 362–88.

Postlewait, Thomas. 2009. *The Cambridge Introduction to Theatre Historiography*. Cambridge: Cambridge University Press.

Price, Helen. 1955. 'Perplexed'. *New York Times*, 5 June.
Pudovkin, V.I., Lewis Jacobs and Ivor Montagu. 1949. *Film Technique and Film Acting*. New York: Lear.
Pullen, Kirsten. 2002. 'They Never Raided Minsky's: Popular Memory and the Performance of History'. *Performance Research* 7 (4): 116–21.
Purkey, Malcolm. 1996. '*Tooth and Nail*. Rethinking Form for the South African Theatre'. *Theatre and Change in South Africa*, ed. Geoffrey V. Davis and Anne Fuchs, 155–72. Amsterdam: Harwood Academic.
Purkey, Malcolm. 1997. 'Productive Misreadings: Brecht and Junction Avenue Theatre Company in South Africa'. *Brecht Yearbook* 23: 13–18.
Purkey, Malcolm. 2015. Interview with the author, 1 October.
'Queen West Gains Arts Hub as Theatre Centre Moves In'. 2014. CBC.ca, 19 March. Web.
Rabinbach, Anson. 1990. *The Human Motor: Energy, Fatigue, and the Origins of Modernity*. Berkeley: University of California Press.
Raheja, Michelle H. 2010. *Reservation Reelism: Redfacing, Visual Sovereignty, and Representation of Native Americans in Film*. Lincoln: University of Nebraska Press.
Rayner, Alice. 2006. *Ghosts: Death's Double and the Phenomena of Theatre*. Minneapolis: University of Minnesota Press.
Rich, Frank. 1989. 'Critics Notebook: The Asterisks of "Oh! Calcutta!"'. *New York Times*, 8 August.
Richards, David. 1994. 'Would-Be Lovers Find Little but Sex In an Endless Dance'. *The New York Times*, 31 January. Web.
Ridout, Nicholas. 2006. *Stage Fright, Animals and Other Theatrical Problems*. Cambridge: Cambridge University Press.
Ridout, Nicholas, and Rebecca Schneider, eds. 2012. 'Precarity and Performance'. *TDR* 56 (4).
Riggs, Lynn Rollie. 1961. *Green Grow the Lilacs*. In *Best American Plays: Supplementary Volume, 1918–1958*, ed. John Gassner. New York: Crown Publishers.
Rimini Protokoll, 2012. 'Trailer of Call Cutta – Mobile Phone Theatre'. Vimeo.com. Web.
Roach, Joseph. 1996. *Cities of the Dead: Circum-Atlantic Performance*. New York: Columbia University Press.
Robb, Martha. 1998. *Irish Dancing Costume*. Dublin: Country House.
Rokem, Freddie. 1986. *Theatrical Space in Ibsen, Chekhov, and Strindberg: Public Forms of Privacy*. Ann Arbor, MI: UMI Research Press.
Romance of the Far Fur Country. 2015 [1920]. Dirs. Harold Wyckoff and Bill Derr. Five Door Films. DVD.
Rudnitsky, Konstantin. 1988. *Russian and Soviet Theater: 1905–1932*, ed. Lesley Milne, trans. Roxane Permar. New York: Harry Abrams.
Russell, Robert. 1990. 'The First Soviet Plays'. In *Russian Theatre in the Age of Modernism*, ed. Robert Russell and Andrew Barratt, 148–71. New York: St Martin's Press.
Said, Edward W. 1979. *Orientalism*. New York: Vintage.
Salter, Chris. 2010. *Entangled: Technology and the Transformation of Performance*. Boston: MIT Press.
Sandberg, Mark 2001. 'Ibsen and the Mimetic Home of Modernity'. *Ibsen Studies* 1 (2): 32–58.
Sandberg, Mark. 2015. *Ibsen's Houses: Architectural Metaphor and the Modern Uncanny*. Cambridge: Cambridge University Press.

Sardi, Vincent, Jr. and Thomas Edward West. 1991. *Off the Wall at Sardi's*. New York: Applause.

Saunders, Graham. 2015. 'Beckett Goes Nude: "Breath", *Oh! Calcutta!* and the Sexual Revolution'. STR Lecture, 16 April. STR.org.uk. Web.

Sayler, Oliver M. 1920. *The Russian Theatre under the Revolution*. Boston: Little, Brown, and Company.

Schlissel, Lillian, ed. 1997. *Three Plays by Mae West:* Sex, The Drag *and* Pleasure Man. London: Routledge, 1997.

Schlossberg, Tatiana. 2014. 'What Elmo and Spidey Want You To Know: They Have Rights'. *New York Times,* 19 August. Web.

Schneider, Herbert. 1972. Personal letter to Harriet DeLong. Getty Research Institute Archive, Los Angeles, CA.

Schneider, Rebecca. 2011. *Performing Remains: Art and War in Times of Theatrical Reenactment*. New York: Routledge.

Schnitzler, Arthur. 1982 [1920]. *La Ronde*. Trans. Frank and Jacquelline Marcus. London: Bloomsbury Methuen.

Schweber, Seymour. 1973. Interview by Harriett De Long. Phone Interview. Experiments in Art and Technology records, Getty Research Institute.

Schweitzer, Marlis. 2009. *When Broadway Was the Runway: Theater, Fashion, and American Culture*. Philadelphia: University of Pennsylvania Press.

Schweitzer, Marlis. 2015. *Transatlantic Broadway: The Infrastructural Politics of Global Performance*. Basingstoke: Palgrave.

'Science: Plastic Ball'. 1951. *Time*, 17 September. Web.

Sears, Ann. 2008. 'The Coming of the Musical Play: Rogers and Hammerstein'. In *The Cambridge Companion to the Musical*, ed. William A. Everett and Paul R. Laird. Second ed. New York: Cambridge University Press. Web.

Sellars, Peter. 2003. 'The Question of Culture'. In *Theatre in Crisis? Performance Manifestos for a New Century*, ed. Caridad Svitch and Maria M. Delgado, 127–44. Manchester: Manchester University Press.

Senelick, Laurence. 1997. 'Early Photographic Attempts to Record Performance Sequence'. *Theatre Research International* 22 (3). Web.

Senelick, Laurence and Sergei Ostrovsky, trans. and ed. 2014. *The Soviet Theater: A Documentary History*. New Haven: Yale University Press.

Shapiro, Doris. 1993. *We Danced All Night: My Life Behind the Scenes with Alan Jay Lerner*. New York: Barricade Books.

Shields, David S. 2014. 'Seeing the Stage | Broadway Photographs'. *Photography and the American Stage*. Broadway.cas.sc.edu. Web.

Shklovskij, Viktor. 1998. 'Art as Technique'. In *Literary Theory: An Anthology,* ed. Julie Rivkin and Michael Ryan, 16. Malden: Blackwell Publishing Ltd.

Short, John Rennie. 1999. 'Foreword'. In *At Home: An Anthropology of Domestic Space*, ed. Irene Cieraad, ix–x. Syracuse, NY: Syracuse University Press.

Shteir, Rachel. 2005. *Striptease: The Untold History of the Girlie Show*. New York: Oxford University Press.

Simpson, Leanne. 2011. *Dancing on Our Turtle's Back*: *Stories of Nishnaabeg Re-Creation, Resurgence and a New Emergence*. Winnipeg: Arbeiter Ring.

Singer, Benjamin. 2001. *Melodrama and Modernity: Early Sensational Cinema and Its Contexts*. New York: Columbia University Press.

Smith, Allan Lloyd. 1996. 'Postmodernism/Gothicism'. In *Modern Gothic: A Reader*, ed. Victor Sage and Allan Lloyd Smith, 6–19. Manchester: Manchester University Press.

Solnit, Rebecca. 2003. *River of Shadows: Eadweard Muybridge and the Technological Wild West*. New York: Penguin.
Sontag, Susan. 1966. 'Film and Theatre'. *The Tulane Drama Review* 11 (1).
Sova, Dawn B. 2004. *Banned Plays: Censorship Histories of 125 Stage Dramas*. New York: Facts on File.
Stansell, Christine. 2000. *American Moderns: Bohemian New York and the Creation of a New Century*. New York: Metropolitan.
Steichen, James. 2009. 'The Metropolitan Opera Goes Public: Peter Gelb and the Institutional Dramaturgy of The Met: Live in HD'. *Music and the Moving Image* 2 (2): 24–30.
Stein, Gertrude. 1935. *Lectures in America*. New York: Random House.
Stephey, Molly. 2010. 'Native American Theatre and Lynn Riggs'. Public talk. The National Museum of the American Indian. 4 November.
Stratford Festival. 2015. 'Stratford Festival: Archives and History: Artistic Directors'. Stratfordfestival.ca. Web.
Stufft, Monica. 2011. 'Chorus Girl Collective: Early 20th Century American Performance Communities and Urban Networking'. PhD dissertation, University of California, Berkeley.
subRosa. 2014. 'Down with Self-Management! Re-boot Ourselves as Feminist Servers'. Cyberfeminism.net. Web.
Syssoyeva, Kathryn Mederos. 2013. 'Revolution in the Theatre I: Meyerhold, Stanislavsky, and in Collective Creation, Russia 1905'. In *A History of Collective Creation*, ed. Kathryn Syssoyeva and Scott Proudfit, 37–57. New York: Palgrave.
Taubman, Howard. 1963. 'Modern Primer: Helpful Hints to Tell Appearances vs. Truth'. *New York Times*, 28 April.
Taylor, Diana. 1997. *Disappearing Acts: Spectacles of Gender and Nationalism in Argentina's 'Dirty War'*. Durham, NC: Duke University Press.
Taylor, Diana. 2003. *The Archive and the Repertoire: Performing Cultural Memory in the Americas*. Durham, NC: Duke University Press.
Taylor, Jane. 2007. 'Writer's Note'. *Ubu and the Truth Commission* playbill, Market Theatre, Johannesburg, 31 July–30 August, n.p.
Taylor, Jane, ed. 2009. *Handspring Puppet Company*, Parkwood: David Krut.
Taylor, Jane. 2010. *Ubu and the Truth Commission*. Cape Town: University of Cape Town Press.
Taylor, Jane. 2015. Interview with the author, 24 September.
The Grand Council of the Haudenosaunee. 2002. *Polishing the Silver Covenant Chain: Building Relationships between Federal, State Agencies, and the Haudenosaunee*. Haudenosaunee Environmental Task Force. Web.
The Theatre Centre. N.d. 'Our New Home; A New Live Arts Hub & Incubator'. Thetheatrecentre.org. Web.
Tobin, Joseph J. 1994. *Re-Made in Japan: Everyday Life and Consumer Taste in a Changing Society*. New Haven: Yale University Press.
Toronto Arts Council. 2014. '2014 Allocations'. Toronto: Toronto Arts Council.
Trimingham, Melissa. 2012. *The Theatre of the Bauhaus: The Modern and Postmodern Stage of Oskar Schlemmer*. Reprint ed. London: Routledge.
Triplett, William. 1998. '*Ubu*: Horror with a Silver Lining of Hope'. *Washington Post*, 22 September. Web.
Tuan, Yi-Fu. 1977. *Space and Place: The Perspective of Experience*. Minneapolis: University of Minnesota Press.

Turkle, Sherry. 2012. *Alone Together: Why We Expect More from Technology and Less from Each Other*. New York: Basic.

Tynan, Kenneth, Samuel Beckett and John Lennon. 1969. *Oh! Calcutta!: An Entertainment with Music Devised by Kenneth Tynan, Directed by Jacques Levy*. New York: Grove Press.

Ubu and the Truth Commission. 1997. Dir. William Kentridge, script by Jane Taylor, design and perf. by Handspring Puppet Company. Market Theatre, Johannesburg. DVD.

Urry, John. 2007. *Mobilities*. Cambridge: Polity.

Van Hulle, Dirk, and Mark Nixon. 2013. *Samuel Beckett's Library*. Cambridge: Cambridge University Press.

Vartanian, Hrag. 2014. 'The Facebook Martyrdom of a Digital Activist'. Hyperallergic.com. Web.

Vertov, Dziga. 1984. *Kino-Eye: The Writings of Dziga Vertov*. Berkeley, CA: University of California Press.

Vidler, Anthony. 1992. *The Architectural Uncanny: Essays in the Modern Unhomely*. Cambridge, MA: MIT Press.

Vizenor, Gerald. 1994. *Manifest Manners: Narratives on Postindian Survivance*. Hanover, NH: Wesleyan University Press.

Vizenor, Gerald. 1998. *Fugitive Poses: Native American Indian Scenes of Absence and Presence*. Lincoln: University of Nebraska Press.

Von Eschen, Penny M. 2006. *Satchmo Blows Up the World: Jazz Ambassadors Play the Cold War*. Cambridge, MA: Harvard University Press.

Von Geldern, James. 1993. *Bolshevik Festivals, 1917–1920*. Berkeley, CA: University of California Press.

Walker, Roy. 1980. 'Love, Chess and Death'. In *Samuel Beckett, Krapp's Last Tape: A Theatre Workbook*, ed. James Knowlson, 48–51. London: Brutus.

Walkowitz, Judith. 2012. *Nights Out: Life in Cosmopolitan London*. New Haven: Yale University Press.

Weaver, Jace 2014. *The Red Atlantic: American Indigenes and the Making of the Modern World, 1000–1927*. Chapel Hill: University of North Carolina Press.

Werman, Marco. 2012. 'Electronic Pow Wow with "A Tribe Called Red"'. *PRI's The World*, 21 November. Web, 7 August 2015.

Werry, Margaret. 2014. 'Oceanic Imagination, Intercultural Performance, Pacific Historiography'. *The Politics of Interweaving Performance Cultures*, ed. Erika Fischer-Lichte, Torsten Jost and Saskya Iris Jain, 97–118. New York and London: Routledge.

Wetmore, Kevin J., Siyuan Liu and Erin B. Mee. 2014. *Modern Asian Theatre and Performance 1900–2000*. London: Bloomsbury Methuen Drama.

White, Timothy R. 2014. *Blue-Collar Broadway: The Craft and Industry of American Theater*. Philadelphia: University of Pennsylvania Press.

Wickstrom, Maurya. 2006. *Performing Consumers: Global Capital and Its Theatrical Seductions*. New York: Routledge.

Wilkie, Fiona. 2014. *Performance, Transport, and Mobility*. Basingstoke: Palgrave.

Willett, John, trans. and ed. 1964. *Brecht on Theatre: The Development of an Aesthetic*. New York: Hill and Wang.

Willett, John. 1998. 'Brecht and Piscator'. In *Brecht in Context*, 101–20. New York and London: Bloomsbury.

Williams, Kirk. 2006. 'Anti-theatricality and the Limits of Naturalism'. In *Against Theatre: Creative Destructions of the Modernist Stage*, ed. Alan Ackerman and Martin Puchner, 95–111. Basingstoke: Palgrave MacMillan.

Williams, Raymond. 1989. *The Politics of Modernism: Against the New Conformists*, ed. Tony Pinkney. London: Verso.

Wollman, Elizabeth L. 2002. 'The Economic Development of the "New" Times Square and Its Impact on the Broadway Musical'. *American Music* 20 (4): 445–65.

Wollman, Elizabeth L. 2008. 'Emancipation or Exploitation?: Gender Liberation and Adult Musicals in 1970s New York'. *Studies in Musical Theatre* 2 (1): 5–32.

Wollman, Elizabeth L. 2013. *Hard Times: The Adult Musical in 1970s New York City*. Oxford and New York: Oxford University Press.

Womack, Craig. 1999. *Red on Red: Native American Literary Separatism*. Minneapolis: University of Minnesota Press.

Woolf, Brandon. 2009. 'Our Fishy Nonprofit Sector'. *The Arts Politic* 1 (1): 18–19.

Worrall, Nick. 1996. *The Moscow Art Theatre*. London: Routledge.

Wright, Oliver. 2014. 'Exclusive: David Cameron's Big Society in tatters as charity watchdog launches investigation into claims of Government funding misuse'. *Independent*, 26 July. Web.

Zagorskii, Mikhail. 1922. 'Teatr i zritel' epokhi revolyutsii (Iz chernovykh nabroskov po anketnym materialam Pervogo Teatra RSFSR)'. In *O teatre*, 102–12. [Tver'] : Tverskoe izdatel'stvo.

Zarhy-Levo, Yael. 2008. *The Making of Theatrical Reputations: Studies from the Modern London Theatre*. Iowa City: University of Iowa Press.

Ziolkowski, Theodore. 2009. *Scandal on Stage: European Theater as Moral Trial*. Cambridge and New York: Cambridge University Press.

Zola, Émile. 1974. 'Naturalism in the Theatre'. In *Dramatic Theory and Criticism: Greeks to Grotowski*, ed. Bernard F. Dukore, 692–720. New York: Holt, Rinehart and Winston.

INDEX

Theatres are listed under the city in which they are located. Theatre and performance works are listed under the name/s of their creator/s.

Abenaki 109
Aboriginal. *See* Indigenous
absurdism 76, 161
actors 55, 82, 123–7, 146, 168, 206, 214–15
  audience interest in 13
  as collaborators 67, 85, 100, 119
  crew as 16
  film 210, 213
  live (contrasted with puppet) 132, 134
  method 84
  modernist 184–5, 190, 191–2
  nude 57
  spect- 7, 46, 118
  politicized 53, 139, 142
  as travellers 179
  as theatre workers 40, 149, 152–4
  virtual 197–200
Actors Equity Association (AEA) (U.S.) 142
Actor's Equity Strike, 1919 (U.S.) 140
Adler, Rudolph 147
Adler, Stella 84
Adorno, Theodor 39–40, 48–9, 52
aesthetics 142, 161, 183–6, 189–90, 196–7
African National Congress (ANC) (South Africa) 130
agency 13, 14, 131, 136–7, 154, 210

agitation 120
agitprop 120
Agnew, Jean-Christophe 20, 22
agonism 22, 26
AIDS. *See* HIV/AIDS
Aksenov, Ivan 123
Albanese, Denise 2, 4
Albee, Edward 66
  Who's Afraid of Virginia Woolf 58
Alberta 102
Allakariallak (aka Nanook) 100–1
Allen, Joe 156
American Music Theatre 193
American Tenth Cavalry 196
Anderson, Gillian 89
Anderson, Joel 216
Anderson, Laurie 193
Anderson, Robert
  Tea and Sympathy 58
Andrews, Benedict 89–90
Anishinaabe 97, 109, 110
Anishinaabeg 108, 110
Anishinaabekwe 107
anti-Semitism 55
Antoine, André 10
  The Butchers 169
apartheid 120, 128–32, 134–6, 151

Appia, Adolphe 184
Arapaho 96
Architectural Digest 80
Argelander, Ronald 67
Aristophanes
    Assembly Women, The 22
Armstrong, Louis 154
Arnaquq-Baril, Aletheia 101–2, 104
Artaud, Antonin 6, 12, 37, 161, 176, 182, 186, 188–9, 191–2, 200
Arthur, Helen 150
Arts Council of England (ACE) 88, 92
Astaire, Fred 152
Aston, Elaine 9
Atkinson, Brooks 71
audience 76, 79, 83, 89, 108, 145, 152, 170, 195–6, 202, 209, 216. *See also* spectator
    activation 122–3, 128, 135
    as actor 93, 197
    Broadway 63, 73, 113
    challenging the 5, 14, 52, 64–5, 127, 134
    as consumers 150
    engagement 3, 49, 53, 119, 125, 130–2, 136, 137, 147, 160–1
    global 12, 136, 154, 175–6, 203
    Indigenous 99, 100, 105
    instruction 189–90
    local 43, 136, 166–7, 171, 173, 178
    mass 43–4
    middle-class 44, 60, 136
    non-Indigenous 97, 100, 105, 106
    one-person 198
    opera 50–1
    promenading 91
    as public 37
    reception 66, 118
    rural 45
    screen 204–9, 218–19
    and sex 56–7, 59–67, 70–1, 73, 192
    as theatrical space 80, 124, 127, 188
    tourist 12, 141, 173
    urban 44, 166
    view of the stage 15, 192
    water as 108
    as witness 134
    working-class 44, 125
Auslander, Philip 210, 218
Austin, J.L. 2
Australia 95, 152. *See also* Melbourne

avant-garde 121, 209. *See also* absurdism; Dadaism; experimental; Expressionism; Futurism; Marseille, Festival d'Avant-Garde; modernism; Surrealism.
    artists 194, 202–3, 216
    contemporary 25, 182
    historical 25, 37, 58, 59, 63, 70, 161, 207, 210
    Japanese 176
    queer spirit of 67, 71
    venues for 69, 80
Avignon
    Festival d' 106

Bachelard, Gaston 82–4, 94
Baker, Bobby 179
Balla, Giacomo 162
Ball, Hugo 155
    Flight Out of Time 207
Balme, Christopher B. 22–3, 25
Bangladesh 41
Barnes, Clive 65
Barrymore, Ethel 142
Bases, Pat 149
Basinski, Sean 158
Basso, Keith 105
Bauhaus 188–9, 208
Bear Witness 106–7, 134–5
Bebutov, Valery 124
Beckett, Samuel 9, 40, 63–5
    Krapp's Last Tape 210–14
    Waiting For Godot 76
Beck, Julian 191
Beer, Alice 149
Belasco, David 63
    Lulu Belle 60
Bel Geddes, Barbara 71
Bel Geddes, Norman 148
Bell Labs 194
belonging 77–8, 82
below-market rent (BMR) agreements 29
Bengali Renaissance (theatre) 36, 42–4
Benjamin, Walter 202
Benton-Banai, Edward 107–8
Berlin 8, 21, 38, 48, 55, 62, 118, 190, 194, 198
    Opera House 28
    Theatre am Nollendorfplatz 189
    Wall 129

Berliner Ensemble 64, 189
Bernstein, Aline 149
Beskin, E. 127
Bharucha, Rustom 42–5
Biblical 121
Big Society (UK) 88–9
Billboard 60
Black-Eyed Susan 68, 79
blackface (tradition of) 14
Blau, Herbert 193
Bleeker, Maaike 219
Blium, Vladimir (aka Sadko) 127
Boal, Augusto 7, 42–6, 53, 118
body. *See also* gender; nudity; sexuality
   gendered 59, 196
   in performance 56–7, 61, 85, 132, 188–9, 194 (*see also* costume)
   and national ideologies 163–4, 170–1, 173–6, 178–9
   sexualized 59, 65, 167, 194
   and/as technology 15, 143, 181–6, 200
Boer War 91
Borowoy, Michael 20
Borsodi, Ralph 62
Boston 153
   Opera 147
Bottoms, Stephen 66–7, 69
Boucicault, Dion 166, 174
   The Colleen Bawn 164, 167
bourgeois. *See also* middle class
   private life 10, 75, 79
   public sphere 38
Brantley, Ben 56–7
Bray, William Robert 73
Brazil 7, 42, 46
Bread and Puppet Theater company 131
Brecht, Bertolt 81, 89, 117–18, 176, 181, 186, 195–6, 198
   alienation effect 131, 190
   Aufstieg und Fall der Stadt Mahagonny 48–50, 52–3
   epic theatre 7, 117, 161, 181
   gestus 190
   as influence 3, 9, 167, 182, 191–2, 195, 200
   learning plays (Lehrstücke) 53, 117–18
   Mother Courage and Her Children 9, 190
   No-Sayer, The (*Der Neinsager*) 118
   Threepenny Opera, The 49
   Yes-Sayer, The (*Der Jasager*) 117–18
Brecht, Stefan 193
British Columbia
   Alert Bay 102, 104
British Film Institute (BFI) 99
Brockett, Oscar G. 185, 188
Brockmeyer, John 69,
Brookfield Center 146,
Brook, Peter 12
Brown, Ford Maddox 164
   The Irish Girl 164
Brush, Charles 215
Brussels
   Expo '58 192
Buenos Aires 38, 46, 194
Buffalo Bill's Wild West Show 98
Builders' Association (U.S.) 198, 200
Burke, Augustus Nicholas 164
   Connemara Girl, A 164
burlesque 60–3, 65, 71, 73, 134
Burnett, John 79
Burton, Frederic William 164
   Aran Fisherman's Drowned Child, The 164
Butler, Jean 174–5
Butler, Judith 2
byt/bytie 127–8

cabaret 48, 62, 154, 207
Cage, John 194
   4'33' 118
   9 Evenings: Theatre and Engineering 194–6
Cai Guo-Chiang 193
Caitlin, George 97
Cameron, David 88
Campeau, Ian (aka DJ NDN) 106
Canada 12, 17, 21, 58, 95, 98–107. *See also* Alberta; Lake Superior; Montreal; Nova Scotia; Nunavut; Ontario; Peterborough; Quebec; Quebec City; Toronto; Turtle Island; Winnipeg; Yellowknife
Canning, Charlotte 154
Cantor, Eddie 142
capitalism 1–10, 35, 38–9, 42, 48–9, 92, 108, 158, 183, 190, 198
Cárdenas, Micha 198–200
   Technésexual 198–9

Carlson, Marvin 28
Carroll, Earl 60, 62
Castellucci, Romeo 37
Cayuga First Nation 106
censorship 60, 65, 121
Chakrabarthy, Dipesh 42
chamber music 40
Chatterjee, Partha 36–7, 41–2
Chatterjee, Sudipto 42
Chaudhuri, Una 77, 81, 89
   Staging Place 79–80
Cheek by Jowl 80–1
Chekhov, Anton 58, 76, 85, 123, 188
   Cherry Orchard, The 89
   Three Sisters 89, 153
Cherokee Nation 112, 114
Chicago 82, 153, 164, 174
Childs, Lucinda
   9 Evenings: Theatre and Engineering 194–6
Choctaw 96
chorus girls 62, 143–4, 158
Churchill, Caryl 82, 209
   Far Away 9
   Seven Jewish Children 9
   Top Girls 7
Cima, Gay Gibson 209–10, 214
Cineplex Odeon 12
circus 122, 125, 207
civic institution 19, 28
Civil War (Soviet Russia) 121, 123
Clurman, Harold
   Fervent Years, The 146
Cocteau, Jean 202
   Wedding on the Eiffel Tower, The 203
Coetzee, Yvette 132
Cold War 8, 66–7, 83, 153–4
collective 35, 37, 78, 96, 142, 146, 197–9
colonialism 4, 36, 42, 98, 154
   neo- 41–2, 45
   settler 4, 95–6, 99, 104–5, 109–11, 115–16
commedia dell'arte 122
Commissariat of Enlightenment (Narkompros) (Soviet Russia) 121
Communism 66, 130
Communist Party of India (CPI) 43
community 8, 39, 80, 85, 89, 94, 114–15
   arts 17, 21, 88

   centres 32
   critical 69
   Indigenous 100–2, 106–7,
   local 29, 55, 148–9, 166
   network 2, 78
   organizations 30
   production 140–2, 146, 150–2, 154–8
   theatrical 71
consumerism 141, 161
consumers 13, 35–53, 154–5, 157, 203
consumption 26, 38, 43, 48–9, 53, 77, 81, 141, 155–8
Constructivist 184–5, 197
Corpus Christi mystery play 122
Cort, John 60
Costa, Dia Da 42–4, 47–8
costume. *See also* body
   ceremonial 103
   experimental 125, 162, 185, 191, 197, 207–8
   and genre 160–1
   mascot 157–8
   national 163–70, 173–9
   traditional 70, 147
Coward, Noël 58
craftspeople 141, 147–9, 174
Craig, Edward Gordon 6, 184, 189, 208
Crawford, Cheryl 146
'creative city' strategy 21, 30
Cree 90
Creek Nation 113
criticism
   conservative 60–7, 169
   critical acclaim 15
   Euro-American 96, 113
   modern 79–80, 94
   newspaper 51, 56, 69–70, 105, 107, 124, 127
Critical Art Ensemble (CAE) 200
Cronin, Anthony 210
Crosby, Bing 152
Crowley, Matt
   Boys in the Band, The 58
cubism 118, 121
cultural
   activism 43, 48
   archives 201
   autonomy 22
   capital 12, 14, 33, 195, 197
   codes 53, 79, 81, 100

context 119–20, 179, 189
counter-85
dominance 98
economy 155, 190
event 65, 106, 174
genocide 9, 13, 35, 95–6
heritage 42, 67
history 27, 35, 77, 153–4, 210
impact 73, 200
infrastructure 29
institutions 20, 23, 26
knowledge 159–60, 204
margins 163
marketplace 88
mediatized 198–9, 218–20
memory 202
mimesis 169, 171
modernity 3–6, 8, 9, 35–6, 94, 209
portfolio 30–1
practice 52, 175
primitivism 37
productions 181
project 168
reception 175
references 194
resurgence, Indigenous 103, 105, 107, 109
shift 183, 188, 192
spaces 32, 47, 57, 91
theory 2
value 24, 76
work 42, 45, 56, 59
Cusco 109
Czech National Theatre 192

Dadaism 11, 26, 76, 80, 155–6, 161, 206–9, 219
Daldry, Stephen 75
dance 45, 83, 149, 153, 155, 192, 197
　Balinese 12
　chorus line 183
　erotic 62, 64
　Indigenous 98–9, 107
　Irish 173–6
　and media 202, 216–19
　modern 177–8, 186
　Western 163, 173
Datta, Michael Madusudhan 43
Davids, Nadia 135

Davies, Paul
　Living Rooms 91
Davis, Tracy C. 13, 160
Davis, Donald 213
De Certeau, Michel 2, 10, 141
de Klerk, F.W. 130
De Mille, Agnes 115
Dene 99, 102, 104, 109
Derr, Bill 99
Diamond, Elin 5, 81–3, 85, 94
Dick, Philip K. 201–2, 220
Disney
　Lion King, The 156–7
Disneyfication 156–8
Dixon, Steve 185
DJ BuddaBlaze 107
Dodge, Mable 144
domestic drama 58, 76, 78–80, 91–2, 134
Donnellan, Declan 81
Douglas, Mary 78
Dressler, Marie 142
Dublin 26, 63, 104, 145, 166–7, 174
　Abbey Theatre 26, 63, 145, 163–4 184
　Fringe Festival 104
　Irish Literary Theatre 164
Dumb Type 200
　[OR] 197
Duncan, Isadora 177
Dunnock, Mildred 71
Dunsany, Lord
　The Glittering Gate 145
Duran Duran 158
Dutt, Utpal 43–4
dystopian 109, 202

East India Company 41
economics 20, 37, 39, 216
Edinburgh
　Festival 106
Edison, Thomas
　Buffalo Dance 98
Edwards, Alan 151
Einstein, Albert 6
Eisenstein, Sergei 118, 206
Elevator Repair Service 200
　Great Gatsby, The 197
　Sound and the Fury, The 197
　Sun Also Rises, The 197
Elliott, Marianne 152

Ellul, Jacques 212
entertainment industry 36, 143, 147, 157, 216
Epidaurus 22
Eskimo stereotype 99–100
Esslin, Martin 209
ethics 3, 81, 118–19, 130, 134, 136–7
ethnography 95, 99
Euripides
   The Bacchae 192
Eurocentrism 13
Eurovision Song Contest 174
Eurozone 22
Ex Machina 7, 82. *See also* Lepage, Robert
   Geometry of Miracles 83
exile 9, 46, 77, 79, 81–2, 91, 94
experimental. *See also* absurdism; avant-garde; Dadaism; Expressionism; Futurism; modernism; Surrealism
   artist 6, 81, 161
   art theatre 37
   company 21, 28, 149
   performance 17
   practice 43, 45, 53, 122–3, 125, 200, 210
   queer 67–70
   spaces 58, 85
   use of technology 181–2, 189, 191–5, 197, 205–6, 214
Expressionism 11, 26, 118, 161

Facebook 199, 219
Falstrom, Oyvind
   9 Evenings: Theatre and Engineering 194–6
fantasy
   consumer 10, 78–9, 82 176
   dystopian 202
   Euro-Western 100, 162, 164, 173, 176
   of modernity 1, 4
farce 132
fascism 43–4, 128
feminism 9, 82, 83, 143, 182, 185–6, 193, 196–7
   first-wave 59
   second-wave 179
   neoliberal 7
Fevralsky, A.V. 120, 125

film 2, 3, 6, 15, 56–7, 67, 122, 152, 156, 181
   adapted to the stage 218
   broadcasts of live theatre 218
   Indigenous 98–105
   modernist 188–9, 192, 202–3, 206, 209, 216
   performances recorded on 3, 186, 208, 216–18
   plays adapted to 73, 113
   silent 205–6, 216
   techniques used in theatre 192, 203, 210, 213
   used in stage productions 15–16, 80, 216
Flaherty, Robert 99–101, 105
Flatley, Michael
   Riverdance 174–6
FLUXUS 194
Fontanne, Lynn 58
Forced Entertainment 6
Foreman, Richard 192
formalism 118, 127, 186
Forsythe, William 193
Fort Chipewyan 102–3
Forum Theatre 46–7, 53
Foucault, Michel 57–8
Four Directions Walk 108
fourth wall 15, 76, 80, 119, 189, 191
Franklin, Benjamin 111
Freire, Paulo 46
Freud, Sigmund 2, 5, 81, 84, 143
   uncanny (*unheimlichkeit*) 9, 79, 82
Frohman, Charles 154
Frow, John 159, 161
Fuller, Loïe 186–7, 196
Futurism 26, 161, 186, 210, 212–14
   Italian 6, 162, 185
   Russian 121, 123, 127, 178, 182, 197

Gambaro, Griselda
   Information for Foreigners 91
Ganguly, Sanjoy 45, 47,
Garner, Stanton 208
gathering 141, 144
gaze 98, 99, 132
Gazzara, Ben 71–2
Geldern, James von 139
Geller, Peter
   On the Trail of the Far Fur Country 99–100, 104

Gellert, Roger
  Quaint Honor 58
gender. *See also* body; queer; sexuality
  codes 79, 149
  cross- 67–9, 173
  difference 5
  discourse 55–6, 58–9, 65, 73
  inequity 57
  non-normative 4
  -segregated 169–71
  -sensitive 51
  and technology 182, 186, 196, 200
  trans- 15
Ghosh, Girish Chandra 43
Glaspell, Susan 144
globalization 141, 162, 176, 178–9
  capitalist 35, 92
  cosmopolitanism 175
  of cultural performance 106
  neoliberal 76, 77, 94
  urban 28, 88
gothic 68, 71
Gray, Spalding 192
Great Law of Peace 111–12
Great Migration 108–10
Greece
  Ancient 178
  contemporary 22
Green, Paul
  House of Connelly, The 146
Gregory, Augusta (Lady) 164, 166, 167, 174
Grene, Nicholas 167
Griffith, D.W. 216
Grimshaw, Anna 100
Grotowski, Jerzy 161, 191
Group Theatre, The 153
Gumbrecht, Hans Ulrich 8
Gussow, Mel 69

Habermas, Jürgen 38
Hair Coat 98
Hamilton, Marybeth 61
Handspring Puppet Company (Handspring Theatre Company)
  Tooth and Nail 129–30
  Ubu and the Truth Commission 119, 130–7
  War Horse 136, 151–2
  Woyzeck on the Highveld 131–2
Hansen, Mark 197

Haraway, Donna 197
Hardberger, Linda 185
Hare, David
  The Blue Room 56
Haudenosaunee 111–12, 114–15
Hauptmann, Elizabeth 117
Hay, Alex
  Grass Field 195–6
  9 Evenings: Theatre and Engineering 194–6
Hay, Deborah
  9 Evenings: Theatre and Engineering 194–6
Haydon, Andrew 56
heterosexuality. *See* sexuality
Hill, Tim (aka 2oolman) 106
historiography 3, 130, 202, 214
  Indigenous 96, 98
history 8
  capitalist 48
  cultural 19, 22, 35, 77–8, 182, 219
  Indigenous 13, 95–8, 101–2, 109, 114
  material 91–2
  and memory 210, 212
  of modernity 36
  national 136, 139, 154, 173
  performance 193–4, 196, 200
  production 14
  theatre 20, 25–6, 28, 38–9, 63, 76, 82, 140
  world 189
HIV/AIDS 67, 182, 197
Hobsbawm, Eric 76, 78–9
Hollander, Anne 160
Hollywood 73, 152, 173, 204. *See also* film
Holmes, Sean P. 142
Holocaust 3, 209–10
Holzapfel, Amy Strahler 204–5
home 6, 9–11, 76, 80–5, 93
  Heim/Heimat 79, 91–2
  modern 78
  on-stage 15, 75, 93, 132,
  physical 12
  territory 100, 106, 113
  theatre as 66, 77, 79, 85, 88–9
  for theatre company 17, 19, 27, 31, 33, 146
  as workspace 150
homosexuality. *See* sexuality

Hopi 109
Horkheimer, Max 39
House of Commons (UK) 111
Howe, LeAnne 95–6, 98
Hudson's Bay Company (HBC) 99, 103, 108, 111
Hudson Scenic Studios 148–9
Hurston, Zora Neale 81
hybridity 43, 162, 163, 171, 173–4, 182, 191

Ibsen, Henrik 43, 76, 81, 84–5, 168
  Doll's House, A 75, 78, 79, 94
  Enemy of the People, An 89
  Hedda Gabler 15, 79
  Little Eyolf 63
identity 114, 162, 217, 219
  community 140
  critique 182, 185
  gender. *See* gender
  Indigenous 97, 101, 105–6
  narratives of 56, 81, 96
  national 66, 112, 153, 163, 166, 171, 173–4, 178–9
  sexual. *See* sexuality
  theatre company 144, 146, 150
  urban 142
ideology 23, 38, 47, 88
  anti-capitalist 22
  of gender and sexuality 196
  of modernity 4–5, 37, 42
  nationalist 178
India 4, 13, 198. *See also* Mumbai; West Bengal
Indian People's Theatre Association (IPTA) 43–4
Indigenous. *See also* Abenaki; Anishinaabe; Arapaho; Cayuga First Nation; Cherokee Nation; Choctaw; Cree; Creek Nation; Dene; Hopi; Inuit; Iroquois; Kogi; Kwakwaka'wakw; Lakota Sioux; Métis; Micmac; Mississauga; Mohawk; Nippissing First Nation; Seminole Nation; Seneca; Six Nations of the Grand River; Western Apache
  audiences 99–100, 102–3
  ceremony 108–10
  creation stories 111
  history 114

homelands 12
  pan- 96
  performers 95, 104–7
  performance 42, 44, 95, 115
  sovereignty 97–8, 116
  worldviews 13
industrialization 45, 111, 141, 182–4
Inge, William 66
  Bus Stop 73
  Picnic 73
Ingmilayuk 101
institutions 9, 36
  national 26, 173
  theatres as 19–25, 28, 33, 77
international 8, 27, 76, 92, 122–3, 140, 147, 193, 199, 219. *See also* national, trans
  touring 106–7, 136, 153–4
Inuit 99–102, 104–5
Ionesco, Eugene 76, 209
Ireland 159, 163–4, 166, 178. *See also* Dublin
  Gaelic League 174
Iroquois 112
irrationality 37, 164, 207
Ito, Michio 177–8
Ives, Burl 71, 73

Jackson, Andrew (President, U.S.) 112
Jackson, Shannon 25
Jana Sanskriti (theatre) 42–6, 53
  Unnayan 47
Janco, Marcel 155
Jannarone, Kimberly 128
Japan 13, 117, 159, 162, 177–9, 197, 201
  Meiji Restoration 163, 168, 170
  modern girl (*moga*) 170–1, 173
  Takarazuka Revue 171–4, 176
  Westernization (*bunmei kaika*) 168–9, 171, 176
Jaques-Dalcroze, Émile 177
Jarry, Alfred
  Ubu Roi 25, 80, 131, 132, 134
jatra 43, 44
jazz 62, 154
Johannesburg 150
  Market Theatre 234
John, Elton 158
Jonas, Joan 193

Jones, Basil 129, 131, 134, 150. *See also* Handspring Theatre Company
Jones, Robert Edmond 145
Jordan, John
   And While London Burns 92
Joubert, Jill 150
Junction Avenue Theatre Company (South Africa)
   Tooth and Nail 129

kabuki 122, 168, 169–70, 173
Kamerzell, Max 147
Kane, Sarah
   Blasted 15, 76
   Cleansed 15
Kaplan, Donald 66
Kaprow, Allan 194
Katz, Pamela 117
Kauffman, Stanley 66
Kaufman, David 68
Kaye, Danny 152
Kazan, Elia 71, 73
Kennedy, Adrienne 209
Kentridge, William 131, 134, 137. *See also* Handspring Theatre Company
Khrakovsky, Vladimir 125
Kidman, Nicole 56
Klein, Yves 193
Klüver, Billy 194–5
Koeck, Karl 147–8
Kogi 109
Kohler, Adrian 131. *See also* Handspring Theatre Company
Kolkata (Calcutta) 36, 41–5, 198
   Academy of Fine Arts 44
   Surendranath Park 44
Kracauer, Siegfried 183, 184, 186
Krizanc, John
   Tamara 91
Kwakwaka'wakw 99, 102–3

labour
   backstage 13, 89, 147
   and capital 9, 39, 117
   domestic 78
   efficiency 183–4
   improvisational 7
   indentured 35
   mechanized 206
   paratheatrical 13

   post-revolutionary 185
   production 140–1
   productive 42, 47–8
   service 15
   theatrical 47, 59, 76, 155–8
   unions 142–3
Lacan, Jacques 222
LaChiusa, Michael John
   Hello Again 56
Lake Superior 108
Lakota Sioux 98, 109
Lamanova, Nadezhda 162
landscape 6, 95, 98, 141, 150, 190
Last Horse 98
Lavinsky, Anton 124
LaViolette, Chief Alexander 104
LeCompte, Elizabeth 192
Le Corbusier (Charles-Édouard Jeanneret) 10, 193
Lee, Young Jean
   Shipment, The 14
Lefebvre, Henri 158
Léger, Fernand 206
Leipzig 48
leisure 9, 37, 39–41, 50, 62
Lenin, Vladimir 120–1, 128, 139
Lenze, Christine 105
Lepage, Robert 7, 12. *See also* Ex Machina
Levinson, Andrei 123
Levy, Jacques 63
Lewisohn, Alice 149
Lewisohn, Irene 149
Ley-Piscator, Maria 189
Little Theatre Group 44
Littlewood, Joan
   Oh! What a Lovely War 118
Living Theatre
   Paradise Now 191
London 15, 37, 41, 56, 65, 82, 149, 154, 167, 213
   And While London Burns 77, 91–4
   Drury Lane 113
   Ideal Home Show 78–9
   Imperial International Exhibition 164
   National Theatre 12, 64, 75, 85, 151–2, 218
   Occupy 76
   Old Vic 217
   Royal Maritime Museum 219
   Royal Opera House 50, 52

Shakespeare's Globe 85
South Bank arts venues 28, 85–6, 88
West End theatre district 59
Windmill Theatre, The 62
Young Vic 76–7, 85–91, 94
Loy, Mina
   Pamperers, The 185
Lucas, Midge 148–9
Ludlam, Charles
   Bluebeard 59, 67–70
Lumière Brothers 186, 205–6, 216
Lunacharsky, Anatoly 121–2
Lunt, Alfred 58

McBurney, Simon 12
McCartney, Paul 158
McCauley, Robbie
   Indian Blood 196–7
McGrath, Aoife 177
McNamara, Brooks 73
Madonna 158
Maeterlinck, Maurice 145
Malevich, Kazimir 122
Malina, Judith 191
Mamet, David
   Sexual Perversity in Chicago 58
Mandamin, Josephine 106–9
Mandela, Nelson 130
Man Ray (Emmanuel Radnitzky) 216
marginalization 5, 15, 59, 70, 107
Marker, Michael 96
market economy. *See* capitalism
marketing 38, 85
marketization 20, 21, 29, 33
Marriot, James
   And While London Burns 91–4
Marseille
   Festival d'Avant-Garde 193
Martin, Jean 104
Martin, Randy 48
Marxism 20, 85, 130, 189
   dialectics 3, 118
Massachusetts 145, 147
Maungwudaus, Chief (Mississauga) 97
May, Elaine Tyler 66
Mayakovsky, Vladimir 178
   Mystery-Bouffe 119–29, 136–7
Mayer, David 215–16
Mehrmand, Elle 198–200
   Technésexual 198–9

Melbourne 91
memory 3, 84, 134
   cultural 202
   historical 142, 210
   mediated 211–12, 214, 217, 219
   project 136
Merritt, Russell 216
Métis 99
Meyerhold, Vsevolod 118, 178, 189, 191–2. *See also* Mayakovsky, Vladimir, *Mystery Bouffe*
   body mechanics of 182, 184–5
Meyer-Plantureux, Chantal 215
Micmac 109
middle class 44, 78, 161. *See also* bourgeois
   activists 45–6
   audiences 43, 60, 62, 77, 88, 136, 191
Midewahnikwe 108
Midewewin 107, 110
Miller, Arthur 76
   Death of a Salesman 72
   View from the Bridge, A 72, 89
mimesis 43, 83–4, 169
Minnaar, Dawid 133
Minujín, Marta 194
mise-en-scène 59, 78, 215
Mississauga 97
Mitchell, Katie
   Cherry Orchard, The 89
   Fraulein Julie 15
Mitchell, Margaret 185, 188
Mitra, Dinabandhu 43
Mnouchkine, Ariane 82
modern 1–16. *See also* Japan, modern girl (*moga*); modernity
   acting practice 84
   artists 177
   dance 186
   drama 80–1
   home 75–9, 85
   media 201–2, 204, 210, 214–16
   performance studies 97
   political theatre 119–20, 128
   production communities 146–9
   sex 56–7, 59, 63, 65, 73
   spatial experience 82, 93–4
   technology 104, 181–3, 193, 206
   theatre 19–28, 39, 137, 145, 160–3, 179, 200

theatrical touring 105
transportation 141, 152
urban development 32–3
warfare 207, 209
modernism. *See also* Absurdism; avant-garde; Dadaism; experimental; Expressionism; Futurism; Surrealism; theatrical modernism
  art 26, 202, 219
  Indigenous 107
  politics of 22, 141
modernity 2–6, 8–15, 174, 207. *See also* modern
  Bengali 41–6, 53
  and domestic space 76–7, 79–82, 94
  globalizing 161–3,
  Indigenous 98–100, 107, 110–11
  Irish 166–7, 176
  Japanese 168–71
  sex as condition of 58, 61–2
  urban 28
  Western 35–8, 96
modernization 47–8
Mohawk 106
Moholy-Nagy, László 188–9, 192, 202, 207–8
Molière (Jean-Baptiste Poquelin) 70
Montez, Mario 69
Montreal 99
Moorman, Charlotte 196
  'TV Bed' (1972) 194
  'TV Bra for Living Sculpture' (1969) 193–4
Morgan, Agnes 149
Morgenstern, C.W. 60
Morley, David 78
Morris, Tom 152
Moscow 123–4, 126, 141
  Moscow Art Theatre (MAT) 146, 153, 184
Mother Earth Water Walkers 106, 108–10
movement 2, 6, 8, 83, 95, 108, 152, 186. *See also* body; dance
  Brechtian 189, 191, 196
  mass 122
  mechanization of 182–5
  mediated 210, 214
  of spectators 198
  Transmotion 98, 106
  vocabulary 176

Mroué, Rabih 200
  33rpm and a few seconds 199
Mueller, Roswitha 118
Mumbai 43
Mumford, Lewis 204, 214
music 45, 49–52, 56, 159, 184, 190
  chamber 40
  geisha 169
  Indigenous 104, 107
  jazz 154
  modernist 118
  recording technologies 201–2
musical theatre 112, 113–15
  acts 60
  adult content 59, 63, 65
  Broadway 37, 71, 143, 156–7, 173, 218
  Hollywood 152
  music hall 216
  revue 171–2, 176
  West End
Muybridge, Eadweard 6, 7, 16

Nanook. *See* Allakariallak
narrative
  cinematic 99–100
  counter- 154, 184–5, 188, 199–200, 210
  drama 15, 75–6, 79, 89, 145, 206
  historical 3, 26, 214
  of identity 56
  Indigenous 95, 97
  kabuki 168, 173
  multiple 91–3
  popular 12
  of progress 4–5, 81, 171
  of sexuality 59, 65, 67, 69, 73
  socialist 44
National Theatre Society 26
national 120, 128
  costume 163, 174–7, 179
  cultural capacity 42
  history 139
  identity 36, 141
  newspaper 143, 156
  post- 77
  theatres 12, 26, 39, 42–5, 66, 146, 192
  trans- 12, 150, 162, 163 (*see also* international)

nationalism 26, 28 160
   German 178
   Indian 43–5
   Irish 26, 164, 166–7, 171
   Japanese 168, 171, 173
   Soviet 153
naturalism
   critiques of 5, 11,
   examples of 10, 15, 63, 74, 77, 121, 169, 184, 186, 214
   'Naturalism in the Theatre' (Émile Zola) 161, 203
   in stage design 79, 80–1
Nazism 178, 209
Nemirovich-Danchenko, Vladimir 146–53
neoliberalism 76–7, 81, 89, 94,
New Stagecraft 145, 148
New York Artists United for a Smile (union) 157
New York City 38, 59, 82, 115, 143, 145, 146, 154
   Abrons Art Center 150
   Bandbox Theatre 145
   Belasco Theatre 63
   Boni Brothers' bookstore 144–5
   Brevoort Hotel Bar 144
   Christopher's End 69, 70
   critics 65–6, 70–1, 73, 113
   Daly Theatre 60
   Edison Theatre 63
   Greenwich Village 143–4
   La MaMa 70, 83
   Liberal Club 144–5
   Lincoln Center 28, 56
   Metropolitan Opera 148, 218
   McHales 156
   Mitzi Newhouse Theatre (Lincoln Center) 56
   Morosco Theatre 71
   Neighborhood Playhouse 149–50
   New Amsterdam Theatre 157
   New York Public Library 217, 218
   Occupy Wall Street 143
   Performing Garage 70, 192
   Polly Holiday's restaurant 144
   Sardi's 156
   Second Stage Theatre 56
   69th Street Armory 194
   Theatre Guild 145–6
   Times Square 141, 158
   Woolworth Building 10
   Ziegfeld's *Follies* 60, 147
New York Critics Circle Award 71
Nijinsky, Vaslav 177
19th Amendment (U.S.) 58
Nippissing First Nation 106
Noah's flood 121, 129
noh 117, 168–70, 176–8
non-profit 21, 23, 30, 31, 88, 143, 149
Norman, Marsha 76
Nova Scotia
   College of Art and Design 104
nudity 56, 59, 62, 64–5, 73, 192, 193. *See also* body
Nunavut 102
   Baffin Island 100
   Cambridge Bay 104

obscenity 65, 71
   charges 55
Obie Awards 63, 70
O'Brien, Edna 63–4
O'Brien, Nellie 174
O'Casey, Sean 164, 166
   Juno and the Paycock 63
Occupy. *See* London; New York
O'Connor, Barbara 166
O'Connor, John 70
O'Curry, Eugene 174
Odets, Clifford 43
Ogel, Sandra 179
Ojibwe 97, 109
Oklahoma 112–13
O'Neill, Eugene
   Great God Brown, The 63
   Hairy Ape, The 206
Ontario 27, 31, 107. *See also* Peterborough; Toronto
   Stratford Festival 153
   Trent University 109
Ontological Hysteric Theatre 192
opera 48–52, 161, 184
   Chinese 176
   culinary 49
   'school' 117
Operación Alfabetización Integral (ALFIN) 46
Ophüls, Max 56–7

orations (Haudenosaunee) 111, 115
orchestra 51
Orkin, Martin 129–30
Ormerod, Nick 81

Paik, Nam June 196
    'TV Bed' (1972) 194
    'TV Bra for Living Sculpture' (1969) 193
Pakistan 41
Palmer, R. Barton 73
pansexuality. *See* sexuality
Pappus, Frederick 71
Paris 21, 25, 82
    Colonial Exhibition 176
    Comédie Française 39
    Folies Bergère 62
    Moulin Rouge 62
    Opéra 28
    'Paris Ojibwe' (George Caitlin) 97
    showgirls 171, 173, 176
Parks, Suzan-Lori 82
Parts His Hair 98
Pashalinski, Lola 68
Pasmaquaddy 109
Pavis, Patrice 217
Paxton, Steve
    9 Evenings: Theatre and Engineering 194–6
percepticide 91, 137
performance 4–7, 12–15, 153–5. *See also* circus; dance; music; stage; theatre
    analysis 25
    artists 82
    consumer 157
    cosmopolitan 177
    and costume 160–2, 166, 168–71, 173, 179
    conventions 134
    documentation 3
    experimental 207–8
    folk 45, 122
    immersive 76–7, 82, 219
    Indigenous 95–9, 105–8, 110, 111, 115
    left-wing 117, 119, 121, 123–6, 128, 139, 142
    live 113
    modern 75–7
    open-air 44
    opera 50–1
    processional 43

queer 71
recordings 202–6, 214–19
responses to 26, 38
ritual 178
sexualized bodies in 59–63
site-specific 11, 76–7, 82, 91–2, 219
sites 21, 22, 28–9, 152
space 84
studies 42, 159
styles 23, 81, 176, 190
and technology 181–4, 186, 188–9, 191–200, 210
workshop 44, 47, 88, 139, 146,
Performance Group 191
    Dionysus in '69 58, 192
performance venues 83, 147
    cruise ship 141, 154–5
    downtown 17, 30, 69, 143, 150
    experimental 6, 58, 69–70, 149
    found space 11–12
    off-Broadway 56, 59, 63, 65, 69, 71, 73
    online 197–8
    street 163
performative 169, 186
    act 2
    embodiment 10
    gesture 188
    politics 143, 198
    technologies 200
Peru 46. *See also* Cusco
Peterborough 109
Petrograd (aka St Petersburg, Leningrad)
    Musical Drama Theatre 122
    Winter Palace 139, 158
Phelan, Peggy 217–18
Philadelphia 153
Pic, Roger 215
Pilkington, Lionel 26
Ping Chong 193
Pinter, Harold 201, 214
    Old Times 209
Pirandello, Luigi
    Si Gira (Shoot!) 213
Piscator, Erwin 118, 189–90, 192
Platform (production company) 92
Play-House of the Ridiculous 67
playwrights 7, 26, 59, 65–7, 145, 166, 174, 181, 185, 202–4, 209
Poel, William 92
Poland 129, 153

Polanyi, Karl 20
Polieri, Jacques 192–3
political activism 42, 45–7, 82, 110, 129, 143, 196–7, 199
Porgy and Bess 154
Postlewait, Thomas 25–6
postmodernism 82, 95–6, 118, 161, 163, 173, 174
power
    economic and political 9, 14, 32, 42, 120
    emotional 43, 76, 102, 105
    empowerment 45, 47, 88, 106
    imperial 168, 170
    performative 169
    royal 189
    sensuous 52
    star 154
    state 36, 39, 46
    transformative 95, 98, 111
    workers' 158
Prampolini, Enrico 185
Price, Helen 71
Priestley, J.B.
    An Inspector Calls 75
Producing Manager's Association (PMA) 142
proletarian 119–20, 122–3, 125, 127, 137
Proletkult 120
propaganda 38, 115, 120
props 7, 15, 83, 140, 153, 147, 151, 207
proscenium tradition 42, 44, 188–9
prostitution 48–50, 55, 58, 60–1, 73
Provincetown Players 63, 144–6
public financing/planning variances
    Section 37 (planning act, Toronto) 31–2
    Section 106 (England and Wales) 31
public sphere 20, 38, 57, 59, 63, 65, 70, 162
Pudovkin, Erwin 203
Pulitzer Prize 71–2
Punchdrunk 82, 219
puppetry 3, 80, 119, 129–36, 150–2, 188
Purkey, Malcolm 128–9

Quebec 82, 83, 223. *See also* Montreal; Quebec City
Quebec City
    La Caserne 83

queer 4. *See also* sexuality, homosexuality
    activism 196–7
    artists 14, 59, 83
    narratives 69–70
    plays 15, 58, 65–73
    playwrights 15, 65–73
    sex 57
    space 65–73, 83
    theory 2

race 36, 82, 132, 154, 182, 196
racism 100–2, 105, 107, 111, 210
Rado, James
    Hair 58
Ragni, Gerome
    Hair 58
Raheja, Michelle 98–100
railroad 9, 152
Rainer, Yvonne
    9 Evenings: Theatre and Engineering 194–6
Rauschenberg, Robert
    9 Evenings: Theatre and Engineering 194–6
Rawlings, Sir Peter 65
realism
    and domestic settings 76–84, 88
    Euro-American 5, 10–11, 14–15, 161, 166–7, 203–5
    and Japanese theatre 168–71, 176
    modernist critiques of 184, 188–9
    and sexuality 62–3
    Soviet Socialist 127–8, 153
relativity 6
religion 15, 37, 41, 111, 123, 142
repertoire 13, 14, 23, 26, 49, 153, 157–8, 159–79
Report of the Departmental Committee on Homosexual Offences and Prostitution (Wolfenden Report) (UK) 58
representation
    abstract 202
    critical 15, 39
    forms of 1, 40, 170
    media 107, 197, 217
    mis- 14, 99–100, 102, 105, 166–7
    self- 43
    of sexuality 55–60, 63, 65–7, 73, 194

theatre as 48, 76, 106, 184, 190, 203, 209
  verisimilitude of 206–7
resistance
  Indigenous 98–9, 102–5, 115
  political 42, 129
  theatre as 25, 200
revitalization 17, 156, 176, 178
Reza, Yasmina 76
Rice, Elmer
  Adding Machine, The 206
Ridiculous Theatrical Company 69
  Mystery of Irma Vep, The 67–8
Riggs, Lynn
  Green Grow the Lilacs 112–15, 231
Rimini Protokoll (Germany) 6
  Call Cutta 198
Robeson, Paul 154
Robins, Elizabeth
  Votes for Women! 15
Rockettes 183
Rodgers, Richard and Oscar Hammerstein II
  Oklahoma! 112–15
Rolling Stones, The 158
Ross, Ian
  fareWell 105–6
Royal Shakespeare Company 39
Rubin, Ben 197
Rudnitsky, Konstantin 121, 125
rural 4, 37, 42–5, 47, 142, 166
Russell, Lillian 142
Russia 175, 177. See also Moscow; Petrograd
  October Revolution 1917 8, 120–2, 189
  Soviet Union (aka USSR, Soviet Russia) 3, 120–9, 137, 139, 142, 153, 178

Sahtu Dene 109
Said, Edward
  Orientalism 13, 176–8
Sandberg, Mark 84
Saneh, Lina 199
São Paulo
  Arena Theatre 46
Sardi, Vincent, Jr. 156
Satabdi theatre company 44
satire 100, 127
Saunders, Graham 65

Sayler, Oliver 137
Schechner, Richard 66, 70
  Dionysus in '69 58, 192, 217
Schneider, Alan 213
Schneider, Herbert 195
Schnitzler, Arthur
  La Ronde (Reigen) 55–6, 73
Schumann, Peter 131
Schweber, Seymour 195
scientific 211. See also technology
  experiments 197
  innovations 2, 4, 6
  management 183–6
  theatre 161
Sears, Djanet
  Harlem Duet 14–15
Seboko, Louis 135
Sellars, Peter
Seminole Nation 113
Seneca 98
Senelick, Laurence 214
sex. See also representation, of sexuality; sexuality
  representations of 55–73, 192, 206
  symbol 166
  workers 97 (*see also* prostitution)
Sex Disqualification Act 1919 (England) 58
sexual revolution 58–9, 63, 65
sexuality 55–7, 192. See also body; sex
  asexual 100
  female 59–61, 167
  hetero- 58, 62–5, 67, 71
  homo- 58, 65–71, 73, 143 (*see also* queer)
  pan- 67
  and technology 182, 196, 198–200
Shakespeare, William 14, 44, 58, 85, 161–2
  Macbeth 132
Shaw, George Bernard 58, 145, 161
Shaw, Peggy
  Dress Suits to Hire 83
Shepard, Sam 63, 76
Shields, David S. 215
shingeki 168–71, 176
shinpa (*shimpa*) 168–72, 176
Shklovsky, Viktor 118
Short, John Rennie 78
Shterenberg, David 121

Shubert, J.J.
    Passing Show of 1919, The 143
Shubert, Lee 143
    Passing Show of 1919, The
Simpson, Leanne 98, 106–8
Singapore 43
Singer, Ben 2, 81
Sircar, Badal 43–5
    Bhoma 44
    Spartacus 44
Six Nations of the Grand River 106, 114
social
    activism 42, 197
    alienation 213
    aspirations 15
    change 2, 6, 25, 47, 57–8, 73, 161, 195
    crisis 76, 187
    critique 37, 43, 166, 197
    Darwinism 5
    function of theatre 36–9, 46–7, 85, 117–18, 128, 189
    genre 169, 179
    impact 194
    institutions 20–5, 29
    justice 3
    life 77, 144, 152
    media 199–200, 214, 219 (*see also* Facebook; Twitter)
    morality 207
    psycho- 80
    relations 14, 36, 38, 149, 154, 168, 181
    spaces 38, 59
    structures 13, 30, 111
    unease 21, 27, 29
    value 12
socialism 128, 130
    actually-existing 35, 38
    theatrical 43–5, 48, 119, 121
Solnit, Rebecca 5–8
Sontag, Susan 203
sovereignty 95–9, 104, 106, 116
Soviet Union. *See* Russia
space
    gendered 55–9, 79, 143, 149
    modern 4–6, 8–9, 11–13, 62, 77, 79–82, 94, 110
    mythic 81, 83, 94
    palimpsestic 12
    private 11, 57, 62, 78–9, 91–4

    public 11, 38, 57, 61–2, 65, 70, 88, 163
    rhetorical 95–6
    social 38, 59
    stage 15, 69, 77–85, 89, 92–4, 145, 184, 186–93
    urban 5, 9, 29–30, 107, 141–3, 146, 155–8, 206
    virtual 6, 38, 85, 197–8, 219
spatio-temporal 4, 6, 8, 25. *See also* space; time
spectators 57, 89, 133, 139, 153, 174, 200. *See also* audience
    actor- 117
    agency of 46, 91, 122–5, 188
    Brecht and 189–91
    as consumer 41, 155, 166
    European 103, 106
    female 164
    Indigenous 102
    as interpreter 3, 83, 84, 92–3, 118–19, 127, 131, 134
    mediated 202, 215
    mobile 198
    politicized 37, 38, 136–7
speech act 2, 111, 114
Split Britches 82
Sri Lanka 41
stage. *See also* performance; theatre
    celebrities 142
    design 5, 15, 124–5, 145, 148, 151, 184–6, 188, 206
    directions 112–13, 212
    effects 160
    hand 149
    -Irish 164–7, 174
    magician 216
    photography 214–15
    recordings 216–17
    society of 37–8
    space (*see also* space, stage)
    technology 189–200
    writing for 9 (*see also* playwrights)
Stalin, Joseph (General Secretary, Soviet Russia) 128
Stanislavsky, Konstantin 7, 80, 84–5, 121, 146, 153, 184
Stein, Gertrude 203
Stewart, Ellen 69
Sting 258

INDEX 275

Stockholm
   Intimate Theatre 80
Strasberg, Lee 84, 146
Stravinsky, Igor
   Rite of Spring 118
Street Vendors Project 158
Strindberg, August 37, 76, 188, 203, 205
   Ghost Sonata 80
   Miss Julie 15
Subotnick, Morton
   Jacob's Room 193
subRosa 200
   'Expose EmmaGenics' 197
suburbs 27, 32
suprematism 121, 168
Surrealism 11, 26
survivance 96, 98–100, 110, 114, 115
Svoboda, Josef
   Laterna Magika 192
   Ring, The 192
Synge, J.M. 164, 174–5
   Playboy of the Western World, The 26, 166–7, 170

Tagaq, Tanya 101–2, 104–5
Takarazuka Revue 171–4, 176
Taubman, Harold 65–6, 71
Taylor, Diana 91, 159
Taylor, Jane
   Ubu and the Truth Commission 119, 130–7
Taylor, Robert Winslow 183
Taylorism 183, 185, 195
Taymor, Julie 12
technology 2, 6, 15–16, 100, 104, 161, 181–200, 201–16
television 67, 73, 150, 182, 201, 203–4, 209, 219
   live broadcast 130, 174, 217–18
   use in live performance 191, 192, 194
Third Theatre 44
theatre. *See also* performance; stage
   of the absurd 209
   architecture 25
   building 21–2, 28
   companies 12, 19–32, 39, 76, 85, 146–54, 159, 162, 217
   of critique 37–8, 166, 196
   of cruelty 6, 37, 161. 188
   environmental 2, 76
   financing 21, 25, 29, 31, 33
   folk 44–5
   institutionalization of 23–7
   makers 3, 9, 11, 37, 41–3, 45, 47, 76–7, 128, 161, 176
   meta- 14–15, 216
   of modernity 5–6, 37–8, 41–6,
   of the oppressed 42, 44–7
   political 3, 42–9, 117–23, 137, 182, 189–90
   popular 43–5, 61–3, 77, 160–4, 171–2, 218,
   raid 60
   riot 26, 55, 163, 166
   site-specific (*see* performance, site-specific)
   workers 13, 112, 120–1, 140, 147, 155–6
Theatre Guild 146
Theatre RSFSR 1 123–7
Theatrical Division (TEO) (Soviet Union) 121
theatrical modernism 15, 81–2, 92, 122, 206, 209. *See also* avant-garde; modernism
   early 76, 79
   Irish 163–4, 166–7, 176, 178
   narratives of 5, 13, 25, 37, 94–5
   technological 186, 202–4
throat singing 104–5
Tiananmen Square 129
Tiller, John 183
   Tiller Girls 183–4, 186
time
   cinematic 203, 206–7
   historical 2–3
   Indigenous 95–9, 101, 104, 110–13, 115
   leisure 37, 41
   modern 5, 9, 117
   perception of 6–8
   performance in 7, 185–6, 210, 215, 217
   real 93
   televisual 204
Timony, John 60
Tolstoy, Leo
   Rasputin 189
topoanalysis 84, 94
Toronto
   Buddies in Bad Times Theatre 30

Canadian Stage Berkeley Street 30
Luminato Festival 104
Strachan House 91
Theatre Centre (Toronto) 17–19, 21–2, 27–33
Theatre District 59
Theatre Passe Muraille 30
Toronto Arts Council (TAC) 30
Young People's Theatre 30
Trail of Tears 112–13, 115
transgender 15
transmotion 95, 98, 106, 110
Transport Group, The 56
transportation 32, 141, 152
trauma 2, 9, 11, 81, 89, 134, 189
Treadwell, Sophie
  Machinal 206
tribalography 95–6, 98, 110–12, 115
Tribe Called Red, A (ATCR) 106
  Electric Pow Wow 107
Truth and Reconciliation Commission (TRC) (South Africa) 119, 130, 131
Tuan, Yi-Fu 82–4, 94
Tucker, Gary 69
Tudor, David
  9 Evenings: Theatre and Engineering 194–6
Turkle, Sherry 213
Turtle Island 12, 115
Tutu, Desmond 130
Twitter 219
Tynan, Kennth
  Oh! Calcutta! 63–5, 71, 73
Tzara, Tristan 155
  Gas Heart, The 208–9

uncanniness. *See* Freud, Sigmund
United States. *See also* Boston; Chicago; Lake Superior; New York; Philadelphia ; Turtle Island; Wisconsin
  civil rights 209
  Cold War 195
  emancipation 120
  free trade campaign 168
  Indigenous performers in 97–8, 107, 111–15,
  market-dominated model 21
  Progressive Era 58
  public television 204, 217

urban 5, 10, 36, 161
  audience 44
  commercial space 155–6
  development 17–19, 27, 29, 33
  Indigenous 107
  infrastructure 32
  planning 21–2, 28, 30–1
  populations 78, 146, 169
  protests 143
  space (*see* space, urban)
  theatre as 13, 37, 43
Urban, Gretl 148
Urban, Joseph 147–8, 156
urbanism 141–2
urbanization 9, 21, 80
Urry, John 152
utopia 4, 62, 82, 89, 119, 128–9, 178

Vaccaro, John 67–8
van der Rohe, Mies 10
Van Druten, John
  I Am a Camera 58
Van Hove, Ivo 89
Vasulka, Steina 193
Vasulka, Woody 193
Vehr, Bill 68
Venice
  Bienniale 193
Vertov, Dziga
  Man With a Movie Camera 206
video 157, 182, 193–4, 196, 198, 203, 214, 216–19
Vienna 55, 148
violence
  apartheid 130, 134–5, 150
  cultural 12
  domestic 47, 81, 94, 97
  intellectual 35
  militarized 8, 206, 208–9
  non- 191
  political 36
  racial 196
  stage 9, 15, 80
virtuosity 51, 83, 123, 173, 175, 184
Vizenor, Gerald 98, 106
Von Eschen, Penny M. 154
Vostell, Wolf 194

Wabanaki. *See* Abenaki
Wagner, Richard 184, 192

war 2, 11, 161
  Civil War (Republic of Ireland) 164
  Civil War (Soviet Union) 121, 123
  Cold War 8, 154
  colonial 111
  crimes 137
  First World War 8, 118, 140, 148, 155–6, 189, 206–9
  Iraq wars 8
  modern 201–2
  nuclear 8, 201, 210, 212
  Second World War 8, 21, 27, 113, 115, 178, 191, 209
  total 9
  Vietnam War 8, 191
War Revenue Act of 1917 (U.S.) 24
Washburn, Anne
  Mr. Burns: A Post-Electric Play 219
Washington Square Players 144–5
Wasserstein, Wendy 58
Weaver, Jace 107
Weaver, Lois 83, 179
  Dress Suits to Hire 83
Weber, Otto 147
Weems, Marianne 198
Weigel, Helena 190
Weill, Kurt
  Aufstieg und Fall der Stadt Mahagonny 48–50, 52–3
  Die Dreigroschenoper 48–9
  Yes-Sayer, The 117
Werry, Margaret 96
West Bengal 41–5, 47, 53
West, Mae
  Sex 60–1
Western Apache 105
Whitman, Robert
  9 Evenings: Theatre and Engineering 194–6
Wickstrom, Maurya 157
Wiener, Norbert 213
Williams, Raymond 141–2
Williams, Tennessee 64, 66, 76
  Cat on a Hot Tin Roof 59, 67, 71–3
  Streetcar Named Desire, A 15, 89
Wilson, August 76
Wilson, Robert 193

Winnipeg
  Prairie Theatre Exchange 105–6
Wisconsin
  Three Fires Midewiwin Lodge 107–8
Wollman, Elizabeth 63
women. *See also* gender; sexuality, female
  audiences 62
  auteurs 12, 196
  bodies 13–15, 197
  ceremony 108–9
  Irish 164, 167, 174
  Japanese 169–71, 173
  performers 59–61, 63, 186, 104, 143, 149
  representations of 58, 63, 66, 71, 194, 216
  suffrage 15, 59
  trans- 198
Wooster Group 82, 192, 198
work. *See* labour
working class
  audience 43–4, 62, 127, 146
  forms 122
  neighbourhood 19
  and race 154
  theatremakers 77
workshop (craft) 147–51
Wright, Frank Lloyd 10–11, 83
Wyckoff, Harold 99–100

Xu Bing 193, 184

Yeats, William Butler 26, 145, 164, 166–7, 174–5,
  At the Hawk's Well 163, 177–8
Yellowknife 104

Zagorsky, Mikhail 125, 127
Ziegfeld, Florenz
  Ziegfeld Follies 60, 147
Ziolkowski, Theodore 55
Zokufa, Busi 132
Zola, Émile 161, 203
Zubot, Jesse 104
Zurich
  Café Voltaire 140, 155, 207